TAKING SCIENCE TO SCHOOL
Learning and Teaching Science in Grades K-8

Committee on Science Learning, Kindergarten Through Eighth Grade

Richard A. Duschl, Heidi A. Schweingruber,
and Andrew W. Shouse, Editors

Board on Science Education
Center for Education
Division of Behavioral and Social Sciences and Education

NATIONAL RESEARCH COUNCIL
OF THE NATIONAL ACADEMIES

THE NATIONAL ACADEMIES PRESS
Washington, D.C.
www.nap.edu

THE NATIONAL ACADEMIES PRESS • 500 Fifth Street, N.W. • Washington, D.C. 20001

NOTICE: The project that is the subject of this report was approved by the Governing Board of the National Research Council, whose members are drawn from the councils of the National Academy of Sciences, the National Academy of Engineering, and the Institute of Medicine. The members of the committee responsible for the report were chosen for their special competences and with regard for appropriate balance.

This study was supported by Grant No. ESI-0348841 between the National Academy of Sciences and the National Science Foundation with support from the National Institute of Child Health and Human Development. Support was also provided through a separate grant from the Merck Institute for Science Education. Any opinions, findings, conclusions, or recommendations expressed in this publication are those of the author(s) and do not necessarily reflect the views of the organizations or agencies that provided support for the project.

Library of Congress Cataloging-in-Publication Data

Taking science to school : learning and teaching science in grades K-8 / Committee on Science Learning, Kindergarten Through Eighth Grade ; Richard A. Duschl, Heidi A. Schweingruber, and Andrew W. Shouse, editors.
    p. cm.
  ISBN 0-309-10205-7 (hardback) — ISBN 0-309-66069-6 (pdf) 1. Science—Study and teaching (Elementary)—United States. I. Duschl, Richard A. (Richard Alan), 1951- II. Schweingruber, Heidi A. III. Shouse, Andrew W. IV. National Research Council (U.S.). Committee on Science Learning, Kindergarten Through Eighth Grade.
LB1585.3.T35 2007
372.3'5—dc22

                              2006038027

Additional copies of this report are available from the National Academies Press, 500 Fifth Street, N.W., Lockbox 285, Washington, DC 20055; (800) 624-6242 or (202) 334-3313 (in the Washington metropolitan area); Internet, http://www.nap.edu.

Suggested citation: National Research Council. (2007). *Taking Science to School: Learning and Teaching Science in Grades K-8.* Committee on Science Learning, Kindergarten Through Eighth Grade. Richard A. Duschl, Heidi A. Schweingruber, and Andrew W. Shouse, Editors. Board on Science Education, Center for Education. Division of Behavioral and Social Sciences and Education. Washington, DC: The National Academies Press.

THE NATIONAL ACADEMIES
Advisers to the Nation on Science, Engineering, and Medicine

The **National Academy of Sciences** is a private, nonprofit, self-perpetuating society of distinguished scholars engaged in scientific and engineering research, dedicated to the furtherance of science and technology and to their use for the general welfare. Upon the authority of the charter granted to it by the Congress in 1863, the Academy has a mandate that requires it to advise the federal government on scientific and technical matters. Dr. Ralph J. Cicerone is president of the National Academy of Sciences.

The **National Academy of Engineering** was established in 1964, under the charter of the National Academy of Sciences, as a parallel organization of outstanding engineers. It is autonomous in its administration and in the selection of its members, sharing with the National Academy of Sciences the responsibility for advising the federal government. The National Academy of Engineering also sponsors engineering programs aimed at meeting national needs, encourages education and research, and recognizes the superior achievements of engineers. Dr. Wm. A. Wulf is president of the National Academy of Engineering.

The **Institute of Medicine** was established in 1970 by the National Academy of Sciences to secure the services of eminent members of appropriate professions in the examination of policy matters pertaining to the health of the public. The Institute acts under the responsibility given to the National Academy of Sciences by its congressional charter to be an adviser to the federal government and, upon its own initiative, to identify issues of medical care, research, and education. Dr. Harvey V. Fineberg is president of the Institute of Medicine.

The **National Research Council** was organized by the National Academy of Sciences in 1916 to associate the broad community of science and technology with the Academy's purposes of furthering knowledge and advising the federal government. Functioning in accordance with general policies determined by the Academy, the Council has become the principal operating agency of both the National Academy of Sciences and the National Academy of Engineering in providing services to the government, the public, and the scientific and engineering communities. The Council is administered jointly by both Academies and the Institute of Medicine. Dr. Ralph J. Cicerone and Dr. Wm. A. Wulf are chair and vice chair, respectively, of the National Research Council.

www.national-academies.org

COMMITTEE ON SCIENCE LEARNING, KINDERGARTEN THROUGH EIGHTH GRADE

RICHARD A. DUSCHL (*Chair*), Department of Learning and Teaching, Rutgers University

CHARLES W. ANDERSON, Department of Teacher Education, Michigan State University, East Lansing

THOMAS B. CORCORAN, Department of Policy, Management and Evaluation, University of Pennsylvania

KEVIN J. CROWLEY, Department of Instruction and Learning, University of Pittsburgh

FRANK C. KEIL, Department of Psychology, Yale University

DAVID KLAHR, Department of Psychology, Carnegie Mellon University

OKHEE LEE, Department of Teaching and Learning, University of Miami, Coral Gables

DANIEL M. LEVIN, Montgomery Blair High School, Silver Spring, MD

KATHLEEN E. METZ, Department of Cognition and Development, University of California, Berkeley

HELEN R. QUINN, Stanford Linear Accelerator Center, Stanford University

BRIAN J. REISER, Department of Learning Sciences, Northwestern University

DEBORAH L. ROBERTS, Maryland State Department of Education, Baltimore

LEONA SCHAUBLE, Department of Teaching and Learning, Vanderbilt University

CAROL L. SMITH, Department of Psychology, University of Massachusetts, Boston

HEIDI A. SCHWEINGRUBER, *Co-Study Director*
ANDREW W. SHOUSE, *Co-Study Director*
C. JEAN MOON, *Director, Board on Science Education*
VICTORIA N. WARD, *Senior Program Assistant*

SCIENCE CONSULTANTS FOR THE COMMITTEE ON SCIENCE LEARNING, KINDERGARTEN THROUGH EIGHTH GRADE

PETER RAVEN, Director, Missouri Botanical Garden, St. Louis

EDWARD C. ROY, JR., Department of Geology (emeritus), Trinity University, San Antonio, TX

MAXINE SINGER, President Emeritus, Carnegie Institution of Washington, DC

SUSAN R. SINGER, Department of Biology, Carleton College, Northfield, MN

Foreword

This report brings together research literatures from cognitive and developmental psychology, science education, and the history and philosophy of science to synthesize what is known about how children in grades K through 8 learn the ideas and practice of science. The resulting conclusions challenge the science education community, writ large, to examine some tenacious assumptions about children's potential for learning about science and, as a result, the priority of science in elementary schools. We believe this research synthesis and the implications from it have the potential to change science education in fundamental ways.

For example, the repeated challenge from science educators is that science education should be for "all" the children. This has been a difficult challenge to meet. Although there is general agreement that all children will and must learn to read, historically there has been far less agreement that all children will and must learn science regardless of gender, race, or socioeconomic circumstances.

That issue is addressed in this report. *Taking Science to School* speaks in a clear, evidentiary-based voice. All young children have the intellectual capability to learn science. Even when they enter school, young children have rich knowledge of the natural world, demonstrate causal reasoning, and are able to discriminate between reliable and unreliable sources of knowledge. In other words, children come to school with the cognitive capacity to engage in serious ways with the enterprise of science.

This finding leads to a sobering insight: as educators, we are underestimating what young children are capable of as students of science—the bar is almost always set too low. Moreover, the current organization of science curriculum and instruction does not provide the kind of support for science learning that results in deep understanding of scientific ideas and an ability to engage meaningfully in the practices of science. In sum, science education as currently structured does not leverage the knowledge and capabilities students bring to the classroom. For students from diverse backgrounds, this problem is even more profound.

While sobering, this news also offers hope. At a time when significant resources, thought, and hand-wringing are devoted to the state of science, technology, engineering, and mathematics education in this country, it is welcome news that children come to school far more ready and far more capable to be science learners than previously thought. Indeed, this knowledge should come as a breath of fresh air, a reason for renewed commitment to science education, and most importantly, an invitation to action on the part of researchers, school practitioners, and state and federal policy makers.

In addition to addressing the issue of children's capacity to engage in science, this report provides a redefinition of what it means to be proficient in science. It is a compelling and comprehensive framework. It will stretch us to think beyond the artificial dichotomy between content and process in science. It is comprehensive because it attends to the whole of science learning.

Taking Science to School makes an important contribution to science education. It has been some time since science education has received an infusion of knowledge so central to the intersection of learning and science. The Board on Science Education at the National Academies is pleased to have coordinated this study. We think it exemplifies the central purpose of the National Academies and the National Research Council (NRC), to advise the nation on matters critical to science and policy in science, engineering, and medicine. We are especially grateful to the sponsors of this study—the National Science Foundation (NSF), the National Institute of Child Health and Human Development (NICHD), and the Merck Institute for Science Education (MISE). Through their sponsorship, each demonstrated a deep commitment to the importance of science, science education, and learning.

Consulting scientists for this study—Peter Raven, director, Missouri Botanical Garden; Edward C. Roy, Jr., Department of Geology (emeritus), Trinity University; Maxine Singer, Carnegie Institution of Washington, DC (president emeritus); and Susan R. Singer, Department of Biology, Carleton College—made important contributions to the study process for which they deserve special recognition. They provided the study committee and staff with advice and reflections from the perspective of individuals with significant expertise in science content.

Finally, the intellectual leadership demonstrated by co-study directors Heidi Schweingruber and Andrew Shouse in guiding the work of this study committee and the final report was outstanding. The board is grateful for their significant contributions along with those of every member of the study committee. The importance of this report to the science education community was recognized early in the committee's work. It became a standard to inspire and guide their work throughout the process. We recognize and thank them for their major contributions to the field of science education.

Carl E. Wieman, *Chair*
C. Jean Moon, *Director*
Board on Science Education

Acknowledgments

The consensus report, *Taking Science to School: Learning and Teaching Science in Grades K-8,* would not have been possible without the important contributions from study committee members, NRC leadership and staff, and many other individuals and organizations.

First, we acknowledge the support of NSF, the NICHD, and MISE. We particularly thank NSF senior program officer Janice Earle, whose initial and continuing engagement with the study committee supported and encouraged the development of the report. We are also grateful to Dan Berch from NICHD who encouraged the committee to focus on the basic science of learning (e.g., infant studies, developmental change, and brain mechanisms) as we addressed the goals and agenda for the study committee. Significant recognition and thanks must go to Carlo Parravano, MISE executive director, for his foresight in knowing how central this report would be for science education and for his strong support throughout the process of the study. This report would not have been possible without the collaborative sponsorship provided by NSF, NICHD, and MISE.

Members of the committee benefited from discussions and presentations by the many individuals who participated in our five meetings. In particular, our initial framing of the K-8 science learning domains underwent significant revisions and refinements as a result of the scholarly and thoughtful contributions made by commissioned paper writers, presenters, responders, science consultants, and members of the Practitioner Study Oversight Group. At our first meeting, Clark Chinn, Rutgers University; Christine Massey, University of Pennsylvania; and Ala Samarapungavan, Purdue University, presented their research on young children's science concept learning, reasoning, and argumentation discourse processes. Maureen Callanan, University of California-Santa Cruz, and Greg Kelly, Pennsylvania State University, provided thoughtful responses to the three presentations. The three presentations and two responses guided the committee to a discussion on the need to delineate the kinds of research to consider regarding children's science learning. Jeremy Kilpatrick, chair, NRC study committee for the report *Adding It Up*, helped committee members grasp the magnitude of the enterprise upon which we were about to embark and comforted us with the information that the NRC leadership, study directors, and staff would, as they most certainly did, provide guidance and acumen in the preparation of the report you have before you.

At the second committee meeting, we extended our explorations of research on children's science learning though a commissioned paper presentation by Deanna Kuhn, Teachers College, Columbia University, and a presentation by Corinne Zimmerman, Illinois State University. We next took up the topic of "what is science?" with a presentation and a response on "model-based reasoning practices in science" from philosophers of science Nancy Nersessian, Georgia Institute of Technology, and Richard Grandy, Rice University, respectively, and a presentation on teaching "ideas-about-science" from Jonathan Osborne, King's College, London, England. Also at the second meeting, we had a presentation on assessment practices in science education from Janet Coffey, University of Maryland-College Park, and a response from Dylan William, then at the Educational Testing Service and currently at the Institute of Education, London, England.

For the third committee meeting, we turned our attention to the relationship between instruction and contexts that support science learning. A perspective on early childhood was presented by Rochel Gelman, professor and codirector of the Rutgers University Center for Cognitive Sciences; and the focus on elementary and middle school years was presented by Sister Gertrude Hennessey, (St. Ann's School, Stoughton, WI). Beth Warren and Josiane Hidicourt-Barnes, both from TERC, presented on the instruction and contexts for science learning issue from the perspective of diverse learners. The committee discussions on assessment were further informed by Senta Raizen from West Ed. Her presentation provided the committee with information on using research on science learning to inform large-scale assessments in science. Science learning in out-of-school contexts was a critically important topic for the committee, and Reed Stevens, University of Washington, and Kirsten Ellenbogen, Science Museum of Minnesota, completed a commissioned paper on this topic, which was presented by Dr. Ellenbogen. Another critical topic was sociocultural perspectives on science learning. The commissioned paper on this topic for the third meeting was one by Ellice Forman and Wendy Sink, University of Pittsburgh, and was quite helpful to the committee.

At the next two committee meetings we were occasionally joined by members of the Science Consultants Advisory Board—Peter Raven, Missouri Botanical Garden; Edward C. Roy, Jr., Trinity University (emeritus); Maxine Singer, president emeritus, Carnegie Institution of Washington, DC; and Susan R. Singer, Carleton College. Feedback from our science consultants helped the committee to clarify messages and issues of audience for the report. A special acknowledgment goes to Susan R. Singer, chair of the NRC study committee that produced the report, *America's Lab Report: Investigations in High School Science*, who offered sage advice and feedback to the chair and to our committee on the process and procedures of our deliberations.

At the last several meetings, we were also joined by members of the Practitioner Study Oversight Group for the science learning study practitioner book—Sister Mary Gertrude Hennessey, Stoughton, WI; Deborah C. Smith, Lansing Public School, MI; Sarah Michaels, Clark University; and Janet English, a middle school teacher on leave of absence and who is now with KOCE-TV, PBS. We are grateful to each member of the group for providing excellent feedback to the committee as well as compelling examples of exemplar practices in K-8 science classrooms. This practitioner book, sponsored by MISE, will be released by the NRC approximately six months after the release of this formal report.

We also would like to thank Erin Furtak, Stanford University, who completed a commissioned paper on assessment; Mark Olson, University of Connecticut, and Carla Zembal-Saul, Pennsylvania State University, who provided additional expertise.

Many individuals at the NRC assisted the committee. The study would not have been possible without the efforts and guidance of C. Jean Moon and Patricia Morison. Both were active participants in the deliberations of the study committee, helping us to focus on key messages and conclusions from the study. Additionally, they also made profound contributions to the development of the report through periodic leadership meetings with the committee chair and the NRC study co-directors. We are grateful to Victoria Ward who arranged logistics for our meetings and facilitated the proceeding of the meetings themselves.

Jeremy Kilpatrick also informed us at the first meeting about the critical role study reviews have in bringing the report together. How very right he was!

This report has been reviewed in draft form by individuals chosen for their diverse perspectives and technical expertise, in accordance with procedures approved by the Report Review Committee of the NRC. The purpose of this independent review is to provide candid and critical comments that will assist the institution in making its published report as sound as possible and to ensure that the report meets institutional standards for objectivity, evidence, and responsiveness to the charge. The review comments and draft manuscript remain confidential to protect the integrity of the deliberative process.

We wish to thank the following individuals for their review of this report: Rolf K. Blank, Education Indicators, Council of Chief State School Officers, Washington, DC; Brian P. Coppola, Department of Chemistry, University of Michigan; Liang-Shih Fan, School of Engineering, Ohio State University; Susan Gelman, Department of Psychology, University of Michigan; Lynda J. Goff, UC Science and Mathematics Initiative, University of California-Davis; Barbara Koslowski, Department of Human Development and Family Studies, Cornell University; Richard Lehrer, Teaching and Learning Department, Vanderbilt University; Douglas L. Medin, Department of Psychology, Northwestern University; Brett D. Moulding, Utah Office of Education, Salt Lake City, UT; Annemarie Sullivan Palincsar, School of Education, University of Michigan; Kathleen Roth, Research Institute, LessonLab, Santa Monica, CA; Norman H. Sleep, Department of Geophysics, Stanford University; Cary Sneider, Educator Programs, Museum of Science, Boston, MA; Nancy Butler Songer, School of Education, University of Michigan.

Although the reviewers listed above provided many constructive comments and suggestions, they were not asked to endorse the conclusions and recommendations nor did they see the final draft of the report before its release. The review of this report was overseen by Catherine Snow, Harvard Graduate School of Education, Harvard University, and Johanna Dwyer, Tufts University School of Medicine and Friedman School of Nutrition and Science Policy, Tufts-New England Medical Center. Appointed by the NRC, they were responsible for making certain that an independent examination of this report was carried out in accordance with institutional procedures and that all review comments were carefully considered. Responsibility for the final content of this report rests entirely with the authoring committee and the institution.

Richard A. Duschl, *Chair*
Committee on Science Learning,
Kindergarten Through Eighth Grade

Contents

Executive Summary

At no time in history has improving science education been more important than it is today. Major policy debates about such topics as cloning, the potential of alternative fuels, and the use of biometric information to fight terrorism require a scientifically informed citizenry as never before in the nation's history. Yet after 15 years of focused standards-based reform, improvements in U.S. science education are modest at best, and comparisons show that U.S. students fare poorly in comparison with students in other countries. In addition, gaps in achievement persist between majority group students and both economically disadvantaged and non-Asian minority students. In part, these achievement gaps mirror inequities in science education and take on greater significance with the looming mandate of the No Child Left Behind Act that states assess science beginning in the 2006-2007 school year. Thus, science education in the United States has become a subject of grave and pressing concern.

The charge to this committee was to answer three broad questions: (1) How is science learned, and are there critical stages in children's development of scientific concepts? (2) How should science be taught in K-8 classrooms? (3) What research is needed to increase understanding about how students learn science?

Our answers to the first question are embodied in our conclusions. Our answers to the second question are embodied in our recommendations. We also offer recommendations on professional development, a topic that demands attention because of its relationship to the second question: how science is taught ultimately depends on the teachers. Extensive rethinking of how teachers are prepared before they begin teaching and as they continue teaching—and as science changes—is critical to improving K-8 science education in the United States.

PROFICIENCY IN SCIENCE

Underlying all our conclusions and recommendations is a redefinition of and a new framework for what it means to be proficient in science. This framework rests on a view of science as both a body of knowledge and an evidence-based, model-building enterprise that continually extends, refines, and revises knowledge. This framework moves beyond a focus on the dichotomy between either content knowledge or process skills because content and process are inextricably linked in science.

Students who are proficient in science:

1. know, use, and interpret scientific explanations of the natural world;
2. generate and evaluate scientific evidence and explanations;
3. understand the nature and development of scientific knowledge; and
4. participate productively in scientific practices and discourse.

These strands of proficiency represent learning goals for students as well as a broad framework for curriculum design. They address the knowledge and reasoning skills that students must acquire to be proficient in science and, ultimately, able to participate in society as educated citizens. They also incorporate the scientific practices that students need to demonstrate their proficiency. The process of achieving proficiency in science involves all four strands—advances in one strand support and advance those in another.

CONCLUSIONS: WHAT CHILDREN KNOW AND HOW THEY LEARN

Changes in understanding of what children know and how they learn have been profound in the past several decades. This new understanding is central to formulating how science should be taught. In summary:

• Children entering school already have substantial knowledge of the natural world, much of which is implicit.
• What children are capable of at a particular age is the result of a complex interplay among maturation, experience, and instruction. What is developmentally appropriate is not a simple function of age or grade, but rather is largely contingent on their prior opportunities to learn.
• Students' knowledge and experience play a critical role in their science learning, influencing all four strands of science understanding.

- Race and ethnicity, language, culture, gender, and socioeconomic status are among the factors that influence the knowledge and experience children bring to the classroom.
  - Students learn science by actively engaging in the practices of science.
  - A range of instructional approaches is necessary as part of a full development of science proficiency.

The commonly held view that young children are concrete and simplistic thinkers is outmoded; research shows that children's thinking is surprisingly sophisticated. Yet much current science education is based on the old assumptions and so focuses on what children cannot do rather than what they can do. Children can use a wide range of reasoning processes that form the underpinnings of scientific thinking, even though their experience is variable and they have much more to learn.

Contrary to conceptions of development held 30 or 40 years ago, young children can think both concretely and abstractly. As with most human characteristics, there is variation across children at a given age and even variation within an individual child. Development is not a kind of inevitable unfolding in which one simply waits until a child is cognitively "ready" for abstract or theory-based forms of content. Instead, parents and teachers can assist children's learning, building on their early capacities. Adults play a central role in promoting children's curiosity and persistence by directing their attention, structuring their experiences, supporting their learning attempts, and regulating the complexity and difficulty of levels of information for them. In the sciences, both teachers and peers can and must fill these critical roles.

Children's rich but naïve understandings of the natural world can be built on to develop their understandings of scientific concepts. At the same time, their understandings of the world sometimes contradict scientific explanations and pose obstacles to learning science. It is thus critical that children's prior knowledge is taken into account in designing instruction that capitalizes on the leverage points and adequately addresses potential areas of misunderstanding. To be successful in science, students need carefully structured experiences, instructional support from teachers, and opportunities for sustained engagement with the same set of ideas over weeks, months, and even years.

Children's experience varies with their cultural, linguistic, and economic background. Such differences mean that students arrive in the classroom with varying levels of exposure to science and varying degrees of comfort with the norms of scientific practice. These differences require teachers' sensitivity to cultural and other background differences and their willingness and skill to adjust instruction in light of these differences. Adjusting for variation in students' background and experience does not mean dumbing down the science curriculum or instruction. All children bring basic reasoning skills, personal knowledge of the natural world, and curiosity, which can be built on to achieve proficiency in science.

At present, a variety of factors result in inequities in science education that limit the opportunities for many students to learn science. Classroom-level factors related to instruction, such as teachers' expectations or strategies for grouping students, play a role in producing inequitable learning opportunities for economically disadvantaged and minority children. At the school, district, state, and federal levels, inequities in the quality of instruction and the qualifications of teachers, resources, facilities, and time devoted to science result in widely different learning opportunities for different groups of students. These inequities demand attention from policy makers, education leaders, and school administrators, as well as researchers.

Students' knowledge growth and reasoning are components of a large ensemble of activities that constitute "doing science." These activities include conducting investigations; sharing ideas with peers; specialized ways of talking and writing; mechanical, mathematical, and computer-based modeling; and development of representations of phenomena. To develop proficiency in science, students must have the opportunity to participate in this full range of activities.

Instruction occurs in sequences of designed, strategic encounters between students and science. Any given unit of study may include episodes that are highly teacher-directed as well as structured student-led activities. Across time, quality instruction should promote a sense of science as a process of building and improving knowledge and understanding. Students should have experiences in generating researchable questions, designing methods of answering them, conducting data analysis, and debating interpretations of data.

RECOMMENDATIONS: WHAT, WHEN, AND HOW TO TEACH

Our recommendations for standards, curricula, assessment, and instruction follow from our conclusions. However, in some areas the research base is not robust enough to offer a detailed, step-by-step roadmap for nationwide action. Given the urgent need for improvement in science education, the committee focused on the "best bets" that represent the most promising work. They require additional documentation through continued research and careful evaluation of implementation: by evaluating school, district, and state initiatives, these best bets can be transformed into well-researched alternatives for policy and practice. Our specific recommendations for research are in Chapter 11.

Science standards, curriculum, assessment, and instruction—as well as professional development for teachers—should be conceived of, designed, and implemented as a coordinated system. Standards and curriculum should lay out specific, coherent goals for important scientific ideas and practices that can be realized through sustained instruction over several years of K-8 schooling. Assessment should provide teachers and students with timely feedback about students' knowledge that, in turn, supports teachers' efforts to improve instruction. Teacher preparation and professional development should be focused on developing teachers' knowledge of the science they teach, how students learn science, and specific methods and technologies that support science learning for all students.

Recommendation 1: Developers of standards, curriculum, and assessment should revise their frameworks to reflect new models of children's thinking and take better advantage of children's capabilities.

Currently, standards and many widely used curriculum materials fail to reflect what is now known about children's thinking, particularly the cognitive capabilities of younger children.

Recommendation 2: The next generation of standards and curricula at both the national and state levels should be structured to identify a few core ideas in a discipline and elaborate how those ideas can be cumulatively developed over grades K-8.

Focusing on core ideas requires eliminating ideas that are not central to the development of science understanding. Core ideas should be both foundational in terms of connection to many related scientific concepts and have the potential for sustained exploration at increasingly sophisticated levels across grades K-8. Although existing national and state standards have been a critical first step in narrowing the focus of science in grades K-8, they do not go far enough. Future revisions to the national standards—and the subsequent interpretation of these standards at the state and local levels and by curriculum developers—need to be built around core scientific ideas and clearly identify the knowledge and practices that can be developed in science education over K-8.

Recommendation 3: Developers of curricula and standards should present science as a process of building theories and models using evidence, checking them for internal consistency and coherence, and testing them empirically. Discussions of scientific methodology should be introduced in the context of pur-

suing specific questions and issues rather than as templates or invariant recipes.

The processes and methodology that students encounter in the classroom need to reflect the range of investigatory forms in science. The range of methodology needs to include not only experiments, which have traditionally been the focus of school science, but also examples from scientific work that uses observational methods, historical reconstruction and analysis, and other nonexperimental methods.

Recommendation 4: Science instruction should provide opportunities for students to engage in all four strands of science proficiency.

In order to provide meaningful opportunities for science learning, policy makers, education leaders, and school administrators need to ensure that adequate time and resources are provided for science instruction at all grade levels for all students. They must also ensure that teachers have adequate knowledge of science content and process and are provided with adequate professional development.

Recommendation 5: State and local leaders in science education should provide teachers with models of classroom instruction that provide opportunities for interaction in the classroom, where students carry out investigations and talk and write about their observations of phenomena, their emerging understanding of scientific ideas, and ways to test them.

RECOMMENDATIONS: PROFESSIONAL DEVELOPMENT

Professional development is key to supporting effective science instruction. We call for a dramatic departure from current professional development practice, both in scope and kind. Teachers need opportunities to deepen their knowledge of the science content of the K-8 curriculum. They also need opportunities to learn how students learn science and how to teach it. They need to know how children's understanding of core ideas in science builds across K-8, not just at a given grade or grade band. They need to learn about the conceptual ideas that students have in the earliest grades and their ideas about science itself. They need to learn how to assess children's developing ideas over time and how to interpret and respond (instructionally) to the results of assessment. In sum, teachers need opportunities to learn how to teach science as an integrated body of knowledge and practice—to teach for scientific proficiency. They need to learn how to teach science to diverse student populations, to provide adequate opportunities for all students to learn science. These needs represent a significant change from what virtually all active teachers learned in college and what most colleges teach aspiring teachers today.

> **Recommendation 6: State and local school systems should ensure that all K-8 teachers experience sustained science-specific professional development in preparation and while in service. Professional development should be rooted in the science that teachers teach and should include opportunities to learn about science, about current research on how children learn science, and about how to teach science.**

> **Recommendation 7: University-based science courses for teacher candidates and teachers' ongoing opportunities to learn science in service should mirror the opportunities they will need to provide for their students, that is, incorporating practices in the four strands that constitute science proficiency and giving sustained attention to the core ideas in the discipline. The topics of study should be aligned with central topics in the K-8 curriculum.**

> **Recommendation 8: Federal agencies that support professional development should require that the programs they fund incorporate models of instruction that combine the four strands of science proficiency, focus on core ideas in science, and enhance teachers' science content knowledge, knowledge of how students learn science, and knowledge of how to teach science.**

In Chapter 11 the committee offers its recommendations for research—the work that should begin now to inform the future recommendations for science teaching.

To improve science education in the United States, changes are urgently needed throughout the system. Beginning with what is known about how children learn science, changes in teaching and in the education of teachers can and should begin now.

Part I

INTRODUCTION

1

Science Learning Past and Present

This report comes at a time when both science and science education are regular topics of national media attention and urgent policy debates. Scientists have used the discovery of DNA to help map the human genome, can prevent diseases like polio and rheumatic fever, and have landed probes on Mars. Today the scientific knowledge to see and manipulate atoms is available, whereas just 100 years ago people debated the existence of atomic matter. Major public policy issues, such as cloning, climate change, and alternative fuels, require a scientifically informed citizenry as never before. Underrepresentation of women and minorities in the sciences is a widely recognized problem of increasing concern amid policy debates about the adequacy of the nation's scientific and technical workforce. Yet as scientific knowledge develops and grows, as new scientific tools and technologies emerge and work their way further into civic life, there is grave concern and debates about the quality of science education.

After 15 years of focused standards-based reform, improvements in U.S. science education are modest at best. International comparisons show that many U.S. students fare poorly relative to their peers in other countries. In addition, large achievement gaps between majority students and both economically disadvantaged and non-Asian minority students persist in all school subjects, and they are especially strong and persistent in science (National Center for Education Statistics, 2000, 2003). These trends in achievement take on even greater significance with the looming deadline in the No Child Left Behind legislation, which mandates state-level assessments in science beginning in the 2007-2008 school year. Meanwhile, state and local school boards around the country, backed by large numbers of citizens, are embroiled in battles over the teaching of evolution. Science educators continue to debate the place of inquiry approaches in the teaching of science. The convergence of these factors has thrust science education into the center of national concern. Thus, there is an urgent need for a concerted effort to examine and improve science education. Science education has been a perennial issue of national concern, and its recent history warrants attention, a stock-taking of the current knowledge base and the prospects for promising directions in the future.

THE HISTORICAL CONTEXT OF U.S. SCIENCE EDUCATION

The current context of science education is shaped by initiatives undertaken over the past few decades. We briefly review these trends with an eye toward how they can inform future directions.

The 1950s and 1960s saw the first federal foray into science teacher education and curriculum reform under the auspices of the National Science Foundation's (NSF) summer institutes and curriculum development projects. A milestone in science education, the NSF curriculum development projects focused on upgrading the teaching of science by modernizing the content of science courses. These projects laid the foundation for the succeeding decades of science education research and reform.

The reform of science education, however, was not devoid of controversy. In the 1970s serious challenges were raised to NSF that, through its curriculum programs, a national curriculum was being advanced. NSF-sponsored teacher professional development programs ceased to operate for several years. In the 1980s, policy makers examined K-12 student achievement rates and declared the nation "at risk" of economic catastrophe. They prescribed ramping up high school graduation requirements, especially in science and mathematics, a recommendation that was a precursor to the standards-based reforms of the 1990s. These crises and the reforms they stimulated are milestones that have defined and redefined the landscape of K-8 science education. They continue to influence the practices and attitudes of educators, researchers, policy makers, and the public.

The Legacy of the 1960s Science Curriculum Reforms

At the height of the cold war, the American scientific establishment enjoyed a lofty but uncertain status. On one hand, scientific productivity was seen as essential to U.S. security, and federal science spending was on the rise. On the other hand, postwar science entailed large-scale, coordinated efforts involving hundreds of scientists. It required a steady flow of well-trained students, scientists, and scientific workers to maintain growth. Policy makers worried that, without large numbers of well-prepared high school graduates to fill the science pipeline, the United States could lose ground to Soviet science, weakening its cold war position (Rudolph, 2002).

While policy makers worried about security and the economy, the scientific community had a slightly different concern. Scientists saw limited public understanding of their work, and in particular, they cited a common misperception that science was equivalent to technological innovation. As they saw it, the public failed to appreciate the value of basic knowledge production. The scientific community recognized that expanding science programs would require a pipeline of new scientists and that growing science budgets would require popular support. The goal was to broaden and deepen the public's understanding of scientific knowledge, inquiry, and institutions.

With this public engagement agenda in mind, NSF by 1964 sponsored some 20 innovative large-scale K-12 science curriculum development projects, such as the Physical Science Study Committee, ChemStudy, the Biological Sciences Curriculum Study, and the Earth Science Curriculum Study (Duschl, 1990). Under the leadership of natural scientists working in collaboration with psychologists, these curricula aimed to provide students with early exposure to "authentic" science. Developers hoped such exposure would both bolster public understanding of science and attract talented students to advanced study. Dubbed "science for scientists," the curricula broadly aimed to help students learn to think and act like scientists, a dramatic departure from contemporary instructional practice and its emphasis on final form science and textbook-driven instruction. The curricula were also novel from a policy perspective. This was the first effort to influence curriculum nationally, traditionally a local issue. National curriculum was (and still is) a politically contentious notion, which further complicated an already immense implementation challenge.

The NSF curricula called for an active learner who engaged in hands-on activities. As characterized by scientist and philosopher Joseph Schwab (1962), science education should be an "enquiry into enquiry."[1] The various curriculum development teams, comprised primarily of scientists, envisioned students learning science by reasoning from direct observations of natural phenomena. Federal funds were made available to school districts for the construction of science teaching laboratories. Teachers could then set up hands-on or investigative science experiences through which students would encounter empirical truths, much as a scientist might in the lab.

Curriculum developers believed that opportunities for students to engage in direct observations of phenomena illustrate the process of basic

---

[1]Schwab chose this variation on the spelling of "inquiry."

scientific research. This seemed a plausible strategy both for attracting more students to science as a career and countering popular views of science as isolated facts.

An important feature common to the curricula—especially those designed for elementary students—was the emphasis placed on general learning, the development of "process skills" that would theoretically generalize to one's thinking across the sciences and beyond.[2] Such skills include making observations and measurements of natural phenomena, articulating hypotheses, and designing and carrying out experiments. These curricula specified behavioral outcomes (e.g., able to make predictions, work with one or two variables) that, according to then-emergent thought in developmental psychology, could be learned in the abstract, retained, and applied across a range of settings irrespective of students' substantive understanding of content areas.

Although influenced by the psychology of the day, the NSF curricula were driven by theories of teaching, and less so by theories of learning explicitly. For example, the Science Curriculum Improvement Study proposed the "learning cycle" (Atkin and Karplus, 1962). The learning cycle included (1) exploration of a concept, often through a laboratory experiment; (2) conceptual invention, in which the student or teacher derived the concept from the experimental data, usually during a classroom discussion; and (3) concept application (Karplus and Their, 1967). The curriculum framed discrete actions for teachers and students to create interactive science classes. However, it did not anticipate students' entering ideas, nor did it envision teachers as diagnosticians of student learning and codesigners of instruction. It presumed that given a cycle of instruction, student learning would unfold rather unproblematically.

These curricula had substantial reach, and in 1977 some 60 percent of U.S. school districts reported using one or another of the NSF-sponsored science curricula (Rudolph, 2002). However, further distribution and use was limited by the cost of curriculum reform. Publishers shied away from the materials, as the estimated costs to school systems far exceeded typical curriculum budgets. Furthermore, they presented new approaches to teaching and learning that would be hard to pitch to their market and that would also require expensive teacher training.

The new curriculum also carried hefty political costs. These were linked to the challenges of promoting a national curriculum, and they were exacerbated by the fact that these curricula, rooted in the disciplines, presented

---

[2]This was also the case for some of the middle grades curricula, though not all. The middle grades curriculum Integrated Physical Science, for example, certainly paid attention to disciplinary conceptual structure. The secondary curricula (physics, chemistry, biology) paid a lot of attention to disciplinary conceptual structures and their justification.

content that was unfamiliar and occasionally disturbing to parents and educators. In particular, Man: A Course of Study, a curriculum unit on human evolution, elicited a backlash of local opposition across the country (Dow, 1991). Parent groups complained that the curriculum was godless and failed to present the proper moral image of humanity. These concerns eventually reached Congress (Lagemann, 2000) and contributed to a precipitous drop in NSF precollege education funding (Duschl, 1980, 1990; Welch, 1973).

The legacy of the 1960s reform is mixed. On one hand, it represented an unparalleled investment in precollege science curriculum and brought disciplinary experts into K-12 science education. The curricula pushed educators to think about what students were doing in class and to portray a broader notion of science to students. However, defining authentic science that could also result in increased student understanding proved more complex than developers had envisioned. Developers seemed to underestimate (1) the influence that students' prior knowledge and ideas had on meaningful learning; (2) the impact of students' and teachers' naïve ideas about scientific inquiry on engagement with investigations; and (3) the tremendous challenge of improving science instruction on a large scale. In the mid-1970s, evaluations conducted to determine the impact of the curricula on science education revealed that the impact was spotty at best, with many teachers (see Crane, 1976) and programs returning to textbook-driven teaching practices (Weiss et al., 2003).

The Emergence of Standards-Based Reform

There was another spike in attention to science education in the 1980s, as once again pundits voiced concerns about U.S. economic competitiveness (this time with Japan and the Pacific Rim nations) and waning American scientific production (Bloch, 1986). The National Commission for Excellence in Education, a group of university presidents, professors, and K-12 educators appointed by Secretary of Education Terrel H. Bell, offered a grave assessment of U.S. K-12 education. Their report, A Nation at Risk, contended that the "once unchallenged [U.S.] preeminence in commerce, industry, science, and technological innovation" was being overtaken as U.S. schools had "lost sight of the high expectations and disciplined effort needed to attain" the necessary goals of education (National Commission for Excellence in Education, 1983, p. 5). Scientific and political leaders assembled at the National Academy of Sciences Convocation on Science and Mathematics Education echoed these concerns. In his statement to the convocation, President Ronald Reagan spoke of curtailing a "20-year decline" in K-12 science and mathematics education that could result in "direct harm to our American economy and standard of living" (National Academy of Sciences and National Academy of Engineering, 1982, p. 1).

Policy makers called for a renewed focus on excellence and prescribed ratcheting up course content and high school graduation requirements broadly. Secretary Bell urged attendees to make science "one of the basics" and to provide additional opportunities for students to learn science during the summer and after school. The National Commission for Excellence in Education urged school systems to create a minimum requirement of three years each of science and mathematics for high school graduation and "more rigorous and measurable standards."

By the 1990s reformers rolled out "systemic" strategies to reach national goals for excellence in education. There was a broadly shared sentiment that ambitious national goals like those laid out in *A Nation at Risk* were attainable only through a coherent, system-wide effort. The "unruly nonsystem" of American education—a concoction of federal, state, and innumerable local policy systems—would be drawn together and organized. Standards for content, instruction, assessment, and professional development would provide a framework for coordinated efforts toward a common goal: offering all students a sufficient level of knowledge and skills across the core academic subjects.

Ever aware of Americans' distaste for centralized education policy, proponents of systemic reform trod lightly in the 1990s. They called for each layer in the education system to play a specific, semiautonomous role within a coordinated policy system, still ultimately driven by state and local decisions. The K-12 subject matter communities, comprised of education researchers, curriculum developers, scientists, teacher educators, and teachers, developed frameworks to guide state and local authorities with curriculum development. In science these were *Benchmarks for Science Literacy* (American Association for the Advancement of Science, 1993) and *The National Science Education Standards* (National Research Council, 1996). These two documents served as guiding frameworks for the development or refinement of each state's own science frameworks, which in turn were used to format the content basis for curriculum and state-level assessments (Council of Chief State School Officers, 1995, 1997). Local education authorities also developed standards and curriculum that aligned with state and national standards, so that they would provide students with opportunities to learn content that would be tested on state assessments.

Standards also created a framework for focused science education funding from federal agencies and philanthropic foundations. Prominent among these were the NSF systemic initiatives, including statewide systemic initiatives, urban systemic initiatives, rural systemic initiatives, and local systemic change initiatives. For example, the local systemic change initiatives were "designed to broaden the impact, accelerate the pace and increase the effectiveness of improvements in K-12 science and mathematics education" (Lawrenz and Post, 1999). This program reflected the logic of standards-based reform and sought to help local authorities achieve standards through teacher enhancement, standards-based curriculum, and the broader participation of parents, informal science institutions, business, and higher education.

The systemic initiatives, which benefited from concurrent evaluation efforts, showed some promising effects on student learning, which were particularly salient for students from traditionally underserved groups. Furthermore, gains were greater for school systems that had participated in the reform for a longer period of time. Results from the local systemic initiatives further helped identify conditions that supported meaningful system-wide changes across urban, rural, and suburban districts (Boyd et al., 2003). It became clear that instructional improvement could be accomplished through system-wide efforts and that many actors—including teachers, students, parents, administrators, and professional development staffs—were implicated in reform (Kim, et al., 2001). The results across the various initiatives also made clear, however, that system-wide reform is often difficult to initiate and maintain (Council of Chief State School Officers, 2000).

Despite recurrent efforts to improve science education through curriculum and standards-based reform, there is still a long way to go. In hindsight, several factors may help to explain the limited impact of these substantial reform efforts. They include the complex political and technical aspects of implementation, insufficient teacher preparation and professional development, discontinuous streams of reform, mismatches between the goals of the initiatives and assessments, and insufficient and inequitable material resources devoted to education and reform (Berliner, 2005; Kozol, 2005; Spillane, 2001). These factors are invariably part of the education reform problem and necessarily constrain how theories of teaching and learning are enacted in school settings.

While science education reform will necessarily bump up against these material, political, and structural factors, this report focuses on the intellectual, research-driven basis for science education. We draw from current research on learning, cognitive development, child development, and the design of effective learning environments, as well as science studies, among others, in an effort to illuminate both *what science is and how students learn science,* to point toward clear possibilities for improvement in current instructional practice and to provide a strategic agenda for future research. Underlying any effort to reform science education is a notion, sometimes tacit, of learning. What does it mean to understand science? How do students come to understand it? What do effective science learning environments look like, and what can be done to create and sustain them? These foundational questions are at the core of this report.

With the adoption of the No Child Left Behind Act in 2001, the federal role in education reform again broadened. This legislation requires schools to report student test scores across demographic groups and to work toward yearly incremental improvements for all students. In 2007 for the first time, the legislation will require science testing to be carried out nationwide.

RECENT DEVELOPMENTS IN SCIENCE, LEARNING, AND TEACHING

Research and development in science education, science, and the science of learning have progressed substantially since the first NSF curriculum efforts. Research-based understandings of learning also diverge from that which informed the recent efforts at systemic, standards-based reform. Since the 1960s, philosophers of science have challenged fundamental assumptions about what science is and how it operates. While considerable disagreement exists within the field, philosophers have long questioned the empiricist assumptions of science as pure discovery or the uncovering of truth, ideas that permeated the mid-century curriculum reforms. They, as well as scholars in the history of science and the sociology of science, see scientific inquiry as model or theory based, increasingly conducted by groups and communities of scientists, and influenced by investigators' conceptual understandings about the phenomena under study. Scholars have also shed light on the elaborate social and technical apparatus on which the conduct of science depends, including instruments, tools, charts and graphs, research articles, journals, research groups, universities, and the larger society.

Philosophers, scientists, and social scientists also describe changes in contemporary science itself (Klahr and Simon, 1999). Whereas direct causal models once prevailed as natural explanations, advances in scientific instrumentation, computer technology, and a deepening of scientific knowledge have given rise to statistical models of natural phenomena that are rooted in probabilistic reasoning. What constitutes scientific practices today is very different from the practices just 50 to 100 years ago. Current models of natural phenomena are strongly grounded in mathematical and computational reasoning and rightly challenge intuitive expectations about direct cause and effect. At the core, science is fundamentally about establishing lines of evidence and using the evidence to develop and refine explanations using theories, models, hypotheses, measurements, and observations.

Over time, scientists have learned how to learn about nature, deepening scientific understandings and methods of inquiry. The disciplinary boundaries between the life and the physical sciences have blurred, as have boundaries between scientific and technological development, with the emergence of new fields, such as biochemistry, geophysics, bioinformatics, computational biology, advanced chemical synthesis, and nanoscience.

The growing sophistication of digital technology and media may also distance people from the everyday experiences that used to hook young people into science. For example, just a few decades ago, it was common for youth to learn to perform repairs on automobiles, a context ripe with scientific concepts (work, efficiency, gas compression and combustion, etc.). Such repairs are impractical now, as automotive systems are governed by microcomputers. Similarly, a malfunctioning iPod cannot be opened and rewired as could a 1960s-era turntable. As the frequency of such encounters wanes, one wonders what the effect will be on children's interest and motivation to understand the scientific underpinnings of the phenomena at play in designed systems.

Expectations of what it means to be competent in doing science and understanding science have also broadened. Beyond skillful performance and recall of factual knowledge, contemporary views of learning prize understanding and application or knowledge in use. Learners who understand can use and apply novel ideas in diverse contexts, drawing connections among multiple representations of a given concept. They appreciate the foundations of knowledge and consider the warrants for knowledge claims. Accomplished learners know when to ask a question, how to challenge claims, where to go to learn more, and they are aware of their own ideas and how these change over time.

Understanding of how learners develop ideas about the natural world has advanced considerably in the last few decades. In particular, contemporary thinking reflects an important role for prior knowledge, which was severely underacknowledged in earlier theories of learning. Even young children have well-established ideas about the natural world. These ideas may be more or less cohesive, and they may serve as resources or distracters in children's efforts to understand and apply new knowledge. The presence of prior knowledge has important implications for instruction and other efforts to influence student thinking. Furthermore, understanding that scientific reasoning is linked tightly to conceptual understanding casts serious doubt on the wisdom of teaching scientific reasoning in the absence of specific content.

Learning environments and understanding of them also have changed. Children learn science from books, television, the Internet, visits to museums and national parks, as well as the science classroom and the scientific and technological world around them. These various sites of learning are now sites of research on learning. Looking inside diverse environments where learning happens, researchers point to the cognitive and social dimensions of learning. Young learners, not unlike scientists, *use* knowledge and language to ask questions and make sense of the world. There is a need to represent their understanding in efforts to challenge and persuade others. Learners talk with peers, classmates, and family members. Through group processes, they share and develop their understanding of, and relationship to, science.

Immigrants, children of color, and children living in poverty have become an increasing fraction of the U.S. student population, and science achievement gaps persist. For example, while the gap between the average performance of black and white students on the National Assessment of Educational Progress narrowed in the early 1980s, white students on average still scored significantly higher than black students on the test administered in 2000. The gap between the average performance of Hispanic and white students has remained relatively stable, with whites outperforming Hispanic students. Furthermore, high-income students consistently outperform low-income students, and the gap in average performance appears to be widening (National Center for Education Statistics, 2000, 2003). The sources of such gaps are complex and include aspects of the structure and organization of schools that go beyond science education, as evidenced by the fact that similar gaps appear in reading and mathematics (National Center for Education Statistics, 2000). However, the emerging body of literature on learning indicates that children from all backgrounds have the capacity to be successful in science and begins to identify the cultural and linguistic resources that nonmainstream students bring to the science classroom.

The new and emergent perspectives on science learning raise questions about the appropriateness of the nation's current approach to science education. Do current standards, curricula, and textbooks reflect an appropriate range of science outcomes? Do they lay out a series of learning goals that reflect the learning capacities of students across the grades? Or are they "a mile wide and an inch deep," as is often suggested? For example, standards, curricula, and textbooks that do not reflect knowledge about students' learning of science will limit what they can learn. Similarly, standards and curricula that are too broad will lead to an unnecessarily diffuse instructional effort. Without a reasonable set of learning objectives to target, research capacity is diluted and efforts to inform practice, in a clear and coherent manner about what is known and what can be done to support children's science learning, will fall short.

Many of today's challenges in science education echo those of the past. Long-standing demands for a better scientifically trained workforce persist, while evidence mounts that scientific literacy is far from what it could or should be. It is essential to bring the best of knowledge to bear on these persistent problems. Other challenges are new, or at least they are salient in ways that they have not been in the past. The historical patterns of inequity in science are no longer tolerable, nor are they inevitable, as children from all backgrounds have the potential to learn science. The standards call for a commitment to all science learners and reflect a moral imperative to make it available in research-supported ways. As educators, researchers, and policy makers tackle these problems, new and old, they will require clear guidance.

ABOUT THIS REPORT

The Committee on Science Learning, Kindergarten Through Eighth Grade, was established by the National Research Council (NRC) to undertake this study. Composed of 14 members selected to reflect a diversity of perspectives and a broad range of expertise, the committee included experts in cognitive and developmental psychology, educational policy and implementation, classroom-based science education research, the natural sciences, the practice of science teaching, and science learning in informal environments. The committee was charged to respond to specific guiding questions (which are laid out in Box 1-1).

Scope and Approach

The committee carried out its charge through an iterative process of gathering information, deliberating on it, identifying gaps and questions, gathering further information to fill these gaps, and holding further discussions. In its search for relevant information, the committee held three public fact-finding meetings, reviewed published reports and unpublished research, and commissioned experts to prepare and present papers. At its fourth and fifth meetings, the committee intensely analyzed and discussed its findings and conclusions.

The report is primarily concerned with characterizing the state of knowledge about how students learn science. However, this interest quickly slips beyond the classroom, museum, or other immediate contexts in which chil-

BOX 1-1 Committee Charge

What does research on learning, culling from a variety of research fields, suggest about how science is learned? What, if any, are "critical stages" in children's development of scientific concepts? Where might connections between lines of research need to be made?

Given a comprehensive review of this research, how does it help clarify how to teach science in K-8 classrooms? How can the existing body of research that is applicable to K-8 science learning be made useful for science educators, teacher educators, professional organizations, researchers, and policy makers?

What other lines of research need to be pursued to make understanding about how students learn science more complete?

dren interact with science. In schools, for example, the organizational, human capital, policy, and material considerations that support science learning emerge as influential. This report also delves into particular parts of this broader picture and includes analysis of supports for teaching science (e.g., instructional systems, teacher knowledge, and professional development). Wherever possible we have tried to focus on the qualities of learning and contexts that are unique to science. Consequently, we steer clear of a broad range of factors that have clear implications for student learning of science (e.g., inequitable school funding, teacher workforce), but that are beyond the scope of this study.

Focus of the Report

This report is an effort to reconcile multiple evidence bases on science learning, in order to render a clear image of what is known collectively about how students across grades K-8 learn science. Synthesizing research from across diverse scholarly perspectives, the report details what is known about how K-8 students learn science in and out of school; what is known about curriculum, assessment, and instructional environments that support learning; and what are the science-specific resources and policies that support instructional systems. The report is intended to inform policy makers, researchers, and education practitioners.

This report builds on an earlier NRC report, *How People Learn* (1999a), which provided a concise description of the state of cognitive research, and it follows in the tradition of a series of reports that focus on learning in specific subject matter areas. These include *Starting Out Right* (National Research Council, 1999b) and *Adding It Up* (National Research Council, 2001a), consensus studies on reading and mathematics, respectively. The discussion of assessment of student learning expands on the research synthesis presented in *Knowing What Students Know* (National Research Council, 2001b). Discussion of large-scale assessment systems to meet the demands of the No Child Left Behind Act is beyond the scope of the current report. This topic is addressed in the report *Systems for State Science Assessment* (National Research Council, 2005).

The current volume also serves as the basis for a forthcoming guide on science learning targeted to K-8 practitioners. Whereas the current report is addressed to policy, research, and practice audiences, the practitioner guide will be addressed specifically to science education practitioners, ranging from classroom teachers, to curriculum developers, and to people who specialize in teacher professional development and assessment. The practitioner guide will focus on the findings from the current volume that are most relevant to practitioners and translate them in a clear, nontechnical manner through extended classroom-based scenarios illustrating how students learn science and constructive practices K-8 science educators can enact in local settings.

Organization of the Report

The report has four major parts. Part I sets the stage for and includes this introductory chapter and Chapter 2, which addresses the goals of science education and our working model of scientific proficiency. What we call the *strands of scientific proficiency* are a touchstone throughout the report. We view science proficiency as multifaceted and the strands as interrelated, although for descriptive and analytic purposes we discuss the strands individually.

Part II tackles how students learn science. Chapter 3 provides a summary of the building blocks for science learning that are in place before children enter school. Chapters 4 through 7 map roughly onto the strands of scientific proficiency and summarize research that provides insight into how students' proficiencies in each strand develop and can be supported across grades K-8. Chapter 4 describes children's understanding of the natural world and how their understanding of scientific explanations can be fostered. Chapter 5 describes the processes involved in generating and evaluating scientific knowledge with specific attention to the role of prior knowledge and experience. Chapter 6 describes what students understand and what they can learn about epistemology and the nature of science. Chapter 7 describes the challenges to engaging students in science and the experiences that can help them become full participants in science classrooms.

Part III addresses the implications of research on science learning for educational settings, focusing in particular on K-8 schools. Chapter 8 builds from the research findings in Part II to develop the idea of learning progressions in science, which characterize how student learning of complex scientific notions might unfold given sustained instructional support over grades K-8. Chapter 9 summarizes current research on pedagogy, examining the central features that are common to current research-based instructional programs. This chapter includes a discussion of classroom-based assessment in science. In Chapter 10 we describe conditions in K-8 classrooms and schools that support quality science instruction, including the teachers' knowledge of science, teaching, and learning; the necessary ongoing opportunities for teacher learning; and a coherent instructional system.

Part IV spells out our conclusions and recommendations for practice and research. Drawing from across the volume, Chapter 11 recapitulates the major findings and implications of the current research base on K-8 science learning. Here we also make recommendations for specific actors in the education system and lay out an agenda for the next generation of science learning research.

REFERENCES

American Association for the Advancement of Science. (1993). *Benchmarks for science literacy*. New York: Oxford University Press.

Atkin, J.M., and Karplus, R. (1962). Discovery or invention? *The Science Teacher, 29,* 45-51.

Berliner, D. (2005). *Our impoverished view of educational reform.* Published in Teachers College Record. Available: http://www.asu.edu/educ/epsl/EPRU/documents/EPSL-0508-116-EPRU.pdf [accessed 2005].

Bloch, E. (1986). Basic research and economic health: The coming challenge. *Science, 232,* 595-599.

Boyd, S.E., Banilower, E.R., Pasley, J.D., and Weiss, I.R. (2003). *Progress and pitfalls: A cross-site look at local systemic change through teacher enhancement.* Chapel Hill, NC: Horizon Research.

Council of Chief State School Officers. (1995). *State curriculum frameworks in math and science: How are they changing across the states?* Washington, DC: Author.

Council of Chief State School Officers. (1997). *Mathematics and science standards and curriculum frameworks: States' progress on development and implementation.* Washington, DC: Author.

Council of Chief State School Officers. (2000). *Summary of findings from SSI and recommendations for NSF's role with states: How NSF can encourage state leadership in improvement of science and mathematics education.* Washington, DC: Author.

Crane, I. (1976). *The National Science Foundation and pre-college science education 1950-75.* (No. 61-660). Washington. DC: U.S. Government Printing Office.

Dow, P. (1991). *Schoolhouse politics: Lessons from the Sputnik era.* Cambridge, MA: Harvard University Press.

Duschl, R.A. (1980). The elementary level science methods course: Breeding ground for an apprehension toward science? A case study. *Journal of Research in Science Teaching, 20*(8), 745-754.

Duschl, R.A. (1990). *Restructuring science education: The importance of theories and their development.* New York: Teachers College Press.

Karplus, R., and Their, H.D. (1967). *A new look at elementary school science: Science Curriculum Improvement Study.* Chicago, IL: Rand McNally.

Kim, J.J., Crasco, L.M., Smith, R.B., Johnson, G., Karantonis, A., and Leavitt, D.J. (2001). *Academic excellence for all urban students: Their accomplishments in science and mathematics.* Norwood, MA: Systemic Research.

Klahr, D., and Simon, H.A. (1999). Studies of scientific discovery: Complementary approaches and convergent findings. *Psychological Bulletin, 125*(5), 524-543.

Kozol, J. (2005). Still separate, still unequal. *Harper's Magazine, 311*(1864), 41-54.

Lagemann, E. (2000). *An elusive science: The troubling history of education research.* Chicago, IL: University of Chicago Press.

Lawrenz, F., and Post, T. (1999). Local systemic change initiatives in science and mathematics. *Research/Practice, 7*(1), Spring. Available: http://education.umn.edu/CAREI/Reports/Rpractice/Spring99/initiatives.html [accessed June 2006].

National Academy of Sciences and National Academy of Engineering. (1982). *Mathematics in the schools: Report of a convocation*. Washington, DC: National Academy Press.

National Center for Education Statistics. (2000). *NAEP 1999 trends in academic progress: Three decades of student performance*. Washington, DC: U.S. Department of Education.

National Center for Education Statistics. (2003). *The national report card: Science 2000*. Washington, DC: U.S. Department of Education.

National Commission on Excellence in Education. (1983). *A nation at risk: The imperative for educational reform*. Washington, DC: U.S. Government Printing Office.

National Research Council. (1996). *National science education standards*. National Committee on Science Education Standards and Assessment. Washington, DC: National Academy Press.

National Research Council. (1999a). *How people learn: Brain, mind, experience, and school*. Committee on Developments in the Science of Learning. J.D. Bransford, A.L. Brown, and R.R. Cocking (Eds.). Washington, DC: National Academy Press.

National Research Council. (1999b). *Starting out right: A guide to promoting children's reading success*. Committee on the Prevention of Reading Difficulties in Young Children. M.S. Burns, P. Griffin, and C.E. Snow (Eds.). Washington, DC: National Academy Press.

National Research Council. (2001a). *Adding it up: Helping children learn mathematics*. Mathematics Learning Study Committee. J. Kilpatrick, J. Swafford, and B. Findell (Eds.). Washington, DC: National Academy Press.

National Research Council. (2001b). *Knowing what students know: The science and design of educational assessment*. Committee on the Foundations of Assessment. J.W. Pellegrino, N. Chudowsky, and R. Glaser (Eds.). Washington, DC: National Academy Press.

National Research Council. (2005). *Systems for state science assessment*. Committee on Test Design for K-12 Science Achievement. M.R. Wilson and M.W. Bertenthal (Eds.). Washington, DC: The National Academies Press.

Rudolph, J.L. (2002). *Scientists in the classroom: The cold war reconstruction of American science education*. New York: Palgrave.

Schwab, J.J. (1962). The teaching of science as enquiry. In J.J. Schwab and P.F. Brandwein (Eds.), *The teaching of science* (pp. 3-103). Cambridge, MA: Harvard University Press.

Spillane, J. (2001). All students: Policy, practitioners, and practice. In S. Fuhrman (Ed.), *From the capitol to the classroom: Standards-based reform in the states*. (National Society for the Study of Education (NSSE) Yearbook). Chicago, IL: University of Chicago Press.

Weiss, I.R., Pasley, J.D., Smith, P.S., Banilower, E.R., and Heck, D.J. (2003). *Looking inside the classroom: A study of K-12 mathematics and science education in the United States*. Chapel Hill, NC: Horizon Research.

Welch, W. (1973). Review of the investigation and evaluation program of Harvard Project Physics. *Journal of Investigation in Science Teaching, 10*, 365-378.

2

Goals for Science Education

Science is built up of facts as a house is of stones, but a collection of facts is no more a science than a pile of stones is a house.

Henri Poincare, *La Science et l'Hypothese* (1908)

Before one can discuss the teaching and learning of science, consensus is needed about what science is and why it should occupy a place in the K-8 curriculum. One must ask: "What is science"? and "Why teach it"? A consensus answer to these fundamental questions is not easily attained, because science is characterized in different ways not only by different categories of people interested in it—practitioners, philosophers, historians, educators—but also by people *within* each of these broad categories. In this chapter, we describe some different characterizations of science and consider implications for what is taught in science classrooms. Although the characterizations share many common features, they vary in the emphasis and priority they place on different aspects of scientific activity, with potential consequences for what is emphasized in science classrooms. We then describe the goals of science education associated with each perspective.

WHAT IS SCIENCE?

Science is both a body of knowledge that represents current understanding of natural systems and the process whereby that body of knowledge has been established and is being continually extended, refined, and revised. Both elements are essential: one cannot make progress in science without an understanding of both. Likewise, in learning science one must come to understand both the body of knowledge and the process by which this knowledge is established, extended, refined, and revised. The various perspectives on science—alluded to above and described below—differ mainly with respect to the process of science, rather than its product. The body of knowledge includes specific facts integrated and articulated into highly developed and well-tested theories. These theories, in turn, can explain bodies of data and predict outcomes of experiments. They are also tools for further development of the subject. An important component of science is the knowledge of the limitations of current theories, that is, an understanding of those aspects of a theory that are well tested and hence are well established, and of those aspects that are not well tested and hence are provisional and likely to be modified as new empirical evidence is acquired.

The process by which scientific theories are developed and the form that those theories take differ from one domain of science to another, but all sciences share certain common features at the core of their problem-solving and inquiry approaches. Chief among these is the attitude that data and evidence hold a primary position in deciding any issue. Thus, when well-established data, from experiment or observation, conflict with a theory or hypothesis, then that idea must be modified or abandoned and other explanations must be sought that can incorporate or take account of the new evidence. This also means that models, theories, and hypotheses are valued to the extent that they make testable (or in principle testable) precise predictions for as yet unmeasured or unobserved effects; provide a coherent conceptual framework that is consistent with a body of facts that are currently known; and offer suggestions of new paths for further study.

A process of argumentation and analysis that relates data and theory is another essential feature of science. This includes evaluation of data quality, modeling, and development of new testable questions from the theory, as well as modifying theories as data dictates the need. Finally, scientists need to be able to examine, review, and evaluate their own knowledge. Holding some parts of a conceptual framework as more or less established and being aware of the ways in which that knowledge may be incomplete are critical scientific practices.

The classic scientific method as taught for many years provides only a very general approximation of the actual working of scientists. The process of theory development and testing is iterative, uses both deductive and inductive logic, and incorporates many tools besides direct experiment. Modeling (both mechanical models and computer simulations) and scenario building (including thought experiments) play an important role in the development of scientific knowledge. The ability to examine one's own knowledge and conceptual frameworks, to evaluate them in relation to new information or competing alternative frameworks, and to alter them by a deliberate and conscious effort are key scientific practices.

Different Perspectives on the Process of Science

Those who study the nature of science and the learning of science have a variety of perspectives not only on key elements of scientific practice and skills (Stanovich, 2003; Grandy and Duschl, 2005), but also on different ways to study the nature of science (Klahr and Simon, 1999; Proctor and Capaldi, 2005; Giere, 1999). The committee recognizes that these different perspectives are not mutually exclusive and that, in considering how best to teach science, each can identify certain elements that need to be given their due attention. We summarize the key elements of a number of these viewpoints.[1]

Science as a Process of Logical Reasoning About Evidence

One view of science, favored by many psychologists who study scientific reasoning, emphasizes the role of domain-general forms of scientific reasoning about evidence, including formal logic, heuristics, and problem-solving strategies. Among psychologists, this view was pioneered by the work of Inhelder and Piaget (1958) on formal operations, by the studies of Bruner, Goodnow, and Austin (1956) on concept development, and by investigations by Wason (1960, 1968) of the type of evidence that people seek when testing their hypotheses. The image of scientist-as-reasoner continues to be influential in contemporary research (Case and Griffin, 1990). In this view, learning to think scientifically is a matter of acquiring problem-solving strategies for coordinating theory and evidence (Klahr, 2000; Kuhn, 1989), mastering counterfactual reasoning (Leslie, 1987), distinguishing patterns of evidence that do and do not support a definitive conclusion (Amsel and Brock, 1996; Beck and Robinson, 2001; Fay and Klahr, 1996; Vellom and Anderson, 1999), and understanding the logic of experimental design (Tschirgi, 1980; Chen and Klahr, 1999). These heuristics and skills are considered important targets for research and for education because they are assumed to be widely applicable and to reflect at least some degree of domain generality and transferability (Kuhn et al., 1995; Ruffman et al., 1993).

Science as a Process of Theory Change

This view places emphasis on the parallel between historical and philosophical aspects of science (Kuhn, 1962) and the domains of cognitive development (Carey, 1985; Koslowski, 1996) in which domain-specific knowledge evolves via the gradual elaboration of existing theories through the accretion of new facts and knowledge (normal science, according to Kuhn), punctuated, occasionally, by the replacement of one theoretical framework by another. The science-as-theory perspective places its emphasis less on the mastery of domain-general logic, heuristics, or strategies and more on

---

[1]This discussion of the different views of science is based on Lehrer and Schauble (2006).

processes of conceptual or theory change. In this view, at critical junctures, as evidence anomalies build up against the established theory, there can occur wholesale restructurings of the theoretical landscape—a paradigm shift, according to Kuhn (1962). For example, in both Kuhn's account of scientific revolutions and Chi's (1992) and Carey's (1988, 1991) accounts of critical points of conceptual restructuring in cognitive development, not only do new concepts enter a domain, but also existing concepts change their meaning in fundamental ways because the theoretical structure within which they are situated radically changes (e.g., changes in concepts like force, weight, matter, combustion, heat, or life). Nersessian (1989) provides a good example of the semantic changes that occur when motion and force are examined across Aristotelian, Galilean, and Newtonian frameworks.

Science as a Process of Participation in the Culture of Scientific Practices

The view of science as practice is emphasized by anthropologists, ethnographers, social psychologists, and the cognitive and developmental psychologists who study "situated cognition" (Brown, Collins, and Duguid, 1989; Lave and Wenger, 1991; Latour, 1990, 1999; Rogoff and Lave, 1984). This view focuses on the nature of scientific activity, both in the short term (e.g., studies of activity in a particular laboratory or a program of study) and historically (e.g., studies of laboratory notebooks, published texts, eyewitness accounts). Science as practice suggests that theory development and reasoning are components of a larger ensemble of activity that includes networks of participants and institutions (Latour, 1999; Longino, 2002); specialized ways of talking and writing (Bazerman, 1988); modeling, using either mechanical and mathematical models or computer-based simulations (Nersessian, 2005); and development of representations that render phenomena accessible, visualizable, and transportable (Gooding, 1989; Latour, 1990; Lehrer and Schauble, 2006).

This perspective serves as a useful foil to the tendency of "pure" cognitive approaches to science to minimize the fact that individual scientists or groups of scientists are always part of a wider social environment, inside and outside science, with which they are in constant communication and which has strongly shaped their knowledge, skills, resources, motives, and attitudes. This interaction between social and cognitive factors is well illustrated in Thagard's (1999a, 1999b) account of the pioneering research by Barry Marshall and Robin Warren. They received the Nobel prize in medicine in 2005 for their discovery of the bacterial origins of stomach ulcers. Until 1983, the prevailing view was that gastric ulcers were caused by lifestyle and stress. When Marshall and Warren suggested that ulcers were caused by the bacterium *Helicobacter pylori,* their claim was viewed as preposterous by the medical research establishment, but the weight of empirical evidence soon overwhelmed deeply entrenched and widely accepted scientific beliefs. The reasons for both the initial and final positions in the field clearly involve important social mechanisms that go beyond simple evidence-based reasoning processes. However, to acknowledge the influence of situated, social, and noncognitive factors in the process of scientific discovery is not to deny the existence of an external physical reality that science attempts to discover and explain (see, e.g., Pickering, 1995).

Language of Science

In science, words often are given very specific meanings that are different from and often more restrictive than their everyday usage. A few such cases are important to discuss before we proceed further in this report. It is also important for teachers to be aware of the confusion that can arise from these multiple usages of familiar words, clarifying the specific scientific usage when needed.

Theory and Hypothesis

A scientific theory (particularly one that is referred to as "the theory of ___," as in the theory of electromagnetism or the theory of thermodynamics or the theory of Newtonian mechanics) is an explanation that has undergone significant testing. Through those tests and the resulting refinement, it takes a form that is a well-established description of, and predictor for, phenomena in a particular domain. A theory is so well established that it is unlikely that new data within that domain will totally discredit it; instead, the theory may be modified and revised to take into account new evidence. There may be domains in which the theory can be applied but has yet to be tested; in those domains the theory is called a working hypothesis. Indeed the term "hypothesis" is used by scientists for an idea that may contribute important explanations to the development of a scientific theory. Scientists use and test hypotheses in the development and refinement of models and scenarios that collectively serve as tools in the development of a theory.

"Theory" has at least two other meanings, and these other meanings differ in important ways from the above use of the term. One alternative use of the term comes from psychological research. Researchers in cognitive development have investigated the way in which children come to understand the world around them and have attributed to them a wide variety of immature and inadequate—albeit pervasive—"theories" about the world. Psychologists use the term "theory" here as a shorthand for the set of ideas and beliefs that forms the child's conceptual framework for explaining phenomena and mechanisms. This usage is closer to the everyday usage of the word "theory" as an idea or conjecture rather than as a complex explanation supported by evidence. It does not imply that a child's theory is a scientific theory in the sense defined above. However, a conceptual framework takes the place of a scientific theory in the way that the child uses it to process information and to view and interact with external events; hence the interplay between instruction and a child's conception of the world is an important issue for the teaching of science.

The second alternative meaning comes from everyday language, in which "theory" is often indistinguishable in its use from "guess," "conjecture," "speculation," "prediction," or even "belief" (e.g., "My theory is that indoor polo will become very popular" or "My theory is that it will rain tomorrow"). Such "theories" are typically very particular and have no broader conceptual scope. Popular usage also confuses the ideas of scientific fact and a scientific theory, which we distinguish by example in the discussion below.

Data and Evidence

A datum is an observation or measurement recorded for subsequent analysis. The observation or measurement may be of a natural system or of a designed and constructed experimental situation. Observation here includes indirect observation, which uses inference from well-understood science, as well as direct sensory observations. Thus the assertion that a particular skeleton comes from an animal that lived during a particular geological period is based on acceptance of the body of knowledge that led to the widely accepted techniques used to date the bones, techniques that are themselves the products of prior scientific study. "Observations" in the research laboratory, particularly observations of events and phenomena whose duration or size is inaccessible to the unaided human perceptual system, often include a substantial chain of such inferences. In the elementary and middle school classroom, observation usually involves fewer inferences. For example, students may begin by conducting unaided observations of natural phenomena and then progress to using simple measurement tools or instruments such as microscopes.

Some use the term "scientific claim" for a well-established property, correlation, or occurrence, directly based on well-validated observation or measurement. When a scientific claim is demonstrated to occur forever and always in any context, scientists will refer to the claim as a fact (e.g., the sun rises in the east). Facts are best seen as evidence and claims of phenomena that come together to develop and refine or to challenge explanations. For example, the fact that earthquakes occur has been long known, but the explanation for the fact that earthquakes occur takes on a different meaning if one adopts plate tectonics as a theoretical framework. The fact that there are different types of earthquakes (shallow and deep focus) helps to deepen and expand the explanatory power of the theory of plate tectonics.

A century ago the atomic substructure of matter was a theory, which became better established as new evidence and inferences based on this evidence deepened the complexity and explanatory power of the theory. Today, atoms are an established component of matter due to the modern capability of imaging individual atoms in matter with such tools as scanning-tunneling microscopes. This kind of progression from theoretical construct to observed property leads to some confusion in the minds of many people about the nature of theory and the distinctions among theory, evidence, claims, and facts. The history of science further reveals that theories progress from hypotheses or tentative ideas to core explanations.

Thus, another source of confusion for the public understanding of science is the use of the term "theory" to represent promising ideas as well as core explanatory theories. Core explanatory theories are those that are firmly established through accumulation of a substantial body of supporting evidence and have no competitors (e.g., cell theory, periodic law, theory of evolution, theory of plate tectonics). For much of science, theories are broad conceptual frameworks that can be invalidated by contradictions with data but can never be wholly validated.

To give a specific example: it is an observed property that things fall down when dropped near the surface of the earth. Repeated observations give the rate of acceleration in this event, both its global average and local variations from that average. Newton's law of universal gravitation and Einstein's general theory of relativity are two successive theories that incorporate this observation and give quantitative predictions for the size of the gravitational effects in any situation, not just on earth. These theories describe but do not actually explain gravitation in the conventional sense of that word; they invoke no underlying mechanism due to substructure and subsystems. The general theory of relativity includes Newton's law of gravitation as a special limited case (an approximation or idealization, valid to high accuracy under certain conditions), but it is a more general theory that makes predictions for cases not covered by Newton's law (e.g., the bending of light paths by the sun or other stars).

In this example, drawn from physics, the theories are expressed in mathematical form and their predictions are thus both precise and specific. They lend themselves readily to computer modeling and simulation. In other areas of science, theories can take more linguistic forms and involve other types of models. What is general is that scientific theories are valued when they (a) incorporate a significant body of evidence in a single conceptual framework and (b) offer predictive suggestions about future directions for study that are specific enough that one can test the theory's validity and domain of applicability. A theory may or may not include a mechanism for the effects it describes and predicts.

Another important feature of the example is that it challenges a common perception of scientific revolutions. Einstein's general theory of relativity was a true scientific revolution, in that it challenged and redefined conceptions of the nature of space and time. However, it did not invalidate all that had gone before; instead, it showed clearly both the limitations of the previous theory *and* the domain in which the previous theory is valid as an excellent (close) approximation, useful because it is much simpler (both conceptually and mathematically) than the full general theory of relativity.

This is a key understanding: science is subject to development and change, yet well-tested and established theories remain true in their tested domain even when dramatic new ideas or knowledge changes the way one views that domain. Such theories are tentative in domains in which they have not yet been tested, or in which only limited data are available, so that the tests are not yet conclusive but are far from tentative in the domains in which they have repeatedly been tested through their use in new scientific inquiries.

Argument

In everyday usage, an argument is an unpleasant situation in which two or more people have differing opinions and become heated in their discussion of this difference. A somewhat different view of the term "argument" comes from the tradition of formal debate, in which contestants are scored on arguments that favor a particular position or point of view or disfavor the opposing one. Argumentation in science has a different and less combative or competitive role than either of these forms (Kuhn, 1991). It is a mode of logical discourse whose goal is to tease out the relationship between ideas and the evidence—for example, to decide what a theory or hypothesis predicts for a given circumstance, or whether a proposed explanation is consistent or not with some new observation. The goal of those engaged in scientific argumentation is a common one: to tease out as much information and understanding from the situation under discussion as possible. Alternative points of view are valued as long as they contribute to this process within the accepted norms of science and logic, but not when they offer alternatives that are viewed as outside those norms. Because the role, mode, and acceptance of argument, in its everyday sense, are cultural variables, it is important to teach skills and acceptable modes of scientific argumentation, and for both teachers and students to learn by experience the difference between this form of discourse and their preconceived notions of what "wins" an argument.

SCIENCE EDUCATION

Why Teach Science?

In the modern world, some knowledge of science is essential for everyone. It is the opinion of this committee that science should be as nonnegotiable a part of basic education as are language arts and mathematics. It is important to teach science because of the following:

1. Science is a significant part of human culture and represents one of the pinnacles of human thinking capacity.
2. It provides a laboratory of common experience for development of language, logic, and problem-solving skills in the classroom.
3. A democracy demands that its citizens make personal and community decisions about issues in which scientific information plays a fundamental role, and they hence need a knowledge of science as well as an understanding of scientific methodology.
4. For some students, it will become a lifelong vocation or avocation.
5. The nation is dependent on the technical and scientific abilities of its citizens for its economic competitiveness and national needs.

What Should Be the Goals of Elementary and Middle School Science?

To quote Albert Einstein, the goal of education is "to produce independently thinking and acting individuals." The eventual goal of science education is to produce individuals capable of understanding and evaluating information that is, or purports to be, scientific in nature and of making decisions that incorporate that information appropriately, and, furthermore, to produce a sufficient number and diversity of skilled and motivated future scientists, engineers, and other science-based professionals.

The science curriculum in the elementary grades, like that for other subject areas, should be designed for all students to develop critical basic knowledge and basic skills, interests, and habits of mind that will lead to productive efforts to learn and understand the subject more deeply in later grades. If this is done well, then all five of the reasons to teach science will be well served. It is not necessary in these grades to distinguish between those who will eventually become scientists and those who will chiefly use their knowledge of science in making personal and societal choices. A good elementary science program will provide the basis for either path in later life.

The specific content of elementary school science has been outlined in multiple documents, including the *National Science Education Standards*, the *Benchmarks for Science Literacy,* and multiple state standards documents. Teachers are held accountable to particular state and local requirements. It is not the role of this report to specify a list of content to be taught. However, it is important to note that what this report says about science learning always assumes that there is a strong basis of factual knowledge and conceptual development in the science curriculum, and that the goal of any methodology for teaching is to facilitate student learning and understanding of this content, as well as developing their skills in, and understanding of, the methods of scientific observation, experimentation, modeling, and analysis.

It is often said that children are natural scientists. Experts in child development have debated this issue, not on the basis of the basic facts of children's behavior, but rather on the relation between that behavior and the essential aspects of scientific thinking (Giere, 1996; Gopnik, 1996; Gopnik and Wellman, 1992; Harris, 1994; Kuhn, 1989; Metz, 1995, 1997; Vosniadou and Brewer, 1992, 1994). Rather than attempting to resolve this debate, we simply acknowledge the fact that children bring to science class a natural curiosity and a set of ideas and conceptual frameworks that incorporate their experiences of the natural world and other information that they have learned. Since these experiences vary, children at a given age have a wide range in their skills, knowledge, and conceptual development. A teacher therefore needs to be able to evaluate each child's knowledge and conceptual and skill development, as well as the child's level of metacognition about his or her own knowledge, skills, and concepts, in order to provide a learning environment that moves each child's development in all these areas. A key question for instruction is thus how to adapt the instructional goals to the existing knowledge and skills of the learners, as well as how to choose instructional techniques that will be most effective.

Each of the views of science articulated above highlights particular modes of thought that are essential to that view. These views are not mutually exclusive descriptions of science, but rather each stresses particular aspects. Since students need to progress in all aspects, it is useful for teachers to have a clear understanding of each of these components of scientific development, just as they need a clear understanding of the subject matter, the specific science content, that they are teaching. It is also useful at times to focus instruction on development of specific skills, in balance with a focus on the learning of specific facts or the understanding of a particular conceptual framework.

Thus, if one looks from the perspective of science as a process of reasoning about evidence, one sees that logical argumentation and problem-solving skills are important. Certain aspects of metacognition are also highlighted, such as the ability to be aware when one's previously held convictions are in conflict with an observation. If one looks at science as a process of theory change, one sees that teachers must recognize the role of students' prior conceptions about a subject and facilitate the necessary processes of conceptual change and development. Finally, when one looks at science as a process of participation in the culture of scientific practice, attention is drawn to the ways in which children's individual cultural and social backgrounds can, on one hand, create barriers to science participation and learning due to possible conflicts of cultural norms or practices with those of science, and, on the other hand, provide opportunities for contributions, particularly from students from nonmainstream cultures, that enrich the discourse in the science classroom. One also sees a range of practices, such as model building and data representation, that each in itself is a specific skill and thus needs to be incorporated and taught in science classrooms.

It is thus clear that multiple strategies are needed, some focused primarily on key skills or specific knowledge, others on particular conceptual understanding, and yet others on metacognition. The issues of what children bring to school and of how teaching can build on it to foster robust science learning with this rich multiplicity of aspects are the core topics of this report.

Strands of Scientific Proficiency

Understanding science is multifaceted. Research has often treated aspects of scientific proficiency as discrete. However, current research indicates that proficiency in one aspect of science is closely related to proficiency in others (e.g., analytic reasoning skills are greater when one is reasoning about familiar domains). Like strands of a rope, the strands of scientific proficiency are intertwined. However, for purposes of being clear about learning and learning outcomes, the committee discusses these four strands separately (see Box 2-1 for a summary).

The strands of scientific proficiency lay out broad learning goals for students. They address the knowledge and reasoning skills that students must eventually acquire to be considered fully proficient in science. They are also a means to that end: they are practices that students need to participate in and become fluent with in order to develop proficiency.

Students who are proficient in science:

1. know, use, and interpret scientific explanations of the natural world;
2. generate and evaluate scientific evidence and explanations;
3. understand the nature and development of scientific knowledge; and
4. participate productively in scientific practices and discourse.

The strands are not independent or separable in the practice of science, nor in the teaching and learning of science. Rather, the strands of scientific proficiency are interwoven and, taken together, are viewed as science as

BOX 2-1 **Strands of Scientific Proficiency**

Strand 1: Know, use, and interpret scientific explanations of the natural world.

This strand includes acquiring facts and the conceptual structures that incorporate those facts and using these ideas productively to understand many phenomena in the natural world. This includes using those ideas to construct and refine explanations, arguments, or models of particular phenomena.

Strand 2: Generate and evaluate scientific evidence and explanations.

This strand encompasses the knowledge and skills needed to build and refine models based on evidence. This includes designing and analyzing empirical investigations and using empirical evidence to construct and defend arguments.

Strand 3: Understand the nature and development of scientific knowledge.

This strand focuses on students' understanding of science as a way of knowing. Scientific knowledge is a particular kind of knowledge with its own sources, justifications, and uncertainties. Students who understand scientific knowledge recognize that predictions or explanations can be revised on the basis of seeing new evidence or developing a new model.

Strand 4: Participate productively in scientific practices and discourse.

This strand includes students' understanding of the norms of participating in science as well as their motivation and attitudes toward science. Students who see science as valuable and interesting tend to be good learners and participants in science. They believe that steady effort in understanding science pays off—not that some people understand science and other people never will. To engage productively in science, however, students need to understand how to participate in scientific debates, adopt a critical stance, and be willing to ask questions.

These strands of scientific proficiency represent learning goals for students as well as providing a broad framework for curriculum design. They address the knowledge and reasoning skills that students must eventually acquire to be considered fully proficient in science. They are also a means to that end: they are practices that students need to participate in and become fluent with in order to develop proficiency. Evidence to date indicates that in the process of achieving proficiency in science, the four strands are intertwined, so that advances in one strand support and advance those in another.

The committee thinks, and emerging evidence suggests, the development of proficiency is best supported when classrooms provide learning opportunities that interweave all four strands together in instruction.

practice (see Lehrer and Schauble, 2006). The science-as-practice perspective invokes the notion that learning science involves learning a system of interconnected ways of thinking in a social context to accomplish the goal of working with and understanding scientific ideas. This perspective stresses how conceptual understanding of natural systems is linked to the ability to develop explanations of phenomena and to carry out empirical investigations in order to develop or evaluate knowledge claims.

The strands framework emerged through the committee's syntheses of disparate research literatures on learning and teaching science, which define science outcomes differently and frequently do not inform one another. The framework offers a new perspective on what is learned when students learn science. First, the strands emphasize the idea of knowledge in use. That is, students' knowledge is not static, and proficiency involves deploying knowledge and skills across all four strands in order to engage successfully in scientific practices. The content of each strand described below is drawn from research and differs from many typical presentations of goals for science learning. For example, we include an emphasis on theory building and modeling, which is often missing in existing standards and curricular frameworks. And, the fourth strand is often completely overlooked, but research indicates it is a critical component of science learning, particularly for students from populations that are typically underrepresented in science.

These strands illustrate the importance of moving beyond a simple dichotomy of instruction in terms of science as content or science as process. That is, teaching content alone is not likely to lead to proficiency in science, nor is engaging in inquiry experiences devoid of meaningful science content. Rather, students across grades K-8 are more likely to advance in their understanding of science when classrooms provide learning opportunities that attend to all four strands.

Know, Use, and Interpret Scientific Explanations of the Natural World

Knowing, using, and interpreting scientific explanations encompasses learning the facts, concepts, principles, laws, theories, and models of science. As the *National Science Education Standards* state (National Research Council, 1996, p. 23):

> Understanding science requires that an individual integrate a complex structure of many types of knowledge, including the ideas of science, relationships between ideas, reasons for these relationships, ways to use the ideas to explain and predict other natural phenomena, and ways to apply them to many events.

Understanding natural systems requires knowledge of conceptually central ideas and facts integrated in well-structured knowledge systems, that is, facts integrated and articulated into highly developed and well-established theories. In the science-as-practice framework, we emphasize that these theories or models—the "big ideas" or powerful explanatory models of science—are what enable learners to construct explanations about natural phenomena, including novel cases not exactly like those previously experienced. This strand stresses acquiring facts, building organized and meaningful conceptual structures that incorporate these facts, and employing these conceptual structures during the interpretation, construction, and refinement of explanations, arguments, or models.

Generate and Evaluate Scientific Evidence and Explanations

Generating and evaluating scientific evidence and explanations encompasses the knowledge and skills used for building and refining models and explanations (conceptual, computational, mechanistic), designing and analyzing empirical investigations and observations, and constructing and defending arguments with empirical evidence. This strand also incorporates the social practices (e.g., critiquing an argument) and tools (conceptual, mathematical, physical, and computational) fundamental to constructing and evaluating knowledge claims. Hence, it includes a wide range of practices involved in designing and carrying out a scientific investigation, including asking questions, deciding what to measure, developing measures, collecting data from the measures, structuring the data, interpreting and evaluating the data, and using the empirical results to develop and refine arguments, models, and theories.

Understand the Nature and Development of Scientific Knowledge

This strand focuses attention on students' understanding of science as a way of knowing: the nature of scientific knowledge, the nature of theory and evidence in science, and the sources for, justification of, and certainty of scientific knowledge. It also includes students' reflection on the status of their own knowledge.

This strand includes developing a conception of "doing science" that extends beyond experiment to include modeling, systematic observation, and historical reconstruction. It also includes an awareness that science entails the search for core explanatory constructs and connections between them. More specifically, students must recognize that there may be multiple interpretations of the same phenomena. They must understand that explanations are increasingly valuable as they account for the available evidence more completely, and as they generate new, productive research questions. Students should be able to step back from evidence or an explanation and consider whether another interpretation of a particular finding is plausible with respect to existing scientific evidence and other knowledge that they hold with confidence. This entails embracing a point of view as *possible* and worthy of further investigation, but subject to careful scrutiny and consideration of alternative perspectives (which may be deemed more valuable in the end).

Participate Productively in Scientific Practices and Discourse

To understand science, one must use science and do so in a manner that reflects the values of scientific practice. Participation is premised on a view that science and scientific knowledge are valuable and interesting, seeing oneself as an effective learner and participant in science, and the belief that steady effort in understanding science pays off. These attitudes toward science and science learning develop as a consequence of students' experience of educational, social, and cultural environments. The educational environment in particular is an important influence on how students view themselves as science learners and whether they feel supported to participate fully in the scientific community of the classroom.

Viewing the science classroom as a scientific community akin to communities in professional science is advantageous (although K-8 students are clearly not engaged in professional science). Science advances in large part through interactions among members of research communities as they test new ideas, solicit and provide feedback, articulate and evaluate emerging explanations, develop shared representations and models, and reach consensus. Likewise, participation in scientific practices in the classroom helps students advance their understanding of scientific argumentation and explanations; engage in the construction of scientific evidence, representations, and models; and reflect on how scientific knowledge is constructed.

To participate fully in the scientific practices in the classroom, students need to develop a shared understanding of the norms of participation in science. This includes social norms for constructing and presenting a scientific argument and engaging in scientific debates. It also includes habits of mind, such as adopting a critical stance, a willingness to ask questions and seek help, and developing a sense of appropriate trust and skepticism.

Interconnections Among the Strands

Interconnections among the strands in the process of learning are supported by research, although the strength of the research evidence varies across the strands. The cognitive research literatures support the value of teaching content in the context of the practices of science. For example, the knowledge factor, that is, the depth of one's knowledge of the domain, has repeatedly been identified as a primary factor in the power or limitations of one's scientific reasoning (Brewer and Samarapungavan, 1991; Brown, 1990;

Carey, 1985; Chi, Feltovich, and Glaser, 1981; Goswami and Brown, 1989; see also the discussion in Chapter 5). Not surprisingly, both children's and adults' scientific reasoning tends to be strongest in domains in which their knowledge is strongest. Therefore, if the goal is to advance the leading edge of children's scientific reasoning, their instruction needs to be grounded in contexts that also build on their relatively robust understanding of content. There is also mounting evidence that knowledge of scientific explanations of the natural world is advanced through generating and evaluating scientific evidence. For example, instruction designed to engage students in model-based reasoning advances their conceptual understanding of natural phenomena (see, for example, Brown and Clement, 1989; Lehrer et al., 2001; Stewart, Cartier, and Passmore, 2005; White, 1993; Wiser and Amin, 2001; see also the discussions in Chapter 4 and Chapter 9).

Evidence for links between Strands 3 and 4 and the other two strands is less robust, but emerging findings are compelling. Motivation, which is an element of Strand 4, clearly plays an important role in learning (see Chapter 7). Furthermore, instruction that makes the norms for participating in science explicit supports students' ability to critique evidence and coordinate theory and evidence (Herrenkohl and Guerra, 1998; for further discussion, see Chapters 7 and 9).

Although we have teased apart aspects of understanding and learning to do science as four interrelated strands, we do not separate these as separate learning objectives in our treatment of the pedagogical literature. Indeed, there is evidence that while the strands can be assessed separately, students use them in concert when engaging in scientific tasks (Gotwals and Songer, 2006). Therefore, we contend that to help children develop conceptual understanding of natural systems in any deep way requires engaging them in scientific practices that incorporate all four strands to help them to build and apply conceptual models, as well as to understand science as a disciplinary way of knowing.

DEVELOPMENT, LEARNING, AND INSTRUCTION

An important theme throughout this report is the complex interplay among development, learning and instruction, and the implications for science education. The evidence base for this report draws from several, mostly independent bodies of research, each emerging from different research traditions that operate within different theoretical frameworks. These frameworks differ in the relative emphasis placed on development versus learning and instruction. As a result, the different bodies of research often provide differing and somewhat conflicting pictures of children's competence. Reconciling these visions of competence and understanding their implications for how to support science learning require careful consideration of the assumptions underlying both research and current practices in science education.

In science education, there has been a frequent assumption that development is a kind of inevitable unfolding and that one must simply wait until a child is cognitively "ready" for more abstract or theory-based forms of content. In other words, through maturation with age, children will achieve certain cognitive milestones naturally, with little direct intervention from adults. Many science educators and policy makers have assumed that the power and limitations of children's scientific reasoning at different grade levels could be derived from the stages delineated in the cognitive developmental literature. In this view, "developmentally appropriate" education would thus require keeping instruction within these bounds.

There are significant problems with this assumption. First, it assumes that the power and limitations of children's scientific thinking within an age band can be described and predicted by stage-defining criteria, with limited variability or change therein. As we show in the chapters in Part II, the cognitive developmental literature simply does not support this assumption. In the words of John Flavell, a seminal cognitive developmentalist (1994), "Virtually all contemporary developmentalists agree that cognitive development is not as general stage-like or grand stage-like as Piaget and most of the rest of the field once thought" (p. 574). The foundation of research undermining a broad stage-like conception of cognitive development goes back at least three decades (e.g., Wollman, 1997a, 1997b).

In fact, variability in scientific reasoning within any age group is large, sometimes broader than the differences that separate contiguous age bands. In self-directed experimentation tasks, there are always some adults whose performance looks no better than that of the average child (Klahr, Fay, and Dunbar, 1993; Kuhn, Schauble, and Garcia-Mila, 1992; Kuhn et al., 1995; Schauble, 1996; see also the discussion in Chapter 5). Indeed, many adults never seem to master the heuristics for generating and interpreting evidence. Moreover, education, context, and domain expertise seem to play a strong role in whether and when these heuristics are appropriately used (Kuhn, 1991).

Stage-like conceptualizations of development also ignore the critical role of support and guidance by knowledgeable adults and peers. As noted in the National Research Council report *How People Learn* (1999), children need assistance to learn; building on their early capacities requires catalysts and mediation. Adults play a central role in "promoting children's curiosity and persistence by directing their attention, structuring their experiences, supporting their learning attempts, and regulating the complexity and difficulty of levels of information for them" (p. 223). In the case of the science classroom, both teachers and peers can and must fill these critical roles. The power of schooling is its potential to make available other people, including adults and peers, to learn with; thought-provoking tasks; tools that both boost and shape thinking; and activity structures that encapsulate learning-supportive norms and processes.

Indeed, observational and historical studies of working scientists reaffirm the promise of looking closely at the ways in which environments support learning. These studies demonstrate that theory development and reasoning in science are components of an ensemble of activity that includes networks of participants and institutions (Latour, 1999); specialized ways of talking and writing (Bazerman, 1988); development of representations that render phenomena accessible, visualizable, and transportable (Gooding, 1989; Latour, 1990); and efforts to manage material contingency by making instruments, machines, and other contexts of observation (such as experimental apparatus). The alignment of instruments, measures, and theories is never entirely principled (e.g., Pickering, 1995), and, whether the scientists are professionals or school students, they wrestle with the relationships between these tools and the phenomena they are intended to capture.

A second major problem with assuming children's learning will unfold without support is that what children are capable of doing without instruction may lag considerably behind what they are capable of doing with effective instruction. Further clouding the picture is that research on cognitive development may not be helpful in illuminating how instruction can advance children's knowledge and skill. Often, studies in developmental psychology do not have an instructional component and therefore may be more informative about starting points than about children's potential for developing scientific proficiency under effective instructional conditions.

For example, the idea that prior to middle school children are incapable of designing controlled experiments has been a ubiquitous assumption in the elementary school science community. This claim can be traced to Inhelder and Piaget's (1958) influential study, *The Growth of Logical Thinking from Childhood to Adolescence*. Indeed the *Benchmarks for Scientific Literacy* (American Association for the Advancement of Science, 1993) included design of controlled experiments in their list of limitations of the scientific reasoning of third to fifth graders:

> Research studies suggest that there are some limits on what to expect at this level of student intellectual development. One limit is that the design of carefully controlled experiments is still beyond most students in middle grades.

Consider the *Benchmarks'* crucial—and unusual—caveat (p. 11):

> However, the studies say more about what students at this level do not learn in today's schools than about what they might possibly learn if instruction were more effective.

Indeed, instructional studies have documented success at teaching controlled experimental design to children in this grade span (see Klahr and Nigam, 2004; Toth, Klahr, and Chen, 2000).

As another example, consider the issue of reasoning about theory and evidence. In their delineation of the limitations on third to fifth graders' scientific reasoning, the *Benchmarks* also claim that third to fifth graders "confuse theory (explanation) with evidence for it." In accordance with this deficiency stance, most science curricula for young children avoid consideration of theory and evidence.

The developmental literature related to this fundamental aspect of scientific reasoning is more complex, with some studies in support of the *Benchmarks* stance and some studies suggesting greater competence. For example, Kuhn, Amsel, and O'Loughlin (1988) conclude that, in the preadolescent, theory and evidence "meld into a single representation as 'the way things are'" (p. 221), whereas the research of Sodian, Zaitchek, and Carey (1991) indicates that, in some form and under some conditions, even preschoolers can make this distinction and reason accordingly.

Once again, the instructional literature indicates that children's capabilities in this regard are to some degree amenable to instruction. The instructional design research literature provides an existence proof that elementary schoolchildren's reasoning about theory and evidence in the context of doing science can be advanced under particular instructional conditions (see Smith et al., 2000). In Chapter 5 we discuss evidence related to both of these examples.

The problem with reducing the power and limitations of children's scientific reasoning to developmental stages is further undermined by the enduring challenges that many of these issues have posed to much older students and even to practicing scientists. For example, although one can read Inhelder and Piaget's work (1958) as contending that an understanding of experimental control emerges with formal operational thought, we continue to train students well beyond adolescence in the logic of experimental design. Continuing with the examples used above, the differentiation of theory and evidence poses even more challenges. Indeed, the philosopher of science Stephen Toulmin (1972) has argued that observation and theory are at some level inevitably entangled; in his words, "the semantic and empirical elements are not so much wantonly confused as unavoidably fused" (p. 189). Delaying instruction until such a capability emerges through "development" cannot constitute a strategic tactic, as development alone cannot adequately elaborate the competence. Furthermore, there is mounting evidence that instruction can advance these capabilities as well as many others.

In short, young children have a broad repertoire of cognitive capacities directly related to many aspects of scientific practice, and it is problematic to view these as simply a product of cognitive development. Current research indicates that students do not go through general stages of cognitive development, and there are no "critical periods" for learning particular aspects of science. Rather, cognitive capacities directly related to scientific practice usually do not fully develop in and of themselves apart from instruction, even in older children or adults. These capacities need to be nurtured, sustained, and elaborated in supportive learning environments that provide effective scaffolding and targeted as important through assessment practices.

Although there is much that is not understood about the relationships between development and learning, the evidence is clear that a student's instructional history plays a critical role in her scientific knowledge, scientific reasoning, and readiness to do and learn more science. Components of the cognitive system (e.g., processing speed and capacity, strategies and heuristics, metacognition) certainly are factors that contribute to a student's learning history, but so do other mechanisms that are manipulable by educators and constitute the "design tools" that a teacher can deploy to most directly affect science learning.

REFERENCES

American Association for the Advancement of Science. (1993). *Benchmarks for science literacy*. New York: Oxford University Press.

Amsel, E., and Brock, S. (1996). The development of evidence evaluation skills. *Cognitive Development, 11,* 523-550.

Bazerman, C. (1988). *Shaping written knowledge: The genre and activity of the experimental article in science.* Madison: University of Wisconsin Press.

Beck, S.R., and Robinson, E.J. (2001). Children's ability to make tentative interpretations of ambiguous messages. *Journal of Experimental Child Psychology, 79,* 95-114.

Brewer, W.F., and Samarapungavan, A. (1991). Child theories versus scientific theories: Differences in reasoning or differences in knowledge? In R.R. Hoffman and D.S. Palermo (Eds.), *Cognition and the symbolic processes: Applied and ecological perspectives* (pp. 209-232). Hillsdale, NJ: Lawrence Erlbaum Associates.

Brown, A.L. (1990). Domain-specific principles affect learning and transfer in children. *Cognitive Science, 14,* 107-134.

Brown, D.E., and Clement, J. (1989). Overcoming misconceptions by analogical reasoning: Abstract transfer versus explanatory model construction. *Instructional Science, 18,* 237-261.

Brown, J.S., Collins, A., and Duguid, P. (1989). Situated cognition and the culture of learning. *Educational Researcher, 18*(1), 32-41.

Bruner, J.S., Goodnow, J.J., and Austin, G.A. (1956). *A study of thinking.* New York: Wiley.

Carey, S. (1985). *Conceptual change in childhood.* Cambridge, MA: MIT Press.

Carey, S. (1988). Conceptual differences between children and adults. *Mind and Language, 3,* 167-181.

Carey, S. (1991). Knowledge acquisition: Enrichment or conceptual change? In S. Carey and R. Gelman (Eds.), *The epigenesis of mind: Essays on biology and cognition* (pp. 257-291). Hillsdale, NJ: Lawrence Earlbaum Associates.

Case, R., and Griffin, S. (1990). Child cognitive development: The role of central conceptual structures in the development of scientific and social thought. In E.A. Hauert (Ed.), *Developmental psychology: Cognitive, perceptuo-motor, and neurological perspectives* (pp. 193-230). Amsterdam: Elsevier.

Chen, Z., and Klahr, D. (1999). All other things being equal: Acquisition and transfer of the control of variables strategy. *Child Development, 70*(5), 1098-1120.

Chi, M.T.H. (1992). Conceptual change within and across ontological categories: Examples from learning and discovery in science. In R. Giere (Ed.), *Cognitive models of science: Minnesota studies in the philosophy of science* (pp. 129-186). Minneapolis: University of Minnesota Press.

Chi, M.T.H., Feltovich, P.J., and Glaser, R. (1981). Categorization and representation of physics problems by experts and novices. *Cognitive Science, 5,* 121-152.

Fay, A., and Klahr, D. (1996). Knowing about guessing and guessing about knowing: Preschoolers' understanding of indeterminacy. *Child Development, 67,* 689-716.

Flavell, J.H. (1994). Cognitive development: Past, present, and future. In R.D. Parke, P.A. Ross, J. Rieser Ornstein, and C. Zahn-Waxler (Eds.), *A century of developmental psychology* (pp. 569-587). Washington, DC: American Psychological Association.

Giere, R.N. (1996). The scientist as adult. *Philosophy of Science, 63,* 538-541.

Giere, R.N. (1999). *Science without laws.* Chicago, IL: University of Chicago Press.

Gooding, D. (1989). "Magnetic curves" and the magnetic field: Experimentation and representation in the history of a theory. In D. Gooding, T. Pinch, and S. Schlffer (Eds.), *The uses of experiment: Studies on the natural sciences* (pp. 183-223). New York: Cambridge University Press.

Gopnik, A. (1996). The scientist as child. *Philosophy of Science, 63*(4), 485-514.

Gopnik, A., and Wellman, H.M. (1992). Why the child's theory of mind really is a theory. *Mind and Language, 7,* 145-171.

Goswami, U., and Brown, A.L. (1989). Melting chocolate and melting snowmen: Analogical reasoning and causal relations. *Cognition, 35,* 69-95.

Gotwals, A., and Songer, N. (2006). *Measuring students' scientific content and inquiry reasoning,* Proceedings of the 7th International Conference of the Learning Sciences, International Society of the Learning Sciences, June 27-July 1, Indiana University, Bloomington, IN.

Grandy, R., and Duschl, R. (2005). *Reconsidering the character and role of inquiry in school science: Analysis of a conference.* Paper presented at the meeting of the International HPS and Science Teaching Group, July 15-18, Leeds, England.

Harris, P.L. (1994). Thinking by children and scientists: False analogies and neglected similarities. In L.A. Hirschfeld and S.A. Gelman (Eds.), *Mapping the mind: Domain specificity in cognition and culture* (pp. 294-315). New York: Cambridge University Press.

Herrenkohl, L.R., and Guerra, M.R. (1998). Participant structures, scientific discourse, and student engagement in fourth grade. *Cognition and Instruction, 16*(4), 431-473.

Inhelder, B., and Piaget, J. (1958). *The growth of logical thinking from childhood to adolescence.* London, England: Routledge and Kagan Paul.

Klahr, D. (2000). *Exploring science: The cognition and development of discovery processes.* Cambridge, MA: MIT Press.

Klahr, D., Fay, A.L., and Dunbar, K. (1993). Heuristics for scientific experimentation: A developmental study. *Cognitive Psychology, 25*(1), 111-146.

Klahr, D., and Nigam, M. (2004). The equivalence of learning paths in early science instruction: Effects of direct instruction and discovery learning. *Psychological Science, 15,* 661-667.

Klahr, D., and Simon, H.A. (1999). Studies of scientific discovery: Complementary approaches and convergent findings. *Psychological Bulletin, 125*(5), 524-543.

Koslowski, B. (1996). *Theory and evidence: The development of scientific reasoning.* Cambridge, MA: MIT Press.

Kuhn, D. (1989). Children and adults as intuitive scientists. *Psychological Review, 96,* 674-689.

Kuhn, D. (1991). *The skills of argument.* New York: Cambridge University Press.

Kuhn, D., Amsel, E., and O'Loughlin, M. (1988). *The development of scientific thinking skills.* San Diego, CA: Academic Press.

Kuhn, D., Garcia-Mila, M. Zohar, A., and Andersen, C. (1995). *Strategies of knowledge acquisition.* (Monographs of the Society for Research in Child Development, serial no. 245, vol. 60, no. 4). Chicago: Child Development Publications, University of Chicago Press.

Kuhn, D., Schauble, L., and Garcia-Mila, M. (1992). Cross-domain development of scientific reasoning. *Cognition and Instruction, 9*(4), 285-327.

Kuhn, T.S. (1962). *The structure of scientific revolutions.* Chicago, IL: University of Chicago Press.

Latour, B. (1990). Drawing things together. In M Lynch and S. Woolgar (Eds.), *Representation in scientific practice* (pp. 19-68). Cambridge, MA: MIT Press.

Latour, B. (1999). *Pandora's hope: Essays on the reality of science studies.* London, England: Cambridge University Press.

Lave, J., and Wenger, E. (1991). *Situated learning: Legitimate peripheral participation.* London, England: Cambridge University Press.

Lehrer, R., and Schauble, L. (2006). Scientific thinking and science literacy. In W. Damon, R. Lerner, K.A. Renninger, and I.E. Sigel (Eds.), *Handbook of child psychology, 6th edition, volume 4, child psychology in practice.* Hoboken, NJ: Wiley.

Lehrer, R., Schauble, L., Strom, D., and Pligge, M. (2001). Similarity of form and substance: Modeling material kind. In D. Klahr and S. Carver (Eds.), *Cognition and instruction: 25 years of progress* (pp. 39-74). Mahwah, NJ: Lawrence Erlbaum Associates.

Leslie, A.M. (1987). Pretense and representation: The origins of "theory of mind." *Psychological Review, 94*(4), 412-426.

Longino, H. (2002). *The fate of knowledge.* Princeton: Princeton University Press.

Metz, K.E. (1995). Reassessment of developmental constraints on children's science instruction. *Review of Educational Research, 65,* 93-127.

Metz, K.E. (1997). On the complex relation between cognitive developmental research and children's science curricula. *Review of Educational Research, 67,* 151-163.

National Research Council. (1996). *National science education standards.* National Committee on Science Education Standards and Assessment. Washington, DC: National Academy Press.

National Research Council. (1999). *How people learn: Brain, mind, experience, and school.* Committee on Developments in the Science of Learning. J.D. Bransford, A.L. Brown, and R.R. Cocking (Eds.). Washington, DC: National Academy Press.

Nersessian, N.J. (1989). Conceptual change in science and in science education. *Synthese, 80*(1), 163-184.

Nersessian, N.J. (2005). Interpreting scientific and engineering practices: Integrating the cognitive, social, and cultural dimensions. In M. Gorman, R. Tweney, D. Gooding, and A. Kincannon (Eds.), *Scientific and technological thinking* (pp. 17-56). Mahwah, NJ: Lawrence Erlbaum Associates.

Pickering, A. (1995). *The mangle of practice: Time, agency and science.* Chicago, IL: University of Chicago Press.

Poincaré, J.H. (1908). *La science et l'hypothese.* Paris, France: Flammarion.

Proctor, R.W., and Capaldi, E.J. (2005). *Why science matters: Understanding the methods of psychological research.* London, England: Blackwell.

Rogoff, B., and Lave, J. (1984). *Everyday cognition: Its development in social context.* Cambridge, MA: Harvard University Press.

Ruffman, T., Perner, J., Olson, D.R., and Doherty, M. (1993). Reflecting on scientific thinking: Children's understanding of the hypothesis-evidence relation. *Child Development, 64,* 1617-1636.

Schauble, L. (1996). The development of scientific reasoning in knowledge-rich contexts. *Developmental Psychology, 32*(1), 102-119.

Smith, C., Maclin, D., Houghton, C., and Hennessey, M.G. (2000). Sixth-grade students' epistemologies of science: The impact of school science experiences on epistemological development. *Cognition and Instruction, 18*(3), 349-422.

Sodian, B., Zaitchik, D., and Carey, S. (1991). Young children's differentiation of hypothetical beliefs from evidence. *Child Development, 62,* 753-766.

Stanovich, K.E. (2003). Understanding the styles of science in the study of reading. *Scientific Studies of Reading, 7*(2), 105-126.

Stewart, J., Cartier, J.L., and Passmore, C.M. (2005). Developing understanding through model-based inquiry. In National Research Council, Committee on How People Learn, M.S. Donovan and J.D. Bransford (Eds.), *How students learn: Science in the classroom* (pp. 515-565). Washington, DC: The National Academies Press.

Thagard, P. (1999a). Explanation. In R. Wilson and F. Keil (Eds.), *MIT encyclopedia of cognitive science* (pp. 300-301). Cambridge, MA: MIT Press.

Thagard, P. (1999b). Induction. In R. Wilson and F. Keil (Eds.), *MIT encyclopedia of cognitive science* (pp. 399-400). Cambridge, MA: MIT Press.

Toth, E.E., Klahr, D., and Chen, Z. (2000). Bridging research and practice: A cognitively-based classroom intervention for teaching experimentation skills to elementary school children. *Cognition and Instruction, 18*(4), 423-459.

Toulmin, S.E. (1972). *Human understanding, vol. I*. Oxford, England: Clarendon Press.

Tschirgi, J.E. (1980). Sensible reasoning: A hypothesis about hypotheses. *Child Development, 51*, 1-10.

Vellom, R.P., and Anderson, C.W. (1999). Reasoning about data in middle school science. *Journal of Research in Science Teaching, 36*, 179-199.

Vosniadou, S., and Brewer, W.F. (1992). Mental models of the earth: A study of conceptual change in childhood. *Cognitive Psychology, 24*, 535-585.

Vosniadou, S., and Brewer, W.F. (1994). Mental models of the day/night cycle. *Cognitive Science, 18*, 123-183.

Wason, P.C. (1960). On the failure to eliminate hypotheses in a conceptual task. *Quarterly Journal of Experimental Psychology, 12*(4), 129-140.

Wason, P.C. (1968). Reasoning about a rule. *Quarterly Journal of Experimental Psychology, 20*, 273-281.

White, B. (1993). ThinkerTools: Causal models, conceptual change, and science education. *Cognition and Instruction, 10*(1), 1-100.

Wiser, M., and Amin, T. (2001). Is heat hot? Inducing conceptual change by integrating everyday and scientific perspective on thermal phenomena. *Learning and Instruction, 11*, 331-355.

Wollman, W. (1997a). Controlling variables: Assessing levels of understanding. *Science Education, 61*(3), 371-383.

Wollman, W. (1997b). Controlling variables: A neo-Piagetian developmental sequence. *Science Education, 61*(3), 385-391.

Part II

HOW CHILDREN LEARN SCIENCE

In Part II, we present reviews of the research on science learning in early childhood through early adolescence. Over the past 50 years, new tools, techniques, and theories about learning—coinciding with the emergence of computer technology, cognitive and sociocultural learning theories, and new theory-building views of the nature of science—have expanded and focused understandings of the ways in which science learning occurs. The chapters in this part, organized around the four strands of science proficiency (see Box 2-1), synthesize research on learning, science learning, and the dynamics involved in the growth of scientific knowledge.

Across the five chapters, we examine the literature on concept learning, scientific reasoning, children's understanding of the structure of scientific knowledge, and the ways in which communication and representation practices that characterize scientific discourse and decision making impact learning. In most cases, we draw on research that was not explicitly organized around the strands framework but is useful nonetheless in illuminating the process of science learning within and across the four strands.

Chapter 3 reviews research on young children and provides an overview of the knowledge and skills they bring to school which provide a foundation for learning science. Chapter 4 reviews literature related to Strand 1: Know, use, and interpret scientific explanations of the natural world. Chapter 5 discusses evidence related to Strand 2: Generate and evaluate scientific evidence and, explanations. Chapter 6 summarizes the research evidence related to Strand 3: Understand the nature and development of scientific knowledge. Finally, Chapter 7 discusses research related to Strand 4: Participate productively in scientific practices and discourse.

A major theme across the chapters is how findings from research have increasingly revealed interconnections between the four strands as children develop scientific understanding at all grade levels. The evidence is especially strong that knowledge of the natural world (Strand 1, Chapter 4) and the ability to generate and evaluate evidence and explanations (Strand 2, Chapter 5) are closely intertwined. Work on the connections between Strands 1 and 2 and Strand 3—understanding the nature and development of scientific knowledge (Chapter 6)—is more recent. However, this connection has strong theoretical support, and emergent empirical work documenting the links is compelling. Connections between Strand 4 (Chapter 7), productive participation in science, and the other three strands have less direct empirical support in science. However, work in other subject areas, such as mathematics and reading, supports the idea that there is a connection and that the connection depends on incorporating certain science practices, like modeling, and discourse practices, like argumentation, into science learning environments.

Another major theme across Part II is the strong evidence from current research that children are more capable than was once thought and that implementation of the strands framework could begin as early as kindergarten. In fact, basic research in cognitive development over the past few decades has revolutionized the view of how children's minds develop, from infancy through adolescence. It turns out that children come to school with a great capacity for learning in general as well as for science learning, and they are able to engage in surprisingly sophisticated scientific thinking in the early grades.

Finally, across the four chapters we review research on how science reasoning and the growth of scientific knowledge develops in the elementary and middle school grades. The research reveals surprisingly diverse capabilities within a given age group as well as variation within a single individual depending on the nature of the task, problem, or inquiry at hand.

3

Foundations for Science Learning
in Young Children

Major Findings in the Chapter:

- *In contrast to the commonly held and outmoded view that young children are concrete and simplistic thinkers, the research evidence now shows that their thinking is surprisingly sophisticated. Important building blocks for learning science are in place before they enter school.*
- *Children entering school already have substantial knowledge of the natural world, which can be built on to develop their understanding of scientific concepts. Some areas of knowledge may provide more robust foundations to build on than others, because they appear very early and have some universal characteristics across cultures throughout the world.*
- *By the end of preschool, children can reason in ways that provide helpful starting points for developing scientific reasoning. However, their reasoning abilities are constrained by their conceptual knowledge, the nature of the task, and their awareness of their own thinking.*

Regardless of one's theoretical orientation, by the time children enter elementary school, no one would argue that their minds are empty vessels awaiting enlightenment in the form of instruction. They come to school after years of cognitive growth in which they have developed a wide range of ways of understanding and reasoning about the world around them. Our goal in this chapter is to describe the knowledge and skills that children bring to school, beginning with the earliest understandings of infants. The past 20 to 30 years of research paint a picture of young children as surprisingly competent and able to engage in learning across all four strands of scientific proficiency from the very beginning of their science education.

We begin with a discussion of young children's knowledge of the natural world. This knowledge can emerge as a consequence of a child's everyday interactions with the world as well as a result of the ways in which the culture and its adult members explicitly impart information to children. In some areas of instruction, such as reading, the role of preexisting knowledge and understanding may be relatively modest, but in the area of science education, children bring a great deal that is relevant. A major challenge is to build on students' existing knowledge of the natural world to help them understand and use scientific knowledge.

Next we identify aspects of young children's thinking that can serve as the foundation for developing scientific reasoning in the elementary grades. For example, young children understand that one thing can represent another (such as a toy airplane or a scale model), which provides a starting point for modeling. Finally, we consider precursors to children's understanding of how scientific knowledge is constructed. We include here their understanding of the ideas and beliefs held by other people and their ability to assess the credibility of different sources of knowledge.

ORGANIZING THEMES

Several themes run repeatedly through the research on young children's emerging understandings of natural systems and their reasoning. The following three themes help organize the research summaries that follow:

1. Concern with explanation and investigation are central to children's learning and thinking at all ages. Even the youngest children are sensitive to highly abstract patterns and causal relations. They use this information to guide the ways in which they generalize, make inferences, and make sense of the world. There is increasing recognition of the richness and variability of children's understandings that involve implicit and explicit, nonsymbolic and symbolic, associative and explanatory components. *There is no simple concrete to abstract progression in children's development.*

2. Children develop explanatory insights in specific domains. *Some key domains of understanding may have a privileged status in helping with the emergence of science.* These include mechanics, folk biology, some aspects of chemistry (e.g., an initial understanding of different substances), and folk psychology, as explained below. These four domains have universal shared components throughout the world and for children from all backgrounds in the United States. They form an important cognitive common ground on which to build more sophisticated scientific understandings. Roots of these

domains extend back to preverbal thought and are therefore a legacy of infancy.

3. Not only does the growth of scientific understanding involve a sense of the patterns special to such domains as physics and biology, but it also requires much broader cognitive skills that cut across domains. These include an ability to stand back and look at one's knowledge and learning, heuristics that enable one to efficiently process large amounts of information, and strategies for acquiring, maintaining, and transmitting information. *This interplay between domain-specific forms of learning and domain-general ones is central to any account of the emergence of scientific thought.*

This chapter illustrates these three themes and how they are central to recent research findings concerning how many of the building blocks of scientific understanding emerge prior to school.

Much of the current science education curriculum is based on dated assumptions about the nature of cognitive development and learning, assumptions that lead to suboptimal teaching of science (Metz, 1995). It has been common to view younger children as deficient in some manner, resulting in a focus on what they cannot do rather than what they can do (Gelman and Baillargeon, 1983). That focus is a legacy going back more than 85 years to Jean Piaget's early studies of the ways in which normal children failed on early versions of the standardized tests that later became widely used as intelligence tests. It asks what children are "missing" and leads to analyses asking when they acquire a certain component of thinking. As a result—in a somewhat distorted interpretation of Piaget's work (e.g., Bruner, 1964; Werner and Kaplan, 1963)—cognitive development has often been understood as a series of artificial dichotomies in which children do or do not have a particular skill. The transition from being without the skill to having the skill is understood as going through a developmental stage. Problems with this perspective have long been recognized (Flavell, 1971; Linn, 1978; Pulos and Linn, 1978; see also Metz, 1995, for an extensive discussion of the misapplication of Piagetian ideas).

The emphasis on deficits and stages of abilities tends to look at highly general characterizations of children's capacities, emphasizing global deficits that apply to almost all areas of thought. For example, preschool children have often been claimed to be concrete, preoperational, precausal, prelogical, and lacking the ability to think in relational terms. Only during the elementary school years, or in some cases not until adolescence, were children thought to transition to "higher" forms of thought. If these claims were true as absolute deficits, they would suggest that children bring a radically different way of understanding the world with them when they enter the elementary school classroom.

One review has characterized three false and outmoded views about limitations in elementary children's thinking that are still widely embraced by education practitioners (Metz, 1995): (1) Elementary schoolchildren think in concrete as opposed to abstract terms. (2) Elementary schoolchildren can make sense of their world primarily in terms of ordering and classifying objects and relations and not in terms of explanatory understanding or the building of intuitive theories. (3) Elementary schoolchildren cannot use experimentation to develop their ideas. All three of these views, as well as other views of broad cognitive limitations of elementary schoolchildren, and even many preschoolers, are no longer accepted by the cognitive developmental research community (see Carey, 1985; Gelman and Baillargeon, 1983; Gelman and Kalish, 2005; and Metz, 1995, for reviews).

EARLY CONCEPTUAL UNDERSTANDING OF NATURAL SYSTEMS

In all cultures, whether they are highly technological or profoundly traditional, there are natural systems that everyone encounters in common and must explain. These form our point of departure for discussing what children bring to school in terms of scientific understanding. Four systems have been extensively studied in infants and young children: the simple mechanics of solid bounded objects, the behaviors of psychological agents, the actions and organization of living things, and the makeup of substances and materials. Infants throughout the world seem to understand these four natural systems in the same way and, to the extent that cross-cultural work has been done with older children, there are considerable commonalities for preschoolers as well. Although these common sets of understandings may diverge more and more in the elementary school years and beyond, they do represent a shared understanding that is a critical foundation for the teaching and learning of science. In older children, there has also been considerable study of their understanding of cosmology and larger scale earth systems, such as weather, ecology, and such processes as volcanic eruptions, tides, and mountain formation. Beliefs in these areas can vary dramatically across cultures and form an interesting contrast to systems that seem to be partially grasped at a much earlier age, but even with large-scale earth systems, there are important common threads.

Naïve Physics

Simple and universal rules govern the behaviors of the physical world, or at least seemingly simple ones at a macroscopic scale. Consider, for example, bounded solid objects, such as rubber balls, wooden doors, and rigid sticks. One knows that solid objects cannot move through each other, that any changes in their movements are the result of forces outside them, either through direct contact, such as in a collision, or through gravity. One knows that action at a distance between two objects, such as with magnets, is unusual. One also knows that objects tend to endure over space and time. They cannot blink out of existence and then reappear at a different time or in a different place, except in science fiction.

It might seem that knowledge of this sort takes years to acquire. A baby and a young toddler would have to carefully observe the behaviors of physical objects and gradually, from this observational data, induce a set of beliefs that would become their intuitive theory of physics. Given that the simple and elegant rules of Newtonian mechanics were not apparent until Newton himself labored over the topic for many years, how could one expect an infant or a toddler to have any set of coherent expectations about the physical world? It now is clear that, well before their first birthday, infants do have such expectations and they continue to develop in the preschool years. They are definitely not in the form laid down in Newton's *Principia*, but they do enable infants and children to anticipate and interpret many aspects of their physical worlds.

The research literature on infants' conceptions of physical objects has burgeoned in the past two decades and cannot possibly be fully surveyed here (see Baillargeon, 2004; Cohen and Cashon, 2006; Mandler, 2004; Munakata, Casey, and Diamond, 2004, for discussions of large segments of this literature). Instead, we provide a few examples of the ways in which infants are and are not successful. One set of studies concerns intuitions about object permanence and solidity. It now appears that, at least by the fourth month of life, infants "know" that solid objects cannot interpenetrate and that they continue to exist over space and time even when out of sight.

One now classic line of studies in this area had infants observe a flat barrier swinging both toward and away from them through 180 degrees of arc on a surface, such as a table. Infants were shown the 180 degree event several times until they became disinterested (i.e., habituated) to the stimulus. They were then shown a small solid object that was placed behind the barrier in such a way that would prevent the barrier from swinging through the full 180 degrees (see Box 3-1 for diagram). Infants looked longer at displays in which the barrier went through the full 180 degrees (the hidden object disappeared through a trap door) than at displays in which the barrier stopped, for the first time, at say 110 degrees, a novel stopping position but one that was consistent with assumptions about object solidity and permanence (Baillargeon, 1987; Baillargeon, Spelke, and Wasserman, 1985).

In other studies, infants expected that a small vehicle moving behind a barrier would reemerge only when a block behind the barrier was not directly in its path (Baillargeon, 1986). In still other lines of work, infants looked longer when a vertically dropped object seemed to end up in a

BOX 3-1 Infants' Understanding of the Physical World

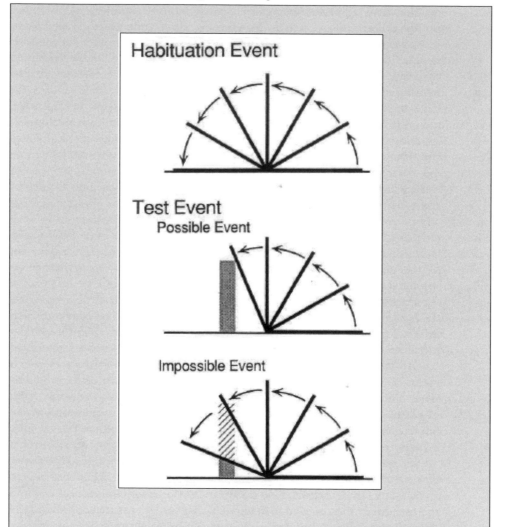

The diagram above shows the kind of apparatus used to study infants' understanding of the barrier phenomena. Infants are first habituated to a screen that rotates through a 180 degree arc, in the manner of a drawbridge. Next, a large box is placed behind the screen. In the possible event, the screen stops when it encounters the box (112 degree arc); in the impossible event, the screen stops after rotating through the top 80 percent of the space occupied by the box (157 degree arc).

SOURCE: Baillargeon (1995).

position that implies it must have moved through an intervening, but oc-cluded, solid platform (Spelke, 1991). Longer looking by infants is widely accepted as an indication that they have seen an event that violates their expectations.

There is also, not surprisingly, considerable learning about the physical world during infancy. For example, younger infants are sensitive only to large and obvious conflicts between the barrier and obscured block and will not notice smaller discrepancies, such as when the barrier stops 30 degrees too early (Baillargeon, 1995). Thus, they need to learn to calibrate the geom-etry of physical events with their consequences. Similarly, an appreciation that an unsupported object will fall down takes time to develop (Spelke and Kyeong, 1992). Other researchers argue that competing ways of thinking about objects during infancy are resolved only gradually, over a period of several months (Munakata et al., 1997). Regardless of the details of how quickly infants gain a single clear view of the nature of the physical world, there is substantial agreement that, by the end of the first year of life, they have expectations about objects that fit with many principles governing the behaviors of bounded physical objects.

By 12 months of age, infants are capable of taking into account physical dimensions and magnitudes and their consequences for events. As noted earlier, they consider the angle of movement of a swinging barrier as it relates to the size of an object behind it. They also understand that bigger objects in motion are likely to have bigger consequences. For example, when 11-month-olds observe a cylinder roll down a ramp and move another object through collision, they infer that a larger novel cylinder will move the object more and that a smaller cylinder will move it less (Kotovsky and Baillargeon, 1994). More broadly, while starting early with some very gen-eral ideas about solidity and spatiotemporal continuity (Spelke et al., 1992, 1995), infants are constantly refining those ideas into forms that enable more subtle inferences about objects and their behaviors over intervals of time and space (Baillargeon, 2004). By the end of the first year, infants also have a clear sense of causation as opposed to mere correlation or contiguity. Thus, even if one event reliably occurs before another one, infants may not infer causation unless there is also some degree of plausible mechanism, such as one object launching another through collision (Leslie and Keeble, 1987). They can also make inferences about unreasonable versus reasonable hidden causes of the motion of an inanimate object (Saxe, Tenenbaum, and Carey, 2005).

Ongoing research is now asking how a 1-year-old's mental representa-tions of the world should be best characterized. Should her ability to antici-pate the behaviors of physical objects be seen as her having beliefs like those of an adult, or could it reflect mental processes that are less explicit and belief-like in nature? (See Leslie, 1994, for further discussion of these issues.) To what extent can the 1-year-old flexibly use those mental representations to understand more novel problems with physical objects? Answers to these questions will help to clarify not only how older children's physical knowledge becomes more explicit but also how that explicit knowledge interacts with earlier preverbal forms.

One intriguing example of the limits of physical understanding in infancy is seen in tasks in which toddlers fail what seem to be the same solidity problems that infants pass. In one task, children observed a display in which several wooden boards could block a ball rolling down a ramp on which the blocks were placed. A low wall was put in front of the blocks and ramp, occluding most of the ramp but keeping the tops of the blocks visible, and a ball was then put into motion on the high part of the ramp that was still visible. When 2-year-olds were asked to open a door where they think a rolling ball will be, they often open the door that would require the ball to move through a salient solid barrier (Keen, 2003). The same children do much better when the two doors are opened simultaneously by another person and they merely have to react to expected and unexpected outcomes. Such actions as retrieval or catching add new levels of complexity in terms of representing the spatial arrangements of hidden objects, levels that can overwhelm 2-year-olds (Freeman et al., 2004; Hood, 2004; Kloos and Keen, 2005).

More broadly, one sees that, in certain tasks, some elements of physical object knowledge are emerging very early, but that the ability to use this knowledge in a wider range of tasks, including those that require planning or coordinating sequences of actions on the part of the child, takes considerable time to develop. In addition, children through their own actions often provide critical feedback that adults might not normally provide. Thus, while adults rarely put objects on surfaces from which they will topple off because they aren't adequately supported, younger children and infants (e.g., Baillargeon, 2004) will do so and will therefore gain valuable new information concerning the mechanics of physical objects. Finally, knowledge can sometimes be implicit in a child's action before it is accessible for other, more explicit uses. For example, 5-year-olds will adjust the angle and strength of their throws of a ball in ways that nicely anticipate the trajectories needed for projectiles to hit particular targets, at the same time showing strong errors in their guesses of correct launch speeds for the same targets (Krist, Fieberg, and Wilkening, 1993; see also Shanon, 1976). Over the next several years, their explicit ability to predict projectile trajectories gradually improves, although even in adults there are vestiges of the kindergarten errors (Krist et al., 1993; Shanon, 1976). Indeed, a large literature has shown that several naïve errors about physical trajectories persist in most adults (Bertamini, Spooner, and Hecht, 2004; Carmazza, McCloskey, and Green, 1981; Clement, 1982; Hecht and Bertamini, 2000).

Preschoolers have a quite sophisticated sense of the sort of mechanical causality that is intrinsic to the motion of simple physical solids. For example, when two events precede another one, they will usually correctly sense which is more physically plausible and then prefer it as the cause (Bullock, Gelman, and Baillargeon, 1982; Gelman and Lucariello, 2002). When preschoolers' spontaneous explanations of various entities are examined in large transcriptions of everyday speech, the children flexibly and easily employ causal reasoning, using different kind of explanations depending on whether the events are thought of as physical, psychological, or biological (Hickling and Wellman, 2001). They show similar distinctions in more experimental tasks (Heyman, Phillips, and Gelman, 2003). Indeed, when asked to explain anomalies in physical regularities, children use very different patterns of reasoning than when explaining anomalies in social conventions of moral rules (Lockhart, 1981).

Preschoolers are also adept at inferring hidden causes. Thus, they assume that similar external motions of animate and inanimate objects are governed by radically different internal causes (Gelman, Durgin, and Kaufman, 1995). They understand that unseen factors must be linked to observable ones in systematic ways that are mechanistically mediated (Yoachim and Meltzoff, 2003). Moreover, preschoolers are quite sophisticated at using complex patterns of covariation over time to infer hidden causes and not just correlations (Gopnik et al., 2004), although often such inferences may be constrained by prior mechanistic theories that they are applying to those tasks (Griffiths, Baraff, and Tenenbaum, 2004). Finally, preschoolers will track a sequence of events occurring in causal chains and infer that the first event in that chain is most likely to be the most important cause (Ahn et al., 2000), a strategy frequently used by adults as well.

A vast literature on science "misconceptions" argues that erroneous beliefs about the physical world are held by many, ranging from preschoolers to adults. And many of these beliefs are highly resistant to change by instruction (Chi, 2005). Much of that literature, especially in the area of mechanics, has focused on high school and college students (e.g., Brown and Clement, 1987; Carmazza, McCloskey, and Green, 1981; Minstrell, 1983, 1988; Clement, 1982); there have been many fewer studies of younger preschool or elementary schoolchildren (Doran, 1972; Ioannides and Vosniadou, 2002; Viennot, 1979). This literature makes clear, however, that the elegant theoretical construction of Newtonian mechanics (including its three primary laws of motion) is by no means obvious even to high school or college students who have had courses in introductory mechanics.

Student misconceptions are sometimes revealed in tasks in which they are asked to predict the trajectories of objects or evaluate whether an observed trajectory is possible or impossible, but even more often when they are asked to identify and explain the forces acting on an object in a given situation. For example, many students predict that a moving object emerging from a circular tube will continue in a circular trajectory once it emerges from the tube (rather than flying off in a straight line path), or they predict that a person running off a cliff will (as in a Wile E. Coyote cartoon) continue a short way off the cliff before abruptly falling straight down.

Although even young children, like adults, have an explicit concept of force that they use to explain what happens in different physical situations, the meaning of force is an intuitive one, very different from the mathematicized notion embodied in Newtonian mechanics. They tend to think of forces as active pushes or pulls that are needed to explain an object's motion, rather than coming in interactive action-reaction pairs that are needed to explain not an object's motion but its change in motion (acceleration). Thus, they see forces in situations in which a physicist has no need to postulate a force (e.g., when a coin is thrown upward, they postulate an upward force is imparted to the object from the hand for the duration of the upward trajectory to explain why it continues to go up), and they fail to see forces that are essential to a Newtonian analysis (e.g., many of the action-reaction pairs that are so central to a Newtonian analysis, such as the force exerted by a table on a book when it is resting on the table). They do not clearly distinguish between force and momentum, acceleration, position, and speed or between instantaneous and average velocity. In light of these findings, some have suggested that high school students may have an alternative naïve theory of motion, akin in many respects to historically naïve impetus views of the sort proposed by Aristotle or the medieval impetus theorists (Caramazza, McCloskey, and Green, 1981; Espinoza, 2005).

Others have argued that viewing these misconceptions as stemming from a highly coherent alternative impetus theory is misleading for several reasons (diSessa, 2004; Smith, diSessa, and Roschelle, 1993). First, it suggests that students are more consistent in their erroneous reasoning than they actually are. Although they may appeal to impetus notions in some tasks, they may not use them in other tasks in which they would be relevant. Second, it overlooks many other notions that students appeal to in their physical explanations, such as balancing, overcoming, or resisting. DiSessa argues that everyday physics is better thought of as exploiting a fairly large and diverse number of these low-level (often inarticulate) explanatory fragments that are evoked, often quite independently, in different contexts. Third, the naïve theories account overlooks many of the points at which students' intuitions are actually in accord with mature physical analysis. For example, although students may not see the balance of forces in the situation of a book on a table, they do provide this analysis when analyzing a book on an outstretched hand. Thus, they are not as devoid of positive intuitions as the misconceptions literature would suggest. On this analysis there is much valuable knowledge, though admittedly often at an inarticulate subconceptual level, acquired from rich everyday experience with objects that can be drawn on as resources in physics teaching.

Considerable research is still needed to map out the ways in which infant expectations about physical objects transition into the expectations and beliefs held by preschoolers and elementary schoolchildren. However those studies turn out, however, it is clear that children entering elementary school should not be characterized as merely having a batch of misconceptions. The many ways in which they do correctly sense some of the behaviors of simple mechanical objects should be central to their teaching and learning of science.

Naïve Psychology

People, as well as many other organisms, behave in ways that are immediately interpreted in terms of their having goals, desires, and beliefs that help to explain their actions. Moreover, their actions have a different quality from those of the inanimate world (Spelke, Phillips, and Woodward, 1995). People can easily act on each other at a distance. A facial expression, a comment, or a gesture can cause another agent to spring into action in ways that are directly related to that first event, even though it may be spatially quite distinct. Causes have no obvious proportionality to their effects. A whisper might cause an eruption of action, while a shout may cause inhibition of action. In a different situation, the opposite may occur. Animate things can change their direction midcourse, while simple objects require an external force to change their trajectories. There are patterns of contingency between people that are quite distinctive, so that one person tends to respond to the actions of the other after a characteristic temporal delay (Scassellati and Gold, in press).

The domain of people (and other intentional agents) and their actions corresponds roughly to the research areas of psychology and cognitive science. Although psychology and cognitive science are not typically areas of science instruction in the elementary school, much of the scholarship in those fields arises from experimental research very much in the tradition of the biological and physical sciences. The contrast between simple mechanical objects and intentional agents is one of the most robust and earliest emerging cognitive distinctions in development. Children's emerging understanding of psychology may be a critical component that they bring to the learning of science in elementary school. For example, understanding and engaging with the beliefs and ideas of other people play an important role in science discourse.

Infants are quite sensitive to the differences in the behavior of people (or other entities considered to be intentional) and inanimate solid objects. They have different expectations about the focus or location of future actions when they perceive an entity to be goal directed. For example, if an inanimate rod reaches out to touch a particular object, such as a teddy bear, in a given location, such as the left of a screen, 5-month-old infants will expect the rod to return to the *same location* regardless of what object is there. By contrast, if a hand reaches out to the teddy bear, they will expect it to go to the *same object* regardless of its location, presumably because they infer that the object is desired by the animate creature possessing the hand (Woodward, 1998). As another example, if an object responds to an infant's vocalizations by making nonsense sounds back with a slight temporal lag, and if the object then turns 90 degrees, 12-month-old infants will turn as well to see where the object is "looking," even though there are no obvious facial features on the side that was initially facing them (Johnson, and Carey, 1998; see also Watson, 1979). In other words, the infant uses the pattern of vocalization to infer that the object is like a person (i.e., it has intentions). In addition, a certain kind of contingency-based movement of a simple triangle is enough to trigger in infants inferences of a social agent with specific intentions when the same triangle might otherwise be seen as a simple inanimate object (Kuhlmeier, Bloom, and Wynn, 2005).

Infants use a wide variety of cues, ranging from facial features to contingent responding, to infer that an object is an intentional agent, and, once they make that categorization, they have radically different expectations about the entity (Johnson, 2003; Woodward, Sommerville, and Guajardo, 2001). They also expect very different paths of movement. They think it odd that a cylinder should act on another one across a spatial gap, but they do not think it odd that people should do so (Spelke, Phillips, and Woodward, 1995), and they assume that animate creatures can move in ways that inanimates cannot (Kuhlmeier, Bloom, and Wynn, 2005). For example, they assume that, if a ball has repeatedly hopped over a barrier on its way to a destination, it will continue to do so when the barrier is removed. Yet if cues are provided that the ball is an intentional agent, 12-month-olds will assume that the intentional ball will now go on an entirely new straight-line trajectory right toward the destination (Gergeley et al., 1995; Csibra et al., 1999). Thus, they seem to assume that the laws of classical mechanics are suspended as soon as an entity is assumed to have goals, desires, and beliefs. As with the case of mechanics, it is still not known to what extent the infant's knowledge of psychology is explicit and within the infant's awareness as opposed to being implicit knowledge that consists mainly of automatic responses (Leslie, 1994).

After infancy, the young child's understanding of the mind develops quite dramatically. One of the most discussed developments concerns the emergence, during the third year of life, of an ability to understand that intentional agents might have false beliefs that lead them to behave differently from when they might have true beliefs (Perner, Leekam, and Wimmer,

1987; see Box 3-2 for examples of tasks used to study theory of mind). Children seem to progress from seeing agents as simply driven by desires to being driven by beliefs and desires that interact in a systematic and reliable way (Wellman, 1990). Over much of childhood, there continue to be advances in thinking in even more subtle ways about how mental states and processes are causally related to actions (Flavell, 1999).

The nature of thought about intentional agents is vividly revealed through the study of individuals with autism. Although their understanding of motion in the physical world may be relatively intact, their understanding of other people's beliefs may be seriously deficient (Baron-Cohen, 1995). Such results give support to the idea that cognitive development proceeds somewhat independently in each domain of knowledge.

In short, from early in infancy, the social world is seen as patterning in dramatically different ways from the physical world. Infants have entirely different sets of expectations about entities in the two worlds, expectations

BOX 3-2 Tasks Used to Study Children's Ideas About the Mind

In a standard test for children's understanding of false belief (Wimmer and Perner, 1983), children watch while a doll puts some chocolate in a cupboard and leaves the room. The chocolate is then moved in the doll's absence, and the doll returns. Children are told that the doll now wants the chocolate, and they are asked to say where the doll will search. Before children have an understanding of others' minds, they are more likely to say the doll will search in the new location. Once they have developed an understanding of false belief, they will predict that the doll will search in the old location. In fact, there is a robust improvement between age 3 and age 5 in children's ability to predict that the doll will search in the old rather than the new location.

A number of other tasks have also been used to explore children's developing understanding of the mind. For example, they may be asked to explain a character's actions in a story (e.g., Jane is looking for her kitty under the piano. Why is she doing that?) (Bartsch and Wellman, 1989). In another task, children watch as Coke is taken out of a Coke can and replaced with milk out of sight of a story character. They are then asked how the character feels about being offered the can to drink, before the character has taken a sip and discovered it is milk; 3- and 4-year-olds often refer to what they themselves know about the contents of the can (it is milk), rather than what the character would believe (it is Coke) (Harris et al., 1989).

that influence later developments in more elaborate and explicit beliefs about the minds of others. There are two ways in which a developing folk psychology and cognitive science are relevant to science education. First, they are domains of scientific activity, and the child's intuitive knowledge can be understood as forming the basis for later explicit instruction on the topic. Second, the cognitive science of science itself is an important part of the science education of the child (Klahr, 2000). For example, an understanding of the subjectivity of knowledge and of potential distortions in communication is essential to being able to engage in science and is deeply dependent on an understanding of the mind and how it acquires and uses knowledge.

Naïve Biology

Given the extraordinary changes in conceptions of the living world over the past few hundred years, it is obvious that the very young child could not possibly have a fully accurate grasp of current biological knowledge. After all, only a few hundred years ago, some of the most learned members of Western society thought that the brain might simply be a large cooling organ for the rest of the body (Zimmer, 2004). Modern molecular biology is a product of the past 60 years or so, and introductory college biology courses of the 1940s have almost no overlap with those of today. In light of these dramatic historical changes, it might seem that a preschooler, let alone an infant, might have no sense whatsoever of the biological world as a distinct domain of causal regularities, mechanisms, and principles.

There is little evidence that infants appreciate the biological world as distinct. They do easily discriminate biological motions, such as walking, from nonbiological ones (Bertenthal, 1993; Booth, Pinto, and Bertenthal, 2002); however, the ability of newborn chicks to make similar discriminations illustrates the point that a mere ability to discriminate biological motion from nonbiological forms should not be overinterpreted in terms of its role in the emergence of biological thought (Vallortigara, Regolin, and Marconato, 2005). Many organisms—whether predator, prey, or both—may have strong reasons for needing a dedicated perceptual system tuned to detect biological motions in the surrounding environment.

Older human infants will classify animals together even when they differ dramatically from each other in appearance, and they will keep apart animals and artifacts (such as birds and toy planes) even when they have strikingly similar appearances (Mandler, 2004). But those acts of categorization, albeit at an apparently abstract level, may be based on seeing the animals as intentional agents compared with the inanimate objects. Along those lines, one view of the emergence of biological thought argues that the infant and the young child initially have no sense of the living world as such and instead only think of living things either as social beings (most animals) or as inanimate objects (most plants) (Carey, 1985). An understanding of the biological world as a domain with its own principles is thought not to emerge until well into the elementary school years (Carey, 1985, 1988). Animals are distinctive only insofar as they are also understood as social agents with desires, goals, and other cognitive and emotional states that help explain their actions. Since young children will often attribute properties to animals on the basis of their psychological similarities to humans (e.g., dogs eat but worms do not because eating is understood as feeling hungry and feeling satiated or as requiring a clearly visible mouth), they often mistakenly underattribute biological properties to simpler organisms in both the animal and plant kingdoms (Carey, 1985, 1988).

Young children can also be remarkably ignorant about many of the mechanisms that underlie biological processes, such as digestion, movement, and reproduction. Thus, preschoolers may grossly misconstrue the inner workings of the body that digest food; they have little sense of how the body breaks down food into simpler compounds through mechanical and chemical means (Gellert, 1962; Nagy, 1953). Similarly, they have no sense of how organic molecules release energy units that are used to contract muscles and enable movement. Nor do most children know about sex gametes, how they come into contact, and how they result in a fertilized egg that differentiates into a fetus. Because of these clear deficits, it is easy to infer that young children have no understanding of the living world. Moreover, their tendency in some contexts to generalize properties based on psychological similarity suggests that they might be understanding biological entities and processes in psychological terms.

At a different level, however, there is considerable evidence suggesting more precocity in children's abilities to track the distinctive nature of causal and relational patterns in the biological world (Inagaki and Hatano, 2006; Keil, 2003). Consider again the case of digestion. Although young children do not understand the physiology of digestion in any sort of detail, they do seem to figure out early on that food is transformed in some manner that gives organisms the ability to grow and to move (Inagaki and Hatano, 2002). They understand that an organism will physically deteriorate if it cannot ingest food, they know that the transformation of food is essential to its being usefully employed by the body, and they know that only plants and animals transform food and need to digest it (Toyama, 2000). It therefore seems that, at a more abstract functional level, preschoolers do have a sense of some of the distinctive operations and processes that are essential to digestion. In that way, they are not so different from adults. Most adults also have poor or mistaken knowledge of biological mechanisms, believing for example that most of the solid mass of plants arises from the soil, often completely missing the huge contribution from gaseous carbon dioxide (Driver et al., 1994). At this mechanistic level of analysis, one can find a huge array of misconceptions about biology not only in children but also in most adults (Driver et al., 1994). Moreover, people of all ages think that they understand such mechanisms far better than they really do, leading to a false impression of having detailed mechanistic understandings (Rozenblit and Keil, 2002; Lawson, in press; Mills and Keil, 2005).

The story for digestion is repeated for most other areas of biology. Both children and adults have glaring gaps in their knowledge and often outright false mechanistic details, at the same time sensing higher level functional patterns quite well. They understand general patterns of growth and re-growth (Hickling and Gelman, 1995; Backscheider, Shatz, and Gelman, 1993), what sorts of properties are likely to be inherited (Springer and Keil, 1989; Gimenez and Harris, 2002), and how something extracted from food helps enable movement (Inagaki and Hatano, 2002). Active debates remain concerning the extent to which children are thinking about living things as a distinct and neatly bounded group. Beyond those debates, children appear to pick up on patterns related to function that help support their thinking about biological kinds (Gelman, 2003; Gelman and Hirschfeld, 1999). Also, children in other cultures may not be swayed by psychological similarity in the same way that North American children are when making judgments about biological properties (Atran et al., 2001; Medin, Unsworth, and Hirschfeld, in press). Indeed, as is the case with physics, a core sense of biological entities as such may often be present but obscured by the context of a task and how it is framed. For example, if preschoolers carrying out a task are given brief cues suggesting that they should attend to internal mechanisms rather than social factors, they will make inductions that are based on biological as opposed to psychological similarity (Gutheil, Vera, and Keil, 1998).

Children may zero in on the domain of living things by realizing that they occur at the intersection of two kinds of causal and relational patterns, each of which individually may apply to entities in multiple domains, but which in concert uniquely pick out the living world (Keil, 1992). Consider, for example, three such patterns: (1) a rich internal, microstructural essence (that is, a true, underlying nature); (2) deep taxonomic embedding (i.e., placed in an ordered system of groups and categories that indicates relationships); and (3) teleological interpretations (i.e., being seen as having a purpose). It is common to think of all categories of natural entities, such as chemical elements and biological species, as having essences (e.g., atomic number, DNA) but artifacts do not (there is no inner essence of chair) (Gelman, 2003; Keil, 1989). This essentialist view for natural kinds is not strictly correct (Keil and Richardson, 1999), but it is a useful heuristic. It is also common to think about parts of biological systems as having purposes, but it is not common to do so for nonliving natural kinds. This teleological stance, in combination with the essentialist bias, helps children pick out all and only living kinds. Finally, the idea that biological entities are embedded in rich and deep taxonomies may not be strictly true for only living things, but when used with the essentialist bias and teleological interpretations, it helps to further demarcate the set of living things. Moreover, there are strong cross-cultural universals in the use of folk biological taxonomies, suggesting a way of organizing the living world that remains robust across both culture and development (Lopez et al., 1997).

The use of a teleological or "design" stance to understand living things is particularly interesting. When children are asked to explicitly reject or accept whether functional attributions can be made about nonliving natural kinds, such as rocks, preschoolers tend to give a functional attribution (Kelemen, 1999). Yet the ability to make explicit judgments about whether a teleological explanation is applicable may emerge later. Young children may in fact have a more tacit understanding that is revealed in their spontaneous use of such explanations in attempts to learn more about the biological and physical worlds. For example, when preschoolers are shown novel artifacts and living things, their spontaneous questions about them reveal sharply contrasting patterns for artifacts and living things. They tend to ask more questions about the purposes of whole artifacts and about the parts of animals rather than about the purposes of whole animals (Greif et al., 2006). Thus, when children later enter a more formal setting of science education, their competence may be underestimated if they are assessed in terms of their judgments of the appropriateness of certain forms of explanation for certain phenomena. Greater competence may be revealed by looking at their spontaneous use of questions.

Overall, well before elementary school begins, children are sensitive to a variety of high-level causal and relational patterns that are particularly useful for reasoning about living things. The most dramatic cases of cognitive change seem to involve learning about more detailed mechanisms of biological systems, much of this occurring during the elementary school years. In addition, an explicit awareness of plants and animals as a distinct domain governed by unique sets of mechanistic principles may undergo considerable development during childhood; it may change from a simple notion of seeing plants and animals as special because of a vital force to seeing them as engaging in unique metabolic activities (Inagaki and Hatano, 2002, 2006).

Substances and Their Transformations

As adults, people think of chemistry as the study of the composition of matter and changes that it can undergo, both in isolation and in combination with other forms of matter. There is a great deal of knowledge involved in mature scientific notions of chemistry, ranging from atomic theory, to mechanisms of chemical bonding, to the dynamics of phase changes. Again, it is clear that children cannot possibly be expected to know the details of organic and inorganic chemistry, the thermodynamics of compounds changing states, or why there are clusters of elements in the periodic table with similar chemical properties. Most adults have only the most shallow grasp of such matters, even those with advanced degrees. As with other domains, it is easy to document a host of dramatic misconceptions if one approaches naïve ideas related to chemistry in this manner. There are, however, other ways of thinking about matter, substance, and transformation that appear to have much earlier developmental roots. Although there has been much less research on infants' and preschool children's understandings of matter and materials than their understandings in other domains, a consistent pattern is suggested.

Infants may have no conception of the makeup of matter, but they do seem early on to know that substance and the stuff that things are made of apply to a different level of conceptual analysis from thinking of things as objects. Preverbally, they seem to know that food is often understood most importantly in terms of the substance it is made of, whereas tools are often most importantly understood in terms of their shapes (Santos, Hauser, and Spelke, 2002). In the earliest stages of word learning, they know that mass nouns (some x) will refer to substance, whereas count nouns (an x) refer to bounded objects, apparently building on a earlier emerging prelinguistic understanding of this fundamental contrast (Imai and Genter, 1997; Soja, Carey, and Spelke, 1992). During the preschool years, children learn not only words that name specific kinds of objects (e.g., boats, cups, airplanes) or bounded entities (e.g., lakes, puddles, rivers), but also words that name specific kinds of materials (e.g., wood, glass, plastic, water, juice, sand) and the perceivable properties of things (e.g., large/small, heavy/light, rough/smooth, red/green, shiny/dull, hot/cold, sweet/salty). Such naming practices could not proceed without some sense of the substances that objects are made of and the ways in which the substance itself confers properties on an object (Gelman and Kalish, 2005).

Although preschoolers still have much to learn about distinguishing and relating object and material levels of description, they are by no means clueless about the patterning of properties at these levels. Indeed, they have several emerging high-level insights that they can build on in subsequent learning. First, in several studies with children from both middle and lower middle-class backgrounds, 3- and 4-year-olds seemed to appreciate the homogeneous structure of materials (Au, 1994). For example, they often judged that an arbitrary portion of a chunk/pile of a given substance was still the same kind of substance as the whole chunk/pile. They also began to distinguish substance-relevant properties (such as taste, smell, whether it melts or burns, the color it turns when in certain reactions) that would be maintained across different portion sizes and more entity-relevant properties (such as coarseness, its capacity to blow away or break another object, fit into a certain space, or its shape) that would not.

Although children were far from perfect in their judgments, especially when materials have been ground into powders or invisible pieces, these and other studies (e.g., Gelman and Markman, 1986, 1987) have shown that preschool children, like adults, can use a notion of material kinds as a basis for making inductive inferences about the properties of things, even when such judgments are pitted against judgments based on global perceptual similarity. In addition, from about age 4, they realize that the same type of object can be made from different materials (e.g., a toy airplane made of paper or wood, a spoon made of plastic or metal) or that two different objects (e.g., a spoon and a cup) could be made of the same materials (Dickinson, 1987). They also realize that transformations (such as cutting, grinding, or breaking) that destroy object identity do not need to change the identity of the kind of material an object is made of. For example, if one cut a wooden toy airplane into pieces, it would no longer be an airplane, but it would still be wood (Smith, Carey, and Wiser, 1985).

Another somewhat early developing notion is the belief in conservation of "amount of matter or stuff" under certain simple transformations in shape, as evidenced in Piaget and Inhelder's famous conservation studies (1974). For example, 5- to 7-year-old children are beginning to realize that changing the shape of an object (rolling a clay ball into a long thin snake-like shape or pouring a liquid from one shaped container to another) does not change the amount of stuff in the object or the amount of liquid in the container. Again, children are beginning to look beyond differences in surface appearance to make inferences about some theoretically important quantity that has been conserved—in this case, "the amount of matter or stuff." These are perhaps some of the most widely studied and replicated findings in all of developmental psychology, although the replications suggest that many features of how the tasks are presented can affect how well the questions are understood, children's pattern of judgment, and the age at which they give "conservation" answers (Gelman and Baillargeon, 1983).

Initially, children who make these conservation judgments base their arguments on references to features of transformation history—nothing appeared to be added or removed—or base their arguments on qualitative compensation arguments (e.g., general trade-off between height and width of containers). They generally have no means yet of directly measuring, quantifying, or comparing the amount of matter in the two samples. Developing a deeper understanding of the (approximate) conservation of amount of matter and mass across a much broader range of transformations (including dissolving and across chemical and phase changes), in contrast, is a protracted process and requires more explicit science instruction and self-conscious theory-building on the child's part, learning to measure volume and weight and, in some cases, developing an atomic-molecular framework of matter (Smith et al., 2006; Stavy, 1995).

Chemistry is a domain in which some of the clearest cases of dramatic conceptual change have been documented during childhood, at both the macroscopic and atomic-molecular levels. For example, although even preschool children understand that objects vary in their size and weight, their initial understanding of these magnitudes is grounded in their perceptual experiences, rather than an explicitly articulated theory of matter. Size is "perceived global bigness," in which different spatial dimensions have not yet been differentiated. Weight is "felt weight," in which weight and density have not yet been differentiated as distinct physical magnitudes. Children often judge that some light objects, like a small piece of Styrofoam, weigh "nothing at all" because they exert no force on their hand (Smith, Carey, and Wiser, 1985; Smith, Solomon, and Carey, 2005). Hence, their understanding of these properties undergoes dramatic change as they construct distinct measures of weight and volume, come to see them as central properties of all matter, and interrelate these quantities in a distinct concept of density tied to their notion of material kind (Lehrer et al., 2001; Smith, Carey, and Wiser, 1985; Smith et al., 1997; Smith, Solomon, and Carey, 2005).

Furthermore, when young children are beginning to develop an explicit concept of matter that includes both solids and liquids, it is initially grounded in more commonsense perceptual properties—something one can see, feel, or touch—rather than as something that takes up space and has mass (Carey, 1991; Stavy, 1991). Thus, children have difficulty recognizing that matter continues to exist when divided into pieces too small to see (Carey, 1991; Smith et al., 1997) and generally do not appreciate the material nature of gases (Lee et al., 1993; Stavy, 1988; Smith et al., 1997).

Even more challenging to their everyday experiences of matter and materials are the assumptions of the atomic-molecular theory of matter. Not only does this theory call for them to imagine matter at a scale far removed from their everyday experiences, but it also makes theoretical commitments that violate their metaphysical beliefs (e.g., there is no vacuum). Everyday experience—the experience that matter is continuous—is deeply entrenched, and the experience that the kinds of materials in the world are infinitely varied is not easily reconciled with the notion that there are only about 100 different kinds of atoms on earth (Nussbaum, 1985; Lee et al., 1993). However, although there is still much for children to learn, even in preschool they are making some distinctions between object and material levels of description in organizing their knowledge of the natural world. They are beginning to ask themselves what are things made of, what changes and what stays the same across different transformations, and learning to count things and even to build some initial causal accounts of why things have the properties that they do. All of these initial insights and interests can and should be drawn on in science teaching.

Earth Systems and Cosmology

In some respects there could hardly be more diversity across cultures than there is with respect to cosmology. Views of the nature of the heavens and of heavenly bodies have varied enormously over the years and from society to society. It might therefore seem that views of the earth, the heavens, extraterrestrial bodies, and the interactions between them would show markedly different developmental patterns depending on the culture involved. Yet the past decade of research suggests a more nuanced pattern. There may be a considerable common ground to early views of the earth and the heavens, with divergence tending to emerge later on.

One view sees preschool children as developing a coarse set of beliefs or "framework theory" (see Wellman, 1990) that helps guide the emergence of later more culture-specific views (Nussbaum, 1979; Nussbaum and Novak, 1976; Nussbaum and Sharoni-Dagan, 1983; Vosniadou, 1994; Vosniadou and Brewer, 1990, 1992, 1994; Vosniadou and Ioannides, 1998). By this account, young children become convinced of two very salient "facts" about their external world: it is essentially flat, and unsupported objects fall down. As they grow older and become immersed in their culture, they strive to fit these two universal framing beliefs with what the culture tells them about the earth, the moon, and the stars. This process of fitting these strong early beliefs with what their culture tells them often results in distortions as they either attempt to reconcile the two or simply develop compartmentalized and internally contradictory beliefs. For example, their firsthand experience of flatness and things falling down may be very difficult to reconcile with being told that the earth is round. Children will try to reinterpret "round" as not meaning a sphere but instead as something like a flat disc or a hollowed out hemisphere in which people live. In fact, the mental models that the children create of the earth, the sun, and the moon tend to come from a relatively small family of alternatives in most cultures (e.g., Samarapungavan, Vosniadou, and Brewer, 1996).

Cosmology and earth sciences offer an especially interesting case in which the history of science and cognitive development can be compared and contrasted for mutually reinforcing insights (Duschl, 2000). Certainly, views of a flat earth, of the heavens as a curtain with pinholes representing stars, or of the sun revolving around the earth are well known for their prominent roles in the Western historical tradition. It is useful to therefore ask about the extent to which very early emerging beliefs, such as those about flatness and about the downward descent of unsupported objects, have had a framing effect on belief systems for millennia and how, as formal science emerged, it managed to override those early belief systems. Those accounts may well help clarify the ways in which science education today might encounter such beliefs and work with them.

There are, of course, many other features of early knowledge that influence the development of cosmology and an intuitive earth science. The large literature on how children conceptualize the spatial layout, for example, is critical to understanding how they start to build models of the arrangement of bodies in space (Newcombe et al., 1998). Similarly, the development of the ability to understand the representational meanings of maps and three-dimensional models (such as globes) undergoes dramatic changes during the preschool and early elementary school years (DeLoache, 1987, 2004; Liben, Kastens, and Stevenson, 2002) and is therefore essential to understanding how cultural artifacts may influence the teaching and learning of earth science. Moreover, the particular symbols and representations used influence the nature of the spatial representations that are constructed (Uttal, 2002), making clear the importance of understanding the ways in which children of different ages naturally conceive of spatial information and the ways in which they are and are not able to glean information from maps and models.

In short, the emergence of a folk cosmology and an intuitive earth science in the preschool and early elementary school years forms a critical skeletal structure within which more formal science curricula must function. Of all five domains considered here, some of the most dramatic changes may occur during the elementary school years with respect to cosmology; but these changes hardly occur in an intellectually empty or unformed mind. Children bring with them a substantial set of interrelated beliefs and expectations about the earth and the heavens that must be taken into account.

UNDERPINNINGS OF SCIENTIFIC REASONING

As we have shown above, young preschoolers can be exquisitely sensitive to abstract patterns in the world and use that sensitivity to guide how they think about the behaviors of objects, the nature of living things, and the layout of things in space, among many other problems (Keil et al., 1998). Young children and preverbal infants seem to have a strong sense of principles of cause and effect and do not merely notice spatial and temporal contiguity (Leslie, 1984). Moreover, they have reasonable expectations about how causes precede effects and how certain kinds of causes are linked to specific kinds of effects (Bullock, Gelman, and Baillargeon, 1982; Koslowski, 1996). Categorization, induction, and many other forms of reasoning seem to be guided by such abstract forms of information. At the same time, infants and young children can have enormous difficulty explicitly talking about abstract patterns, a difficulty that may well contribute to a false impression that they are hopelessly concrete (Simons and Keil, 1995). That difficulty in itself is an important developmental factor to consider in its own right.

Children can use many processes that can be thought of as the underpinnings of scientific reasoning (at least in certain contexts), certainly by the end of the preschool years and often well before. These include deductive reasoning, inductive reasoning, Bayesian reasoning and screening off, sensitivity to covariation, correlation, and contingency patterns in stimulus input, the ability to evaluate simple quantified and if-then rules, the ability to distinguish determinate and indeterminate evidence, and some general problem-solving heuristics and reasoning biases. In this sense, children are more competent than has been commonly supposed and bring a wealth of capacities to the learning process.

For example, reasoning about covariation and cause has been an active area of research on scientific reasoning in older children. Research has demonstrated that even preschool children are adept at using a variety of cues from the environment to identify the cause of an event from a set of potential candidates. Among these cues are temporal contiguity, spatial contiguity, consistent covariation between the candidate cause and the effect, and mechanism—that is, whether there is a plausible mechanism that would account for A causing B (Leslie, 1984; Shultz, 1982). There is mounting evidence that even very young children (ages 2, 3, and 4) are able to draw inferences about cause from viewing patterns of covariation of events.

In a series of investigations, Gopnik and her colleagues (Gopnik et al., 2004; Gopnik and Sobel, 2000; Gopnik, et al., 2001; Kushnir and Gopnik, 2005; Schulz and Gopnik, 2004) explored both how young children learn about new causal relations and whether these learning systems are domain specific or apply across different domains of knowledge, such as biological and physical systems. The strategy was to observe children as they went about learning a novel causal relation that they had not previously encountered or been taught.

In one series of studies, children were shown several small blocks and told that one or more of them were blickets. They were then introduced to the "blicket detector," a machine that lights up and plays music when (and only when) "blickets" are placed on it. Children were asked to identify which of the blocks were the blickets, either by observing the response of the blicket detector as the researcher placed blocks on it, or, in some studies, by themselves placing blocks on the detector. Across trials within a study and across studies, the patterns of evidence that children used to make inferences became increasingly complex, ultimately including multiple causes and probabilistic relationships. In most cases, even the 2-year-olds made correct conclusions about causality by observing patterns of contingency, although younger children did not perform as well as older preschoolers on more complex tasks. Children seemed to use similar kinds of causal learning principles across different content domains of knowledge.

Young children also demonstrate capacities that can be seen as the foundation for modeling. The developmental literature illustrates that there are myriad ways in which even preschool children come to regard one thing as representing another. For example, long before they arrive at school, children have some appreciation of the representational qualities of toys, pictures, scale models, and video representations (DeLoache, 2004; DeLoache, Pierroutsakos, and Uttal, 2003; Troseth, 2003; Troseth and DeLoache, 1998; Troseth, Pierroutsakos, and DeLoache, 2004). In pretend play, children treat objects as stand-ins for others (a block stands in for a teacup; a banana for a telephone), yet they still understand that the object has not really changed its original identity, character, or function (Leslie, 1987). Later in school, they capitalize on very similar understandings to use counters for "direct modeling" to solve simple early arithmetic problems that involve grouping and separating.

Although young children demonstrate many early symbolic capacities that provide a foundation for modeling, they are not yet able to engage in all the key aspects of modeling in science. As Lehrer and Schauble (2000) note, "Mature modeling includes the self-conscious separation of a model and its referent, the explicit consideration of measurement error, and the understanding that alternative models are possible and may in fact be preferable." In contrast, although they certainly know the difference between a model and its referent, children do not usually self-consciously think about the separation of the model and the modeled world. Consequently, they often show a preference for copies over true models, because they tend to resist symbolic depictions that leave out information, even if the information is not important to the current theoretical purposes (Grosslight et al., 1991; Lehrer and Schauble, 2000). For example, children using paper strips to represent the height of plants may insist on the strips being colored green (like the plant stems), and demand that each strip be adorned with a flower (Lehrer and Schauble, 2002).

Children are also unlikely to spontaneously consider issues of precision and error of a representation or the implications of deviations between the model and the modeled world in light of current goals (although they certainly have intuitions that are helpful as starting points; see Masnick and Klahr, 2003; Petrosino, Lehrer, and Schauble, 2003). They also have difficulty entertaining the idea that there are many possible alternative representations. Indeed, the search for and evaluation of rival models in evaluating alternative hypotheses is a form of argument that does not typically emerge spontaneously (Driver et al., 1996; Grosslight et al., 1991).

In sum, the evidence is strong that children can engage in sophisticated forms of reasoning in some contexts. However, there are certainly many problems and tasks in which they do not display these abilities (a fact that explains, in part, why psychologists and teachers have often thought of them as lacking some of these abilities). Researchers are now more aware of the conditions that affect the use of many forms of reasoning. Significantly, many of the same variables that affect adults' use of these forms of reasoning act in similar ways with children. In this sense, there is much greater continuity across development in basic reasoning processes than has been commonly supposed, as well as more variability and context sensitivity for a given individual. Three important conditions on reasoning are (1) knowledge of relevant conceptual relations, (2) whether a problem makes sense to the child, and (3) whether implicit or nonverbal reasoning comes into play.

One of the foremost conditions on reasoning is the role of children's knowledge of relevant conceptual relations in promoting deeper reasoning (i.e., reasoning based on causal, taxonomic relations rather than surface similarity or perceptual cues). Thus, rather than reasoning being independent of knowledge, there are deep interactions between domain knowledge and many forms of reasoning (Gotwals and Songer, 2006). For example, studies of young children's causal reasoning suggest an interaction of domain-general reasoning processes and knowledge of the specific domain being investigated (Gopnik et al., 2001).

Another important condition is that the problem an individual is asked to reason about has to make (pragmatic) sense to him or her. When a problem does not make sense, people often transform it into one that does. When care is taken to present a reasoning problem in a form in which it makes sense to children, they show much more competence. For example, many problems that involve reasoning with counterfactual information do not make sense to either young children or lay adults (e.g., All snow is black. Tom sees some snow. Is it black?). However, even preschool children can reason about counterfactuals if the problem is presented in a context in which such reasoning makes sense. For example, Leevers and Harris (1999, 2000) found that 4- and 5-year-old children could reason syllogistically about incongruent content when the problems were presented in fantasy mode or when they were encouraged to think about the problems and imagine what it would be like if it were true. Many classic tasks showing apparent deep conceptual failures can be changed through pragmatic manipulations into ones where the children succeed.

Finally, in many contexts, reasoning processes are implicit and outside of children's conscious control, rather than explicit. Work in infancy suggests that even nonverbal infants have ways of representing and evaluating ideas, independent of language or other culturally transmitted symbol systems. Thus, there are many implicit and nonverbal aspects to reasoning that need to be understood and that may persist in important ways into the adult years. For example, detecting covariation and contingency and inferring causal relations from this information is likely to be an implicit process for young children (and for adults). That is, they are not fully conscious of the reasoning they use and cannot describe their thinking processes to someone else (Gopnik et al., 2001). Developing more awareness of our reasoning processes can give us conscious control over them and allows us to choose when and how we use different strategies.

YOUNG CHILDREN'S UNDERSTANDING OF KNOWLEDGE AND OF SCIENCE

Understanding how scientific knowledge is constructed and reflecting on the status of one's own knowledge of scientific concepts is challenging for many students and for adults. While young children clearly do not have a complete grasp of the scientific enterprise, research suggests that they do have important insights that can serve as resources to their learning about science as a way of knowing. These resources include children's understanding of their own and others' ideas, beliefs, and knowledge and their ability to assess sources of knowledge.

Understanding Ideas, Beliefs, and Knowledge

An extensive research literature describes young children's understanding of knowledge. The preschool years are a time of enormous accomplishments in this regard. Most notably, children develop an initial theory of mind, which provides a framework for their beginning to think of themselves and others as more or less knowledgeable. The research literature on children's theory of mind is concerned with their increasing sophistication in understanding and predicting the behaviors of others. Central to this development is the transition from a "copy theory" of mind to a "representational" theory of mind (Wellman, 1990), enabling such insights as false belief and how access to different information can lead to different inferences. In the words of Gopnik and Wellman, 5-year-olds appreciate that "all mental life has the same representational character" (Gopnik and Wellman, 1994, p. 267). This work describes an important foundation for children's understanding of knowledge and the construction of scientific knowledge. For example, it reveals the child's growing understanding of the active role of the knower in knowledge construction, negating any simple correspondence between observing and knowing.

Understanding what ideas are and what they are not is prerequisite to doing science in a meaningful way. As early as 2 years of age, children begin to use words like "think" in ways that suggest that ideas carry varying degrees of certainty (Perner, 1991); by age 3, they use a cluster of words that distinguish among different mental states (e.g., "think," "know," "forget," and "pretend"). These are the early markers of their growing awareness of their own minds and the fact that their own understandings may be tentative, incomplete, or incorrect in relation to those of other people. Beyond recognizing ideas as such, by about the age of 4 (if not sooner) children also understand that individuals can believe things that may be false. False belief is an essential component to mature learning as well as scientific practice. The inquiry process hinges on treating ideas as plausible and testing them empirically before determining their value.

By school age, most children will easily distinguish objects from simple symbols representing those objects (e.g., an actual milk bottle from a drawing of one) (see, e.g., DeLoache, 2004). Their ability to understand symbol systems and representational models underpins a capacity to understand and formulate explanatory models in science. This capacity emerges quite early and is in place before children enter school. For example, in studies conducted by DeLoache and her colleagues, children see an object hidden in a small-scale model of a room, and they are asked to find the object in the actual room. To be successful at this task, children must achieve the insight that the scale model is both an object in its own right and that it represents something about the larger room. This task is quite difficult for $2\frac{1}{2}$-year-olds, although on versions of the task using scale models, by 3 years of age, children typically succeed.

Understanding Sources of Knowledge

Young children are also surprisingly sophisticated in the sources of information they consider. Contrary to pervasive views of children as "lone scientists" or "concrete operators" who rely only on firsthand observations and experiments, children actually draw on information from a range of sources. These include their own perception, as well as the testimony of other children and adults, and the inferences they draw from observations and testimony (Harris, 2002). Furthermore, they also track the sources of information that influence their thinking. In the preschool years, children begin to identify clear sources of their beliefs. They accurately attribute their ideas to perception, the testimony of others, or inference from observations (Montgomery, 1992; Perner, 1991; Sodian and Wimmer, 1987; Taylor, 1988; Wellman, 1990).

Scientific practice and mature learning involve making informed judgments of the quality and truthfulness of evidence and arguments, as well as identification of reliable sources of expert knowledge. By the time children reach kindergarten, the rudiments of these intellectual skills are in hand. Children as young as age 2 make basic distinctions in the sources from which they gather information. For example, children viewing the same scene on TV and through a window will treat their observations differently

(Troseth and DeLoache, 1998). By the age of 3 or 4, children acquire a sense of the credibility of reports. Koenig, Clement, and Harris (2004), for example, presented groups of 3- and 4-year-olds with two adult "labelers" who, respectively, identified novel objects correctly and incorrectly. The older preschool children in their sample were quite capable of identifying accurate and inaccurate informants, and many tracked the accurate labeler and tended to rely on that labeler's testimony in novel scenarios.

Learning in science and in general also entails sensing the terrain of knowledge in other minds: determining who is expert on particular topics of interest (Keil, 1989). Children are surprisingly good at getting a sense of the divisions of cognitive labor around them and how to evaluate people's credibility. In preschool and through the first years of schooling, children develop a crude but impressive sense that there are experts in different broad domains corresponding roughly to physics, psychology, biology, chemistry, and political science. They know that expertise is bounded, and that not everyone knows everything. They also show marked changes during late preschool and early elementary school in their ability to discount information given by others if they see that person as having suspect motivations. In addition, they start to understand the general nature of testimony and the different pressure points that can make it fallible.

Another way of thinking about sources of knowledge is distinguishing between one's own beliefs (or theories) and empirical evidence. Kuhn and Pearsall (2000) report a study that provides evidence of an initial fragile contrast between theory and evidence by about age 6. They investigated whether children ages 4 to 6 were sensitive to evidence as a source of knowledge to support the truth of a claim, and as distinguishable from theory that enhances plausibility of the claim. Participants were shown a sequence of pictures in which, for example, two runners compete in a race. Cues in the images suggested a theory as to why one will win (e.g., one runner sports fancy running shoes, the other does not). The final image depicts one runner holding a winner's trophy.

When asked to indicate the outcome and to justify this knowledge, 4-year-olds show a fragile distinction between the two kinds of justification, "How do you know?" and "Why is it so?" (the evidence for the claim versus an explanation). In contrast, 6-year-olds, while still prone to errors, were right most of the time, and adults made no errors. Other researchers have reported similar findings that reveal children's ability to distinguish beliefs from evidence (Sodian, Zaitchick, and Carey, 1991).

Understanding Scientific Knowledge

The research literature has not extensively investigated what young children may know about science as a distinct way of knowing by the start of elementary school. In this category, we include both knowledge of the enterprise of science per se, as well as knowledge about processes that are at the heart of doing science (such as the coordination of theory and evidence). Whereas for the most part, children will have had limited experience with science, there is enormous variability in this regard. For example, some children will have gone to science museums, been read various science books, perhaps seen TV scientists performing experiments, or even had a parent who is a scientist. Such differences in experience are likely to translate into variations in children's ideas about the enterprise of science. However, very little research has explored this issue.

Some suggestions about what first graders may think about science comes from the work of Gertrude Hennessey, a science education researcher as well as a grade 1-6 science teacher, who asked her students to respond to the question "What is science?" Typical responses from first graders indicated that they did not think about science as a unique enterprise of knowledge production. Their responses included that "science is"

- learning about things,
- learning about the human body,
- having fun and learning about what it was like in the olden days, and
- about learning and listening.

These anecdotal responses suggest that early elementary students have some idea that science involves learning new things, although they may not yet have much idea what might be distinctive or special about science as a way of knowing and learning.

CONCLUSION

The notion of young children as hopelessly concrete and incapable of abstract thought is undermined by their early emerging abilities to track all sorts of highly abstract relations in the world around them. They have rich knowledge of natural phenomena. They are able to reason in ways that provide a foundation for scientific thinking, including potential precursors of modeling, designing experiments, and reasoning about theory and evidence. They also enter school with a broad and impressive set of knowledge skills that allow them to use and work with knowledge in sophisticated ways, although they may lack a clear sense of what is unique about science.

Across all five domains of knowledge of the natural world considered in this chapter, there is a consistent pattern in which preschoolers, and often even preverbal infants, are found to be tracking a wide range of relational and causal properties of the world around them. Beyond just tracking those regularities, however, they also come to link them to broad domains, such as those corresponding to physical mechanics, cognitive and motivational processes, matter, the living world, and cosmology. They are not always correct and often have huge gaps in their understandings, but they certainly aren't mere bundles of misconceptions. Instead, they are more profitably construed as active exploratory agents who have successfully learned about regularities in these broad domains in ways that help them interpret, anticipate, and explain their worlds. They do have misconceptions, and some persist into most adults' mental lives, but these misconceptions are more revealing and better understood in the broader context of considering children's positive abilities.

In conjunction with their knowledge of the natural world, young children are also able to engage in reasoning that can be used as starting points for supporting the generation and evaluation of evidence. For example, young children's understanding of symbols and scale models can be used to help them engage in modeling activities. Likewise, their ability to distinguish cause and effect is a critical foundation for designing informative experiments. These early reasoning abilities are constrained, however, by the depth of children's conceptual knowledge, the nature of the task, and their awareness of their own thinking (metacognition). The latter, metacognition or the ability to think about one's own thinking, is recognized as critical to learning in general (see National Research Council, 2000) and emerges again and again as important to science learning.

Finally, children's early beliefs about knowledge may serve as precursors to developing an understanding of how scientific knowledge is constructed. During the preschool years, children develop an awareness of other people's minds that reveals a growing understanding of the active role of the knower in knowledge construction. This ability to consider ideas and beliefs as separate from the material world is foundational for engaging in debates about the interpretation of evidence. Children's beliefs about knowledge also encompass some aspects of the nature of knowledge, such as its degree of uncertainty and the relative credibility of knowledge sources. These epistemological beliefs can function as a starting point for learning about the nature and development of science knowledge in the classroom, providing rich resources on which to build, as well as limitations.

Many questions remain about the mental representations that children use to help make sense of their world, such as how different they are from the more formal theories of science and how easy it is for them to access information for use across a wide range of contexts. It is important for science educators to balance a deep appreciation of what is genuinely conceptually difficult, "non obvious," and novel about many central principles of modern science, with an equally deep appreciation of the many intellectual resources that children bring to the science learning task. It is these resources in combination with the new knowledge and tools provided in science instruction itself that will make successful science learning possible. There is now abundant evidence that, along with whatever misconceptions they may appear to have, children also bring to the classroom a rich and valuable set of knowledge structures and processes that should be exploited more fully as points of departure for science education. Furthermore, their reasoning abilities and understanding of knowledge mean that they can engage in and profit from instruction that incorporates relatively complex scientific practices from the very beginning of their schooling.

REFERENCES

Ahn, W., Gelman, S.A., Amsterlaw, J.A., Hohenstein, J., and Kalish, C.W. (2000). Causal status effects in children's categorization. *Cognition, 76,* 35-43.

Atran, S., Medin, D.L., Lynch, E., Vapnarsky, V., Ucan Ek', E., and Sousa, P. (2001). Folkbiology doesn't come from folkpsychology: Evidence from Yukatec Maya in cross-cultural perspective. *Journal of Cognition and Culture, 1,* 4-42.

Au, T.K. (1994). Developing an intuitive understanding of substance kinds. *Cognitive Psychology, 27*(1), 71-111.

Backscheider, A.G., Shatz, M., and Gelman, S.A. (1993). Preschoolers' ability to distinguish living kinds as a function of regrowth. *Child Development, 64,* 1242-1257.

Baillargeon, R. (1986). Representing the existence and the location of hidden objects: Object permanence in 6- and 8-month-old infants. *Cognition, 23,* 21-41.

Baillargeon, R. (1987). Object permanence in 3.5- and 4.5-month-old infants. *Developmental Psychology, 23,* 655-664.

Baillargeon, R. (1995). A model of physical reasoning in infancy. In C. Rovee-Collier and L. Lipsitt (Eds.), *Advances in infancy research* (vol. 9, pp. 305-371). Norwood NJ: Ablex.

Baillargeon, R. (2004). How do infants learn about the physical world? *Current Directions in Psychological Science, 3,* 133-140.

Baillargeon, R., Spelke, E.S., and Wasserman, S. (1985). Object permanence in five-month-old infants. *Cognition, 20,* 191-208.

Baron-Cohen, S. (1995). *Mindblindness: An essay on autism and theory of mind.* Cambridge, MA: MIT Press.

Bartsch, K., and Wellman, H. (1989). Young children's attribution of action to beliefs and desires. *Child Development, 60,* 946-964.

Bertamini, M., Spooner A., and Hecht, H. (2004). The representation of naive knowledge about physics. In G. Malcolm (Ed.), *Multidisciplinary approaches to visual representations and interpretations.* Amsterdam: Elsevier.

Bertenthal, B.I. (1993). Infants' perception of biomechanical motions: Intrinsic image and knowledge-based constraints. In C. Granrud (Ed.), *Visual perception and cognition in infancy* (pp. 175-214). Hillsdale, NJ: Lawrence Erlbaum Asociates.

Booth, A.E., Pinto, J., and Bertenthal, B.I. (2002). Perception of the symmetrical patterning of human gait by infants. *Developmental Psychology, 38*(4), 554-563.

Bullock, M., Gelman, R., and Baillargeon, R. (1982). The development of causal reasoning. In W.J. Friedman (Ed.), *The developmental psychology of time*. New York: Academic Press.

Brown, D.E., and Clement, J. (1989). Overcoming misconceptions via analogical reasoning: Abstract transfer versus explanatory model construction. *Instructional Science, 18*, 237-261.

Bruner, J. (1964). The course of cognitive growth. *American Psychologist, 19*, 1-15.

Caramazza, A., McCloskey, M., and Green, B. (1981). Naive beliefs in "sophisticated" subjects: Misconceptions about trajectories of objects. *Cognition, 9*, 117-123.

Carey, S. (1985). *Conceptual change in childhood*. Cambridge, MA: MIT Press.

Carey, S. (1988). Conceptual differences between children and adults. *Mind and Language, 3,* 167-181.

Carey, S. (1991). Knowledge acquisition: Enrichment or conceptual change? In S. Carey and R. Gelman (Eds.), *The epigenesis of mind: Essays on biology and cognition* (pp. 257-291). Hillsdale, NJ: Lawrence Erlbaum Associates.

Chi, M.T.H. (2005). Commonsense conceptions of emergent processes: Why some misconceptions are robust. *Journal of the Learning Sciences, 14*(2), 161-199.

Clement, J. (1982). Students' preconceptions in introductory mechanics. *American Journal of Physics, 50*, 66-71.

Cohen, L.B., and Cashon, C.H. (2006). Infant cognition. In W. Damon and R.M. Lerner (Eds.), *Handbook of child psychology, 6th Edition*. Hoboken, NJ: Wiley.

Csibra, G., Gergely, G., Biró, S., Koós, O., and Brockbank, M. (1999). Goal-attribution without agency cues: The perception of 'pure reason' in infancy. *Cognition, 72*, 237-267.

DeLoache, J.S. (1987). Rapid change in the symbolic functioning of very young children. *Science, 238*, 1556-1557.

DeLoache, J.S. (2004). Becoming symbol-minded. *Trends in Cognitive Sciences, 8*, 66-70.

DeLoache, J.S., Pierroutsakos, S.L., and Uttal, D.H. (2003). The origins of pictorial competence. *Current Directions in Psychological Science, 12,* 114-118.

Dickinson, L. (1987). *Self-instruction in language learning*. Cambridge, MA: Cambridge University Press.

diSessa, A.A. (2004). Metarepresentation: Native competence and targets for instruction. *Cognition and Instruction, 22*(3), 293-331.

Doran, R.L. (1972). Misconceptions of selected science held by elementary school students. *Journal of Research in Science Teaching, 9*, 127-137.

Driver, R., Leach, J., Millar, R., and Scott, P. (1996). *Young people's images of science*. Buckingham, England: Open University Press.

Driver, R., Squires, A., Rushworth, P., and Wood-Robinson, V. (1994). *Making sense of secondary science: Research into children's ideas*. New York: Routledge.

Duschl, R. (2000). Making the nature of science explicit. In R. Millar, J. Leech, and J. Osborne (Eds.), *Improving science education: The contribution of research* (pp. 187-206). Philadelphia, PA: Open University Press.

Espinoza, F. (2005). Experience conflicts with and undermines instruction and its legacy: Examples from two-dimensional motion. *Physics Education, 40*(3), 274-280.

Flavell, J. (1971). Stage-related properties of cognitive development. *Cognitive Psychology, 2*, 421-453.

Flavell, J.H. (1999). Cognitive development: Children's knowledge about the mind. *Annual Review of Psychology, 16*, 21.

Freeman, N.H, Hood, B.M., and Meehan, C. (2004). Young children who abandon error behaviorally still have to free themselves mentally: A retrospective test for inhibition in intuitive physics. *Developmental Science, 7*, 277-282.

Gellert, E. (1962). Children's conceptions of the content and function of the human body. *Genetic Psychology Monographs, 65*, 293-405.

Gelman, R., and Baillargeon, R. (1983). A review of some Piagetian concepts. In J.H. Flavell and E.M. Markman (Eds.), *Handbook of child psychology* (vol. 3, pp. 167-230). Hoboken, NJ: Wiley.

Gelman, R., Durgin, F., and Kaufman, L. (1995). Distinguishing between animates and inanimates: Not by motion alone. In D. Sperber, D. Premack, and A.J. Premack (Eds.), *Causal cognition: A multidisciplinary debate* (pp. 150-184). Oxford, England: Clarendon Press.

Gelman, R., and Lucariello, J. (2002). Role of learning in cognitive development. In H. Pashler (Series Ed.) and R. Gallistel (Vol. Ed.), *Stevens' handbook of experimental psychology: Learning, motivation, and emotion* (vol. 3, 3rd ed., pp. 395-443). Hoboken, NJ: Wiley.

Gelman, S.A. (2003). *The essential child: Origins of essentialism in everyday thought.* Oxford, England: Oxford University Press.

Gelman, S.A., and Hirschfeld, L.A. (1999). How biological is essentialism? In D.L. Medin and S. Atran (Eds.), *Folkbiology* (pp. 403-446). Cambridge, MA: MIT Press.

Gelman, S., and Kalish, C. (2005). Conceptual development. In R.S. Siegler and D. Kuhn (Eds.), *Handbook of child psychology volume 2, cognition, perception, and language, 6th edition* (pp. 687-733). Hoboken, NJ: Wiley.

Gelman, S.A., and Markman, E. (1986). Categories and induction in young children. *Cognition, 23*, 183-209.

Gelman, S.A., and Markman, E.M. (1987). Young children's inductions from natural kinds: The role of categories and appearances. *Child Development, 58*, 1532-1541.

Gergeley, G., Nadasdy, Z., Csibra, G., and Biro, S. (1995). Taking the intentional stance at 12 months of age. *Cognition, 56*, 165-193.

Gimenez, M., and Harris, P.L. (2002). Understanding constraints on inheritance: Evidence for biological thinking in early childhood. *British Journal of Developmental Psychology, 20*, 307-324.

Gopnik, A., Glymour, C., Sobel, D., Schulz, L., Kushnir, T., and Danks, D. (2004). A theory of causal learning in children: Causal maps and Bayes nets. *Psychological Review, 111*, 1-31.

Gopnik, A., and Sobel, D.M. (2000). Detecting blickets: How young children use information about novel causal powers in categorization and induction. *Child Development, 71*, 1205-1222.

Gopnik, A., Sobel, D.M., Schulz, L., and Glymour, C. (2001). Causal learning mechanisms in very young children: Two, three, and four-year-olds infer causal relations from patterns of variation and covariation. *Developmental Psychology, 37*, 620-629.

Gopnik, A., and Wellman, H. (1994). The "theory theory." In L. Hirschfield and S. Gelman (Eds.), *Domain specificity in culture and cognition.* New York: Cambridge University Press.

Gotwals, A., and Songer, N. (2006). Measuring students' scientific content and inquiry reasoning. In S. Barab and K. Hay (Eds.), *Proceedings of the international conference of the learning sciences.* Ann Arbor: University of Michigan Press.

Greif, M., Nelson, D., Keil, F., and Gutierrez, F. (2006). What do children want to know about animals and artifacts? Domain-specific requests for information. *Psychological Science, 17*(6), 455-459.

Griffiths, T.L., Baraff, E.R., and Tenenbaum, J.B. (2004). Using physical theories to infer hidden causal structure. In K. Forbes, D. Gentner, and J. Regier (Eds.), *Proceedings of the 26th annual meeting of the cognitive science society* (pp. 500-505). Mahwah, NJ: Lawrence Erlbaum Associates.

Grosslight, L., Unger, C., Jay, E., and Smith, C. (1991). Understanding models and their use in science: Conceptions of middle and high school students and experts. *Journal of Research in Science Teaching, 28*(9), 799-822.

Gutheil, C., Vera, A., and Keil, F.C. (1998). Do houseflies think? Patterns of induction and biological beliefs in development. *Cognition, 66*(1), 33-49.

Harris, P. (2002). What do children learn from testimony? In P. Carruthers, S. Stich, and M. Siegal (Eds.), *The cognitive basis of science* (pp. 316-334). New York: Cambridge University Press.

Harris, P., Johnson, C.N., Hutton, D., Andrews, G., and Cooke, T. (1989). Young children's theory of mind and emotion. *Cognition and Emotion, 3,* 379-400.

Hecht, H.H., and Bertamini, M. (2000). Understanding projectile acceleration. *Journal of Experimental Psychology: Human Perception and Performance, 26*(2), 730-746.

Heyman, G.D., Phillips, A.T., and Gelman, S.A. (2003). Children's reasoning about physics within and across ontological kinds. *Cognition, 89*(1), 43-61.

Hickling, A., and Gelman, S. (1995). How does your garden grow? Evidence of an early conception of plants as biological kinds. *Child Development, 66,* 856-876.

Hickling, A.K., and Wellman, H.M. (2001). The emergence of children's causal explanations and theories: Evidence from everyday conversation. *Developmental Psychology, 5,* 668-683.

Hood, B.M. (2004). Children's understanding of the physical world. In R.L. Gregory (Ed.), *The Oxford companion to the mind, 2nd edition.* New York: Oxford University Press.

Imai, M., and Gentner, D. (1997). A crosslinguistic study of early word meaning: Universal ontology and linguistic influence. *Cognition, 62,* 169-200.

Inagaki, K., and Hatano, G. (2002) *Young children's naïve thinking about the biological world.* New York: Psychology Press.

Inagaki, K., and Hatano, G. (2006). Young children's conception of the biological world. *Current Directions in Psychological Science, 15*(4), 177.

Ioannides, C.H., and Vosniadou, S. (2002). The changing meanings of force. *Cognitive Science Quarterly, 2*(1), 5-62.

Johnson, S.P. (2003). Theories of development of the object concept. In J.G. Bremner and A.M. Slater (Eds.), *Theories of infant development* (pp. 174-203). Cambridge, MA: Blackwell.

Johnson, S., and Carey, S. (1998). Knowledge enrichment and conceptual change in folkbiology: Evidence from Williams Syndrome. *Cognitive Psychology, 37,* 156-200.

Keen, R. (2003). Representation of objects and events: Why do infants look so smart and toddlers look so dumb? *Current Directions in Psychological Science, 12,* 79-83.

Keil, F.C. (1989). *Concepts, kinds, and cognitive development.* Cambridge, MA: MIT Press.

Keil, F.C. (1992). The origins of an autonomous biology. In M.R. Gunnar and M. Maratsos (Eds.), *Modularity and constraints in language and cognition.* The Minnesota Symposia on Child Psychology (vol. 25, pp. 103-137). Hillsdale, NJ: Lawrence Erlbaum Associates.

Keil, F.C. (2003). That's life: Coming to understand biology. *Human Development, 46,* 369-377.

Keil, F.C., and Richardson, D.C. (1999). Species, stuff, and patterns of causation. In R. Wilson (Ed.), *Species: New interdisciplinary essays* (Chapter 10). Cambridge, MA: MIT Press.

Keil, F.C., Smith, C.S., Simons, D., and Levin, D. (1998). Two dogmas of conceptual empiricism. *Cognition, 65,* 103-135.

Kelemen, D. (1999). The scope of teleological thinking in preschool children. *Cognition, 70*(3), 241-272.

Klahr, D. (2000). *Exploring science: The cognition and development of discovery processes.* Cambridge, MA: MIT Press.

Kloos, H., and Keen, R. (2005). An exploration of toddlers' problems in a search task. *Infancy, 7*(1), 7-34.

Koenig, M., Clement, F., and Harris, P. (2004). Trust in testimony: Children's use of true and false statements. *Psychological Science, 15*(10), 694-698.

Koslowski, B. (1996). *Theory and evidence: The development of scientific reasoning.* Cambridge, MA: MIT Press.

Kotovsky, L., and Baillargeon, R. (1994). Calibration-based reasoning about collision events in 11-month-old infants. *Cognition, 51,* 107-129.

Krist, H., Fieberg, E.L., and Wilkening, F. (1993). Intuitive physics in action and judgment: The development of knowledge about projectile motion. *Journal of Experimental Psychology: Learning Memory and Cognition, 19*(4), 952-966.

Kuhlmeier, V., Bloom, P., and Wynn, K. (2005). Do 5-month-old infants see humans as material objects? *Cognition, 94,* 95-103.

Kuhn, D., and Pearsall, S. (2000). Developmental origins of scientific thinking. *Journal of Cognition and Development, 1,* 113-129.

Kushnir, T., and Gopnik, A. (2005). Young children infer casual strength from probabilities and interventions. *Psychological Science, 16*(9), 678-683.

Lawson, R. (in press). The science of cycology: Failures to understand how everyday objects work. *Memory and Cognition.*

Lee, O., Eichinger, D.C., Anderson, C.W., Berkheimer, G.D., and Blakeslee, T.D. (1993). Changing middle school students' conceptions of matter and molecules. *Journal of Research in Science Teaching, 30*(3), 249-270.

Leevers, H.J., and Harris, P.L. (1999). Persisting effects of instruction on young children's syllogistic reasoning with incongruent and abstract premises. *Thinking and Reasoning, 5*, 145-173.

Leevers, H.J., and Harris, P.L. (2000). Counterfactual syllogistic reasoning in normal 4-year-olds, children with learning disabilities, and children with autism. *Journal of Experimental Child Psychology, 76*, 64-87.

Lehrer, R., and Schauble, L. (2000). Inventing data structures for representational purposes: Elementary grade students' classification models. *Mathematical Thinking and Learning, 2*, 51-74.

Lehrer, R., and Schauble, L. (2002). Symbolic communication in mathematics and science: Co-constituting inscription and thought. In J. Byrnes and E.D. Amsel, (Eds.), *Language, literacy, and cognitive development: The development and consequences of symbolic communication* (pp. 167- 192). Mahwah, NJ: Lawrence Erlbaum Associates.

Lehrer, R., Schauble, L., Strom, D., and Pligge, M. (2001). Similarity of form and substance: Modeling material kind. In D. Klahr and S. Carver (Eds.), *Cognition and instruction: 25 years of progress* (pp. 39-74). Mahwah, NJ: Lawrence Erlbaum Associates.

Leslie, A.M. (1984). Spatiotemporal continuity and the perception of causality in infants. *Perception, 13*, 287-305.

Leslie, A.M. (1987). Pretense and representation: The origins of "theory of mind." *Psychological Review, 94*, 412-426.

Leslie, A.M. (1994). ToMM, ToBY, and agency: Core architecture and domain specificity. In L.A. Hirschfeld and S.A. Gelman (Eds.), *Mapping the mind: Domain specificity in cognition and culture* (pp. 119-148). New York: Cambridge University Press.

Leslie, A.M., and Keeble, S. (1987) Do six-month-old infants perceive causality? *Cognition, 25*, 265-288.

Liben, L.S., Kastens, K.A., and Stevenson, L.M. (2002). Real-world knowledge through real-world maps: A developmental guide for navigating the educational terrain. *Developmental Review, 22*, 267-322.

Linn, M.C. (1978). Formal operations: Construct or conglomerate. *Formal Operator, 1*(4), 2-4.

Lockhart, K. (1981). The development of knowledge about uniformities in the environment: A comparative analysis of the child's understanding of social, moral, and physical rules. *Dissertation Abstracts International, 41*(7-B), 2793.

Lopez, A., Atran, S., Coley, J.D., Medin, D.L., and Smith, E.E. (1997). The tree of life: Universal and cultural features of folkbiological taxonomies and induction. *Cognitive Psychology, 32*(3), 251-295.

Mandler, J.M. (2004). *The foundations of mind: Origins of conceptual thought.* Oxford, England: Oxford University Press.

Masnick, A.M., and Klahr, D. (2003). Error matters: An initial exploration of elementary school children's understanding of experimental error. *Journal of Cognition and Development, 4*, 67-98.

Medin, D.L., Unsworth, S.J., and Hirschfeld, L. (in press). Cultures, categorization, and reasoning. In S. Kitayama and D. Cohen (Eds.), *Handbook of cultural psychology.* New York: Guilford Press.

Metz, K.E. (1995). Reassessment of developmental constraints on children's science instruction. *Review of Educational Research, 65*, 93-127.

Mills, C., and Keil, F.C. (2005). The development of cynicism. *Psychological Science, 16*, 385-390.

Minstrell, J. (1983). Getting the facts straight. *Science Teacher, 50*(1), 52-54.

Minstrell, J. (1988). Teaching science for education. In L.B. Resnick and L.E. Klopfer (Eds.), *Toward the thinking curriculum: ASCD yearbook.* Hillsdale, NJ: Lawrence Erlbaum Associates.

Montgomery, D. (1992). Young children's theory of knowing: The development of a folk epistemology. *Developmental Review, 12*, 410-430.

Munakata, Y., Casey, B.J., and Diamond, A. (2004). Developmental cognitive neuroscience: Progress and potential. *Trends in Cognitive Science, 8*, 122-128.

Munakata, Y., McClelland, J.L., Johnson, M.H., and Siegler, R. (1997). Rethinking infant knowledge: Toward an adaptive process account of successes and failures in object permanence tasks. *Psychological Review, 104*, 686-713.

Nagy, M.H. (1953). The representations of "germs" by children. *Journal of Genetic Psychology, 83*, 227-240.

National Research Council. (2000). *How people learn: Brain, mind, experience, and school.* Committee on Developments in the Science of Learning. J.D. Bransford, A.L. Brown, and R.R. Cocking (Eds.). Washington, DC: National Academy Press.

Newcombe, N., Huttenlocher, J., Drummey, A.B., and Wiley, J.G. (1998). The development of spatial location coding: Place learning and dead reckoning in the second and third years. *Cognitive Development, 13*, 185-201.

Nussbaum, J. (1979). Children's conceptions of the earth as a cosmic body: A cross-age study. *Science Education, 63,* 83-93.

Nussbaum, J. (1985). The particulate nature of matter in the gaseous phase. In R. Driver, E. Guesne, and A. Tiberghien (Eds.), *Children's ideas in science.* Philadelphia, PA: Open University Press.

Nussbaum, J. and Novak, J.D. (1976). An assessment of children's concepts of the earth utilizing structured interviews. *Science Education, 60,* 535-550.

Nussbaum, J. and Sharoni-Dagan, N. (1983). Changes in second grade children's preconceptions about the earth as a cosmic body resulting from a short series of audio-tutorial lessons. *Science Education, 67,* 99-114.

Perner, J. (1991). *Understanding the representational mind.* Cambridge, MA: Bradford Books/MIT Press.

Perner, J., Leekam, S.R., and Wimmer, H. (1987). Three-year-olds' difficulty with false belief: The case for a conceptual deficit. *British Journal of Developmental Psychology, 5*, 125-137.

Petrosino, A., Lehrer, R., and Schauble, L. (2003). Structuring error and experimental variation as distribution in the fourth grade. *Mathematical Thinking and Learning, 5*(2-3), 131-156.

Piaget, J., and Inhelder, B. (1974). *The child's construction of quantities.* London, England: Routledge and Kegan Paul.

Pulos, S., and Linn, M.C. (1978). Pitfalls and pendulums. *Formal Operator, 1*(2), 9-11.

Rozenblit, L.R., and Keil, F.C. (2002). The misunderstood limits of folk science: An illusion of explanatory depth. *Cognitive Science, 26*, 521-562.

Samarapungavan, A., Vosniadou, S., and Brewer, W.F. (1996). Mental models of the earth, sun, and moon: Indian children's cosmologies. *Cognitive Development, 11*, 491-521.

Santos, L.R., Hauser, M.D., and Spelke, E.S. (2002). Domain-specific knowledge in human children and non-human primates: Artifact and food kinds. In M. Bekoff (Ed.), *The cognitive animal.* Cambridge, MA: MIT Press.

Saxe, R., Tenenbaum, J.B., and Carey, S. (2005). Inferences about hidden causes by 10 and 12 month old infants. *Psychological Science, 16*(12), 995-1001.

Scassellati, B., and Gold, K. (in press). Learning acceptable windows of contingency. *Connection Science: Special Issue on Developmental Learning, (18)*2.

Schulz, L., and Gopnik, A. (2004). Causal learning across domains. *Developmental Psychology, 40*(2), 162-176.

Shanon, B. (1976). Aristotelianism, Newtonianism and the physics of the layman. *Perception, 5,* 241-243.

Shultz, T.R. (1982). Rules of causal attribution. *Monographs of the Society for Research in Child Development, 47*(1).

Simons, D.J., and Keil, F. (1995). An abstract to concrete shift in the development of biological thought: The insides story. *Cognition, 56,* 129-163.

Smith, C., Carey, S., and Wiser, M. (1985). On differentiation: A case study of the development of size, weight, and density. *Cognition, 21*(3), 177-237.

Smith, C., Maclin, D., Grosslight, L., and Davis, H. (1997). Teaching for understanding: A study of students' preinstruction theories of matter and a comparison of the effectiveness of two approaches to teaching students about matter and density. *Cognition and Instruction, 15,* 317-393.

Smith, C., Solomon, G., and Carey, S. (2005). Never getting to zero: Elementary school students' understanding of the infinite divisibility of number and matter. *Cognitive Psychology, 51*(2), 101-140.

Smith, C.L., Wiser, M., Anderson, C.W., and Krajcik, J. (2006). Implications of research on children's learning for standards and assessment: A proposed learning progression for matter and the atomic molecular theory. *Measurement: Interdisciplinary Research and Perspectives, 4*(1-2), Focus Article.

Smith, J., di Sessa, A., and Roschelle, J. (1993). Misconceptions reconceived: A constructivist analysis of knowledge in transition. *Journal of the Learning Sciences, 3,* 115-163.

Sodian, B., and Wimmer, H. (1987). Children's understanding of inference as a source of knowledge. *Child Development, 58,* 424-433.

Sodian, B., Zaitchik, D., and Carey, S. (1991). Young children's differentiation of hypothetical beliefs from evidence. *Child Development, 62*(4), 753-766.

Soja, N.N., Carey, S., and Spelke, E.S. (1992). Ontological categories guide young children's inductions of word meaning: Object terms and substance terms. *Cognition, 43*(1), 85-91.

Spelke, E.S. (1991). Physical knowledge in infancy: Reflections on Piaget's theory. In S. Carey and R. Gelman (Eds.), *The epigenesis of mind: Essays on biology and cognition* (pp. 133-169). Hillsdale, NJ: Lawrence Erlbaum Associates.

Spelke E.S., Katz, G., Purcell, S.E., Ehrlich, S.M., and Breinlinger, K. (1992). Early knowledge of object motion: Continuity and inertia. *Cognition, 51,* 131-176.

Spelke, E.S., and Kyeong, K.I. (1992). Infants' sensitivity to effects of gravity on visible object motion. *Journal of Experimental Psychology: Human Perception and Performance, 8*(2), 385-393.

Spelke, S.S., Phillips, A.T., and Woodward, A.L. (1995). Infants' knowledge of object motion and human action. In A. Premack (Ed.), *Causal understanding in cognition and culture* (pp. 47-78). Oxford, England: Clarendon Press.

Springer, K., and Keil, F. (1989). On the development of biologically specific beliefs: The case of inheritance. *Child Development, 60*, 637-648.

Stavy, R. (1988). Children's conception of gas. *International Journal of Science Education, 10*(5), 553-560.

Stavy, R. (1991). Children's ideas about matter. *School Science and Mathematics, 91*(6), 240-244.

Stavy, R. (1995). Conceptual development of basic ideas in chemistry. In S. Glynn and R. Duit (Eds.), *Learning science in the schools: Research reforming practice* (pp. 131-154). Hillsdale, NJ: Lawrence Erlbaum Associates.

Taylor, M. (1988) Conceptual perspective taking: Children's ability to distinguish what they know from what they see. *Child Development, 59*, 703-718.

Toyama, N. (2000). What are food and air like inside our bodies? Children's thinking about digestion and respiration. *International Journal of Behavioral Development, 24*(2), 222-230.

Troseth, G.L. (2003). Getting a clear picture: Young children's understanding of a televised image. *Developmental Science, 6*(3), 247-253.

Troseth, G.L., and DeLoache, J.S. (1998). The medium can obscure the message: Young children's understanding of video. *Child Development, 69*, 950-965.

Troseth, G.L., Pierroutsakos, S.L., and DeLoache, J.S. (2004). From the innocent to the intelligent eye: The early development of pictorial competence. *Advances in Child Development and Behavior, 32*, 1-35.

Uttal, W.R. (2002). *A behaviorist looks at form recognition.* Mahwah, NJ: Lawrence Erlbaum Associates.

Vallortigara, G., Regolin, L., and Marconato, F. (2005). Visually inexperienced chicks exhibit spontaneous preference for biological motion patterns. *PLoS Biology, 3*(7), 1312-1316 (e208).

Viennot, L. (1979). Spontaneous reasoning in elementary dynamics. *European Journal of Science Education, 1*, 205-221.

Vosniadou, S. (1994). Capturing and modeling the process of conceptual change. *Learning and Instruction, 4*, 45-69.

Vosniadou, S., and Brewer, W.F. (1990). A cross-cultural investigation of children's conceptions about the earth, the sun, and the moon: Greek and American data. In H. Mandl, E. DeCorte, N. Bennett, and H.F. Friedrich (Eds.), *Learning and instruction: European research in an international context* (pp. 605-629). Oxford, England: Pergamon Press.

Vosniadou, S., and Brewer, W.F. (1992). Mental models of the earth: A study of conceptual change in childhood. *Cognitive Psychology, 24*, 535-585.

Vosniadou, S., and Brewer, W.F. (1994). Mental models of the day/night cycle. *Cognitive Science, 18*, 123-183.

Vosniadou, S., and Ioannides, C. (1998). From conceptual development to science education: A psychological point of view. *International Journal of Science Education, 20*(10), 1213-1230.

Watson, J.S. (1979). Perception of contingency as a determinant of social responsiveness. In E.B. Thoman (Ed.), *Origins of the infant's social responsiveness* (pp. 33-64). Hillsdale, NJ: Lawrence Erlbaum Associates.

Wellman, H.M. (1990). *The child's theory of mind.* Cambridge, MA: MIT Press.

Werner, H., and Kaplan, B. (1963). *Symbol formation: An organismic developmental approach to language and the expression of thought.* Hoboken, NJ: Wiley.

Wimmer, H., and Perner, J. (1983). Beliefs about beliefs: Representations and constraining functions of wrong beliefs in young children's understanding of deception. *Cognition, 13*, 103-128.

Woodward, A.L. (1998). Infants selectively encode the goal object of an actor's reach. *Cognition, 69*(1), 1-34.

Woodward, A.L., Sommerville, J.A., and Guajardo, J.J. (2001). How infants make sense of intentional action. In B.F. Malle, L.J. Moses, and D.A. Baldwin (Eds.), *Intentions and intentionality. Foundations of social cognition* (pp. 149-170). Boston, MA: MIT Press.

Yoachim, C.M., and Meltzoff, A.N. (2003, October). *Cause and effect in the mind of the preschool child.* Poster presented at the biennial meeting of the Cognitive Development Society, Park City, UT.

Zimmer, C. (2004). *Soul made flesh.* New York: Free Press.

4

Knowledge and Understanding
of the Natural World

Major Findings in the Chapter:

- *Children's intuitive concepts of the natural world can be both resources and barriers to emerging understanding. These concepts can be enriched and transformed by appropriate classroom experiences.*
- *Changes in a student's knowledge do not necessarily follow a linear improvement across grades, and an individual's understanding can vary across contexts.*
- *Conceptual development can occur in many different ways. Some kinds of conceptual change occur naturally as a consequence of the child's everyday experiences, whereas others require intentional effort, often by both a learner and a teacher.*
- *Major changes in conceptual frameworks are often difficult to make because they require learners to break out of their familiar frame and reorganize a body of knowledge, often in ways that draw on unfamiliar ideas. Such changes are facilitated by instruction that helps students construct an understanding of the new concepts, and provides opportunities for them to strengthen their understanding of the new ideas through extended application and argumentation.*

In this chapter we summarize research related to Strand 1: know, use, and interpret scientific knowledge of the natural world. We begin with a discussion of how children's knowledge develops as they move through the K-8 years. We consider each of the knowledge domains identified in Chapter 3—physics, biology, psychology, chemistry, and earth sciences—and sketch out how early understanding is extended and revised. In the second half of the chapter, we describe the process of conceptual change, considering the various ways changes can occur and how they can be facilitated.

CHANGES IN CONCEPTUAL UNDERSTANDING DURING THE K-8 YEARS

There is no magic line that divides children's cognitive development before entering elementary school from their cognitive development after the onset of formal schooling. Children continue to refine their abilities to use information at various levels of abstraction and become ever more sophisticated at understanding the nature of good explanations, methods of inquiry, and the role of evidence. They also show substantial increases in the ability to explicitly talk about patterns and principles and realize their relevance across a wider and wider range of settings. In addition, they greatly expand their understandings of pathways to knowledge and how to navigate pathways in ways that exploit the greater expertise of specialists in various areas. All of these patterns of change during the elementary school years have their roots in preschool and earlier, but in many cases the changes greatly accelerate in older children. Explicit instruction and educational experiences in school and other settings clearly help foster many of these changes, but others should be understood as the continuation of processes that started long before school and that now also interact with those of formal education.

In this section we very briefly provide examples of how children's knowledge changes over the K-8 years, building on the knowledge they develop prior to school. We highlight three main ideas. First, there are some (positive) improvements in children's understanding (e.g., increased knowledge, increased understanding of some mechanisms, increased understanding of relations among variables). Second, not all changes necessarily bring children closer to canonical scientific views. For example, children bring naïve conceptions about the natural world that differ from accepted scientific explanation (often referred to as misconceptions). Some of the naïve concepts are persistent and difficult to change. Others are transitory and appear to resolve themselves with time and experience. Third, there is considerable variability in the changes that occur. An individual's understanding can vary across contexts. There is also variation among children when they attain certain understandings. This variation is likely to reflect differences in the kinds of previous educational opportunities or experiences they have had. The latter findings underscore that these changes do not just come for free with increasing age.

It is important to emphasize that changes in knowledge during this period do not necessarily follow a pattern of linear improvement across grades (Siegler, 1998). Instead, there are many twists and turns and misconceptions that develop along the way. In fact, growth can be difficult to gauge, as it sometime follows a U-shaped pattern, with apparent regressions or intermediate constructions developing as part of the process. In this context, misconceptions or wrong ideas are not necessarily a bad thing, nor are they necessarily a sign of a deeply held systematic alternative theory—some are highly context dependent and even quite transitory. However, they do reflect deeper conceptual difficulties, and understanding the *reasons* for those difficulties can be instructive. In some cases, misconceptions develop in part because of limited symbolic tools available to students or limitations in conceptual knowledge in other domains (e.g., having mathematics based on natural rather than rational number, having limitations in geometric understandings).

Some misconceptions may stem from alternative *ontological* commitments that constrain children's ideas. If children assume that an entity or relation belongs to a fundamentally different kind of thing, that assumption can derail attempts to link up their conceptual system with that of adults or older children. For example, if fire is thought of as a kind of stuff rather than a symptom of an event (combustion), that misattribution of fire to the wrong category (a substance instead of an event) can lead to dramatically different inferences about other properties of fires. More broadly, conceptual change may be more difficult when the child's naïve conception assigns entities in a domain to a different ontological category than an adult's conception assigns them (Chi, 2005). In contrast, if a young child initially misconceives an entity as a different sort of thing but in the same ontological category, then conceptual change may be much easier to achieve (Chi, 2005). For example, a child might initially think that germs are like small insects inside the body instead of knowing that they are a different kind of organism, but such a mistake makes the same ontological commitments and would be relatively easy for a child to surmount.

Multiple factors contribute to the changes described in this section. Thus, we need to avoid the trap of looking for a single explanation for such diverse phenomena. Instead, we need to identify the range of important factors and explore how they contribute and interact with one another. Many of these factors may be primarily experiential in nature (rather than maturational in a strict biological sense), and there are a variety of ways that experience can contribute to growth. Even in the case of more maturationally based factors (such as increases in working memory, processing speed, capacity for attention, self-regulation, executive function), there is evidence for interactions with experiential factors in these developments as well. For example, many factors (knowledge, processing speed, strategies) affect measured short-term storage span of memory, and, although measured short-term storage span increases with age, many argue that short-term storage capacity is not changing with age. In both children and adults, richer knowledge bases result in larger memory capacities (Chi, 1978). There is more evidence, however, for an underlying maturational component for changes in processing speed (although some aspects are also clearly affected by experience) (Kail, 1991; Luna et al., 2004; Travis, 1998).

Extending and Changing Understandings of Naïve Physics

Children's understanding of the simple mechanics of bounded objects undergoes considerable change during the elementary school years. One area of dramatic change concerns an appreciation of how to interrelate variables that are concerned with trajectories, most notably, distance, speed, and duration. Many years ago, the Swiss psychologist, Jean Piaget, demonstrated confusions among these variables in young children (Piaget, 1946a, 1946b; Piaget and Inhelder, 1948), but only recently have more systematic studies documented the ways in which children come to make sense of each of these variables and their interrelations. Those studies now suggest that even young preschool children distinguish distance, speed, and time in some contexts (in contrast to Piaget's claim that these notions are initially completely undifferentiated) (Acredelo, Adams, and Schmid, 1984; Matsuda, 1994, 2001; Wilkening, 1981). Some of the differences across tasks depend on what criteria children use in judging each task. Many of the tasks require them to use qualitative criteria (e.g., comparing starting and stopping times); some give them direct information in some symbolic form and examine their ability to integrate it (a clock that says 10 versus 20 seconds; a distance strip; two animals that are known to be fast or slow, like turtles and horses). Development here, however, does not occur in a vacuum. Consider the normal developmental progressions for children in two different cultures that vary in their approach to science and math education. Chinese third graders seem to have no difficulty reasoning about inverse relations, whereas American third graders often do; American fifth graders achieve performance more like Chinese third graders (Zhou et al., 2000). Although further research is needed to confirm the reliability of this difference and to understand its sources, it may reflect differences in the quality of early mathematics and science education. In China, in contrast to the United States, the skills of argument and proof are taught as early as the first grade and mathematics and science topics are pursued more deeply and thoroughly. In addition, the elementary teachers are more highly trained in the teaching of mathematics.

Thus, although there is a clear age trend in learning to understand inverse relations, there can be dramatic differences in the age at which most children understand such relations as a function of educational and cultural environment. The mechanisms behind such age differences are yet to be fully understood, but they make clear the folly of thinking that there are certain ages at which children can or cannot understand specific scientific concepts. And there is a continuing legacy of cognitive challenges in some areas. In more complex tasks, for example, college students have difficulties with inverse relations as well.

There are also developmental lags in how children understand trajectories, with an understanding in terms of catching actions appearing much earlier than those in terms of predictions as more passive observers (Krist, Fieberg, and Wilkening, 1993; Huber, Krist, and Wilkening, 2003; Krist, 2003). In fact, explicit predictions about trajectories are often wrong even in adults (Clement, 1982; McCloskey, 1983). Indeed, in some cases, very young children actually seem to be better at anticipating trajectories, then get worse as they get older and develop a more consistent but incorrect "theory" of motion (Kaiser, McCloskey, and Profitt, 1986). Such U-shaped developmental curves have been documented repeatedly in children's developing conceptions of mechanics (Karmiloff-Smith and Inhelder, 1974).

Children also show substantial improvement during the elementary school years in detailed understanding of physical mechanisms. Consider, for example, research on changes in children's understanding of gears. The mechanism is fully observable in these studies (a set of exposed gears), yet there is much that is not transparent to young children or even adults. One study that compared second and fifth graders showed how children can take an idea that is useful in one context and then overapply it to others (Lehrer and Schauble, 1998). Thus, a child might develop a hunch about gear function from playing with an egg beater and then inappropriately make some extensions to gears on a bicycle. More broadly, it can take years for elementary school children to start to understand systems like gears and levers in more formal terms that allow more correct generalizations across instances (Lehrer and Schauble, 1998). At the same time, children clearly benefit from core concepts that arise in infancy and the preschool years. For example, children of all ages insist that gears must make physical contact with each other in order to form a working system of gears.

Children have great difficulties learning physicists' notions of force. Students tend to associate forces with movement and do not recognize the action of forces in situations of equilibrium. They also tend to focus on forces as active agents and are less likely to recognize passive forces (e.g., they may think forces are needed more to start a motion than to stop one, hence have difficulty recognizing friction as a force). They also think of force as a property of objects rather than as a feature of interaction between two objects—so they identify forces singly, rather than in terms of interaction pairs. Finally, when two forces are acting on an object, they think of one as winning or overcoming the other, rather than interacting through vector addition (Clement, 1982; diSessa, 1982). The developmental story seems to involve several distinct notions of force emerging at different times in childhood, with a final convergence on the physicists' concept usually occurring only in those lucky few who actually get insight from a college-level physics course instead of continuing to cling to developmentally earlier views (Ioannides and Vosniadou, 2002; Watts and Zylberstajn, 1981).

There are many other misconceptions that develop in childhood and often persist into adulthood without appropriate instruction. These include mistaken beliefs about relations between air pressure and gravity (Minstrell, 1982), confusions between momentum and force (diSessa, 1988), and difficulties in understanding magnetism (Barrow, 1987), among many others. As mentioned earlier, misconceptions should be seen as attempts by children to make sense of the world around them, often building on more correct notions that also coexist with the misconceptions (Clement, Brown, and Zietsman, 1989; Confrey, 1990). Misconceptions can often be understood as parts of a larger system of beliefs that do a good deal of cognitive work for the child. They also can reflect mistaken ontological commitments, which when changed allow the child to access other, more relevant, and already present concepts (Chi, 2005). Finally, they can be seen as necessary conceptual steppingstones on a path toward more accurate knowledge.

Extending and Revising Naïve Biology

During the elementary and early middle school years, children show major gains in their understanding of the living world. There is considerable growth in factual knowledge that starts to fill out conceptual frameworks. Children have opportunities to observe particular animals or plants (through caretaking or school activities) and learn more about what they do, what their parts are, what their insides are like, etc. Between preschool and fifth grade, children are able to list more and more internal body parts (Gellert, 1962). They also gain a better understanding of the function of those parts. Of course, that emerging understanding of anatomy and function is hardly complete by middle school. Most adults have huge gaps in their understanding of body structure and function in addition to misconceptions.

Children also learn about many more types of plants and animals. Whether through a visit to the zoo, reading a book about another country, or looking at animals and plants on line, there is a continual expansion in understanding about the diversity of kinds in the living world. There is also an increasing appreciation of the depth of biological taxonomies, with an emerging awareness of different subclasses of species, such as breeds of dogs.

In addition to the accumulation of facts, children in the elementary school years also appear to show restructuring of knowledge. They may reclassify some kinds of plants from nonliving to living (Hatano et al., 1997). Moreover, such shifts seem to be linked to cultural practices as well. For example, in a cross-national study of U.S., Japanese, and Israeli children, only 60 percent of Israeli fourth graders thought that plants were alive compared with over 90 percent of U.S. and Japanese children. Children may well shift to belief in the living nature of plants without explicit instruction or such cultural practices as gardening, but those forms of exposure may accelerate the process.

There is also growth in children's understanding of the human body as a machine (see Carey, 1985, 1995; and Cridier, 1981, for reviews). That is, with the development of an understanding of internal organs comes elaboration of ideas about how they function. Although these ideas may be quite simplistic, they represent an elaboration of their ideas about mechanisms, by combining some ideas of physical mechanism with body structure. Examples are coming to see the heart as a pump, coming to see the insides as consisting of interconnected tubes with vital nutrients transported to different parts of the body (e.g., Arnaudin and Mintez, 1985). Children also come to see that food is taken in, broken down into pieces, and then physically transported. They also gain some idea that human beings take in and breathe out air (exchange of materials). At the same time, they can miss many other mechanisms, such as that food is broken down not only physically but also chemically, or that there are many feedback loops operating between organs and systems.

Again, not only are elementary schoolchildren missing many details about the workings of plants and animals, but they also have a number of misconceptions. For example, as children come to recognize that plants are living things, they begin to overgeneralize that plants eat, sleep, etc. A powerful idea for them is that plants take in their food through their roots, rather than understanding that they synthesize sugars in their leaves from inanimate raw materials (Roth, 1984). There are many reasons why understanding photosynthesis is difficult, including limitations in their understanding of matter and atomic-molecular levels of description. Limitations in their conceptions of matter also affect their understanding of growth and decay.

These sorts of patterns also illustrate how domain knowledge interacts; limitations in one's understanding in one domain, that of matter, can constrain the kinds of ideas one can consider in another, that of metabolism. Again, many of these misconceptions persist in adults, who normally are quite surprised at how much of the mass of plants comes from the air around them.

One area of many misconceptions concerns cellular levels of functioning and mechanisms (Dreyfus and Jungworth, 1989; Flores, Tovar, and Gallegos, 2003). Of course, many of these problems are failures to develop any meaningful level of description or explanation at a cellular level. Students may think of cells as inanimate or confuse atoms and cells. Furthermore, without an atomic-molecular level of description, it is hard to understand what cells are doing (to understand cellular metabolism, etc.). They may have an anthropomorphic view of cells as making decisions and see the nucleus as directing all cell processes. They may also see cells as engaging in miniature versions of macroscopic processes. For example, they think of nutritive processes in cells as analogous to macroscopic digestive processes where food is ground and processed; or they confuse cellular respiration with macroscopic processes of breathing (Flores, Tovar, and Gallegos, 2003). Thus, they lack distinct descriptions of processes at the atomic-molecular and cellular levels that would provide deeper, mechanistic explanations for macroscopic phenomena. Overall, they seem to retain a simple macroscopic conception of the workings of the human body—and a very limited one at that.

At a more systemic level, children's understanding of the origin of living things undergoes considerable change. Between about 8 and 10 years of age, children develop a more explicit creationist explanation of the origins of species, regardless of beliefs in their homes (Evans, 2001). Such beliefs may reflect the formation of an explicit theory based on their initial essentialist bias—that is, their initial tendency to believe that things have a true underlying nature. Thus, a belief that species have fixed essences works against the necessary concept of a species as a probabilistic distribution of traits on which natural selection operates. That essentialist bias, however, is not merely a problem confronted by children. Indeed, it has been argued that the relatively late emergence of evolutionary theory in the history of science was because of the essentialist biases in most adult theories of species (Hull, 1965; Mayer, 1982), leading one scholar to remark that essentialism had resulted in a "2000 year stasis" in evolutionary thought.

This continuing difficulty with evolutionary thought in adulthood is also borne out in work showing that college-educated adults also frequently answer questions about evolution and natural selection in ways that are not in accord with evolutionary theory (Shtulman, 2006). Thus, essentialist biases can distort judgments about a wide range of evolutionary phenomena, including variation, inheritance, adaptation, domestication, speciation, and extinction (Shtulman, 2006). It may also be the case that evolutionary thought is hampered in childhood and beyond by another bias that emerges in the first year of life, that of seeing intentional agents as the only plausible causes of ordered relationships in the world (Newman et al., 2006). When tested as to whether an inanimate entity, such as the wind, or an animate one, such as a person, could cause a disordered array to become ordered, 1-year-olds and preschoolers strongly prefer the animate agent, while showing no preference when the situation is reversed, that is, the cause of an ordered array becoming disordered. This bias may be related to the argument from design, a centuries-old belief that the elaborate functional structure of the living world must be caused by intentional agents who "designed" those living things.

The study of children's intuitive biology has also revealed strong cross-cultural variations that seem to be closely related to cultural practices and traditions. Thus, children in non-Western traditional cultures often seem to have more sophisticated notions about taxonomies, ecology, and what properties are likely to be shared among various groups of animals and plants (Atran et al., 2001; Atran, Medin, and Ross, 2004; Ross et al., 2003; Waxman and Medin, in press). The simple act of raising a goldfish can help a child move to more sophisticated forms of biological thought (Inagaki and Hatano, 2001). One intriguing interpretation of cultural differences has emerged from a comparison between cross-cultural studies and changes in beliefs about biology through the course of history. It appears that with respect to an understanding of the taxonomies of genera, species, and subspecies, there has been a gradual devolution of biological knowledge in Western urbanized cultures over the past 400 years (Wolff, Medin, and Pankratz, 1999; Atran, Medin, and Ross, 2004).

Expanding Understandings of Matter and Its Transformation

We discussed how preschool conceptions of matter and its transformation continue to change in the elementary school years. In addition, we treat this topic in depth in Chapter 8 where we discuss how a learning progression can be developed for teaching about matter and the atomic-molecular theory. We therefore provide only a brief overview here to illustrate the complexity of the terrain children will have to cover, some of the shifts in conceptualization that can occur along the way, and how different ideas interact with each other and with forms of teaching.

There is now an extensive literature of misconceptions in the area broadly known as chemistry. Misconceptions have been documented in concepts of burning (Boujaoude, 1991), the nature of gases (Benson, Wittrock, and Baur, 1993), the particulate nature of matter (De Vos and Verdonk, 1996), and many other areas (Abraham et al., 1992; Andersson, 1990). One major area of difficulty involves coming to conceptualize gases as material bodies. Students tend to think of gases as immaterial and ethereal—belonging to an ontologically different category than solids and liquids.

Another major difficulty involves developing a macroscopic conception of chemical substances (as characterized by its properties such as boiling and melting points, different spectra, etc.) that allows them to identify substances and track the ways substances can go in and out of existence in chemical change (Johnson, 2000, 2002). Although very young children tend to identify material kinds by their perceptual properties, during elementary school children increasingly trace the identity of materials through their transformational history (e.g., sawdust comes from grinding up wood, so it must still be the same kind of stuff with some of its properties). This move can lead them to "hyperconservation of material kind"—a commitment to thinking that the identity of material is generally preserved which prevents them from being able to engage with the idea of chemical change. For example, they may see chemical changes as involving simply the mixture of substances whose identities are maintained during the process. Yet attending to transformation history can spawn productive insights in other contexts. For example, it allows them to think of materials as underlying constituents that maintain some core properties and to explain the properties of large-scale objects in terms of the materials of which they are composed. This move may be quite helpful to them in constructing an initial understanding of density as an intensive characteristic of materials.

Ultimately, however, in developing an understanding of atomic-molecular theory, students will need to reconsider the relation between properties that characterize entities at macro and micro levels and the ways assumptions about entities at the micro level can be used to explain observable phenomena. For example, although some macro-level properties are explained in decompositional terms (e.g., the weight and mass of an object is a function of the weight and mass of the atoms or molecules of which it is composed), other macro-level properties are emergent characteristics explained in terms of interactions among entities at the micro level. For example, objects are solid not because they have solid atoms, but because of bonding patterns among atoms and molecules. Thus, another major area of difficulty concerns linking up micro-level processes and entities with macro-level phenomena (Ben-Zvi, Silberstein, and Mamlok, 1989). Thus, elementary schoolchildren often have difficulty seeing how micro-level entities are related to macro-level ones, sometimes thinking that everything must appear the same at all levels of analysis (Nakhleh and Samarapungavan, 1999).

Unfortunately, an understanding of the distinction and linkages between macro and micro levels is often obscured by current teaching approaches that do not engage students with thinking through these issues and that have not systematically developed students' epistemological understanding of the nature of models and theories. Students may be introduced to atoms and molecules through thought experiments about dividing materials into little pieces. This approach encourages students to think of atoms and molecules as just little pieces of materials that inherit all of their macroscopic properties. They then may not recognize that atoms/molecules are preexisting entities with distinct properties and characteristics (Pfundt, 1981). Students may be taught about the atomic-molecular theory as a "rhetoric of conclusions" or list of facts, rather than being engaged in model-based reasoning and exploring how to explain and make sense of a wide range of phenomena (Lee et al., 1993; Snir, Smith, and Raz, 2003). In addition, they often are presented with such an impoverished view of the atomic-molecular theory (e.g., no discussion of atoms and molecules as discrete particles separated by empty space or of the role of bonds in holding particles together) that students cannot possibly understand how to explain macroscopic phenomena in atomic-molecular terms (Nussbaum, 1998).

Fortunately, innovative approaches to teaching students about atoms and molecules indicate that middle school students can engage with these issues and benefit greatly from teaching approaches that encourage them to think through these issues (Lee et al., 1993; Meheut and Chomat, 1990; Nussbaum, 1998; Snir, Smith, and Raz, 2003; see Chapter 8 for a discussion of some of these innovative teaching approaches.) Further, there is evidence that being able to think about matter in atomic-molecular terms feeds back and helps clarify children's understanding of the material nature of gases, phase change, chemical substance and chemical reactions (Lee et al, 1993; Johnson, 1998, 2002).

In short, it takes many years to work out the subtleties of the appropriate constituents of matter and how they combine to create larger units all the way up to those that are macroscopically observable. As children try to figure out these relations, they do make a large number of mistaken inferences about the nature of matter and its transformation. Above and beyond those mistakes, however, are some more accurate beliefs about the different kinds of matter, some sense of conservation, and what sorts of properties are likely to be the most useful in identifying substances.

An Expanding Theory of Psychology

We have explained that infants and preschoolers are acutely sensitive to intentional agents and that they make a wide range of causal attributions about intentional agents that they do not make for other kinds of agents. By the end of the preschool period, they have learned how to think about the relations between true and false beliefs and actions in contexts related to those beliefs. These insights, however, are only the beginning of a long process of increasingly subtle insights into the workings of the minds of others, insights that continue well into adolescence. For example, only in the middle of elementary school do children start to clearly understand that an individual can simultaneously have two conflicting desires or beliefs (Choe, Keil, and Bloom, 2005). Similarly, it can take many years to understand that different people might see ambiguous events quite differently because of the different expectations or biases they bring to the situation (Barquero, Robinson, and Thomas, 2003; Mills and Keil, 2005; Pillow and Henrichon, 1996). The more subtle consequences of thought, such as that cognitive inferences can be sources of knowledge, also take time to develop (Pillow et al., 2000). As we discuss in Chapter 5, views toward knowledge as constructed and subjective tend to emerge in middle childhood. These increasingly sophisticated views toward knowledge are related to a child's developing understanding of the ways in which knowledge is gained in the sciences as well.

There are, however, signs of a continuing influence of theory of mind errors in children and adults. For example, Keysar, Lin, and Barr (2003) asked adults to play a communication game where one person played the role of a director who directed another person (the participant) to move objects around on a grid. Before receiving instructions, the participant hid an object in a bag such that the director did not know its identity. During the game, the director sometimes described an object in the grid that both people could see in ways that more closely matched the object hidden in the bag. Although the participant knew the director was unaware of the identity of the object in the bag, he or she often thought the director was referring to the hidden object, sometimes even attempting to follow the director's instruction by moving the object in the bag instead of the object on the grid. These kinds of mistakes are predicted from vestiges of failures that young children make about false beliefs (Keysar, Lin, and Barr, 2003). Similarly, egocentrism, a difficulty in taking the points of views of others, can have strong influences on adult inferences into the mental states of others. More subtle misconceptions concerning the nature of perception also persist into adulthood. For example, many adults believe that, in order to see, something must leave the eyes (extramissionist view). That is, the perceiver "projects" rays out of the eyes into the world that "see" objects. This belief often influences adult judgments of how other humans perceive (Cottrell and Winer, 1994).

Toward a Mature Cosmology

As mentioned earlier, much of the work on the child's emerging understanding of cosmology spans the preschool and elementary school years, making a discussion here of later developments less necessary. It is worth briefly noting, however, that a great deal of detailed knowledge about cosmology can be acquired during the elementary school and middle school years, although progress here is typically quite variable. Many children learn more and more about astronomical bodies and their distinctions, such as stars and planets. Some even start to understand more clearly the Copernican view of the solar system, although research has shown that misconceptions about the explanation of day and night and the seasons can extend into the adult years. Furthermore, it can take many more years to correctly understand the basis for the tides, eclipses, and the nature of distances in the universe.

A review of three decades of research on learning about Earth's spherical shape and gravity (Agan and Sneider, 2004) found that until fourth grade it is very difficult for students to fully grasp the spherical Earth concept, with gravity pulling objects toward Earth's center, and that "achieving conceptual change at such a deep level requires clarification of current ideas (even if those ideas may be wrong), listening to the ideas of others, thinking through the logical implications of different models, and then applying conceptual models to explain previously observed phenomena." Yet, taking the time to construct such a robust Earth concept may be worth it for several reasons. First, it provides a foundational framework for constructing explanations of many important phenomena that connect to children's daily lives such as the reasons for day and night and the causes of the seasons. Second, it provides a wonderful opportunity for engaging in model-based reasoning during the elementary school years and developing important epistemological understandings of models.

Critical to an account of cosmology is a recognition that most adults through most of history have held views that are radically different from those held by scientists today. Errors and mistakes are, in that sense, the norm for individuals of all ages and not merely during a period of development.

Summary of Knowledge Growth Across the Domains

A few themes cut across all domains in discussions of knowledge growth after preschool. First, it is clear that older children are building on the products of preschool knowledge growth. The cognitive achievements of infants and toddlers provide older children with foundations for further understandings in each domain. It is easy to see how notions of mechanics, folk psychology and folk biology, for example, persist into later childhood and influence the ways in which more detailed mental models are constructed.

Second, a great deal of development during the elementary school years involves learning about more detailed mechanisms and facts in various domains. The surprisingly abstract frameworks and expectations that develop in the early years are now supplemented by more concrete ways of fleshing them out. Whether it is specific notions of digestion, blood flow, burning, or gear action, children attempt to work out the concrete details in each domain in ways that honor the legacies of preschool and infancy.

Third, children's attempts to develop more concrete models result in a large number of misconceptions. Concreteness can lead to commitments that create mistakes. Children's misconceptions can be dramatic, but they do not really represent a step backward from earlier ages when those misconceptions might be weaker or not even present. In many cases, moving through a series of misconceptions may be the only plausible way for a child to progress toward a more correct and detailed notion of mechanism. In addition, many misconceptions persevere into adulthood, illustrating that misconceptions will always be a by-product of attempts to build more precise accounts of how the world works.

Finally, the elementary school years and beyond can include impressive periods of conceptual change. Children will come to reassign entities to different ontological categories, they will put together concepts to create new ones, and they seem to have dramatic new insights that can change the way they understand a whole domain. It is equally clear that there is a real diversity in the kinds of conceptual change that occur, a diversity that must be understood to have a full account of how the foundations of a scientific knowledge emerge in childhood. That topic is the focus of the next section.

THE NATURE OF CONCEPTUAL CHANGE

As described in the preceding chapter, one of the surprising discoveries of the past few decades of research in developmental psychology is the tendency for children to search for mechanisms and the important ways ideas about mechanisms inform their reasoning and inference in everyday life. As we've said, children are by no means the blank slates or concrete, atheoretical reasoners that previous theorists have claimed. Instead, they have some existing concepts, constrained by either framework theories (Inagaki and Hatano, 2002; Vosniadou and Ioannides, 1998; Wellman and Gelman, 1992), modes of construal (phenomena in a domain are assumed to correspond to certain causal patterns; Keil, 2003), or skeletal principles (innate, abstract guidelines; Gelman and Lucariello, 2002), that help them carve the world up into different domains and organize their expectations about how different types of things should behave. These concepts help them organize and make sense of the world, support categorization, inductive and deductive inference, problem solving, explanation, as well as language learning and comprehension (Carey, 1999; Thagard, 1992; Wellman, 1990).

The research of the past few decades has thus revealed greater similarities between the concepts of children and those of scientists, avoiding simplistic dichotomies in which the concepts of the two are seen to be fundamentally different types. Not only is there now greater recognition of the implicit explanatory and systematic constraints on children's concepts (Carey, 1999; Gelman and Lucariello, 2002; Keil and Lockhart, 1999; Wellman and Gelman, 1992) but also of the implicit, informal aspects of scientific concepts (see the pioneering work of Clement, 1991, 1993, and Nersessian, 1992, in this regard). In addition, philosophers and historians of science have long recognized the role of guiding paradigms and frameworks, in which many deeply entrenched assumptions are not consciously emphasized or subjected to investigation, just assumed (e.g., Kuhn, 1970; Lakatos, 1978).

Greater awareness of the similarities between children's and scientists' concepts also allows one to consider the differences between them. Some researchers suggest that children's concepts may differ from those of scientists because they are embedded in different theories or constrained by somewhat different assumptions about the origins of the natural world and the nature of knowledge. Clearly, the current theories of science are immense intellectual achievements that are the products of centuries of investigation and testing carried out by entire communities of adult experts. Furthermore, the history of scientific ideas documents the profound changes in proposed theories and explanatory ideas that have occurred as scientists have struggled to develop, test, and refine their theories. Many of the concepts in these theories are counterintuitive, far removed from the first guesses one would have made about what the world is like and how it functions. In this view, learning science is difficult not because of what children don't have or lack, but because of what they do have: some initial commitments and ideas that will need to be revised and changed.

Forms of Conceptual Change

Conceptual change can take a variety of forms that can vary in degree and difficulty (Carey, 1991; Chi, 1992; Keil, 1999; Thagard, 1992). A challenge for conceptual change researchers is to provide a typology of important forms of conceptual change that occur, especially in the course of science learning. Most researchers make a distinction between changes that are relatively easy, because they are basically consistent with students' initial conceptual structure, and ones that are more difficult because they call for more fundamental revisions to that structure. In the latter group, some make further distinctions based on the extent of the restructuring involved and the degree that such restructuring violates students' most central ontological commitments.

Science education presents many opportunities for multiple kinds of change that vary in difficulty. Teachers and curriculum developers are often not aware of these different levels of difficulty and hence don't appropriately modify their methods of teaching when confronting different types of cases.

Elaborating on an Existing Conceptual Structure

At one level, students are relatively quick to learn new concepts that fit within an existing conceptual structure, such as new subkinds or superordinates or new parts or properties of particular kinds. For example, learning about new kinds of animals (e.g., aardvarks, emus) or subkinds of dogs (e.g., German shepherds, bulldogs) need not require a change in the child's concept of animals or dogs. The child already knows that animals (or dogs) can vary in size, body type, eating preferences, and temperament. Thus, identifying new kinds that have different clusters of these attributes enriches the child's understanding of the diversity of animals or dogs without fundamentally challenging the organizing principle on which their concept of animal or dog is based. Similarly, adding a new superordinate that unites subkinds (e.g.. learning that bears, dogs, and cats are all mammals) need not be difficult, especially when there are some easy-to-understand common properties that unite these kinds (e.g., they are all warm-blooded and nurse their young) and when the new kind called "mammals" can be understood as a special kind of animal.

Restructuring a Network of Concepts

In other cases, children need to restructure their understandings of an entire network of concepts that are used to understand or explain phenomena in a given domain. In these cases, there are multiple coordinated changes in the conceptual groupings used, and not a simple one-to-one correspondence between the concepts of the earlier and the later network.

In conceptual differentiation, the newer (descendant) theory uses two distinct concepts whereas the initial (parent) theory used only one, and the undifferentiated parent concept unites elements that will subsequently be kept distinct and regarded as fundamentally different kinds. For example, children initially conflate dead/not real/inanimate in an undifferentiated concept of "not alive," which subsequently is rearticulated as separate concepts characterizing fundamentally different kinds of things (Carey, 1985, 1999). In another case, children initially conflate heavy/heavy-for-size in an undifferentiated concept of "felt weight," which is subsequently reanalyzed as weight (an extensive physical quantity) and density (an intensive quantity) (Carey, 1991; Smith, Carey, and Wiser, 1985). Conceptual differentiation is different from simply adding two new subcategories to an existing category (as when one learns to distinguish two different types of dogs), because in those cases the parent concept "dogs" remains intact when the subtypes are added. In differentiation, the parent concept is seen as incoherent from the perspective of the subsequent theory and plays no role in it.

Conceptual differentiations are typically accompanied by conceptual coalescences, another fundamental form of conceptual change. In coalescences, the descendant theory introduces a new concept that unites concepts previously seen to be of fundamentally different types in the parent theory. For example, children initially see solids and liquids as fundamentally different from air (Smith et al., 1997; Stavy, 1991). Later they may come to see them all as distinct forms of matter. For another example, children initially see rest as the opposite of motion. Later, in learning physics, they come to see both rest and uniform motion as "unaccelerated" states resulting from balanced forces. Conceptual coalescence is different from simply adding a more general category by abstracting properties common to more specific categories. In coalescence, the initial concepts are thought to be fundamentally different kinds, and the properties or relations that will be central to defining the new superordinate category are not explicitly represented or considered central to the initial concepts.

Two additional forms of conceptual change frequently accompany conceptual differentiations and coalescences and can contribute to the restructuring: (1) there can be changes in what characteristics are seen as central or peripheral to (multiple) concepts and (2) something that was originally conceptualized as a property may be reconceptualized as a relation (or vice versa). For example, in coming to form a biological concept of living things that includes both plants and animals, children may shift from the view that being active and moving without outside intervention are more central to living things, to the view that having a life cycle (involving reproduction, growth, and death) and engaging in basic processes to sustain life (such as getting food, water, air) are more central. These changes in turn require coordinated changes in children's related conceptions of reproduction, growth, death, eating, drinking, and breathing as well, as they develop a more abstract sense of how these processes can apply to organisms as different as plants and animals.

Similarly, in order to rationalize the inclusion of air, solids, and liquids into a single category of matter, children must move from thinking of matter as something perceptually accessible (as something one can see, feel, touch) to thinking of it as something that takes up space and has weight. This change in turn requires changes in their initial concepts of taking up space and weight—for example, reconceptualizing weight from something that is primarily perceptually defined and assessed (i.e., weight as felt weight) to an objective magnitude that is measured and quantified. This reconceptualization also supports making a principled differentiation between weight and density.

Adding New (Deeper) Levels of Explanation

Learning science with understanding requires that children reconceptualize their initial concepts to describe macroscopically accessible objects and events. It also requires that they add new levels of conceptual description (e.g., descriptions of the behavior and interactions among atoms and molecules, of the structure and functioning of individual cells), in order to provide deeper layers of explanation. Adding these new levels is difficult for several reasons. First, these levels may build on some of the previous restructurings described above and provide deeper explanation of many phenomena. Given that many students do not achieve those understandings, they do not have an appropriate foundation for constructing the next level of explanation.

Second, these new levels can interact and mutually support each other. For example, a deep understanding of cell theory and basic biological processes of living things actually calls for students to integrate atomic-molecular ideas into their analyses of living things. Without that foundation and level of analysis, many of the ideas of cell theory remain hard to explain or understand. Finally, adding these new levels calls for greater sophistication than many students have. For example, it requires that students understand the nature and purpose of explanatory models and how they are evaluated. That is, they are evaluated on the basis of their ability to explain a pattern of evidence rather than on whether they "look like" what is to be explained. If students do not have this kind of understanding, they may reject claims about atoms—such as that they are in constant motion—because these violate their commonsense impressions.

Mechanisms of Conceptual Change

One reason for distinguishing more fundamental, "revolutionary" conceptual changes from belief revision or conceptual elaboration is that these more profound forms of change may require a more complex coordination of a variety of learning mechanisms than more typical learning does. Most everyday learning involves knowledge enrichment and rests on an assumed set of concepts. For example, people use existing concepts to represent new facts, formulate new beliefs, make inductive or deductive inferences, and solve problems. Fundamental conceptual change, in contrast, involves coordinated adjustments of a variety of sorts in students' network of concepts. The concepts of the new theory are ultimately organized and stated in terms of each other, rather than the concepts of the old theory, and there is no simple one-to-one correspondence between some concepts of the old and new theories. By what learning mechanisms, then, can students comprehend a genuinely new set of concepts and interrelations and come to prefer them to their initial set of concepts?

Acquiring New Knowledge Over an Existing Base of Concepts

First, the acquisition of new knowledge about the world (building on an initial base of concepts) is certainly an important part of the process of conceptual change (Carey, 1985; Chi, 1992; Case, 1997). For example, young children certainly won't change their understanding of living things without learning about internal body organs and their function; they won't deepen their understanding of materials without learning about a variety of materials and their characteristics. The claim being advanced by conceptual change researchers, however, is that, although such new knowledge may be necessary for conceptual change, it is not sufficient to produce it (Carey, 1991; Inagaki and Hatano, 2002).

Some of the strongest evidence for this claim comes from the repeated failures of both traditional science instruction and simple discovery learning to produce understanding of scientific ideas for large numbers of students. Such failures have been found in domain after domain, such as photosynthesis (Roth, 1984), atomic-molecular theories of matter (Lee et al., 1993), and weight and density (Smith et al., 1997). Traditional instruction exploits simple knowledge-telling strategies of teaching and conveys science as a rather flat "rhetoric of conclusions" (Schwab, 1962). Simple discovery approaches have students do experiments or make observations with the naïve hope that the scientists' conclusion will emerge unproblematically from the data (Roth, 1990, 2002). Given that both these didactic and discovery teaching approaches are certainly introducing students to a wealth of new knowledge and experiences, these findings underscore that being exposed to new information is not the same as remembering or understanding it. Indeed, in one study of a special cognitively impaired population with Williams Syndrome (Johnson and Carey, 1998), it appeared that simple knowledge accumulation was possible for this group in the area of biology but not the more revolutionary cases of conceptual change, which may require much deeper causal explanatory understandings to occur.

Metacognitively Guided Learning

Children's metacognitive abilities may be critical to many cases of fundamental conceptual change (Beeth, 1998; Case, 1997; Inagaki and Hatano, 2002). Metacognition or "thought about thought" refers to a broad range of processes, including monitoring, detecting incongruities or anomalies, self-correcting, planning and selecting goals, and even reflecting on the structure of one's knowledge and thinking (Gelman and Lucariello, 1992). Even preschool children have some metacognitive abilities, but major expansions in these abilities during the elementary school years may create especially powerful support for more dramatic forms of conceptual change.

Metacognitive abilities may foster conceptual change by detecting and monitoring incongruities in an existing conceptual system. This alerts the learner to potential problems, but it does not itself reveal the nature of the problem or its resolution (Gelman and Lucariello, 2002; Inagaki and Hatano, 2002). When an unexpected result arises, there can be many reasons for the anomalous data: a fluke result, poor data collection technique, a faulty hypothesis, a limited framework theory, among others (Chinn and Brewer, 1993). More explicit metacognitive knowledge (that allows one to identify and describe different sources of problems) can help direct the learner's attention to determine the likely source of the problem given further information. For example, the learner might check to see if the result is reproducible, reexamine the data collection methods, compare results with other groups, etc. Thus, a second function of metacognition is a more directive and reflective one: to consider possible reasons for the incongruity and gathering or selecting further information that helps refine one's understanding of the problem. Adding a reflective component to learning not only speeds up the time it takes to learn, but also makes it possible to learn things that one might never figure out through trial and error (Case, 1997).

Evidence that metacognition plays a key role in conceptual change learning comes from a variety of types of studies. The instructional techniques that have been shown to be effective in producing conceptual understanding of new science content all have a strong metacognitive component (Minstrell, 1982, 1984; Nussbaum and Novick, 1982; Chinn and Brewer, 1993; Roth, 1984; Brown and Campione, 1994; Hennessey, 2003; Beeth and Hewson, 1999; National Research Council, 2000). Typically, activities are introduced to make students aware of their initial ideas and that there may be a *conceptual problem* that needs to be solved. Students may be asked to make a prediction about an event and give reasons for their prediction, a technique that activates their initial ideas and makes students aware of them. Class discussion of the range of student predictions foregrounds alternative ways of thinking about the event, further highlighting the conceptual level of analysis and creating a need to resolve the discrepancy. Gathering data that expose students to unexpected discrepant events or posing challenging problems that they cannot immediately solve are other ways of sending signals to students that they need to stop and think, step outside the normal "apply" conceptual framework mode, to a more metaconceptual "question, generate and examine alternatives, and evaluate" mode. In addition, experimental manipulation of the amount of reflective inquiry and self-assessment in two identical versions of a carefully designed inquiry unit on motion for sixth graders produced greater gain scores for the students in the classroom with enhanced opportunities for reflective self-assessment (White and Frederickson, 1998). Particularly important, the gains were evident for all ability levels; indeed, they were highest for students with lower ability levels.

Elementary schoolchildren have much more capacity for metacognitively guided learning than has been commonly supposed or taken advantage of by existing science curricula (see Hennessey, 2003, for a detailed analysis of the subtle and diverse expressions of metacognitive understandings shown by her students in science class in grades 1 through 6). These abilities are typically overlooked and untapped in traditional approaches to science teaching, and, as a result, they not only fail to develop those abilities further, but also reduce the chances of conceptual change.

Constructing New Conceptual Representations

Conceptual change often requires an ability to imagine and understand alternative ways of conceptualizing the problems under consideration (Strike and Posner, 1985; Inagaki and Hatano, 2002; Carey, 1999). Indeed, research has shown that students are reluctant to abandon an initial idea, however imperfect, if there is not a better idea available (Karmiloff-Smith and Inhelder, 1974; Chinn and Brewer, 1993). Instead they are likely to ignore or discount the challenging data, consider that their idea works most but not all of the time, or make local patches. For this reason, researchers have noted the limitations of "discrepant events" as catalysts of conceptual change. Although they can be helpful in arousing interest, they may be counterproductive if introduced too soon before students have the conceptual resources to resolve them. Furthermore, they are not the only means of motivating conceptual change.

How can students construct a new set of conceptual representations? They need to draw on existing resources in their conceptual system—things they already understand in some context or that make sense to them. Drawing on and connecting to these resources is essential if the new conception is going to be intelligible to them—something often overlooked when they are presented with explicit formal definitions that they cannot understand. Some of these resources may come from *within* their initial theory for a given domain (e.g., as they learn about new internal body parts or organs of human beings, or elaborate on their understanding of eating, growing, and breathing). Others may come from understandings students have *outside* the domain (e.g., as they draw on their knowledge of number in constructing measures of physical quantities, such as weight).

Students then need to use a variety of heuristic procedures and symbolic tools to exploit these resources in constructing new representations of the problem. For example, heuristic procedures, such as analogical and imagistic reasoning, thought experiments involving extreme and limiting case analyses, and inference to best explanation allow students to creatively extend, combine, and modify existing conceptual resources through the construction of new models (Nersessian, 1989, 1992; Clement, 1991; Gentner et al., 1997; Kuhn, 1977; Carey, 1999). Symbolic tools, such as spoken and written language, diagrams, pictures, and algebraic, geometric, and graphical representations of mathematics, and other invented or culturally transmitted notational systems, allow the explicit representation of key relations in the new system of concepts (Gelman and Lucariello, 2002, discuss this as forming rerepresentations) (see also Lehrer et al., 2000).

Even preschool children can use many of these heuristic techniques in limited contexts and in domains they understand, although they certainly do not yet coordinate them in the service of serious model-based reasoning. For example, even 3-year-olds can engage in analogical reasoning (Goswami and Brown, 1990); they can also engage in inference to best explanation, as when they infer a hidden causal mechanism to explain an observable event (Bullock

BOX 4-1 An Example of Discovery Argumentation

An example of a powerful form of discovery argumentation is the "bridging analogies" strategy (Brown and Clement, 1989; Clement, 1993). In this strategy, one identifies a *target situation* in which students' initial intuitions are at variance with the expert analysis. For example, students do not see a book resting on a table as involving balanced forces (i.e., the force of the book on the table is equal and opposite to the force of the table on the book). Instead, they think that only the book is pressing on the table, or that it is pressing down more than the table is pressing up (hence, the book stays down). In fact, they often don't think of a table as the sort of thing that *can* exert a force; it is conceptualized as a passive resistance or support.

Then one looks for an *anchoring intuition*—a situation in which the students' intuition is in line with the expert analysis, even though they may not yet share the same general conception of force with the expert. For example, students see a book resting on an outstretched hand as a clear case of balanced forces, because the student can actively feel and imagine exerting greater and greater force as more books are piled on to actively compensate for the weight of the book.

Students initially see these two situations as entirely different from each other. Then one presents a series of bridging analogies—new situations that are intermediate between the target and the anchor, such as a metal coiled spring. The metal coil shows visible compression when the book is placed on it, which helps the student see the situation as like the hand, with which the student can feel the push and counterpush. Yet unlike the hand, it is an inanimate object. Students can engage in cycles of reasoning about these situations and in the process construct a new model of the situation, in which they can imagine the molecules in the table undergoing compression when the book is placed on it and pushing back with equal and opposite force. They can they test their prediction by checking if, in fact, there is a (slight) compression of the table when the book is placed on it.

and Gelman, 1979). Thus, conceptual change researchers are finding that involving elementary, middle, and high school students in discovery argumentation via cycles of model-based reasoning—practices very similar to those used by scientists themselves—are highly effective means of building these new understandings (Brown and Clement, 1989; Lehrer et al., 2001; Smith et al., 1997; Stewart, Cartier, and Passmore, 2005; White, 1993; Wiser and Amin, 2001). Such modes of teaching and presentation are dramatically different, however, from those employed in traditional instruction (see Box 4-1).

Clement and his colleagues have exploited this bridging analogies strategy, in combination with other techniques, throughout a high school physics curriculum (Camp and Clement, 1994). In addition, they have directly compared the effectiveness of this mode of discovery argumentation with more traditional modes of argumentation in making new ideas intelligible and plausible to students (Brown and Clement, 1989). Both approaches use a variety of everyday examples as well as present an important "big idea," but the examples are organized and presented entirely differently in relation to the big idea.

In the traditional approach, the big idea is stated as a general principle, such as Newton's third law. It is assumed that the general principle is immediately intelligible to students, and that each of the subsequent examples will be compelling and readily interpretable in terms of the general principle. There is no consideration that students may have alternative ideas that are inconsistent with both understanding and accepting this general principle.

In the bridging approach, it is assumed that students have an alternative way of thinking about the target situation, but that they have resources available (in the form of physical intuitions about different physical situations) that can be drawn on in constructing a new representation of the target situation. In addition, students are led to formulate the big idea through a chain of reasoning about specific situations. Finally, the big idea takes the form, not only of an abstract general principle, but also of a model of the situation that incorporates both abstract elements and physical intuitions, which allows them to see the situations in new ways. The results of their study were striking: students were able to understand Newton's third law more thoroughly and apply it to novel situations when presented with text that used the bridging analogy argumentation (Brown and Clement, 1989).

The recent interest in having science instruction focus on helping students to construct and evaluate abstract models of situations fits with the recognition that effective science learning calls for students to construct new representations that differ in important ways from those used in everyday life. Science involves more than gathering new data and making inductive generalizations from those data; it also involves new ways of seeing those data in terms of idealized representations. Although there are many approaches to building these models in different domains, science commonly incorporates mathematical relations in these models (Nersessian, 1992) as well as physical intuitions and sensorimotor schemas (Brown, 1993; Clement, 1991). As Nersessian (1989) points out, "in learning Newtonian mechanics, students must usually also learn how to construct an abstract, mathematical representation of the physical world for the first time." Thus, science educators should not neglect teaching students some of the idealization techniques (such as thought experiments and limiting case analyses) that are central to constructing those abstract representations and that can facilitate their recognition of deep analogies between superficially different phenomena.

Strengthening New Systems of Ideas

Constructing a new system of ideas does not, of course, ensure that these ideas will be internalized (i.e., frequently used in appropriate contexts or that they will even be preferred to one's initial ways of thinking). How does a new conceptual system become strengthened and gain ascendancy over one's initial ideas? Many conceptual change researchers have considered that engaging in argument may be a central part of this process (e.g., Chinn and Brewer, 1993; Strike and Posner, 1985; Thagard, 1992). More specifically, students are asked to evaluate (or debate) the adequacy of the new system with known competitors. For example, the new system will gain ascendancy if seen as more plausible (consistent with prior knowledge and existing data) and fruitful (generative of further questions) (Strike and Posner, 1985). Or the new system will be favored if it is seen as more explanatorily coherent (Thagard, 1992); a variety of aspects contribute to judgments of coherence, such as explanatory breadth, elegance, simplicity (not ad hoc), avoidance of contradiction, and future prospects. Even elementary school students are sensitive to many of these features in judging rival accounts. More specifically, Samarapungavan (1992) found that children prefer accounts that explain more, are not ad hoc, are internally consistent, and fit the empirical data. An important step in evaluating an argument may first be to discuss and construct some shared norms for argumentation not only among students but also with the broader scientific community they are trying to understand (Brown and Campione, 1994; Beeth, 1998; Beeth and Hewson, 1999; Duschl and Osborne, 2002; Sandoval, Reiser, 2004).

Argumentation and repeated application of new ideas are both important and may involve complementary, but also mutually supportive, processes. Argumentation is a more explicit "meta-process," whereas repeated practice in application involves (in part) gaining lower level associative strength. At the same time, argumentation from patterns of evidence involves practice in application, and repeated application can also provide additional opportunities for metacognitive reflection. Indeed, many science educators believe that a key to promoting conceptual change in the classroom is to create a more reflective classroom discourse that is structured around explicit argumentation (Hennessey, 2003; Herrenkohl and Guerra, 1998; van Zee and Minstrell, 1997). In addition, longitudinal studies of conceptual change highlight the importance of elaboration and depth of coverage (Clark and Linn, 2003), opportunities to revisit key ideas introduced in benchmark lessons (diSessa and Minstrell, 1998; Minstrell, 1984; Minstrell and Kraus, 2005; Roth, Peasley, and Hazelwood, 1992), and continued use of key ideas in subsequent courses in which they are further elaborated (Arzi, 1988).

Developmental Change That Is Not Conceptual Change

It is important to note that not all developmental change in performance on science-related tasks involves conceptual change. Some kinds of change can often appear superficially to be conceptual change but in fact may be quite different. Consider cases of increasing access to conceptual systems and increasing relevance. Increasing access can be illustrated by an analogy of a child learning to use a heavy hammer. The child may only be capable of using the hammer to hit nails at eye height or lower, as the hammer is too heavy to use for higher level objects. As her arm gets stronger, she can use the hammer in new tasks. Her basic skills at hammering may not have changed in important ways, only her general arm strength. Similarly, a child may have a conceptual system that she uses to understand a phenomenon, but because of more general memory or attentional limits, she may not be able to use it in as wide a range of tasks as an older child. Change here may not involve new conceptual insight, but merely increasing processing capacity, memory storage, or attentional ability. A child who fails to engage in transitive reasoning with a set of inequalities may be failing not because he doesn't have the concept of transitive relations, but rather because he cannot remember as many relations as an older child. When that memory is assisted, he can see the transitive relations as well (Bryant and Trabasso, 1971). Thus, some tasks may, for cognitive reasons not related to conceptual change, prevent a child from accessing the needed conceptual systems.

In other cases, a child may be able to access a conceptual system but may have a different default bias for thinking about which system of explanation is most relevant to the task at hand. A younger child may think hammers are used for hammering nails and not at first realize that they can also be used for sealing a paint can lid. When she realizes the relevance, she can use the tool immediately. The same pattern can happen with conceptual systems as tools. Shifting relevances in themselves may or may not be related to conceptual change. We have already seen how a child may undergo conceptual change in an area but still fall back on an older system because she doesn't fully realize the relevance or value of the new one. When the relevance is made clear, the child may suddenly use the system with ease.

One example occurs in the development of biological thought: younger children may interpret a property, such as "sleeps," in psychological terms and thereby judge that simple animals do not sleep (Carey, 1985). Yet when the same children are primed with a very brief context indicating that sleeping can also refer to how the body works, they will instantly attribute sleeping to a much broader array of cases (Gutheil, Vera, and Keil, 1998). The most relevant domain of explanation for a particular task may often come from experience with alternative framings or even from general cultural practices (Atran, Medin, and Ross, 2004).

It is therefore essential, when encountering developmental changes in children's ability to reason about various problems in the sciences, not only to understand the kind of conceptual change that is involved, but also to understand that some dramatic changes in performance ability may be largely unrelated to any underlying changes in conceptual understanding. As an adult, one can easily see how this is the case by considering how one's ability to understand a complex scientific phenomena may evaporate in the face of powerful cognitive distractions, massive sleep deprivation, or other factors that reduce the efficiency of cognitive processing. A sleep-deprived person hasn't really undergone regressive conceptual change; he simply has lost access and may not be tracking as well cues to the relevance of the best conceptual system. As mentioned earlier, however, memory and attentional changes can sometimes also be linked to conceptual change and, in such cases, bring conceptual change back into the process of developmental change.

CONCLUSIONS

As children enter elementary school, the pace of change in their knowledge and understanding of the natural world continues and sometimes seems to dramatically accelerate. Thus, while they bring much with them to the classroom from their preschool years, they launch into quite extraordinary expansions of their knowledge and understanding between kindergarten and grade 8. Understanding how their knowledge growth unfolds and can be supported requires an appreciation of the connections with earlier forms of understanding. Importantly, the kindergartener must be seen as far more than a bundle of mistaken ideas that needs to be completely reformed from scratch.

Admittedly, children's understandings of the world sometimes contradict scientific explanations, and these conceptions about the natural world can pose obstacles to learning science. However, their prior knowledge also offers leverage points that can be built on to develop their understanding of scientific concepts and their ability to engage in scientific investigations. Thus, children's prior knowledge must be taken into account in order to design instruction in strategic ways that capitalize on the leverage points and adequately address potential areas of misunderstanding. Young and novice students are likely to profit from study in areas in which their personal, prior experience with the natural world can be leveraged to connect with scientific ideas.

Debates remain about how the early understanding that children bring to school continues to develop across later years. According to one view, these core knowledge domains from infancy remain a nearly invariant framework of ways of understanding the world for much of one's life afterward (Carey and Spelke, 1996). Thus, even as adults, especially when under time pressure or distraction, we may show some of the same errors shown by infants in terms of their understandings of trajectories, collisions, and the like. By these accounts, there is a freezing of core knowledge domains early on because such knowledge can only be elaborated, not fundamentally revised. The later development of both naïve and more formal scientific theories depends on the ability to combine these domains (as well as other constructed understandings) in new ways, perhaps through language, which is said to have a kind of combinatorial glue-like power over these domains. These newer forms of knowledge, unlike core knowledge, are always open to revision, including quite radical forms of conceptual change. They also emerge in a different cognitive format and sit on top of these core domains but not really rewrite them or reinterpret them so much as coexist with them and be more evident when cognition is more reflective, slow, and considered.

An alternative view considers all knowledge to be revisable (Gopnik, 1996) and that these early domains continue to differentiate and become elaborated through childhood and perhaps into adulthood as well (Rogers and McClelland, 2004). For example, the folk sciences may start in infancy but continue to grow, as systems, for many years thereafter. In some accounts they may continue to gradually differentiate, but they always tend to have the same overall structure. In other accounts, quite dramatic patterns of conceptual change, sometimes akin to scientific revolutions in the history of science, are said to occur.

Conceptual change can take on several distinct forms, and the literature uses several different senses of these kinds of change, sometimes not recognizing the differences (Inagaki and Hatano, 2002; Keil, 1999). It is critical to understand the full diversity of kinds of conceptual change and the range of mechanisms that bring it about as well as how developmental changes in scientific thought can occur without obvious conceptual change.

Some conceptual changes are more challenging than others. For example, when children develop commonsense frameworks that deviate substantially from those proposed by scientists, a considerable amount of conceptual work is required to achieve knowledge restructuring. Part of the difficulty of learning a new concept is letting go of a familiar but incorrect set of ideas. Major changes in conceptual frameworks are often difficult to grasp because they require learners to break out of their familiar frame and reorganize a body of knowledge, often in ways that draw on unfamiliar ideas. Making these changes is facilitated when students engage in metacognitively guided learning, when teachers use a variety of techniques (such as bridging analogies, thought experiments, and imagistic reasoning) to help students construct an understanding of new concepts, and when students have opportunities to strengthen their understanding of the new ideas through extended application and argumentation.

Importantly, the difference between students who are less or more proficient in science is not only that the latter know more discrete facts. Instead, gains in proficiency often consist of changes in the organization of knowledge, not just the accretion of more pieces of knowledge. When students develop a coherent understanding of the organizing principles of science, they are more likely to be able to apply their knowledge appropriately and will learn new, related material more effectively. Knowledge of the salient factual details is necessary but not sufficient for developing an understanding of the discipline and its core ideas and principles.

REFERENCES

Abraham, M.R., Grzybowski, E.B., Renner, J.W., and Marek, E.A. (1992). Understandings and misunderstandings of eighth graders of five chemistry concepts found in textbooks. *Journal of Research in Science Teaching, 29*, 105-120.

Acredolo, C., Adams, A., and Schmid, J. (1984). On the understanding of the relationships between speed, duration, and distance. *Child Development, 55*, 2151-2159.

Agan, L., and Sneider, C. (2004). Learning about the Earth's shape and gravity: A guide for teachers and curriculum developers. *Astronomy Education Review, 2*(2), 90-117. Available: http://aer.noao.edu/cgi-bin/new.pl [accessed Dec. 2006].

Andersson, B. (1990). Pupils' conceptions of matter and its transformations (ages 12-16). *Studies in Science Education, 18*, 53-85.

Arnaudin, M.W., and Mintez, J.J. (1985). Students' alternative conceptions of the human circulatory system: A cross-age study. *Science Education, 69*, 721-733.

Arzi, H.J. (1988). From short to long-term: Studying science education longitudinally. *Studies in Science Education, 15*, 17-53.

Atran, S., Medin, D.L., Lynch, E., Vapnarsky, V., Ucan Ek', E., and Sousa, P. (2001). Folkbiology doesn't come from folkpsychology: Evidence from Yukatec Maya in cross-cultural perspective. *Journal of Cognition and Culture ,1*, 4-42.

Atran, S., Medin, D.L, and Ross, N. (2004). Evolution and devolution of knowledge: A tale of two biologies. *Journal of the Royal Anthropological Institute, 10*, 395-420.

Barquero, B., Robinson, E.J., and Thomas, G.V. (2003). Children's ability to attribute different interpretations of ambiguous drawings to a naïve vs. a biased observer. *International Journal of Behavioral Development, 27*, 445-456.

Barrow, L.H. (1987). Magnet concepts and elementary students' misconceptions. In J. Noval (Ed.), *Proceedings of the second international seminar on misconceptions and educational strategies in science and mathematics* (pp. 17-32). Ithaca, NY: Cornell University Press.

Beeth, M.E. (1998). Teaching science in 5th grade: Instructional goals that support conceptual change. *Journal of Research in Science Teaching, 35*(10), 1091-1101.

Beeth, M.E., and Hewson, P.W. (1999). Learning goals in an exemplary science teacher's practice: Cognitive and social factors in teaching for conceptual change. *Science Education, 83*, 738-760.

Benson, D.L., Wittrock, M.C., and Baur, M.E. (1993). Students' preconceptions of the nature of gases. *Journal of Research in Science Teaching, 30*, 587-597.

Ben-Zvi, R., Silberstein, J., and Mamlok, R. (1989). Macro-micro relationships: A key to the world of chemistry. In P. Lijnse, P. Licht, W. de Vos, and A.J. Waarlo (Eds.), *Relating macroscopic phenomena to microscopic particles: A central problem in secondary science education* (pp. 184-197). Utrecht, South Africa: CD-ß Press.

Boujaoude, S.B. (1991). A study of the nature of students' understanding about the concept of burning. *Journal of Research in Science Teaching, 28*, 689-704.

Brown, A.L., and Campione, J.C. (1994). Guided discovery in a community of learners. In K. McGilly (Ed.), *Classroom lessons: Integrating cognitive theory and educational practice* (pp. 229-270). Cambridge, MA: MIT/Bradford Press.

Brown, D.E. (1993). Refocusing core intuitions: A concretizing role for analogy in conceptual change. *Journal of Research in Science Teaching, 30*, 1273-1290.

Brown, D.E., and Clement, J. (1989). Overcoming misconceptions via analogical reasoning: Abstract transfer versus explanatory model construction. *Instructional Science, 18*, 237-261.

Bryant, P.E., and Trabasso, T. (1971). Transitive inferences and memory in young children. *Nature, 232*, 456-458.

Bullock, M., and Gelman, R. (1979). Preschool children's assumptions about cause and effect: Temporal ordering. *Child Development, 50*, 89-96.

Camp, C.W., and Clement, J.J. (1994). *Preconceptions in mechanics. Lessons dealing with students' conceptual difficulties.* Dubuque, IA: Kendall/Hunt.

Carey, S. (1985). *Conceptual change in childhood.* Cambridge, MA: MIT Press.

Carey, S. (1991). Knowledge acquisition: Enrichment or conceptual change? In S. Carey and R. Gelman (Eds.), *The epigenesis of mind: Essays on biology and cognition* (pp. 257-291). Hillsdale, NJ: Lawrence Erlbaum Associates.

Carey, S. (1995). Continuity and discontinuity in cognitive development. In D.N. Osherson (Ed.), *An invitation to cognitive science, vol. 3: Thinking* (pp. 101-129). Cambridge, MA: MIT Press.

Carey, S. (1999). Sources of conceptual change. In E. Scholnick, K. Nelson, S. Gelman, and P. Miller (Eds.), *Conceptual development: Piaget's legacy* (pp. 293-326). Mahwah, NJ: Lawrence Erlbaum Associates.

Carey, S., and Spelke, E. (1996). Science and core knowledge. *Philosophy of Science, 63,* 515-533.

Case, R. (1997). The development of conceptual structures. In D. Kuhn and R.S. Siegler (Eds.), *Handbook of child psychology, vol. 2: Perception, cognition, and language* (pp. 745-800). New York: Wiley.

Chi, M.T.H. (1978). Knowledge structures and memory development. In R. Siegler (Ed.), *Children's thinking: What develops?* (pp. 73-96). Hillsdale, NJ: Lawrence Erlbaum Associates. (Reprinted in Wozniak, R.H. (1993) *Worlds of childhood reader* (pp. 232- 240). New York: Harper/Collins).

Chi, M.T.H. (1992). Conceptual change within and across ontological categories: Examples from learning and discovery in science. In R. Giere (Ed.), *Cognitive models of science: Minnesota studies in the philosophy of science* (pp. 129-186). Minneapolis: University of Minnesota Press.

Chi, M.T.H. (2005). Commonsense conceptions of emergent processes: Why some misconceptions are robust. *Journal of the Learning Sciences, 14*(2), 161-199.

Chinn, C., and Brewer, W. (1993). The role of anomalous data in knowledge acquisition: A theoretical framework and implications for science instruction. *Review of Educational Research, 63,* 1-49.

Choe, K., Keil, F.C., and Bloom, P. (2005). Children's understanding of the Ulysses conflict. *Developmental Science, 8*(5), 387-392.

Clark, D., and Linn, M.C. (2003). Designing for knowledge integration: The impact of instructional time. *Journal of the Learning Sciences, 12*(4), 451-493.

Clement, J. (1982). Students' preconceptions in introductory mechanics. *American Journal of Physics, 50,* 66-71.

Clement, J. (1991). Nonformal reasoning in science: The use of analogies, extreme cases, and physical intuition. In J. Voss, D. Perkings, and J. Segal (Eds.), *Informal reasoning and education.* Hillsdale, NJ: Lawrence Erlbaum Associates.

Clement, J. (1993). Using bridging analogies and anchoring intuitions to deal with students' preconceptions in physics. *Journal of Research in Science Teaching, 30,* 1241-1257.

Clement, J., Brown, D.E., and Zietsman, A. (1989). Not all preconceptions are misconceptions: Finding 'anchoring conceptions' for grounding instruction on students' intuitions. *International Journal of Science Education, 11,* 554-565.

Confrey, J. (1990). A review of the research on student conceptions in mathematics, science and programming. In C. Cazden (Ed.), *Review of research in education* (vol. 16, pp. 3-56). Washington, DC: American Educational Research Association.

Cottrell, J.E., and Winer, G.A. (1994). Development in the understanding of perception: The decline of extramission perception beliefs. *Developmental Psychology, 30*, 218-228.

Crider, C. (1981). Children's conceptions of the body interior. In R. Bibace and M. Walsh (Eds.), *New directions in child development: Children's conceptions of health, illness, and body functions* (pp. 49-65). San Francisco: Jossey-Bass.

De Vos, W., and Verdonk, A.H. (1996). The particulate nature of matter in science education and in science. *Journal of Research in Science Teaching, 33*, 657-664.

diSessa, A. (1982). Unlearning Aristotelian physics: A study of knowledge-based learning. *Cognitive Science, 6*, 37-75.

diSessa, A. (1988). Knowledge in pieces. In G. Forman and P. Pufall (Eds.), *Constructivism in the computer age* (pp. 49-70). Hillsdale, NJ: Lawrence Erlbaum Associates.

diSessa, A., and Minstrell, J. (1998). Cultivating conceptual change with benchmark lessons. In J. Greeno and S. Goldman (Eds.), *Thinking practices* (pp. 155-187). Hillsdale, NJ: Lawrence Erlbaum Associates.

Dreyfus, A., and Jungworth, E. (1989). The pupil and the living cell: A taxonomy of dysfunctional ideas about an abstract idea. *Journal of Biological Education, 23*, 49-55.

Duschl, R., and Osborne, J. (2002). Supporting and promoting argumentation discourse. *Studies in Science Education, 38*, 39-72.

Evans, E.M. (2001). Cognitive and contextual factors in the emergence of diverse belief system: Creation versus evolution. *Cognitive Psychology, 42*, 217-266.

Flores, F., Tovar, M., and Gallegos, L. (2003). Representation of the cell and its processes in high school students: An integrated view. *International Journal of Science Education*, 269-286.

Gellert, E. (1962). Children's conceptions of the content and function of the human body. *Genetic Psychology Monographs, 65*, 293-405.

Gelman, R., and Lucariello, J. (2002). Role of learning in cognitive development. In H. Pashler (Series Ed.) and R. Gallistel (Vol. Ed.), *Stevens' handbook of experimental psychology: Learning, motivation, and emotion* (vol. 3, 3rd ed., pp. 395-443). New York: Wiley.

Gentner, D., Brem, S., Ferguson, R., Markman, A., Levidow, B., Wolff, P., and Forbus, K. (1997). Analogical reasoning and conceptual change: A case study of Johannes Kepler. *Journal of the Learning Sciences, 6*(1), 3-40.

Gopnik, A. (1996). The scientist as child. *Philosophy of Science, 63*(4), 485-514.

Goswami, U., and Brown, A. (1990). Melting chocolate and melting snowmen: Analogical reasoning and causal relations. *Cognition, 35*, 69-95.

Gutheil, C., Vera, A., and Keil, F.C. (1998). Do houseflies think? Patterns of induction and biological beliefs in development. *Cognition, 66*(1), 33-49.

Hatano, G., Siegler, R.S., Richards, D.D., Inagaki, K., Stavy, R., and Wax, N. (1997). The development of biological knowledge: A multinational study. *Cognitive Development, 8*, 47-62.

Hennessey, M.G. (2003). Probing the dimensions of metacognition: Implications for conceptual change teaching-learning. In G.M. Sinatra and P.R. Pintrich (Eds.), *Intentional conceptual change*. Mahwah, NJ: Lawrence Erlbaum Associates.

Herrenkohl, L.R., and Guerra, M.R. (1998). Participant structures, scientific discourse, and student engagement in fourth grade. *Cognition and Instruction, 16*(4), 433-475.

Huber, S., Krist, H., and Wilkening, F. (2003). Judgment and action knowledge in speed adjustment tasks: Experiments in a virtual environment. *Developmental Science, 6,* 197-210.

Hull, D. (1965). The effects of essentialism on taxonomy: Two thousand years of stasis. *The British Journal for the Philosophy of Science, 15,* 314-326 and *16,* 1-18. (Reprinted in *Concepts of species,* C.N. Slobodchikoff (Ed.), Berkeley: University of California Press, 1976; and *The units of selection,* M. Ereshefsky (Ed.), Cambridge, MA: MIT Press, 1992).

Inagaki, K., and Hatano, G. (2001). Children's understanding of mind-body relationships. In M. Siegal and C. Peterson (Eds.), *Children's understanding of biology and health.* Cambridge, England: Cambridge University Press.

Inagaki, K., and Hatano, G. (2002). *Young children's naive thinking about the biological world.* New York: Psychology Press.

Ioannides, C.H., and Vosniadou, S. (2002). The changing meanings of force. *Cognitive Science Quarterly, 2*(1), 5-62.

Johnson, P. (1998). Children's understanding of changes of state involving the gas state, part 2: Evaporation and condensation below boiling point. *International Journal of Science Education, 20,* 695-709.

Johnson, P. (2000). Children's understanding of substances, part 1: Recognizing chemical change. *International Journal of Science Education, 22*(7), 719-737.

Johnson, P. (2002). Children's understanding of substances, part 2: Explaining chemical change. *International Journal of Science Education, 24*(10), 1037-1054.

Johnson, S., and Carey, S. (1998). Knowledge enrichment and conceptual change in folkbiology: Evidence from Williams Syndrome. *Cognitive Psychology, 37,* 156-200.

Kail, R. (1991). Developmental changes in speed of processing during childhood and adolescence. *Psychological Bulletin, 109,* 490-501.

Kaiser, M.K., McCloskey, M., and Proffitt, D.R. (1986). Development of intuitive theories of motion. Curvilinear motion in the absence of external forces. *Developmental Psychology, 22,* 67-71.

Karmiloff-Smith, A., and Inhelder, B. (1974). If you want to get ahead, get a theory. *Cognition, 3,* 195-212.

Keil, F.C. (1999). Conceptual change. In R.A. Wilson and F. Keil (Eds.), *The MIT encyclopedia of the cognitive sciences* (pp. 172-182). Cambridge, MA: MIT Press.

Keil, F.C. (2003). That's life: Coming to understand biology. *Human Development, 46,* 369-377.

Keil, F.C., and Lockhart, K. (1999). Explanatory understanding in conceptual development. In E. Scholnick, K. Nelson, S. Gelman, and P. Miller (Eds.), *Conceptual development: Piaget's legacy* (pp. 103-130). Mahwah, NJ: Lawrence Erlbaum Associates.

Keysar, B., Lin, S., and Barr, D.J. (2003). Limits on theory of mind use in adults. *Cognition, 89,* 25-41.

Krist, H., Fieberg, E.L., and Wilkening, F. (1993). Intuitive physics in action and judgment: The development of knowledge about projectile motion. *Journal of Experimental Psychology: Learning Memory and Cognition, 19*(4), 952-966.

Krist, Y. (2003). Knowing how to project objects: Probing the generality of children's action knowledge. *Journal of Cognition and Development, 4*(4), 383-414.

Kuhn, T. (1970). *The structure of scientific revolutions.* Chicago, IL: University of Chicago Press.

Kuhn, T. (1977). A function for thought experiments. In T. Kuhn (Ed.), *The essential tension: Selected studies in scientific tradition and change.* Chicago, IL: University of Chicago Press.

Lakatos, I. (1978). *The methodology of scientific research programs.* Cambridge, England: Cambridge University Press.

Lee, O., Eichinger, D.C., Andderson, C.W., Berkheimer, G.D., and Blakeslee, T.D. (1993). Changing middle school students' conceptions of matter and molecules. *Journal of Research in Science Teaching, 30*(3), 249-270.

Lehrer, R., and Schauble, L. (1998). Reasoning about structure and function: Children's conceptions of gears. *Journal of Research in Science Teaching, 31*(1), 3-25.

Lehrer, R., Schauble, L., Carpenter, S., and Penner, D. (2000). The inter-related development of inscriptions and conceptual understanding. In P. Cobb, E. Yackel, and K. McClain (Eds.), *Symbolizing and communicating in mathematics classrooms: Perspectives on discourse, tools, and instructional design.* Mahwah, NJ: Lawrence Erlbaum Associates.

Lehrer, R., Schauble, L., Strom, D., and Pligge, M. (2001). Similarity of form and substance: Modeling material kind. In D. Klahr and S. Carver (Eds.), *Cognition and instruction: 25 years of progress* (pp. 39-74). Mahwah, NJ: Lawrence Erlbaum Associates.

Luna, B., Garver, K., Urban, T., Lazar, N., and Sweeney, J. (2004). Maturation of cognitive processes from late childhood to adulthood. *Child Development, 75,* 1357-1372.

Matsuda, F. (1994). Concepts about interrelations among duration, distance, and speed in young children. *International Journal of Behavioral Development, 17,* 553-576.

Matsuda, F. (2001). Development of concepts of interrelationships among duration, distance, and speed. *International Journal of Behavioral Development, 25,* 466-480.

Mayer, E. (1982). *The growth of biological thought: Diversity, evolution, and inheritance.* Cambridge, MA: Harvard University Press.

McCloskey, M. (1983). Naive theories of motion. In D. Gentner and A.L. Stevens (Eds.), *Mental models* (pp. 299-324). Hillsdale, NJ: Lawrence Erlbaum Associates.

Meheut, M., and Chomat, A. (1990). Les limies de l'atomisme enfantin: Experimentation d'une demarche d'elaboration d'un modele particulaire par des eleves de college. *European Journal of Psychology of Education, 4,* 417-437.

Mills, C., and Keil, F.C. (2005). The development of cynicism. *Psychological Science, 16,* 385-390.

Minstrell, J. (1982). Explaining the 'at rest' condition of an object. *Physics Teacher, 20,* 10-14.

Minstrell, J. (1984). Teaching for the development of understanding of ideas: Forces on moving objects. In C.W. Anderson (Ed.), *Observing classrooms: Perspectives from research and practice* (pp. 67-85). Columbus: Ohio State University.

Minstrell, J., and Kraus, P. (2005). Guided inquiry in the science classroom. In National Research Council, J. Bransford and M.S. Donovan (Eds.), *How students learn: Science in the classroom* (pp. 475-513). Washington, DC: The National Academies Press.

Nakhleh, M.B., and Samarapungavan, A. (1999). Elementary school children's beliefs about matter. *Journal of Research in Science Teaching, 36,* 777-805.

National Research Council. (2000). *How people learn: Brain, mind, experience, and school.* Committee on Developments in the Science of Learning. J.D. Bransford, A.L. Brown, and R.R. Cocking (Eds.). Washington, DC: National Academy Press.

Nersessian, N. (1989). Conceptual change in science and in science education. *Synthese,* 163-183.

Nersessian, N.J. (1992). How do scientists think? Capturing the dynamics of conceptual change in science. *Minnesota Studies in the Philosophy of Science, 15,* 3-44.

Newman, G., Keil, F., Kuhlmeier, V. and Wynn, K. (2006). *Infants understand that only intentional agents can create order.* Manuscript submitted for publication.

Nussbaum, J. (1998). History and philosophy of science and the preparation for constructivist teaching: The case for particle theory. In J.J. Mintzes, J.H. Wandersee, and J.D. Novak (Eds.), *Teaching science for understanding* (pp. 165-194). New York: Academic Press.

Nussbaum, J., and Novick, S. (1982). Alternative frameworks, conceptual conflict and accommodation: Toward a principled teaching strategy. *Instructional Science, 11,* 183-200.

Pfundt, H. (1981). The atom—the final link in the division process or the first building block? *Chimica Didactica, 7,* 75-94.

Piaget, J. (1946a). *Le developpement de la notion de temps chez l'enfant.* Paris: Presses Universitaires de France.

Piaget, J. (1946b). *Les notions de mouvement et de vitesse chez l'enfant.* Paris: Presses Universitaires de France.

Piaget, J., and Inhelder, B. (1948). *La representation de l'espace chez l'enfant.* Paris: Presses Universitaires de France.

Pillow, B.H., and Henrichon, A.J. (1996). There's more to the picture than meets the eye: Young children's difficulty understanding interpretation. *Child Development, 67,* 808-819.

Pillow, B.H., Hill, V., Boyce, A., and Stein, C. (2000). Understanding inference as a source of knowledge: Children's ability to evaluate the certainty of deduction, perception, and guessing. *Developmental Psychology, 36,* 169-179.

Rogers, T.T., and McClelland, J.L. (2004). *Semantic cognition: A parallel distributed processing approach.* Cambridge, MA: MIT Press.

Ross, N., Medin, D., Coley, J.D., and Atran, S. (2003). Cultural and experiential differences in the development of folkbiological induction. *Cognitive Development, 18,* 35-47.

Roth, K. (1984). Using classroom observations to improve science teaching and curriculum materials. In C.W. Anderson (Ed.), *Observing science classrooms: Perspective from research and practice.* Columbus, OH: ERIC.

Roth, K.J. (1990). Science education: It's not enough to "do" or "relate." *American Educator, 13*(4), 16-22, 46-48.

Roth, K.J. (2002). Talking to understand science. In J. Brophy (Ed.), *Social constructivist teaching: Affordances and constraints. Advances in research on teaching* (vol. 9). New York: JAI Press.

Roth, K.J., Peasley, K., and Hazelwood, C. (1992). *Integration from the student perspective: Constructing meaning in science. Elementary subjects series No. 63.* East Lansing, MI: Center for Learning and Teaching for Elementary Subjects.

Samarapungavan, A. (1992). Children's judgments in theory choice tasks: Scientific rationality in childhood. *Cognition, 45,* 1-32.

Sandoval, W.A., and Reiser, B.J. (2004). Explanation-driven inquiry: Integrating conceptual and epistemic scaffolds for scientific inquiry. *Science Education, 88,* 345-372.

Schwab, J. (1962). *The teaching of science as enquiry.* Cambridge, MA: Harvard University Press.

Shtulman, A. (2006). Qualitative differences between naïve and scientific theories of evolution. *Cognitive Psychology, 52,* 170-194.

Siegler, R. (1998). *Emerging minds: The process of change in children's thinking.* New York: Oxford University Press.

Smith, C., Carey, S., and Wiser, M. (1985). On differentiation: A case study of the development of size, weight, and density. *Cognition, 21*(3), 177-237.

Smith, C., Maclin, D., Grosslight, L., and Davis, H. (1997). Teaching for understanding: A study of students' pre-instruction theories of matter and a comparison of the effectiveness of two approaches to teaching about matter and density. *Cognition and Instruction, 15*(3), 317-393.

Snir, J., Smith, C.L., and Raz, G. (2003). Linking phenomena with competing underlying models: A software tool for introducing students to the particulate model of matter. *Science Education, 87,* 794-830.

Stavy, R. (1991). Children's ideas about matter. *School Science and Mathematics, 91*(6), 240-244.

Stewart, J., Cartier, J., and Passmore, C. (2005). Developing understanding through model-based inquiry. In National Research Council, J. Bransford and M.S. Donovan (Eds.), *How students learn: Science in the classroom* (pp. 515-565). Washington, DC: The National Academies Press.

Strike, K., and Posner, G. (1985). A conceptual change view of learning and understanding. In L.H.T. West and A.L. Pines (Eds.), *Cognitive structure and conceptual change* (pp. 211-231). Orlando, FL: Academic Press.

Thagard, P. (1992). *Conceptual revolutions.* Princeton, NJ: Princeton University Press.

Travis, E. (1998). Cortical and cognitive development in 4th, 8th, and 12th grade students: The contribution of speed of processing and executive functioning to cognitive development. *Biological Psychology, 48*(1), 37-56.

van Zee, E.H., and Minstrell, J. (1997). Reflective discourse: Developing shared understandings in a high school physics classroom. *International Journal of Science Education, 19,* 209-228.

Vosniadou, S., and Ioannides, C. (1998). From conceptual development to science education: A psychological point of view. *International Journal of Science Education, 20,* 1213-1230.

Watts, D.M., and Zylberstajn, A. (1981). A survey of some children's ideas about force. *Physics Education, 16,* 360.

Waxman, S.R., and Medin, D.L. (in press). Interpreting asymmetries of projection in children's inductive reasoning. In A. Feeny and E. Heit (Eds.), *Inductive reasoning.* New York: Cambridge University Press.

Wellman, H.M. (1990). *The child's theory of mind.* Cambridge, MA: MIT Press.

Wellman, H.M., and Gelman, S. (1992). Cognitive development: Foundational theories of core domains. *Annual Review of Psychology, 43,* 337-375.

White, B. (1993). Thinkertools: Causal models, conceptual change, and science instruction. *Cognition and Instruction, 10,* 1-100.

White, B., and Frederickson, J. (1998). Inquiry, modeling, and metacognition. Making science accessible to all students. *Cognition and Instruction, 16*(1), 3-117.

Wilkening, F. (1981). Integrating velocity, time, and distance information: A developmental study. *Cognitive Psychology, 13,* 231-247.

Wiser, M., and Amin, T. (2001). Is heat hot? Inducing conceptual change by integrating everyday and scientific perspectives on thermal phenomena. *Learning and Instruction, 11*(4-5), 331-355.

Wolff, P., Medin, D.L., and Pankratz, C. (1999). Evolution and devolution of folk biological knowledge. *Cognition, 73,* 177-204.

Zhou, Z., Peverly, S., Boehm, A., and Chongde, L. (2000). American and Chinese children's understanding of distance, time, and speed interrelations. *Cognitive Development, 15,* 215-240.

5

Generating and Evaluating Scientific Evidence and Explanations

Major Findings in the Chapter:

- *Children are far more competent in their scientific reasoning than first suspected and adults are less so. Furthermore, there is great variation in the sophistication of reasoning strategies across individuals of the same age.*
- *In general, children are less sophisticated than adults in their scientific reasoning. However, experience plays a critical role in facilitating the development of many aspects of reasoning, often trumping age.*
- *Scientific reasoning is intimately intertwined with conceptual knowledge of the natural phenomena under investigation. This conceptual knowledge sometimes acts as an obstacle to reasoning, but often facilitates it.*
- *Many aspects of scientific reasoning require experience and instruction to develop. For example, distinguishing between theory and evidence and many aspects of modeling do not emerge without explicit instruction and opportunities for practice.*

In this chapter, we discuss the various lines of research related to Strand 2—generate and evaluate evidence and explanations.[1] The ways in which

---

[1]Portions of this chapter are based on the commissioned paper by Corinne Zimmerman titled, "The Development of Scientific Reasoning Skills: What Psychologists Contribute to an Understanding of Elementary Science Learning."

scientists generate and evaluate scientific evidence and explanations have long been the focus of study in philosophy, history, anthropology, and sociology. More recently, psychologists and learning scientists have begun to study the cognitive and social processes involved in building scientific knowledge. For our discussion, we draw primarily from the past 20 years of research in developmental and cognitive psychology that investigates how children's scientific thinking develops across the K-8 years.

We begin by developing a broad sketch of how key aspects of scientific thinking develop across the K-8 years, contrasting children's abilities with those of adults. This contrast allows us to illustrate both how children's knowledge and skill can develop over time and situations in which adults' and children's scientific thinking are similar. Where age differences exist, we comment on what underlying mechanisms might be responsible for them. In this research literature, two broad themes emerge, which we take up in detail in subsequent sections of the chapter. The first is the role of prior knowledge in scientific thinking at all ages. The second is the importance of experience and instruction.

Scientific investigation, broadly defined, includes numerous procedural and conceptual activities, such as asking questions, hypothesizing, designing experiments, making predictions, using apparatus, observing, measuring, being concerned with accuracy, precision, and error, recording and interpreting data, consulting data records, evaluating evidence, verification, reacting to contradictions or anomalous data, presenting and assessing arguments, constructing explanations (to oneself and others), constructing various representations of the data (graphs, maps, three-dimensional models), coordinating theory and evidence, performing statistical calculations, making inferences, and formulating and revising theories or models (e.g., Carey et al., 1989; Chi et al., 1994; Chinn and Malhotra, 2001; Keys, 1994; McNay and Melville, 1993; Schauble et al., 1995; Slowiaczek et al., 1992; Zachos et al., 2000). As noted in Chapter 2, over the past 20 to 30 years, the image of "doing science" emerging from across multiple lines of research has shifted from depictions of lone scientists conducting experiments in isolated laboratories to the image of science as both an individual and a deeply social enterprise that involves problem solving and the building and testing of models and theories.

Across this same period, the psychological study of science has evolved from a focus on scientific reasoning as a highly developed form of logical thinking that cuts across scientific domains to the study of scientific thinking as the interplay of general reasoning strategies, knowledge of the natural phenomena being studied, and a sense of how scientific evidence and explanations are generated. Much early research on scientific thinking and inquiry tended to focus primarily either on conceptual development or on the development of reasoning strategies and processes, often using very simplified reasoning tasks. In contrast, many recent studies have attempted to describe a larger number of the complex processes that are deployed in the context of scientific inquiry and to describe their coordination. These studies often engage children in firsthand investigations in which they actively explore multivariable systems. In such tasks, participants initiate all phases of scientific discovery with varying amounts of guidance provided by the researcher. These studies have revealed that, in the context of inquiry, reasoning processes and conceptual knowledge are interdependent and in fact facilitate each other (Schauble, 1996; Lehrer et al. 2001).

It is important to note that, across the studies reviewed in this chapter, researchers have made different assumptions about what scientific reasoning entails and which aspects of scientific practice are most important to study. For example, some emphasize the design of well-controlled experiments, while others emphasize building and critiquing models of natural phenomena. In addition, some researchers study scientific reasoning in stripped down, laboratory-based tasks, while others examine how children approach complex inquiry tasks in the context of the classroom. As a result, the research base is difficult to integrate and does not offer a complete picture of students' skills and knowledge related to generating and evaluating evidence and explanations. Nor does the underlying view of scientific practice guiding much of the research fully reflect the image of science and scientific understanding we developed in Chapter 2.

TRENDS ACROSS THE K-8 YEARS

Generating Evidence

The evidence-gathering phase of inquiry includes designing the investigation as well as carrying out the steps required to collect the data. Generating evidence entails asking questions, deciding what to measure, developing measures, collecting data from the measures, structuring the data, systematically documenting outcomes of the investigations, interpreting and evaluating the data, and using the empirical results to develop and refine arguments, models, and theories.

Asking Questions and Formulating Hypotheses

Asking questions and formulating hypotheses is often seen as the first step in the scientific method; however, it can better be viewed as one of several phases in an iterative cycle of investigation. In an exploratory study, for example, work might start with structured observation of the natural world, which would lead to formulation of specific questions and hypotheses. Further data might then be collected, which lead to new questions, revised hypotheses, and yet another round of data collection. The phase of asking questions also includes formulating the goals of the activity and generating hypotheses and predictions (Kuhn, 2002).

Children differ from adults in their strategies for formulating hypotheses and in the appropriateness of the hypotheses they generate. Children often propose different hypotheses from adults (Klahr, 2000), and younger children (age 10) often conduct experiments without explicit hypotheses, unlike 12- to 14-year-olds (Penner and Klahr, 1996a). In self-directed experimental tasks, children tend to focus on plausible hypotheses and often get stuck focusing on a single hypothesis (e.g., Klahr, Fay, and Dunbar, 1993). Adults are more likely to consider multiple hypotheses (e.g., Dunbar and Klahr, 1989; Klahr, Fay, and Dunbar, 1993). For both children and adults, the ability to consider many alternative hypotheses is a factor contributing to success.

At all ages, prior knowledge of the domain under investigation plays an important role in the formulation of questions and hypotheses (Echevarria, 2003; Klahr, Fay, and Dunbar, 1993; Penner and Klahr, 1996b; Schauble, 1990, 1996; Zimmerman, Raghavan, and Sartoris, 2003). For example, both children and adults are more likely to focus initially on variables they believe to be causal (Kanari and Millar, 2004; Schauble, 1990, 1996). Hypotheses that predict expected results are proposed more frequently than hypotheses that predict unexpected results (Echevarria, 2003). The role of prior knowledge in hypothesis formulation is discussed in greater detail later in the chapter.

Designing Experiments

The design of experiments has received extensive attention in the research literature, with an emphasis on developmental changes in children's ability to build experiments that allow them to identify causal variables. Experimentation can serve to generate observations in order to induce a hypothesis to account for the pattern of data produced (discovery context) or to test the tenability of an existing hypothesis under consideration (confirmation/verification context) (Klahr and Dunbar, 1988). At a minimum, one must recognize that the process of experimentation involves generating observations that will serve as evidence that will be related to hypotheses.

Ideally, experimentation should produce evidence or observations that are interpretable in order to make the process of evidence evaluation uncomplicated. One aspect of experimentation skill is to isolate variables in such a way as to rule out competing hypotheses. The control of variables is a basic strategy that allows valid inferences and narrows the number of possible experiments to consider (Klahr, 2000). Confounded experiments, those in which variables have not been isolated correctly, yield indeterminate evidence, thereby making valid inferences and subsequent knowledge gain difficult, if not impossible.

Early approaches to examining experimentation skills involved minimizing the role of prior knowledge in order to focus on the strategies that participants used. That is, the goal was to examine the domain-general strategies that apply regardless of the content to which they are applied. For example, building on the research tradition of Piaget (e.g., Inhelder and Piaget, 1958), Siegler and Liebert (1975) examined the acquisition of experimental design skills by fifth and eighth graders. The problem involved determining how to make an electric train run. The train was connected to a set of four switches, and the children needed to determine the particular on/off configuration required. The train was in reality controlled by a secret switch, so that the discovery of the correct solution was postponed until all 16 combinations were generated. In this task, there was no principled reason why any one of the combinations would be more or less likely, and success was achieved by systematically testing all combinations of a set of four switches. Thus the task involved no domain-specific knowledge that would constrain the hypotheses about which configuration was most likely. A similarly knowledge-lean task was used by Kuhn and Phelps (1982), similar to a task originally used by Inhelder and Piaget (1958), involving identifying reaction properties of a set of colorless fluids. Success on the task was dependent on the ability to isolate and control variables in the set of all possible fluid combinations in order to determine which was causally related to the outcome. The study extended over several weeks with variations in the fluids used and the difficulty of the problem.

In both studies, the importance of practice and instructional support was apparent. Siegler and Liebert's study included two experimental groups of children who received different kinds of instructional support. Both groups were taught about factors, levels, and tree diagrams. One group received additional, more elaborate support that included practice and help representing all possible solutions with a tree diagram. For fifth graders, the more elaborate instructional support improved their performance compared with a control group that did not receive any support. For eighth graders, both kinds of instructional support led to improved performance. In the Kuhn and Phelps task, some students improved over the course of the study, although an abrupt change from invalid to valid strategies was not common. Instead, the more typical pattern was one in which valid and invalid strategies coexisted both within and across sessions, with a pattern of gradual attainment of stable valid strategies by some students (the stabilization point varied but was typically around weeks 5-7).

Since this early work, researchers have tended to investigate children's and adults' performance on experimental design tasks that are more knowledge rich and less constrained. Results from these studies indicate that, in general, adults are more proficient than children at designing informative experiments. In a study comparing adults with third and sixth graders, adults were more likely to focus on experiments that would be informative (Klahr, Fay, and Dunbar, 1993). Similarly, Schauble (1996) found that during the initial 3 weeks of exploring a domain, children and adults considered about the same number of possible experiments. However, when they began experimentation of another domain in the second 3 weeks of the study, adults considered a greater range of possible experiments. Over the full 6 weeks, children and adults conducted approximately the same number of experiments. Thus, children were more likely to conduct unintended duplicate or triplicate experiments, making their experimentation efforts less informative relative to the adults, who were selecting a broader range of experiments. Similarly, children are more likely to devote multiple experimental trials to variables that were already well understood, whereas adults move on to exploring variables they did not understand as well (Klahr, Fay, and Dunbar, 1993; Schauble, 1996). Evidence also indicates, however, that dimensions of the task often have a greater influence on performance than age (Linn, 1978, 1980; Linn, Chen, and Their, 1977; Linn and Levine, 1978).

With respect to attending to one feature at a time, children are less likely to control one variable at a time than adults. For example, Schauble (1996) found that across two task domains, children used controlled comparisons about a third of the time. In contrast, adults improved from 50 percent usage on the first task to 63 percent on the second task. Children usually begin by designing confounded experiments (often as a means to produce a desired outcome), but with repeated practice begin to use a strategy of changing one variable at time (e.g., Kuhn, Schauble, and Garcia-Mila, 1992; Kuhn et al. 1995; Schauble, 1990).

Reminiscent of the results of the earlier study by Kuhn and Phelps, both children and adults display intraindividual variability in strategy usage. That is, multiple strategy usage is not unique to childhood or periods of developmental transition (Kuhn et al., 1995). A robust finding is the coexistence of valid and invalid strategies (e.g., Kuhn, Schuable, and Garcia-Mila, 1992; Garcia-Mila and Andersen, 2005; Gleason and Schauble, 2000; Schauble, 1990; Siegler and Crowley, 1991; Siegler and Shipley, 1995). That is, participants may progress to the use of a valid strategy, but then return to an inefficient or invalid strategy. Similar use of multiple strategies has been found in research on the development of other academic skills, such as mathematics (e.g., Bisanz and LeFevre, 1990; Siegler and Crowley, 1991), reading (e.g., Perfetti, 1992), and spelling (e.g., Varnhagen, 1995). With respect to experimentation strategies, an individual may begin with an invalid strategy, but once the usefulness of changing one variable at a time is discovered, it is not immediately used exclusively. The newly discovered, effective strategy is only slowly incorporated into an individual's set of strategies.

An individual's perception of the goals of an investigation also has an important effect on the hypotheses they generate and their approach to experimentation. Individuals tend to differ in whether they see the overarching goal of an inquiry task as seeking to identify which factors make a difference (scientific) or seeking to produce a desired effect (engineering). It is a question for further research if these different approaches characterize an individual, or if they are invoked by task demand or implicit assumptions.

In a direct exploration of the effect of adopting scientific versus engineering goals, Schauble, Klopfer, and Raghavan (1991) provided fifth and sixth graders with an "engineering context" and a "science context." When the children were working as scientists, their goal was to determine which factors made a difference and which ones did not. When the children were working as engineers, their goal was optimization, that is, to produce a desired effect (i.e., the fastest boat in the canal task). When working in the science context, the children worked more systematically, by establishing the effect of each variable, alone and in combination. There was an effort to make inclusion inferences (i.e., an inference that a factor is causal) and exclusion inferences (i.e., an inference that a factor is not causal). In the engineering context, children selected highly contrastive combinations and focused on factors believed to be causal while overlooking factors believed or demonstrated to be noncausal. Typically, children took a "try-and-see" approach to experimentation while acting as engineers, but they took a theory-driven approach to experimentation when acting as scientists. Schauble et al. (1991) found that children who received the engineering instructions first, followed by the scientist instructions, made the greatest improvements. Similarly, Sneider et al. (1984) found that students' ability to plan and critique experiments improved when they first engaged in an engineering task of designing rockets.

Another pair of contrasting approaches to scientific investigation is the theorist versus the experimentalist (Klahr and Dunbar, 1998; Schauble, 1990). Similar variation in strategies for problem solving have been observed for chess, puzzles, physics problems, science reasoning, and even elementary arithmetic (Chase and Simon, 1973; Klahr and Robinson, 1981; Klayman and Ha, 1989; Kuhn et al., 1995; Larkin et al., 1980; Lovett and Anderson, 1995, 1996; Simon, 1975; Siegler, 1987; Siegler and Jenkins, 1989). Individuals who take a theory-driven approach tend to generate hypotheses and then test the predictions of the hypotheses. Experimenters tend to make data-driven discoveries, by generating data and finding the hypothesis that best summarizes or explains that data. For example, Penner and Klahr (1996a) asked 10- to 14-year-olds to conduct experiments to determine how the shape, size, material, and weight of an object influence sinking times. Students' approaches to the task could be classified as either "prediction oriented" (i.e., a theorist: "I believe that weight makes a difference) or "hypothesis oriented" (i.e., an experimenter: "I wonder if . . ."). The 10-year-olds were more likely to take a prediction (or demonstration) approach, whereas the 14-year-olds were more likely to explicitly test a hypothesis about an attribute without a strong belief or need to demonstrate that belief. Although these patterns may characterize approaches to any given task, it has yet to be determined if such styles are idiosyncratic to the individual and likely to remain stable across varying tasks, or if different styles might emerge for the same person depending on task demands or the domain under investigation.

Observing and Recording

Record keeping is an important component of scientific investigation in general, and of self-directed experimental tasks especially, because access to and consulting of cumulative records are often important in interpreting evidence. Early studies of experimentation demonstrated that children are often not aware of their own memory limitations, and this plays a role in whether they document their work during an investigation (e.g., Siegler and Liebert, 1975). Recent studies corroborate the importance of an awareness of one's own memory limitations while engaged in scientific inquiry tasks, regardless of age. Spontaneous note-taking or other documentation of experimental designs and results may be a factor contributing to the observed developmental differences in performance on both experimental design tasks and in evaluation of evidence. Carey et al. (1989) reported that, prior to instruction, seventh graders did not spontaneously keep records when trying to determine and keep track of which substance was responsible for producing a bubbling reaction in a mixture of yeast, flour, sugar, salt, and warm water. Nevertheless, even though preschoolers are likely to produce inadequate and uninformative notations, they can distinguish between the two when asked to choose between them (Triona and Klahr, in press). Dunbar and Klahr (1988) also noted that children (grades 3-6) were unlikely to check if a current hypothesis was or was not consistent with previous experimental results. In a study by Trafton and Trickett (2001), undergraduates solving scientific reasoning problems in a computer environment were more likely to achieve correct performance when using the notebook function (78 percent) than were nonusers (49 percent), showing that this issue is not unique to childhood.

In a study of fourth graders' and adults' spontaneous use of notebooks during a 10-week investigation of multivariable systems, all but one of the adults took notes, whereas only half of the children took notes. Moreover, despite variability in the amount of notebook usage in both groups, on average adults made three times more notebook entries than children did. Adults' note-taking remained stable across the 10 weeks, but children's frequency of use decreased over time, dropping to about half of their initial usage. Children rarely reviewed their notes, which typically consisted of conclusions, but not the variables used or the outcomes of the experimental tests (i.e., the evidence for the conclusion was not recorded) (Garcia-Mila and Andersen, 2005).

Children may differentially record the results of experiments, depending on familiarity or strength of prior theories. For example, 10- to 14-year-olds recorded more data points when experimenting with factors affecting force produced by the weight and surface area of boxes than when they were experimenting with pendulums (Kanari and Millar, 2004). Overall, it is a fairly robust finding that children are less likely than adults to record experimental designs and outcomes or to review what notes they do keep, despite task demands that clearly necessitate a reliance on external memory aids.

Given the increasing attention to the importance of metacognition for proficient performance on such tasks (e.g., Kuhn and Pearsall, 1998, 2000), it is important to determine at what point children and early adolescents recognize their own memory limitations as they navigate through a complex task. Some studies show that children's understanding of how their own memories work continues to develop across the elementary and middle school grades (Siegler and Alibali, 2005). The implication is that there is no particular age or grade level when memory and limited understanding of one's own memory are no longer a consideration. As such, knowledge of how one's own memory works may represent an important moderating variable in understanding the development of scientific reasoning (Kuhn, 2001). For example, if a student is aware that it will be difficult for her to remember the results of multiple trials, she may be more likely to carefully record each outcome. However, it may also be the case that children, like adult scientists, need to be inducted into the practice of record keeping and the use of records. They are likely to need support to understand the important role of records in generating scientific evidence and supporting scientific arguments.

Evaluating Evidence

The important role of evidence evaluation in the process of scientific activity has long been recognized. Kuhn (1989), for example, has argued that the defining feature of scientific thinking is the set of skills involved in differentiating and coordinating theory and evidence. Various strands of research provide insight on how children learn to engage in this phase of scientific inquiry. There is an extensive literature on the evaluation of evidence, beginning with early research on identifying patterns of covariation and cause that used highly structured experimental tasks. More recently researchers have studied how children evaluate evidence in the context of self-directed experimental tasks. In real-world contexts (in contrast to highly controlled laboratory tasks) the process of evidence evaluation is very messy and requires an understanding of error and variation. As was the case for hypothesis generation and the design of experiments, the role of prior knowledge and beliefs has emerged as an important influence on how individuals evaluate evidence.

Covariation Evidence

A number of early studies on the development of evidence evaluation skills used knowledge-lean tasks that asked participants to evaluate existing data. These data were typically in the form of covariation evidence—that is, the frequency with which two events do or do not occur together. Evaluation of covariation evidence is potentially important in regard to scientific thinking because covariation is one potential cue that two events are causally related. Deanna Kuhn and her colleagues carried out pioneering work on children's and adults' evaluation of covariation evidence, with a focus on how participants coordinate their prior beliefs about the phenomenon with the data presented to them (see Box 5-1).

Results across a series of studies revealed continuous improvement of the skills involved in differentiating and coordinating theory and evidence, as well as *bracketing* prior belief while evaluating evidence, from middle childhood (grades 3 and 6) to adolescence (grade 9) to adulthood (Kuhn, Amsel, and O'Loughlin, 1988). These skills, however, did not appear to develop to an optimal level even among adults. Even adults had a tendency to meld theory and evidence into a single mental representation of "the way things are."

Participants had a variety of strategies for keeping theory and evidence in alignment with one another when they were in fact discrepant. One tendency was to ignore, distort, or selectively attend to evidence that was inconsistent with a favored theory. For example, the protocol from one ninth grader demonstrated that upon repeated instances of covariation between type of breakfast roll and catching colds, he would not acknowledge this relationship: "They just taste different . . . the breakfast roll to me don't cause so much colds because they have pretty much the same thing inside" (Kuhn, Amsel, and O'Loughlin, 1998, p. 73).

Another tendency was to adjust a theory to fit the evidence, a process that was most often outside an individual's conscious awareness and control. For example, when asked to recall their original beliefs, participants would often report a theory consistent with the evidence that was presented, and not the theory as originally stated. Take the case of one ninth grader who did not believe that type of condiment (mustard versus ketchup) was causally related to catching colds. With each presentation of an instance of covariation evidence, he acknowledged the evidence and elaborated a theory based on the amount of ingredients or vitamins and the temperature of the

BOX 5-1 Evaluation of Covariation Evidence

Kuhn and her colleagues used simple, everyday contexts, rather than phenomena from specific scientific disciplines. In an initial theory interview, participants' beliefs about the causal status of various variables were ascertained. For example, sixth and ninth graders were questioned about their beliefs concerning the types of foods that make a difference in whether a person caught a cold (35 foods in total). Four variables were selected on the basis of ratings from the initial theory interview: two factors that the participant believed make a difference in catching colds (e.g., type of fruit, type of cereal) and two factors the participant believed do not make a difference (e.g., type of potato, type of condiment). This procedure allowed the evidence to be manipulated so that covariation evidence could be presented that *confirmed* one existing causal theory and one noncausal theory. Likewise, noncovariation evidence was presented that *disconfirmed* one previously held causal theory and one noncausal theory. The specific manipulations were therefore tailored for each person in the study.

Participants then evaluated patterns of covariation data and answered a series of questions about what the evidence showed for each of the four variables. Responses were coded as evidence based when they referred to the patterns of covariation or instances of data presented (e.g., if shown a pattern in which type of cake covaried with getting colds, a participant who noted that the sick children ate chocolate cake and the healthy ones ate carrot cake would be coded as having made an evidence-based response). Responses were coded as theory based when they referred to the participant's prior beliefs or theories (e.g., a response that chocolate cake has "sugar and a lot of bad stuff in it" or that "less sugar means your blood pressure doesn't go up").

food the condiment was served with to make sense of the data (Kuhn, Amsel, and O'Loughlin, 1988, p. 83). Kuhn argued that this tendency suggests that the student's theory does not exist as an object of cognition. That is, a theory and the evidence for that theory are undifferentiated—they do not exist as separate cognitive entities. If they do not exist as separate entities, it is not possible to flexibly and consciously reflect on the relation of one to the other.

A number of researchers have criticized Kuhn's findings on both methodological and theoretical grounds. Sodian, Zaitchik, and Carey (1991), for example, questioned the finding that third and sixth grade children cannot distinguish between their beliefs and the evidence, pointing to the complexity of the tasks Kuhn used as problematic. They chose to employ simpler tasks that involved story problems about phenomena for which children did not hold strong beliefs. Children's performance on these tasks demonstrated that even first and second graders could differentiate a hypothesis from the evidence. Likewise, Ruffman et al. (1993) used a simplified task and showed that 6-year-olds were able to form a causal hypothesis based on a pattern of covariation evidence. A study of children and adults (Amsel and Brock, 1996) indicated an important role of prior beliefs, especially for children. When presented with evidence that disconfirmed prior beliefs, children from both grade levels tended to make causal judgments consistent with their prior beliefs. When confronted with confirming evidence, however, both groups of children and adults made similar judgments. Looking across these studies provides insight into the conditions under which children are more or less proficient at coordinating theory and evidence. In some situations, children are better at distinguishing prior beliefs from evidence than the results of Kuhn et al. suggest.

Koslowksi (1996) criticized Kuhn et al.'s work on more theoretical grounds. She argued that reliance on knowledge-lean tasks in which participants are asked to suppress their prior knowledge may lead to an incomplete or distorted picture of the reasoning abilities of children and adults. Instead, Koslowski suggested that using prior knowledge when gathering and evaluating evidence is a valid strategy. She developed a series of experiments to support her thesis and to explore the ways in which prior knowledge might play a role in evaluating evidence. The results of these investigations are described in detail in the later section of this chapter on the role of prior knowledge.

Evidence in the Context of Investigations

Researchers have also looked at reasoning about cause in the context of full investigations of causal systems. Two main types of multivariable systems are used in these studies. In the first type of system, participants are involved in a hands-on manipulation of a physical system, such as a ramp (e.g., Chen and Klahr, 1999; Masnick and Klahr, 2003) or a canal (e.g., Gleason and Schauble, 2000; Kuhn, Schauble, and Garcia-Mila, 1992). The second type of system is a computer simulation, such as the Daytona microworld in which participants discover the factors affecting the speed of race cars (Schauble, 1990). A variety of virtual environments have been created in domains such as electric circuits (Schauble et al., 1992), genetics (Echevarria, 2003), earthquake risk, and flooding risk (e.g., Keselman, 2003).

The inferences that are made based on self-generated experimental evidence are typically classified as either causal (or inclusion), noncausal (or exclusion), indeterminate, or false inclusion. All inference types can be further classified as valid or invalid. Invalid inclusion, by definition, is of particular interest because in self-directed experimental contexts, both children and adults often infer based on prior beliefs that a variable is causal, when in reality it is not.

Children tend to focus on making causal inferences during their initial explorations of a causal system. In a study in which children worked to discover the causal structure of a computerized microworld, fifth and sixth graders began by producing confounded experiments and relied on prior knowledge or expectations (Schauble, 1990). As a result, in their early explorations of the causal system, they were more likely to make incorrect causal inferences. In a direct comparison of adults and children (Schauble, 1996), adults also focused on making causal inferences, but they made more valid inferences because their experimentation was more often done using a control-of-variables strategy. Overall, children's inferences were valid 44 percent of the time, compared with 72 percent for adults. The fifth and sixth graders improved over the course of six sessions, starting at 25 percent but improving to almost 60 percent valid inferences (Schauble, 1996). Adults were more likely than children to make inferences about which variables were noncausal or inferences of indeterminacy (80 and 30 percent, respectively) (Schauble, 1996).

Children's difficulty with inferences of noncausality also emerged in a study of 10- to 14-year-olds who explored factors influencing the swing of a pendulum or the force needed to pull a box along a level surface (Kanari and Millar, 2004). Only half of the students were able draw correct conclusions about factors that did not covary with outcome. Students were likely to either selectively record data, selectively attend to data, distort or reinterpret the data, or state that noncovariation experimental trials were "inconclusive." Such tendencies are reminiscent of other findings that some individuals selectively attend to or distort data in order to preserve a prior theory or belief (Kuhn, Amsel, and O'Loughlin, 1988; Zimmerman, Raghavan, and Sartoris, 2003).

Some researchers suggest children's difficulty with noncausal or indeterminate inferences may be due both to experience and to the inherent complexity of the problem. In terms of experience, in the science classroom it is typical to focus on variables that "make a difference," and therefore students struggle when testing variables that do not covary with the outcome (e.g., the weight of a pendulum does not affect the time of swing or the vertical height of a weight does not affect balance) (Kanari and Millar, 2004). Also, valid exclusion and indeterminacy inferences may be conceptually more complex, because they require one to consider a pattern of evidence produced from several experimental trials (Kuhn et al., 1995; Schauble, 1996). Looking across several trials may require one to review cumulative records of previous outcomes. As has been suggested previously, children do not often have the memory skills to either record information, record sufficient information, or consult such information when it has been recorded.

The importance of experience is highlighted by the results of studies conducted over several weeks with fifth and sixth graders. After several weeks with a task, children started making more exclusion inferences (that factors are not causal) and indeterminacy inferences (that one cannot make a conclusive judgment about a confounded comparison) and did not focus solely on causal inferences (e.g., Keselman, 2003; Schauble, 1996). They also began to distinguish between an informative and an uninformative experiment by attending to or controlling other factors leading to an improved ability to make valid inferences. Through repeated exposure, invalid inferences, such as invalid inclusions, dropped in frequency. The tendency to begin to make inferences of indeterminacy suggests that students developed more awareness of the adequacy or inadequacy of their experimentation strategies for generating sufficient and interpretable evidence.

Children and adults also differ in generating sufficient evidence to support inferences. In contexts in which it is possible, children often terminate their search early, believing that they have determined a solution to the problem (e.g., Dunbar and Klahr, 1989). In studies over several weeks in which children must continue their investigation (e.g., Schauble et al., 1991), this is less likely because of the task requirements. Children are also more likely to refer to the most recently generated evidence. They may jump to a conclusion after a single experiment, whereas adults typically need to see the results of several experiments (e.g., Gleason and Schauble, 2000).

As was found with experimentation, children and adults display intraindividual variability in strategy usage with respect to inference types. Likewise, the existence of multiple inference strategies is not unique to childhood (Kuhn et al., 1995). In general, early in an investigation, individuals focus primarily on identifying factors that are causal and are less likely to consider definitely ruling out factors that are not causal. However, a mix of valid and invalid inference strategies co-occur during the course of exploring a causal system. As with experimentation, the addition of a valid inference strategy to an individual's repertoire does not mean that they immediately give up the others. Early in investigations, there is a focus on causal hypotheses and inferences, whether they are warranted or not. Only with additional exposure do children start to make inferences of noncausality and indeterminacy. Knowledge change and experience—gaining a better understanding of the causal system via experimentation—was associated with the use of valid experimentation and inference strategies.

THE ROLE OF PRIOR KNOWLEDGE

In the previous section we reviewed evidence on developmental differences in using scientific strategies. Across multiple studies, prior knowledge emerged as an important influence on several parts of the process of generating and evaluating evidence. In this section we look more closely at the specific ways that prior knowledge may shape part of the process. Prior knowledge includes conceptual knowledge, that is, knowledge of the natural world and specifically of the domain under investigation, as well as prior knowledge and beliefs about the purpose of an investigation and the goals of science more generally. This latter kind of prior knowledge is touched on here and discussed in greater detail in the next chapter.

Beliefs About Causal Mechanism and Plausibility

In response to research on evaluation of covariation evidence that used knowledge-lean tasks or even required participants to suppress prior knowledge, Koslowski (1996) argued that it is legitimate and even helpful to consider prior knowledge when gathering and evaluating evidence. The world is full of correlations, and consideration of plausibility, causal mechanism, and alternative causes can help to determine which correlations between events should be taken seriously and which should be viewed as spurious. For example, the identification of the *E. coli* bacterium allows a causal relationship between hamburger consumption and certain types of illness or mortality. Because of the absence of a causal mechanism, one does not consider seriously the correlation between ice cream consumption and violent crime rate as causal, but one looks for other covarying quantities (such as high temperatures) that may be causal for both behaviors and thus explain the correlation.

Koslowski (1996) presented a series of experiments that demonstrate the interdependence of theory and evidence in legitimate scientific reasoning (see Box 5-2 for an example). In most of these studies, all participants (sixth graders, ninth graders, and adults) did take mechanism into consideration when evaluating evidence in relation to a hypothesis about a causal relationship. Even sixth graders considered more than patterns of covariation when making causal judgments (Koslowksi and Okagaki, 1986; Koslowski et al., 1989). In fact, as discussed in the previous chapter, results of studies by Koslowski (1996) and others (Ahn et al., 1995) indicate that children and adults have naïve theories about the world that incorporate information about both covariation and causal mechanism.

The plausibility of a mechanism also plays a role in reasoning about cause. In some situations, scientific progress occurs by taking seemingly implausible correlations seriously (Wolpert, 1993). Similarly, Koslowski argued that if people rely on covariation and mechanism information in an interdependent and judicious manner, then they should pay attention to implausible correlations (i.e., those with no apparent mechanism) when the implausible correlation occurs repeatedly. For example, discovering the cause of Kawasaki's syndrome depended on taking seriously the implausible cor-

BOX 5-2 The Interdependence of Theory and Evidence in Scientific Reasoning

In studies conducted by Koslowski and her colleagues, participants were given problem situations in which a story character is trying to determine if some target factor (e.g., a gasoline additive) is causally related to an effect (e.g., improved gas mileage). They were then shown either perfect covariation between the target factor and the effect or partial covariation (4 of 6 instances). Perfect correlation was rated as more likely to indicate causation than partial correlation. Participants were then told that a number of plausible mechanisms had been ruled out (e.g., the additive does not burn more efficiently, the additive does not burn more cleanly). When asked to rate again how likely it was that the additive is causally responsible for improved gas mileage, the ratings for both perfect and partial covariation were lower for all age groups.

Koslowski also tried to determine if participants would spontaneously generate information about causal mechanisms when it was not cued by the task. Children and adults were presented with story problems in which a character is trying to answer a question about, for example, whether parents staying in the hospital with them improves the recovery rate of their children. Participants were asked to describe whatever type of information might be useful for solving the problem. Half of the participants were told that experimental intervention (that is, parents and children could not be assigned to particular groups) was not possible, while the other half were not restricted in this manner. Almost all participants showed some concern for a causal mechanism, including expectations about how the target mechanism would operate. Although the sixth graders were less likely to generate a variety of alternative hypotheses, all age groups proposed appropriate contrastive tests.

relation between the illness and having recently cleaned carpets. Similarly, Thagard (1998a, 1998b) describes the case of researchers Warren and Marshall, who proposed that peptic ulcers could be caused by a bacterium, and their efforts to have their theory accepted by the medical community. The bacterial theory of ulcers was initially rejected as implausible, given the assumption that the stomach is too acidic to allow bacteria to survive.

Studies with both children and adults reveal links between reasoning about mechanism and the plausibility of that mechanism (Koslowski, 1996). When presented with an implausible covariation (e.g., improved gas mileage and color of car), participants rated the causal status of the implausible cause (color) before and after learning about a possible way that the cause could bring about the effect (improved gas mileage). In this example, participants learned that the color of the car affects the driver's alertness (which affects driving quality, which in turn affects gas mileage). At all ages, participants increased their causal ratings after learning about a possible mediating mechanism. The presence of a possible mechanism in addition to a large number of covariations (four or more) was taken to indicate the possibility of a causal relationship for both plausible and implausible covariations. When either generating or assessing mechanisms for plausible covariations, all age groups (sixth and ninth graders and adults) were comparable. When the covariation was implausible, sixth graders were more likely to generate dubious mechanisms to account for the correlation.

The role of prior knowledge, especially beliefs about causal mechanism and plausibility, is also evident in hypothesis formation and the design of investigations. Individuals' prior beliefs influence the choice of which hypotheses to test, including which hypotheses are tested first, repeatedly, or receive the most time and attention (e.g., Echevarria, 2003; Klahr, Fay, and Dunbar, 1993; Penner and Klahr, 1996b; Schauble, 1990, 1996; Zimmerman, Raghavan, and Sartoris, 2003). For example, children's favored theories sometimes result in the selection of invalid experimentation and evidence evaluation heuristics (e.g., Dunbar and Klahr, 1989; Schauble, 1990). Plausibility of a hypothesis may serve as a guide for which experiments to pursue. Klahr, Fay, and Dunbar (1993) provided third and sixth grade children and adults with hypotheses to test that were incorrect but either plausible or implausible. For plausible hypotheses, children and adults tended to go about demonstrating the correctness of the hypothesis rather than setting up experiments to decide between rival hypotheses. For implausible hypotheses, adults and some sixth graders proposed a plausible rival hypothesis and set up an experiment that would discriminate between the two. Third graders tended to propose a plausible hypothesis but then ignore or forget the initial implausible hypothesis, getting sidetracked in an attempt to demonstrate that the plausible hypothesis was correct.

Recognizing the interdependence of theory and data in the evaluation of evidence and explanations, Chinn and Brewer (2001) proposed that people evaluate evidence by building a mental model of the interrelationships between theories and data. These models integrate patterns of data, procedural details, and the theoretical explanation of the observed findings (which may include unobservable mechanisms, such as molecules, electrons, enzymes, or intentions and desires). The information and events can be linked by different kinds of connections, including causal, contrastive, analogical, and inductive links. The mental model may then be evaluated by considering the plausibility of these links. In addition to considering the links between, for example, data and theory, the model might also be evaluated by appealing to alternate causal mechanisms or alternate explanations. Essentially, an individual seeks to "undermine one or more of the links in the model" (p. 337). If no reasons to be critical can be identified, the individual may accept the new evidence or theoretical interpretation.

Some studies suggest that the strength of prior beliefs, as well as the personal relevance of those beliefs, may influence the evaluation of the mental model (Chinn and Malhotra, 2002; Klaczynski, 2000; Klaczynski and Narasimham, 1998). For example, when individuals have reason to disbelieve evidence (e.g., because it is inconsistent with prior belief), they will search harder for flaws in the data (Kunda, 1990). As a result, individuals may not find the evidence compelling enough to reassess their cognitive model. In contrast, beliefs about simple empirical regularities may not be held with such conviction (e.g., the falling speed of heavy versus light objects), making it easier to change a belief in response to evidence.

Evaluating Evidence That Contradicts Prior Beliefs

Anomalous data or evidence refers to results that do not fit with one's current beliefs. Anomalous data are considered very important by scientists because of their role in theory change, and they have been used by science educators to promote conceptual change. The idea that anomalous evidence promotes conceptual change (in the scientist or the student) rests on a number of assumptions, including that individuals have beliefs or theories about natural or social phenomena, that they are capable of noticing that some evidence is inconsistent with those theories, that such evidence calls into question those theories, and, in some cases, that a belief or theory will be altered or changed in response to the new (anomalous) evidence (Chinn and Brewer, 1998). Chinn and Brewer propose that there are eight possible responses to anomalous data. Individuals can (1) ignore the data; (2) reject the data (e.g., because of methodological error, measurement error, bias); (3) acknowledge uncertainty about the validity of the data; (4) exclude the data as being irrelevant to the current theory; (5) hold the data in abeyance (i.e., withhold a judgment about the relation of the data to the initial theory); (6) reinterpret the data as consistent with the initial theory; (7) accept the data and make peripheral change or minor modification to the theory; or (8) accept the data and change the theory. Examples of all of these responses were found in undergraduates' responses to data that contradicted theories to explain the mass extinction of dinosaurs and theories about whether dinosaurs were warm-blooded or cold-blooded.

In a series of studies, Chinn and Malhotra (2002) examined how fourth, fifth, and sixth graders responded to experimental data that were inconsistent with their existing beliefs. Experiments from physical science domains were selected in which the outcomes produced either ambiguous or unambiguous data, and for which the findings were counterintuitive for most children. For example, most children assume that a heavy object falls faster than a light object. When the two objects are dropped simultaneously, there is some ambiguity because it is difficult to observe both objects. An example of a topic that is counterintuitive but results in unambiguous evidence is the reaction temperature of baking soda added to vinegar. Children believe that either no change in temperature will occur, or that the fizzing causes an increase in temperature. Thermometers unambiguously show a temperature drop of about 4 degrees centigrade.

When examining the anomalous evidence produced by these experiments, children's difficulties seemed to occur in one of four cognitive processes: observation, interpretation, generalization, or retention (Chinn and Malhotra, 2002). For example, prior belief may influence what is "observed," especially in the case of data that are ambiguous, and children may not perceive the two objects as landing simultaneously. Inferences based on this faulty observation will then be incorrect. At the level of interpretation, even if individuals accurately observed the outcome, they might not shift their theory to align with the evidence. They can fail to do so in many ways, such as ignoring or distorting the data or discounting the data because they are considered flawed. At the level of generalization, an individual may accept, for example, that these particular heavy and light objects fell at the same rate but insist that the same rule may not hold for other situations or objects. Finally, even when children appeared to change their beliefs about an observed phenomenon in the immediate context of the experiment, their prior beliefs reemerged later, indicating a lack of long-term retention of the change.

Penner and Klahr (1996a) investigated the extent to which children's prior beliefs affect their ability to design and interpret experiments. They used a domain in which most children hold a strong belief that heavier objects sink in fluid faster than light objects, and they examined children's ability to design unconfounded experiments to test that belief. In this study, for objects of a given composition and shape, sink times for heavy and light objects are nearly indistinguishable to an observer. For example, the sink times for the stainless steel spheres weighing 65 gm and 19 gm were .58 sec and .62 sec, respectively. Only one of the eight children (out of 30) who chose to directly contrast these two objects continued to explore the reason for the unexpected finding that the large and small spheres had equivalent sink times. The process of knowledge change was not straightforward. For example, some children suggested that the size of the smaller steel ball offset the fact that it weighed less because it was able to move through the water as fast as the larger, heavier steel ball. Others concluded that both weight and shape make a difference. That is, there was an attempt to reconcile the evidence with prior knowledge and expectations by appealing to causal mechanisms, alternate causes, or enabling conditions.

What is also important to note about the children in the Penner and Klahr study is that they did in fact notice the surprising finding, rather than ignore or misrepresent the data. They tried to make sense of the outcome by acting as a theorist who conjectures about the causal mechanisms, boundary conditions, or other ad hoc explanations (e.g., shape) to account for the results of an experiment. In Chinn and Malhotra's (2002) study of students' evaluation of observed evidence (e.g., watching two objects fall simultaneously), the process of noticing was found to be an important mediator of conceptual change.

Echevarria (2003) examined seventh graders' reactions to anomalous data in the domain of genetics and whether they served as a catalyst for knowledge construction during the course of self-directed experimentation. Students in the study completed a 3-week unit on genetics that involved genetics simulation software and observing plant growth. In both the software and the plants, students investigated or observed the transmission of one trait. Anomalies in the data were defined as outcomes that were not readily explainable on the basis of the appearance of the parents.

In general, the number of hypotheses generated, the number of tests conducted, and the number of explanations generated were a function of students' ability to encounter, notice, and take seriously an anomalous finding. The majority of students (80 percent) developed some explanation for the pattern of anomalous data. For those who were unable to generate an explanation, it was suggested that the initial knowledge was insufficient and therefore could not undergo change as a result of the encounter with "anomalous" evidence. Analogous to case studies in the history of science (e.g., Simon, 2001), these students' ability to notice and explore anomalies was related to their level of domain-specific knowledge (as suggested by Pasteur's oft quoted maxim "serendipity favors the prepared mind"). Surprising findings were associated with an increase in hypotheses and experiments to test these potential explanations, but without the domain knowledge to "notice," anomalies could not be exploited.

There is some evidence that, with instruction, students' ability to evaluate anomalous data improves (Chinn and Malhotra, 2002). In a study of fourth, fifth, and sixth graders, one group of students was instructed to *predict* the outcomes of three experiments that produce counterintuitive but unambiguous data (e.g., reaction temperature). A second group answered questions that were designed to promote unbiased observations and interpretations by *reflecting* on the data. A third group was provided with an *explanation* of what scientists expected to find and why. All students reported their prediction of the outcome, what they observed, and their interpretation of the experiment. They were then tested for generalizations, and a retention test followed 9-10 days later. Fifth and sixth graders performed better than did fourth graders. Students who heard an explanation of what scientists expected to find and why did best. Further analyses suggest that the explanation-based intervention worked by influencing students' initial predictions. This correct prediction then influenced what was observed. A correct observation then led to correct interpretations and generalizations, which resulted in conceptual change that was retained. A similar pattern of results was found using interventions employing either full or reduced explanations prior to the evaluation of evidence.

Thus, it appears that children were able to change their beliefs on the basis of anomalous or unexpected evidence, but only when they were capable of making the correct observations. Difficulty in making observations was found to be the main cognitive process responsible for impeding conceptual change (i.e., rather than interpretation, generalization, or retention). Certain interventions, in particular those involving an explanation of what scientists expected to happen and why, were very effective in mediating conceptual change when encountering counterintuitive evidence. With particular scaffolds, children made observations independent of theory, and they changed their beliefs based on observed evidence.

THE IMPORTANCE OF EXPERIENCE AND INSTRUCTION

There is increasing evidence that, as in the case of intellectual skills in general, the development of the component skills of scientific reasoning "cannot be counted on to routinely develop" (Kuhn and Franklin, 2006, p. 47). That is, young children have many requisite skills needed to engage in scientific thinking, but there are also ways in which even adults do not show full proficiency in investigative and inference tasks. Recent research efforts have therefore been focused on how such skills can be promoted by determining which types of educational interventions (e.g., amount of structure, amount of support, emphasis on strategic or metastrategic skills) will contribute most to learning, retention, and transfer, and which types of interventions are best suited to different students. There is a developing picture of what children are capable of with minimal support, and research is moving in the direction of ascertaining what children are capable of, and when, under conditions of practice, instruction, and scaffolding. It may one day be possible to tailor educational opportunities that neither under- or overestimate children's ability to extract meaningful experiences from inquiry-based science classes.

Very few of the early studies focusing on the development of experimentation and evidence evaluation skills explicitly addressed issues of instruction and experience. Those that did, however, indicated an important role of experience and instruction in supporting scientific thinking. For example, Siegler and Liebert (1975) incorporated instructional manipulations aimed at teaching children about variables and variable levels with or without practice on analogous tasks. In the absence of both instruction and extended practice, no fifth graders and a small minority of eighth graders were successful. Kuhn and Phelps (1982) reported that, in the absence of explicit instruction, extended practice over several weeks was sufficient for the development and modification of experimentation and inference strategies. Later studies of self-directed experimentation also indicate that frequent engagement with the inquiry environment alone can lead to the development and modification of cognitive strategies (e.g., Kuhn, Schauble, and Garcia-Mila, 1992; Schauble et al., 1991).

Some researchers have suggested that even simple prompts, which are often used in studies of students' investigation skills, may provide a subtle form of instruction intervention (Klahr and Carver, 1995). Such prompts may cue the strategic requirements of the task, or they may promote explanation or the type of reflection that could induce a metacognitive or metastrategic awareness of task demands. Because of their role in many studies of revealing students' thinking generation, it may be very difficult to tease apart the relative contributions of practice from the scaffolding provided by researcher prompts.

In the absence of instruction or prompts, students may not routinely ask questions of themselves, such as "What are you going to do next?" "What outcome do you predict?" "What did you learn?" and "How do you know?" Questions such as these may promote self-explanation, which has been shown to enhance understanding in part because it facilitates the integration of newly learned material with existing knowledge (Chi et al., 1994). Questions such as the prompts used by researchers may serve to promote such integration. Chinn and Malhotra (2002) incorporated different kinds of interventions, aimed at promoting conceptual change in response to anomalous experimental evidence. Interventions included practice at making predictions, reflecting on data, and explanation. The explanation-based interventions were most successful at promoting conceptual change, retention, and generalization. The prompts used in some studies of self-directed experimentation are very likely to serve the same function as the prompts used by Chi et al. (1994). Incorporating such prompts in classroom-based inquiry activities could serve as a powerful teaching tool, given that the use of self-explanation in tutoring systems (human and computer interface) has been shown to be quite effective (e.g., Chi, 1996; Hausmann and Chi, 2002).

Studies that compare the effects of different kinds of instruction and practice opportunities have been conducted in the laboratory, with some translation to the classroom. For example, Chen and Klahr (1999) examined the effects of direct and indirect instruction of the control of variables strategy on students' (grades 2-4) experimentation and knowledge acquisition. The instructional intervention involved didactic teaching of the control-of-variables strategy, along with examples and probes. Indirect (or implicit) training involved the use of systematic probes during the course of children's experimentation. A control group did not receive instruction or probes. No group received instruction on domain knowledge for any task used (springs, ramps, sinking objects). For the students who received instruction, use of the control-of-variables strategy increased from 34 percent prior to instruction to 65 percent after, with 61-64 percent usage maintained on transfer tasks that followed after 1 day and again after 7 months, respectively. No such gains were evident for the implicit training or control groups.

Instruction about control of variables improved children's ability to design informative experiments, which in turn facilitated conceptual change in a number of domains. They were able to design unconfounded experiments, which facilitated valid causal and noncausal inferences, resulting in a change in knowledge about how various multivariable causal systems worked. Significant gains in domain knowledge were evident only for the instruction group. Fourth graders showed better skill retention at long-term assessment than second or third graders.

The positive impact of instruction on control of variables also appears to translate to the classroom (Toth, Klahr, and Chen, 2000; Klahr, Chen and Toth, 2001). Fourth graders who received instruction in the control-of-variables strategy in their classroom increased their use of the strategy, and their domain knowledge improved. The percentage of students who were able to correctly evaluate others' research increased from 28 to 76 percent.

Instruction also appears to promote longer term use of the control-of-variables strategy and transfer of the strategy to a new task (Klahr and Nigam, 2004). Third and fourth graders who received instruction were more likely to master the control-of-variables strategy than students who explored a multivariable system on their own. Interestingly, although the group that received instruction performed better overall, a quarter of the students who explored the system on their own also mastered the strategy. These results raise questions about the kinds of individual differences that may allow for some students to benefit from the discovery context, but not others. That is, which learner traits are associated with the success of different learning experiences?

Similar effects of experience and instruction have been demonstrated for improving students' ability to use evidence from multiple records and make correct inferences from noncausal variables (Keselman, 2003). In many cases, students show some improvement when they are given the opportunity for practice, but greater improvement when they receive instruction (Kuhn and Dean, 2005).

Long-term studies of students' learning in the classroom with instructional support and structured experiences over months and years reveal children's potential to engage in sophisticated investigations given the appropriate experiences (Metz, 2004; Lehrer and Schauble, 2005). For example, in one classroom-based study, second and fourth and fifth graders took part in a curriculum unit on animal behavior that emphasized domain knowledge, whole-class collaboration, scaffolded instruction, and discussions about the kinds of questions that can and cannot be answered by observational records (Metz, 2004). Pairs or triads of students then developed a research question, designed an experiment, collected and analyzed data, and presented their findings on a research poster. Such studies have demonstrated that, with appropriate support, students in grades K-8 and students from a variety of socioeconomic, cultural, and linguistic backgrounds can be successful in generating and evaluating scientific evidence and explanations (Kuhn and Dean, 2005; Lehrer and Schauble, 2005; Metz, 2004; Warren, Rosebery, and Conant, 1994).

KNOWLEDGE AND SKILL IN MODELING

The picture that emerges from developmental and cognitive research on scientific thinking is one of a complex intertwining of knowledge of the natural world, general reasoning processes, and an understanding of how scientific knowledge is generated and evaluated. Science and scientific thinking are not only about logical thinking or conducting carefully controlled experiments. Instead, building knowledge in science is a complex process of building and testing models and theories, in which knowledge of the natural world and strategies for generating and evaluating evidence are closely intertwined. Working from this image of science, a few researchers have begun to investigate the development of children's knowledge and skills in modeling.

The kinds of models that scientists construct vary widely, both within and across disciplines. Nevertheless, the rhetoric and practice of science are governed by efforts to invent, revise, and contest models. By modeling, we refer to the construction and test of representations that serve as analogues to systems in the real world (Lehrer and Schauble, 2006). These representations can be of many forms, including physical models, computer programs, mathematical equations, or propositions. Objects and relations in the model are interpreted as representing theoretically important objects and relations in the represented world. Models are useful in summarizing known features and predicting outcomes—that is, they can become elements of or representations of theories. A key hurdle for students is to understand that models are not copies; they are deliberate simplifications. Error is a component of all models, and the precision required of a model depends on the purpose for its current use.

The forms of thinking required for modeling do not progress very far without explicit instruction and fostering (Lehrer and Schauble, 2000). For this reason, studies of modeling have most often taken place in classrooms over sustained periods of time, often years. These studies provide a provocative picture of the sophisticated scientific thinking that can be supported in classrooms if students are provided with the right kinds of experiences over extended periods of time. The instructional approaches used in studies of students' modeling, as well as the approach to curriculum that may be required to support the development of modeling skills over multiple years of schooling, are discussed in the chapters in Part III.

Lehrer and Schauble (2000, 2003, 2006) reported observing characteristic shifts in the understanding of modeling over the span of the elementary school grades, from an early emphasis on literal depictional forms, to representations that are progressively more symbolic and mathematically powerful. Diversity in representational and mathematical resources both accompanied and produced conceptual change. As children developed and used new mathematical means for characterizing growth, they understood biological change in increasingly dynamic ways. For example, once students understood the mathematics of ratio and changing ratios, they began to conceive of growth not as simple linear increase, but as a patterned rate of change. These transitions in conception and representation appeared to support each other, and they opened up new lines of inquiry. Children wondered whether plant growth was like animal growth, and whether the growth of yeast and bacteria on a Petri dish would show a pattern like the growth of a single plant. These forms of conceptual development required a context in which teachers systematically supported a restricted set of central ideas, building successively on earlier concepts over the grades of schooling.

Representational Systems That Support Modeling

The development of specific representational forms and notations, such as graphs, tables, computer programs, and mathematical expressions, is a critical part of engaging in mature forms of modeling. Mathematics, data and scale models, diagrams, and maps are particularly important for supporting science learning in grades K-8.

Mathematics

Mathematics and science are, of course, separate disciplines. Nevertheless, for the past 200 years, the steady press in science has been toward increasing quantification, visualization, and precision (Kline, 1980). Mathematics in all its forms is a symbol system that is fundamental to both expressing and understanding science. Often, expressing an idea mathematically results in noticing new patterns or relationships that otherwise would not be grasped. For example, elementary students studying the growth of organisms (plants, tobacco hornworms, populations of bacteria) noted that when they graphed changes in heights over the life span, all the organisms studied produced an emergent S-shaped curve. However, such seeing depended on developing a "disciplined perception" (Stevens and Hall, 1998), a firm grounding in a Cartesian system. Moreover, the shape of the curve was determined in light of variation, accounted for by selecting and connecting midpoints of intervals that defined piece-wise linear segments. This way of representing typical growth was contentious, because some midpoints did not correspond to any particular case value. This debate was therefore a pathway toward the idealization and imagined qualities of the world necessary for adopting a modeling stance. The form of the growth curve was eventually tested in other systems, and its replications inspired new questions. For example, why would bacteria populations and plants be describable by the same growth curve? In this case and in others, explanatory models and data models mutually bootstrapped conceptual development (Lehrer and Schauble, 2002).

It is not feasible in this report to summarize the extensive body of research in mathematics education, but one point is especially critical for science education: the need to expand elementary school mathematics beyond arithmetic to include space and geometry, measurement, and data/uncertainty. The National Council of Teachers of Mathematics standards (2000) has strongly supported this extension of early mathematics, based on their judgment that arithmetic alone does not constitute a sufficient mathematics education. Moreover, if mathematics is to be used as a resource for science, the resource base widens considerably with a broader mathematical base, affording students a greater repertoire for making sense of the natural world.

For example, consider the role of geometry and visualization in comparing crystalline structures or evaluating the relationship between the body weights and body structures of different animals. Measurement is a ubiquitous part of the scientific enterprise, although its subtleties are almost always overlooked. Students are usually taught procedures for measuring but are rarely taught a theory of measure. Educators often overestimate children's understanding of measurement because measuring tools—like rulers or scales—resolve many of the conceptual challenges of measurement for children, so that they may fail to grasp the idea that measurement entails the iteration of constant units, and that these units can be partitioned. It is reasonably common, for example, for even upper elementary students who seem proficient at measuring lengths with rulers to tacitly hold the theory that measuring merely entails the counting of units between boundaries. If these students are given unconnected units (say, tiles of a constant length) and asked to demonstrate how to measure a length, some of them almost always place the units against the object being measured in such a way that the first and last tile are lined up flush with the end of the object measured. This arrangement often requires leaving spaces between units. Diagnostically, these spaces do not trouble a student who holds this "boundary-filling" conception of measurement (Lehrer, 2003; McClain et al., 1999).

Data

Researchers agree that scientific thinking entails the coordination of theory with evidence (Klahr and Dunbar, 1988; Kuhn, Amsel, and O'Loughlin, 1988), but there are many ways in which evidence may vary in both form and complexity. Achieving this coordination therefore requires tools for structuring and interpreting data and error. Otherwise, students' interpretation of evidence cannot be accountable. There have been many studies of students' reasoning about data, variation, and uncertainty, conducted both by psychologists (Kahneman, Solvic, and Tversky, 1982; Konold, 1989; Nisbett et al., 1983) and by educators (Mokros and Russell, 1995; Pollatsek, Lima, and Well, 1981; Strauss and Bichler, 1988). Particularly pertinent here are studies that focus on data modeling (Lehrer and Romberg, 1996), that is, how reasoning with data is recruited as a way of investigating genuine questions about the world.

Data modeling is, in fact, what professionals do when they reason with data and statistics. It is central to a variety of enterprises, including engineering, medicine, and natural science. Scientific models are generated with acute awareness of their entailments for data, and data are recorded and structured as a way of making progress in articulating a scientific model or adjudicating among rival models. The tight relationship between model and data holds generally in domains in which inquiry is conducted by inscribing, representing, and mathematizing key aspects of the world (Goodwin, 2000; Kline, 1980; Latour, 1990).

Understanding the qualities and meaning of data may be enhanced if students spend as much attention on its generation as on its analysis. First and foremost, students need to grasp the notion that data are constructed to answer questions (Lehrer, Giles, and Schauble, 2002). The National Council of Teachers of Mathematics (2000) emphasizes that the study of data should be firmly anchored in students' inquiry, so that they "address what is involved in gathering and using the data wisely" (p. 48). Questions motivate the collection of certain types of information and not others, and many aspects of data coding and structuring also depend on the question that motivated their collection. Defining the variables involved in addressing a research question, considering the methods and timing to collect data, and finding efficient ways to record it are all involved in the initial phases of data modeling. Debates about the meaning of an attribute often provoke questions that are more precise.

For example, a group of first graders who wanted to learn which student's pumpkin was the largest eventually understood that they needed to agree whether they were interested in the heights of the pumpkins, their circumferences, or their weights (Lehrer et al., 2001). Deciding what to measure is bound up with deciding how to measure. As the students went on to count the seeds in their pumpkins (they were pursuing a question about whether there might be relationship between pumpkin size and number of seeds), they had to make decisions about whether they would include seeds that were not full grown and what criteria would be used to decide whether any particular seed should be considered mature.

Data are inherently a form of abstraction: an event is replaced by a video recording, a sensation of heat is replaced by a pointer reading on a thermometer, and so on. Here again, the tacit complexity of tools may need to be explained. Students often have a fragile grasp of the relationship between the event of interest and the operation (hence, the output) of a tool, whether that tool is a microscope, a pan balance, or a "simple" ruler. Some students, for example, do not initially consider measurement to be a form of comparison and may find a balance a very confusing tool. In their mind, the number displayed on a scale *is* the weight of the object. If no number is displayed, weight cannot be found.

Once the data are recorded, making sense of them requires that they be structured. At this point, students sometimes discover that their data require further abstraction. For example, as they categorized features of self-portraits drawn by other students, a group of fourth graders realized that it would not be wise to follow their original plan of creating 23 categories of "eye type" for the 25 portraits that they wished to categorize (DiPerna, 2002). Data do not come with an inherent structure; rather, structure must be imposed (Lehrer, Giles, and Schauble, 2002). The only structure for a set of data comes from the inquirers' prior and developing understanding of the phenomenon under investigation. He imposes structure by selecting categories around which to describe and organize the data.

Students also need to mentally back away from the objects or events under study to attend to the data as objects in their own right, by counting them, manipulating them to discover relationships, and asking new questions of already collected data. Students often believe that new questions can be addressed only with new data; they rarely think of querying existing data sets to explore questions that were not initially conceived when the data were collected (Lehrer and Romberg, 1996).

Finally, data are represented in various ways in order to see or understand general trends. Different kinds of displays highlight certain aspects of the data and hide others. An important educational agenda for students, one that extends over several years, is to come to understand the conventions and properties of different kinds of data displays. We do not review here the extensive literature on students' understanding of different kinds of representational displays (tables, graphs of various kinds, distributions), but, for purposes of science, students should not only understand the procedures for generating and reading displays, but they should also be able to critique them and to grasp the communicative advantages and disadvantages of alternative forms for a given purpose (diSessa, 2004; Greeno and Hall, 1997). The structure of the data will affect the interpretation. Data interpretation often entails seeking and confirming relationships in the data, which may be at varying levels of complexity. For example, simple linear relationships are easier to spot than inverse relationships or interactions (Schauble, 1990), and students often fail to entertain the possibility that more than one relationship may be operating.

The desire to interpret data may further inspire the creation of statistics, such as measures of center and spread. These measures are a further step of abstraction beyond the objects and events originally observed. Even primary grade students can learn to consider the overall shape of data displays to make interpretations based on the "clumps" and "holes" in the data. Students often employ multiple criteria when trying to identify a "typical value" for a set of data. Many young students tend to favor the mode and justify their choice on the basis of repetition—if more than one student obtained this value, perhaps it is to be trusted. However, students tend to be less satisfied with modes if they do not appear near the center of the data, and they also shy away from measures of center that do not have several other values clustered near them ("part of a clump"). Understanding the mean requires an understanding of ratio, and if students are merely taught to "average" data in a procedural way without having a well-developed sense of ratio, their performance notoriously tends to degrade into "average stew"— eccentric procedures for adding and dividing things that make no sense (Strauss and Bichler, 1988). With good instruction, middle and upper elementary students can simultaneously consider the center and the spread of the data. Students can also generate various forms of mathematical descriptions of error, especially in contexts of measurement, where they can readily grasp the relationships between their own participation in the act of measuring and the resulting variation in measures (Petrosino, Lehrer, and Schauble, 2003).

Scale Models, Diagrams, and Maps

Although data representations are central to science, they are not, of course, the only representations students need to use and understand. Perhaps the most easily interpretable form of representation widely used in science is scale models. Physical models of this kind are used in science education to make it possible for students to visualize objects or processes that are at a scale that makes their direct perception impossible or, alternatively, that permits them to directly manipulate something that otherwise they could not handle. The ease or difficulty with which students understand these models depends on the complexity of the relationships being communicated. Even preschoolers can understand scale models used to depict location in a room (DeLoache, 2004). Primary grade students can pretty readily overcome the influence of the appearance of the model to focus on and investigate the way it functions (Penner et al., 1997), but middle school students (and some adults) struggle to work out the positional relationships of the earth, the sun, and the moon, which involves not only reconciling different perspectives with respect to perspective and frame (what one sees standing on the earth, what one would see from a hypothetical point in space), but also visualizing how these perspectives would change over days and months (see, for example, the detailed curricular suggestions at the web site http://www.wcer.wisc.edu/ncisla/muse/).

Frequently, students are expected to read or produce diagrams, often integrating the information from the diagram with information from accompanying text (Hegarty and Just, 1993; Mayer, 1993). The comprehensibility of diagrams seems to be governed less by domain-general principles than by the specifics of the diagram and its viewer. Comprehensibility seems to vary with the complexity of what is portrayed, the particular diagrammatic details and features, and the prior knowledge of the user.

Diagrams can be difficult to understand for a host of reasons. Sometimes the desired information is missing in the first place; sometimes, features of the diagram unwittingly play into an incorrect preconception. For example, it has been suggested that the common student misconception that the earth is closer to the sun in the summer than in the winter may be due in part to the fact that two-dimensional representations of the three-dimensional orbit make it appear as if the foreshortened orbit is indeed closer to the sun at some points than at others.

Mayer (1993) proposes three common reasons why diagrams miscommunicate: some do not include explanatory information (they are illustrative or decorative rather than explanatory), some lack a causal chain, and some fail to map the explanation to a familiar or recognizable context. It is not clear that school students misperceive diagrams in ways that are fundamentally different from the perceptions of adults. There may be some diagrammatic conventions that are less familiar to children, and children may well have less knowledge about the phenomena being portrayed, but there is no reason to expect that adult novices would respond in fundamentally different ways. Although they have been studied for a much briefer period of time, the same is probably true of complex computer displays.

Finally, there is a growing developmental literature on students' understanding of maps. Maps can be particularly confusing because they preserve some analog qualities of the space being represented (e.g., relative position and distance) but also omit or alter features of the landscape in ways that require understanding of mapping conventions. Young children often initially confuse maps of the landscape with pictures of objects in the landscape. It is much easier for youngsters to represent objects than to represent large-scale space (which is the absence of or frame for objects). Students also may struggle with orientation, perspective (the traditional bird's eye view), and mathematical descriptions of space, such as polar coordinate representations (Lehrer and Pritchard, 2002; Liben and Downs, 1993).

CONCLUSIONS

There is a common thread throughout the observations of this chapter that has deep implications for what one expects from children in grades K-8 and how their science learning should be structured. In almost all cases, the studies converge to the position that the skills under study develop with age, but also that this development is significantly enhanced by prior knowledge, experience, and instruction.

One of the continuing themes evident from studies on the development of scientific thinking is that children are far more competent than first suspected, and likewise that adults are less so. Young children experiment, but their experimentation is generally not systematic, and their observations as well as their inferences may be flawed. The progression of ability is seen with age, but it is not uniform, either across individuals or for a given individual. There is variation across individuals at the same age, as well as variation within single individuals in the strategies they use. Any given individual uses a collection of strategies, some more valid than others. Discovering a valid strategy does not mean that an individual, whether a child or an adult, will use the strategy consistently across all contexts. As Schauble (1996, p. 118) noted:

> The complex and multifaceted nature of the skills involved in solving these problems, and the variability in performance, even among the adults, suggest that the developmental trajectory of the strategies and processes associated with scientific reasoning is likely to be a very long one, perhaps even lifelong. Previous research has established the existence of both early precursors and competencies . . . and errors and biases that persist regardless of maturation, training, and expertise.

One aspect of cognition that appears to be particularly important for supporting scientific thinking is awareness of one's own thinking. Children may be less aware of their own memory limitations and therefore may be unsystematic in recording plans, designs, and outcomes, and they may fail to consult such records. Self-awareness of the cognitive strategies available is also important in order to determine when and why to employ various strategies. Finally, awareness of the status of one's own knowledge, such as recognizing the distinctions between theory and evidence, is important for reasoning in the context of scientific investigations. This last aspect of cognition is discussed in detail in the next chapter.

Prior knowledge, particularly beliefs about causality and plausibility, shape the approach to investigations in multiple ways. These beliefs influence which hypotheses are tested, how experiments are designed, and how evidence is evaluated. Characteristics of prior knowledge, such as its type, strength, and relevance, are potential determinants of how new evidence is evaluated and whether anomalies are noticed. Knowledge change occurs as a result of the encounter.

Finally, we conclude that experience and instruction are crucial mediators of the development of a broad range of scientific skills and of the degree of sophistication that children exhibit in applying these skills in new contexts. This means that time spent doing science in appropriately structured instructional frames is a crucial part of science education. It affects not only the level of skills that children develop, but also their ability to think about the quality of evidence and to interpret evidence presented to them. Students need instructional support and practice in order to become better at coordinating their prior theories and the evidence generated in investigations. Instructional support is also critical for developing skills for experimental design, record keeping during investigations, dealing with anomalous data, and modeling.

REFERENCES

Ahn, W., Kalish, C.W., Medin, D.L., and Gelman, S.A. (1995). The role of covariation versus mechanism information in causal attribution. *Cognition, 54,* 299-352.

Amsel, E., and Brock, S. (1996). The development of evidence evaluation skills. *Cognitive Development, 11,* 523-550.

Bisanz, J., and LeFevre, J. (1990). Strategic and nonstrategic processing in the development of mathematical cognition. In. D. Bjorklund (Ed.), *Children's strategies: Contemporary views of cognitive development* (pp. 213-243). Hillsdale, NJ: Lawrence Erlbaum Associates.

Carey, S., Evans, R., Honda, M., Jay, E., and Unger, C. (1989). An experiment is when you try it and see if it works: A study of grade 7 students' understanding of the construction of scientific knowledge. *International Journal of Science Education, 11,* 514-529.

Chase, W.G., and Simon, H.A. (1973). The mind's eye in chess. In W.G. Chase (Ed.), *Visual information processing.* New York: Academic.

Chen, Z., and Klahr, D. (1999). All other things being equal: Children's acquisition of the control of variables strategy. *Child Development, 70,* 1098-1120.

Chi, M.T.H. (1996). Constructing self-explanations and scaffolded explanations in tutoring. *Applied Cognitive Psychology, 10,* 33-49.

Chi, M.T.H., de Leeuw, N., Chiu, M., and Lavancher, C. (1994). Eliciting self-explanations improves understanding. *Cognitive Science, 18,* 439-477.

Chinn, C.A., and Brewer, W.F. (1998). An empirical test of a taxonomy of responses to anomalous data in science. *Journal of Research in Science Teaching, 35,* 623-654.

Chinn, C.A., and Brewer, W. (2001). Model of data: A theory of how people evaluate data. *Cognition and Instruction, 19*(3), 323-343.

Chinn, C.A., and Malhotra, B.A. (2001). Epistemologically authentic scientific reasoning. In K. Crowley, C.D. Schunn, and T. Okada (Eds.), *Designing for science: Implications from everyday, classroom, and professional settings* (pp. 351-392). Mahwah, NJ: Lawrence Erlbaum Associates.

Chinn, C.A., and Malhotra, B.A. (2002). Children's responses to anomalous scientific data: How is conceptual change impeded? *Journal of Educational Psychology, 94,* 327-343.

DeLoache, J.S. (2004). Becoming symbol-minded. *Trends in Cognitive Sciences, 8,* 66-70.

DiPerna, E. (2002). Data models of ourselves: Body self-portrait project. In R. Lehrer and L. Schauble (Eds.), *Investigating real data in the classroom: Expanding children's understanding of math and science. Ways of knowing in science and mathematics series.* Willington, VT: Teachers College Press.

diSessa, A.A. (2004). Metarepresentation: Native competence and targets for instruction. *Cognition and Instruction, 22*(3), 293-331.

Dunbar, K., and Klahr, D. (1989). Developmental differences in scientific discovery strategies. In D. Klahr and K. Kotovsky (Eds.), *Complex information processing: The impact of Herbert A. Simon* (pp. 109-143). Hillsdale, NJ: Lawrence Erlbaum Associates.

Echevarria, M. (2003). Anomalies as a catalyst for middle school students' knowledge construction and scientific reasoning during science inquiry. *Journal of Educational Psychology, 95,* 357-374.

Garcia-Mila, M., and Andersen, C. (2005). Developmental change in notetaking during scientific inquiry. Manuscript submitted for publication.

Gleason, M.E., and Schauble, L. (2000). Parents' assistance of their children's scientific reasoning. *Cognition and Instruction, 17*(4), 343-378.

Goodwin, C. (2000). Introduction: Vision and inscription in practice. *Mind, Culture, and Activity, 7,* 1-3.

Greeno, J., and Hall, R. (1997). Practicing representation: Learning with and about representational forms. *Phi Delta Kappan,* January, 361-367.

Hausmann, R., and Chi, M. (2002) Can a computer interface support self-explaining? *The International Journal of Cognitive Technology, 7*(1).

Hegarty, M., and Just, A. (1993). Constructing mental models of machines from text and diagrams. *Journal of Memory and Language, 32,* 717-742.

Inhelder, B., and Piaget, J. (1958). *The growth of logical thinking from childhood to adolescence.* New York: Basic Books.

Kahneman, D., Slovic, P, and Tversky, A. (1982). *Judgment under uncertainty: Heuristics and biases.* New York: Cambridge University Press.

Kanari, Z., and Millar, R. (2004). Reasoning from data: How students collect and interpret data in science investigations. *Journal of Research in Science Teaching, 41*, 17.

Keselman, A. (2003). Supporting inquiry learning by promoting normative understanding of multivariable causality. *Journal of Research in Science Teaching, 40*, 898-921.

Keys, C.W. (1994). The development of scientific reasoning skills in conjunction with collaborative writing assignments: An interpretive study of six ninth-grade students. *Journal of Research in Science Teaching, 31*, 1003-1022.

Klaczynski, P.A. (2000). Motivated scientific reasoning biases, epistemological beliefs, and theory polarization: A two-process approach to adolescent cognition. *Child Development, 71*(5), 1347-1366.

Klaczynski, P.A., and Narasimham, G. (1998). Development of scientific reasoning biases: Cognitive versus ego-protective explanations. *Developmental Psychology, 34*(1), 175-187.

Klahr, D. (2000). *Exploring science: The cognition and development of discovery processes.* Cambridge, MA: MIT Press.

Klahr, D., and Carver, S.M. (1995). Scientific thinking about scientific thinking. *Monographs of the Society for Research in Child Development, 60*, 137-151.

Klahr, D., Chen, Z., and Toth, E.E. (2001). From cognition to instruction to cognition: A case study in elementary school science instruction. In K. Crowley, C.D. Schunn, and T. Okada (Eds.), *Designing for science: Implications from everyday, classroom, and professional settings* (pp. 209-250). Mahwah, NJ: Lawrence Erlbaum Associates.

Klahr, D., and Dunbar, K. (1988). Dual search space during scientific reasoning. *Cognitive Science, 12*, 1-48.

Klahr, D., Fay, A., and Dunbar, K. (1993). Heuristics for scientific experimentation: A developmental study. *Cognitive Psychology, 25*, 111-146.

Klahr, D., and Nigam, M. (2004). The equivalence of learning paths in early science instruction: Effects of direct instruction and discovery learning. *Psychological Science, 15*(10), 661-667.

Klahr, D., and Robinson, M. (1981). Formal assessment of problem solving and planning processes in preschool children. *Cognitive Psychology, 13*, 113-148.

Klayman, J., and Ha, Y. (1989). Hypothesis testing in rule discovery: Strategy, structure, and content. *Journal of Experimental Psychology: Learning, Memory, and Cognition, 15*(4), 596-604.

Kline, M. (1980). *Mathematics: The loss of certainty.* New York: Oxford University Press.

Konold, C. (1989). Informal conceptions of probability. *Cognition and Instruction, 6*, 59-98.

Koslowski, B. (1996). *Theory and evidence: The development of scientific reasoning.* Cambridge, MA: MIT Press.

Koslowski, B., and Okagaki, L. (1986). Non-human indices of causation in problem-solving situations: Causal mechanisms, analogous effects, and the status of rival alternative accounts. *Child Development, 57*, 1100-1108.

Koslowski, B., Okagaki, L., Lorenz, C., and Umbach, D. (1989). When covariation is not enough: The role of causal mechanism, sampling method, and sample size in causal reasoning. *Child Development, 60,* 1316-1327.

Kuhn, D. (1989). Children and adults as intuitive scientists. *Psychological Review, 96,* 674-689.

Kuhn, D. (2001). How do people know? *Psychological Science, 12,* 1-8.

Kuhn, D. (2002). What is scientific thinking and how does it develop? In U. Goswami (Ed.), *Blackwell handbook of childhood cognitive development* (pp. 371-393). Oxford, England: Blackwell.

Kuhn, D., Amsel, E., and O'Loughlin, M. (1988). *The development of scientific thinking skills.* Orlando, FL: Academic Press.

Kuhn, D., and Dean, D. (2005). Is developing scientific thinking all about learning to control variables? *Psychological Science, 16*(11), 886-870.

Kuhn, D., and Franklin, S. (2006). The second decade: What develops (and how)? In W. Damon, R.M. Lerner, D. Kuhn, and R.S. Siegler (Eds.), *Handbook of child psychology, volume 2, cognition, peception, and language, 6th edition* (pp. 954-994). Hoboken, NJ: Wiley.

Kuhn, D., Garcia-Mila, M., Zohar, A., and Andersen, C. (1995). Strategies of knowledge acquisition. *Monographs of the Society for Research in Child Development, Serial No. 245*(60), 4.

Kuhn, D., and Pearsall, S. (1998). Relations between metastrategic knowledge and strategic performance. *Cognitive Development, 13,* 227-247.

Kuhn, D., and Pearsall, S. (2000). Developmental origins of scientific thinking. *Journal of Cognition and Development, 1,* 113-129.

Kuhn, D., and Phelps, E. (1982). The development of problem-solving strategies. In H. Reese (Ed.), *Advances in child development and behavior* (vol. 17, pp. 1-44). New York: Academic Press.

Kuhn, D., Schauble, L., and Garcia-Mila, M. (1992). Cross-domain development of scientific reasoning. *Cognition and Instruction, 9,* 285-327.

Kunda, Z. (1990). The case for motivated reasoning. *Psychological Bulletin, 108,* 480-498.

Larkin, J.H., McDermott, J., Simon, D.P, and Simon, H.A. (1980). Expert and novice performance in solving physics problems. *Science, 208,* 1335-1342.

Latour, B. (1990). Drawing things together. In M. Lynch and S. Woolgar (Eds.), *Representation in scientific practice* (pp. 19-68). Cambridge, MA: MIT Press.

Lehrer, R. (2003). Developing understanding of measurement. In J. Kilpatrick, W.G. Martin, and D.E. Schifter (Eds.), *A research companion to principles and standards for school mathematics* (pp. 179-192). Reston, VA: National Council of Teachers of Mathematics.

Lehrer, R., Giles, N., and Schauble, L. (2002). Data modeling. In R. Lehrer and L. Schauble (Eds.), *Investigating real data in the classroom: Expanding children's understanding of math and science* (pp. 1-26). New York: Teachers College Press.

Lehrer, R., and Pritchard, C. (2002). Symbolizing space into being. In K. Gravemeijer, R. Lehrer, B. van Oers, and L. Verschaffel (Eds.), *Symbolization, modeling and tool use in mathematics education* (pp. 59-86). Dordrecht, The Netherlands: Kluwer Academic.

Lehrer, R., and Romberg, T. (1996). Exploring children's data modeling. *Cognition and Instruction, 14*, 69-108.

Lehrer, R., and Schauble, L. (2000). The development of model-based reasoning. *Journal of Applied Developmental Psychology, 21*(1), 39-48.

Lehrer, R., and Schauble, L. (2002). Symbolic communication in mathematics and science: Co-constituting inscription and thought. In E.D. Amsel and J. Byrnes (Eds.), *Language, literacy, and cognitive development: The development and consequences of symbolic communication* (pp. 167-192). Mahwah, NJ: Lawrence Erlbaum Associates.

Lehrer, R., and Schauble, L. (2003). Origins and evolution of model-based reasoning in mathematics and science. In R. Lesh and H.M. Doerr (Eds.), *Beyond constructivism: A models and modeling perspective on mathematics problem-solving, learning, and teaching* (pp. 59-70). Mahwah, NJ: Lawrence Erlbaum Associates.

Lehrer, R., and Schauble, L., (2005). Developing modeling and argument in the elementary grades. In T.A. Rombert, T.P. Carpenter, and F. Dremock (Eds.), *Understanding mathematics and science matters* (Part II: Learning with understanding). Mahwah, NJ: Lawrence Erlbaum Associates.

Lehrer, R., and Schauble, L. (2006). Scientific thinking and science literacy. In W. Damon, R. Lerner, K.A. Renninger, and I.E. Sigel (Eds.), *Handbook of child psychology, 6th edition* (vol. 4). Hoboken, NJ: Wiley.

Lehrer, R., Schauble, L., Strom, D., and Pligge, M. (2001). Similarity of form and substance: Modeling material kind. In D. Klahr and S. Carver (Eds.), *Cognition and instruction: 25 years of progress* (pp. 39-74). Mahwah, NJ: Lawrence Erlbaum Associates.

Liben, L.S., and Downs, R.M. (1993). Understanding per son-space-map relations: Cartographic and developmental perspectives. *Developmental Psychology, 29*, 739-752.

Linn, M.C. (1978). Influence of cognitive style and training on tasks requiring the separation of variables schema. *Child Development, 49*, 874-877.

Linn, M.C. (1980). Teaching students to control variables: Some investigations using free choice experiences. In S. Modgil and C. Modgil (Eds.), *Toward a theory of psychological development within the Piagettian framework*. Windsor Berkshire, England: National Foundation for Educational Research.

Linn, M.C., Chen, B., and Thier, H.S. (1977). Teaching children to control variables: Investigations of a free choice environment. *Journal of Research in Science Teaching, 14*, 249-255.

Linn, M.C., and Levine, D.I. (1978). Adolescent reasoning: Influence of question format and type of variables on ability to control variables. *Science Education, 62*(3), 377-388.

Lovett, M.C., and Anderson, J.R. (1995). Making heads or tails out of selecting problem-solving strategies. In J.D. Moore and J.F. Lehman (Eds.), *Proceedings of the seventieth annual conference of the Cognitive Science Society* (pp. 265-270). Hillsdale, NJ: Lawrence Erlbaum Associates.

Lovett, M.C., and Anderson, J.R. (1996). History of success and current context in problem solving. *Cognitive Psychology, 31*(2), 168-217.

Masnick, A.M., and Klahr, D. (2003). Error matters: An initial exploration of elementary school children's understanding of experimental error. *Journal of Cognition and Development, 4,* 67-98.

Mayer, R. (1993). Illustrations that instruct. In R. Glaser (Ed.), *Advances in instructional psychology* (vol. 4, pp. 253-284). Hillsdale, NJ: Lawrence Erlbaum Associates.

McClain, K., Cobb, P., Gravemeijer, K., and Estes, B. (1999). Developing mathematical reasoning within the context of measurement. In L. Stiff (Ed.), *Developing mathematical reasoning, K-12* (pp. 93-106). Reston, VA: National Council of Teachers of Mathematics.

McNay, M., and Melville, K.W. (1993). Children's skill in making predictions and their understanding of what predicting means: A developmental study. *Journal of Research in Science Teaching, 30,* 561-577.

Metz, K.E. (2004). Children's understanding of scientific inquiry: Their conceptualization of uncertainty in investigations of their own design. *Cognition and Instruction, 22*(2), 219-290.

Mokros, J., and Russell, S. (1995). Children's concepts of average and representativeness. *Journal for Research in Mathematics Education, 26*(1), 20-39.

National Council of Teachers of Mathematics. (2000). *Principles and standards for school mathematics.* Reston, VA: Author.

Nisbett, R.E., Krantz, D.H., Jepson, C., and Kind, Z. (1983). The use of statistical heuristics in everyday inductive reasoning. *Psychological Review, 90,* 339-363.

Penner, D., Giles, N.D., Lehrer, R., and Schauble, L. (1997). Building functional models: Designing an elbow. *Journal of Research in Science Teaching, 34(2),* 125-143.

Penner, D.E., and Klahr, D. (1996a). The interaction of domain-specific knowledge and domain-general discovery strategies: A study with sinking objects. *Child Development, 67,* 2709-2727.

Penner, D.E., and Klahr, D. (1996b). When to trust the data: Further investigations of system error in a scientific reasoning task. *Memory and Cognition, 24,* 655-668.

Perfetti, CA. (1992). The representation problem in reading acquisition. In P.B. Gough, L.C. Ehri, and R. Treiman (Eds.), *Reading acquisition* (pp. 145-174). Hillsdale, NJ: Lawrence Erlbaum Associates.

Petrosino, A., Lehrer, R., and Schauble, L. (2003). Structuring error and experimental variation as distribution in the fourth grade. *Mathematical Thinking and Learning, 5*(2-3), 131-156.

Pollatsek, A., Lima, S., and Well, A.D. (1981). Concept or computation: Students' misconceptions of the mean. *Educational Studies in Mathematics, 12,* 191-204.

Ruffman, T., Perner, I., Olson, D.R., and Doherty, M. (1993). Reflecting on scientific thinking: Children's understanding of the hypothesis-evidence relation. *Child Development, 64*(6), 1617-1636.

Schauble, L. (1990). Belief revision in children: The role of prior knowledge and strategies for generating evidence. *Journal of Experimental Child Psychology, 49*(1), 31-57.

Schauble, L. (1996). The development of scientific reasoning in knowledge-rich contexts. *Developmental Psychology, 32*(1), 102-119.

Schauble, L., Glaser, R., Duschl, R., Schulze, S., and John, J. (1995). Students' understanding of the objectives and procedures of experimentation in the science classroom. *Journal of the Learning Sciences, 4*(2), 131-166.

Schauble, L., Glaser, R., Raghavan, K., and Reiner, M. (1991). Causal models and experimentation strategies in scientific reasoning. *Journal of the Learning Sciences, 1*(2), 201-238.

Schauble, L., Glaser, R., Raghavan, K., and Reiner, M. (1992). The integration of knowledge and experimentation strategies in understanding a physical system. *Applied Cognitive Psychology, 6,* 321-343.

Schauble, L., Klopfer, L.E., and Raghavan, K. (1991). Students' transition from an engineering model to a science model of experimentation. *Journal of Research in Science Teaching, 28*(9), 859-882.

Siegler, R.S. (1987). The perils of averaging data over strategies: An example from children's addition. *Journal of Experimental Psychology: General, 116,* 250-264.

Siegler, R.S., and Alibali, M.W. (2005). *Children's thinking* (4th ed.). Upper Saddle River, NJ: Prentice Hall.

Siegler, R.S., and Crowley, K. (1991). The microgenetic method: A direct means for studying cognitive development. *American Psychologist, 46,* 606-620.

Siegler, R.S., and Jenkins, E. (1989). *How children discover new strategies.* Hillsdale, NJ: Lawrence Erlbaum Associates.

Siegler, R.S., and Liebert, R.M. (1975). Acquisition of formal experiment. *Developmental Psychology, 11,* 401-412.

Siegler, R.S., and Shipley, C. (1995). Variation, selection, and cognitive change. In T. Simon and G. Halford (Eds.), *Developing cognitive competence: New approaches to process modeling* (pp. 31-76). Hillsdale, NJ: Lawrence Erlbaum Associates.

Simon, H.A. (1975). The functional equivalence of problem solving skills. *Cognitive Psychology, 7,* 268-288.

Simon, H.A. (2001). Learning to research about learning. In S.M. Carver and D. Klahr (Eds.), *Cognition and instruction: Twenty-five years of progress* (pp. 205-226). Mahwah, NJ: Lawrence Erlbaum Associates.

Slowiaczek, L.M., Klayman, J., Sherman, S.J., and Skov, R.B. (1992). Information selection and use in hypothesis testing: What is a good question, and what is a good answer. *Memory and Cognition, 20*(4), 392-405.

Sneider, C., Kurlich, K., Pulos, S., and Friedman, A. (1984). Learning to control variables with model rockets: A neo-Piagetian study of learning in field settings. *Science Education, 68*(4), 463-484.

Sodian, B., Zaitchik, D., and Carey, S. (1991). Young children's differentiation of hypothetical beliefs from evidence. *Child Development, 62*(4), 753-766.

Stevens, R., and Hall, R. (1998). Disciplined perception: Learning to see in technoscience. In M. Lampert and M.L. Blunk (Eds.), *Talking mathematics in school: Studies of teaching and learning* (pp. 107-149). Cambridge, MA: Cambridge University Press.

Strauss, S., and Bichler, E. (1988). The development of children's concepts of the arithmetic average. *Journal for Research in Mathematics Education, 19*(1), 64-80.

Thagard, P. (1998a). Ulcers and bacteria I: Discovery and acceptance. *Studies in History and Philosophy of Science. Part C: Studies in History and Philosophy of Biology and Biomedical Sciences, 29,* 107-136.

Thagard, P. (1998b). Ulcers and bacteria II: Instruments, experiments, and social interactions. *Studies in History and Philosophy of Science. Part C: Studies in History and Philosophy of Biology and Biomedical Sciences, 29*(2), 317-342.

Toth, E.E., Klahr, D., and Chen, Z. (2000). Bridging research and practice: A cognitively-based classroom intervention for teaching experimentation skills to elementary school children. *Cognition and Instruction, 18*(4), 423-459.

Trafton, J.G., and Trickett, S.B. (2001). Note-taking for self-explanation and problem solving. *Human-Computer Interaction, 16,* 1-38.

Triona, L., and Klahr, D. (in press). The development of children's abilities to produce external representations. In E. Teubal, J. Dockrell, and L. Tolchinsky (Eds.), *Notational knowledge: Developmental and historical perspectives.* Rotterdam, The Netherlands: Sense.

Varnhagen, C. (1995). Children's spelling strategies. In V. Berninger (Ed.), *The varieties of orthographic knowledge: Relationships to phonology, reading and writing* (vol. 2, pp. 251-290). Dordrecht, The Netherlands: Kluwer Academic.

Warren, B., Rosebery, A., and Conant, F. (1994). Discourse and social practice: Learning science in language minority classrooms. In D. Spencer (Ed.), *Adult biliteracy in the United States* (pp. 191-210). McHenry, IL: Delta Systems.

Wolpert, L. (1993). *The unnatural nature of science.* London, England: Faber and Faber.

Zachos, P., Hick, T.L., Doane, W.E.I., and Sargent, C. (2000). Setting theoretical and empirical foundations for assessing scientific inquiry and discovery in educational programs. *Journal of Research in Science Teaching, 37*(9), 938-962.

Zimmerman, C., Raghavan, K., and Sartoris, M.L. (2003). The impact of the MARS curriculum on students' ability to coordinate theory and evidence. *International Journal of Science Education, 25,* 1247-1271.

6

Understanding How Scientific Knowledge Is Constructed

Major Findings in the Chapter:

- *The research base on children's understanding of how scientific knowledge is constructed is limited. Most studies have been conducted in laboratory settings and do not take into account instructional history and children's opportunity to learn about this aspect of science.*
- *Most children do not develop a sophisticated understanding of how scientific knowledge is constructed.*
- *Methods of science dominate the school science curriculum, with little emphasis on the role of theory, explanation, or models.*
- *Children's understanding of science appears to be amenable to instruction. However, more research is needed that provides insight into the experiences and conditions that facilitate their understanding of science as a way of knowing.*

Science is not only a body of knowledge, but also a way of knowing. One important underpinning for learning science is students' understanding of the nature and structure of scientific knowledge and the process by which it is developed. Our vision of K-8 science features this understanding as one of the four strands. We have elevated this focus to the status of a strand for several reasons. We view understanding of the nature and structure of scientific knowledge and the process by which it is developed as a worthy end in and of itself. In addition, emerging research evidence suggests that students' grasp of scientific explanations of the natural world and their ability to engage successfully in scientific investigations are advanced when they understand how scientific knowledge is constructed. In this chapter we address how children come to understand both "how we know" in science and "why we believe" scientific evidence.

For more than a century, educators have argued that students should understand how scientific knowledge is constructed (Rudolph, 2005). One rationale that is often invoked, but not empirically tested, is that understanding science makes for a more informed citizenry and supports democratic participation. That is, citizens who understand how scientific knowledge is produced will be careful consumers of scientific claims about public scientific issues (e.g., global warming, ecology, genetically modified foods, alternative medicine) both at the ballot box and in their daily lives.

A second justification among educators is that understanding the structure and nature of science makes one better at doing and learning science (see review by Sandoval, 2005). That is, if students come to see science as a set of practices that builds models to account for patterns of evidence in the natural world, and that what counts as evidence is contingent on making careful observations and building arguments, then they will have greater success in their efforts to build knowledge. Viewing these processes from a distance—not merely enacting them—enhances students' ability to practice science. Schauble and colleagues (1995), for example, found that fifth grade students designed better experiments after instruction about the purpose of experimentation.

We begin the chapter with an elaboration on science as a way of knowing, sketching the goals of the enterprise, the nature and structure of scientific knowledge, and the process by which it is constructed. This elaboration is intended to provide a sense of the target we have for students' learning. That is, it represents currently accepted ideas about the nature of scientific knowledge that are important to teach in grades K-8.

Building on this model of science, we first turn to the cognitive research literatures to examine the intellectual resources relevant to this strand that children bring to kindergarten. In an earlier chapter (Chapter 3), we discussed the developmental research on children's early "theory of mind," that is, their growing awareness of their own and other's minds and their understanding of expertise. In this chapter, we first discuss how during the K-8 years, they build on these understandings to develop some initial epistemological ideas about what knowledge is and how it is constructed. Next, we consider how they begin to think about what scientific knowledge is and how it is constructed. In the field of science education, this research is often found under the general heading of students' understanding of the nature of science. Finally, we consider external influences on students' understanding of science as a way of knowing, including teacher knowledge, the epistemic model that may underlie the curriculum, and the literature—albeit extremely small—that has been focused on classroom-based interventions in epistemic advancements.

Before delving into this research, one major caveat is in order. Almost all of the research investigating children's thinking relevant to this strand has been conducted in the research laboratory, examining how their thinking develops over time irrespective of instructional history or opportunities to learn. It allows us to point to developmental trends and base-level competencies that can be expected in a given age span in normally developing children. However, inferences from this research base about the upper limits of children's capability are inappropriate and are likely to yield underestimates. Furthermore, as almost all of this research attends to development and not opportunities to learn, it provides little insight into the kinds of experiences and conditions that facilitate children's understanding of science and thinking about their own knowledge. A few studies have begun to explore the effects of teaching approaches on the development of epistemological understanding. We offer a limited discussion of this literature here. Later, in Chapters 6 and 9, we discuss in more depth studies that provide insight as to supportive classroom conditions and provide better proxies for what is possible when those conditions exist.

UNDERLYING MODEL OF THE NATURE AND DEVELOPMENT OF SCIENTIFIC KNOWLEDGE

Before considering the research that may elucidate the intellectual resources and challenges that learning this strand might pose to children in the K-8 years, we briefly review approaches the field has taken to articulate the underlying model of building scientific knowledge. In this explication, we consider the goals of the enterprise, the nature and structure of scientific knowledge, and how knowledge is developed, with a focus on what is most relevant for student learning. (For a more complete discussion of our view of the nature of science, see Chapter 2.) While we acknowledge there is no simple correspondence with this model of science and the epistemic goals of the curriculum at any particular grade level, consideration of both relevant cognitive research and instructional design is informed by close consideration of the normative model.

Osborne and colleagues (2003) have proposed taking a consensus view to identify the ideas about science that should be part of the school science curriculum. They conducted a study to examine the opinions of scientists, science educators, individuals involved in promoting the public understanding of science, and philosophers, historians, and sociologists of science. They identified nine themes encapsulating key ideas about the nature of science that were considered to be an essential component of school science curriculum. These included science and certainty, analysis and interpretation of data, scientific method and critical testing, hypothesis and prediction, creativity/science and questioning, cooperation and collaboration in the development of scientific knowledge, science and technology, historical development of scientific knowledge, and diversity of scientific thinking.

Sandoval reviewed Osborne and others' definitions of science epistemology (e.g., Driver et al., 1996; Lederman et al., 2002; McComas and Olson, 1998) and presented a more manageable list of four broad epistemological themes, which we pause to discuss briefly. First, Sandoval asserts that viewing scientific knowledge as constructed is of primary importance that underscores a dialectical relationship between theory and evidence. Students, if they are to understand what science is, must accept that it is something that people do and create. From this flows the implication that science involves creativity and that science is not science because it is "true" but because it is persuasive.

The second theme is that scientific methods are diverse: there is no single "method" which generically applies to all scientific inquiries (experiments may be conducted in some fields, but not in others). Rather than relying on one or several rote methods, science depends on ways of evaluating scientific claims (e.g., with respect to systematicity, care, and fit with existing knowledge).

Third, scientific knowledge comes in different forms, which vary in their explanatory and predictive power (e.g., theories, laws, hypotheses; for more on this, see Chapter 2). This is a theme often overlooked in traditional analyses (including Osborne's) but one that is central to understanding the constructive nature of science and the interaction of different knowledge forms in inquiry. Fourth, Sandoval asserts that scientific knowledge varies in certainty. Acknowledging variable certainty, Sandoval argues, invites students to engage the ideas critically and to evaluate them using epistemological criteria.

Another approach to defining the aspects of understanding the epistemology of science that science curriculum should inhere is to consider the aspects of epistemology that have been linked to enhancing the development of science understanding. Although the literature does not offer a systematic treatment of this notion, there are pockets of evidence that suggest a relationship between aspects of epistemology and students' understanding and use of scientific knowledge.

For example, there is evidence that when students come to view argumentation as a central feature of science, this can have considerable positive effects on their understanding and use of investigative strategies (see, e.g., Sandoval and Reiser, 2004; Toth, Suthers, and Lesgold, 2002). Songer and Linn (1991) have also analyzed the effects of a dynamic versus a static view of science and found that a dynamic view is conducive to knowledge integration. Hammer (1994) has identified a relationship between views of knowledge (in terms of coherence, authoritativeness, and degree to which knowledge is constructed) and achievement differences in science among undergraduate physics students.

In addition, there is also evidence that students' epistemology of models—an aspect of epistemology that receives little attention in the normative and consensus views of the nature of science—has important implications for a range of conceptual and practical outcomes. Gobert and colleagues have studied the epistemology of models of students in the middle grades, high school, and college, including their understanding of models as representations of causal or explanatory ideas, that there can be multiple models of the same thing, that models do not need to be exactly like the thing modeled, and that models can be revised or changed in light of new data. They have documented correlations between measures of students' sophistication in the epistemology of models and their ability to draw inferences from texts and transfer causal knowledge to new domains, as well as conceptual development (Gobert and Discenna, 1997; Gobert and Pallant, 2001).

Similarly, Schwartz and White (2005) studied seventh grade student learning using a software environment that allowed the students to design, test, and revise models. They examined a battery of pre- and postmeasures of physics content knowledge, inquiry, and knowledge of modeling. They found that students' pretest modeling knowledge was the only variable that was a significant predictor of success for all three posttest measures, and it was the best predictor of both posttest content and modeling knowledge. While these studies examine but a few slices of epistemology, they suggest that certain features of epistemological understanding can offer students powerful leverage for science learning. These studies also suggest an important way to think about defining what students should learn about epistemology and the nature of science and call attention to an area worthy of future study.

UNDERSTANDING SCIENCE AND KNOWLEDGE IN THE K-8 YEARS

In this section, we separate the research literature into that concerned with the development of children's understanding of knowledge in general and that more specifically concerned with the development of their understanding of scientific knowledge. Changes across the K-8 grades reflect increasing variability in students' opportunities to learn about knowledge construction in science and increasing variability in their understanding of science as a way of knowing. Also contributing to the complexity of this picture, multiple literatures with fundamentally different methodological tactics and analytical lenses have contributed contrasting models of the limitations and emerging competences of K-8 students.

Understanding Knowledge Construction

There are multiple lines of research, largely disjointed, that are relevant to K-8 students' understanding of knowledge construction. This research encompasses both a continuation of the developmental research literature and the "epistemic cognition" literature investigating stages in older students' stances toward knowledge and knowing.

One line of research in the developmental literature involves a continuation of the theory of mind frame into the elementary school years. There is evidence that 6-year-olds (in limited contexts) are beginning to develop a view of mind as an "active interpreter." That is, they become more aware that people actively construct their own understanding of the world and are aware of the role of prior knowledge in seeing. At the same time, the literature suggests, children continue to elaborate on their understanding of mind (and different mental states) throughout elementary school.

Young children's understanding of the constructive nature of knowledge itself has not been studied extensively, but the limited research suggests that upper elementary school students tend to fall short of viewing knowledge as rooted in a theoretical world view. Kuhn and Leadbeater (1988), for example, fictionalized two conflicting historical accounts of the "Livian Wars." They asked students to interpret the accounts in response to a variety of probe questions that they were asked after reading the two accounts. Students were asked to articulate differences between the accounts, consider reasons for the differences, and discuss whether both accounts could be correct. They were scored in terms of epistemological level, from treating the two pieces as factual accounts that might differ only in specific facts reported, to understanding that they reflect contrasting interpretations, filtered through world views. They found that no sixth graders responded in terms of the higher levels.

The work of Perry (1970/1999), consisting of longitudinal studies of Harvard male undergraduates, constitutes an early and influential line of research on stages in understanding knowledge construction. Researchers have made substantial methodological and conceptual advances since Perry's time (see the discussion of instructional intervention studies in the next section). However, work that continues in the tradition of Perry maintains his general findings that, over the early to late adolescent years, individuals display shifts in their general stance toward knowledge and knowing. Specifically, many young people enter early adolescence embracing an "absolutist" or dualist view of knowledge and truth, one that assumes that there is one right answer to every question and differences of opinion are explainable by misinformation or faulty reasoning. At some point, usually during adolescence, youngsters become aware that others may disagree with them on matters about which they hold strong beliefs.

As these young people begin to understand that knowing necessarily involves interpretation and its consequent ambiguities, they may enter an epistemological crisis, characterized by what Chandler, Boyes, and Ball (1990) called "epistemic doubt." In this state, they struggle with the erosion of their certainty and may lose confidence altogether that it is possible to be certain about anything. The temporary result may be subjective relativism, a stance epitomized in the quintessential adolescent remark, "Whatever." Subjective relativism is the notion that as all beliefs are subjectively held, it is impossible to verify any of them with certainty, so no one's beliefs or opinions are better or worse than those of anyone else.

This relativism is regarded as an early reaction to the recognition that knowledge is conjectural and uncertain, open to and requiring interpretation. In later adolescence or early adulthood, some individuals may pass through relativism to embrace a contextualist commitment to reasoned judgment, although this move is by no means typical or inevitable. The individual continues to understand that knowledge is neither certain nor complete but comes nevertheless to accept that, with good judgment and careful reason, it is possible over time to achieve successively closer approximations of the truth.

Much of this research has been performed with college undergraduates, and the homogeneity of the participants may in part account for the degree of general agreement in the findings about the overall nature of change. However, different models propose different numbers of sublevels along the way. Moreover, there are some disagreements about the extent to which change is regarded as universal or not, the ages at which shifts typically occur, and also the extent to which it is regarded as stage-like and structurally integrated, or composed of a series of relatively independent beliefs about knowledge and learning. Some accounts emphasize change that is primarily linear and hierarchical, whereas others propose that change is merely adaptation to one's immediate or global environment and thus may not be unidirectional.

Most of the models appear to assume that epistemology is trait-like, so that it is a relatively stable feature of the individual. However, a few (e.g., Hammer and Elby, 2002; Sandoval, 2005) argue that epistemology is situational, an interaction of the individual's cognitive and historical resources and environmental features that cue or elicit patterns of those resources.

At first glance, some of these ideas appear to be inconsistent with research that suggests that much earlier—indeed, by the time they begin elementary school—children already are well aware that individuals can hold different beliefs about the same objects and events. Beliefs are not simply copies of reality; they are products of the activity of knowing—therefore, they are subject to verification and are potentially disconfirmable by evidence (Perner, 1991). If young elementary schoolchildren understand these concepts, how can adolescents be deemed to hold an "absolutist" position toward knowledge? Chandler, Hallett, and Sokol (2002) suggest that, although young children are aware of representational diversity, this does not mean that they consider it a necessary or legitimate aspect of knowledge. Instead, they are more likely to believe that there is one right answer and that other interpretations are simply wrong or misinformed.

Chandler, Hallett, and Sokol (2002) propose that young children do not understand that diversity of interpretations is "somehow intrinsic to the knowing process;" that is, that interpretation is an unavoidable aspect of all knowledge. Hence, the criteria for knowledge cannot easily be specified, and all knowing is associated with an unavoidable degree of ambiguity.

Understanding the Nature of Science and How It Is Constructed

Multiple lines of research are relevant to the issue of children's understanding of the nature of science and how it is constructed. And once again, the relations between the lines of research are complex. Relevant lines of research include the science-specific developmental literature, the epistemic cognition literature focused on understanding of science as a way of knowing, and survey-based data focused on children's beliefs about the nature of scientific knowledge and how it is constructed. Finally, we consider how science curricula, instructional interventions, and teachers' notions of science may influence children's understanding of science as a way of knowing.

It is straightforward to imagine how holding either absolutist or relativist epistemologies could lead to a distorted view of the nature of science. Indeed, research directed more explicitly at young students' grasp of the nature of scientific knowledge and practice has produced findings with interesting parallels to the more general developmental literature. For example, Carey and Smith (1993) point out that many students do not understand that science is primarily a theory-building enterprise. They may learn about observation, hypotheses, and experiment from their science textbooks, but they rarely understand that theories underlie these activities and are responsible for both the generation and interpretation of both hypotheses and experiments. The commonsense epistemology that young students typically hold is unreflective; to the extent that they think about it at all, children often think of knowledge as stemming directly from sensory experience, even though they do know that some knowledge is inferred rather than observed (Sodian and Wimmer, 1987), and they are even aware that the same object may be interpreted differently by different observers (Taylor, Cartwright, and Bowden, 1991).

Carey and Smith (1993) suggest that children may not make clear distinctions between theory, specific hypotheses, and evidence, and they may expect to find simpler and more direct relations between data and conclusions than are warranted. Like the absolutists described in the developmental psychology literature, they tend to regard differences in conclusions or observations as being due to lack of information or misinformation, rather than legitimate differences in perspective or interpretation. There is limited or no awareness that one's beliefs may be connected into coherent frameworks, and that these frameworks may have an influence on what one observes via the senses. For this reason, Kitchener and King (1981) argue students fail to understand that controversy is a part of science and that authorities are deemed, by definition, to share a common set of true beliefs. We suggest, however, an additional factor that may explain this finding, but that is not considered in this body of research. Children are rarely taught about controversy in science, so why would they come to view scientific knowledge as contested?

Carey et al. (1989) asked seventh graders a series of questions about the goals and practice of science and about the relationships between scientists' ideas, experiments, and data. Students' responses to these interviews were coalesced into three global perspectives about the nature of science, ranging from Level 1, in which scientists were regarded simply as collecting facts about the world, to Level 3, in which scientists were seen as concerned with building ever more powerful and explanatorily adequate theories about the world. A second interview study (Grosslight, Unger, Jay, and Smith, 1991) probed middle school students' understanding of models and modeling and achieved similar results. Many children regarded models merely as copies of the world, a Level 1 perspective. Level 2 children understood that models involve both the selection and omission of features, but emphasis remained on the models themselves rather than on the scientists' ideas behind the model. Finally, in Level 3 epistemology, models were regarded as tools developed for the purpose of testing theories.

Almost all seventh graders in these studies were at Levels 1 or 2, described by the researchers as "knowledge unproblematic" because from this view, disagreements about the nature of reality are considered due to ignorance or misinformation and knowledge is regarded as relatively straightforward. In contrast, in "knowledge problematic" epistemologies, seldom or never achieved by the students in these studies, knowledge is regarded as being organized into theories about the world that are actively constructed via a process of critical inquiry and that are often successively revised over extended periods of time.

The science education research on learners' and teachers' views about the nature of science is mixed (McComus and Olson, 1998; Lederman et al., 2002; Lederman, 1999; Osborne et al., 2003). When data are gathered employing survey instruments that probe learners' views of science outside any specific context of inquiry, the results indicate that even high school and undergraduate students do not develop accurate views about the theory revision and responsiveness to evidence.

Similarly, Driver et al. (1996) interviewed same-age pairs of students at ages 9, 12, and 16 about the purposes of scientific work, their understanding of the nature and status of scientific knowledge, and their understanding of science as a social enterprise. They classified students' responses about epistemology into three overall levels, with the lowest levels reflecting little acknowledgment of interpretation and successive levels indicating the importance of forms of thinking that do not rely solely on sensory input. The reasoning considered at the lowest level was reasoning grounded in phenomena; at the next, empirical reasoning based on relationships between variables; and finally, the highest level was reasoning that uses imagined models. Like the Carey and Unger studies, Driver et al. (1996) characterized children as moving from perspectives that emphasize unproblematic, sensory-based knowledge in which truth is considered a relatively simple objective to attain, to views in which science is acknowledged to depend on active interpretations of staged events (experiments), mental manipulations, and coherent, connected bodies of knowledge that may include many areas of uncertainty.

Much of this research literature suggests that K-8 students have a limited understanding of how scientific knowledge is constructed. However, it is not clear to what extent one can attribute such limitations to developmental stage, as opposed to adequacy of instructional opportunity or other experiences. In the words of Carey and Smith (1993, p. 243): "Two questions of urgent importance to educators now arise. First, in what sense are these levels developmental? Second (and distinctly), do these levels provide barriers to grasping a constructivist epistemology if such is made the target of the science education?"

Consider first the model of science as a way of knowing underlying the science children experience in the science curriculum, their primary source of information about the nature of the discipline. As noted in other chapters, in the upper elementary school years, the process of scientific knowledge construction is typically represented as experiment, with negligible acknowledgment of the role of interpretation or, more generally, the active role of the scientist in the process of knowledge construction. In the early grades, the typical emphasis on description of phenomenology through the basic science process skills of observation, categorization, measurement, etc., also reflects a distorted image of science, far removed from a constructivist epistemology.

In the same vein, science aspires to construct conceptual structures, with robust explanatory and predictive power, yet this is seldom either explicit or implicit in the K-8 science curriculum. An analysis of science curriculum by the American Association for the Advancement of Science (AAAS) indicates that all curricular content is typically represented as of equal importance, with little attention to its interconnections or functionality. According to Roseman, Kesidou, Stern, and Caldwell (1999), authors of the AAAS report, the science texts evaluated by AAAS included many classroom activities that either were irrelevant to learning key science ideas or failed to help students relate their activitiy to science ideas.

Science curriculum has long been criticized as reflecting an impoverished and misleading model of science as a way of knowing (e.g., Burbules and Linn, 1991; Hewson and Hewson, 1988). Methods of science dominate the school science curriculum, with little emphasis on the role of theory, explanation, or models. More contemporary views of science (Giere, 1991, 1999; Solomon, 2001; Longino, 1990) "as a multidimensional interaction among the models of scientists, empirical observation of the real world, and their predictions" are seldom included (Osborne et al., 2003, p. 715).

Although there are notable exceptions to this pattern, most K-8 curricula would appear to at least exacerbate the epistemological shortcomings with which children enter school. In the words of Reif and Larkin (1991, p. 733): "Science taught in schools is often different from actual science and from everyday life. Students' learning difficulties are thus increased because scientific goals are distorted and scientific ways of thinking are inadequately taught."

Another factor that needs to be considered in understanding and attribution of children's shortcomings in this regard is teachers' understanding of science as a way of knowing (Akerson, Abd-El-Khalick, and Lederman, 2000). The epistemic cognition literature has documented shortcomings in students at all levels of study, including college and beyond. It is not surprising that shortcomings in the understanding of science as a way of knowing have been identified in K-8 teachers.

A small literature of classroom-based design studies indicates that these limitations may be at least to some degree ameliorable by instruction. Design studies, in which researchers create conditions favorable to students' learning about the scientific enterprise, show that elementary and middle school students can develop their understanding of how scientific knowledge develops (Carey et al., 1989; Khishfe and Abd-El-Khalick, 2002), including a more sophisticated understanding of the nature and purpose of scientific models (Gobert and Pallant, 2001; Schwartz and White, 2005). With appropriate supports for learning strategies of investigation, children can generate meaningful scientific questions and design and conduct productive scientific investigations (e.g., Metz, 2004; Smith et al., 2000).

For example, in the small elementary school in which she was the lone science teacher, Gertrude Hennessey was able to systematically focus the lessons on core ideas built cumulatively across grades 1-6. She chose to emphasize generating, communicating, and evaluating theories via the intelligibility, plausibility, fruitfulness, and conceptual coherence of the alternatives (see Table 6-1). Research on her sixth grade students' understanding of the nature of science suggested that they had a much better sense of the constructive, knowledge problematic nature of the enterprise than did sixth graders from a comparable school (Smith et al., 2000).

In another example, students showed improved understanding of the process of modeling after they engaged in the task of designing a model that works like a human elbow (Penner et al., 1997). In this study, students in first and second grade in two classrooms participated in a model-building task over three consecutive 1-hour sessions. They began by discussing different types of models they had previously seen or made. They considered the characteristics of those models, and how models are used for understanding phenomena. They were then introduced to the task of designing a model that functions like their elbow. After discussing how their own elbows work, children worked in pairs or triads to design and build models that illustrated the functional aspects of the human elbow. After generating an initial model, each group demonstrated and explained their model to the class followed by discussion of the various models. Students were then given an opportunity to modify their models or start over. In interviews conducted after the session, students improved in their ability to judge the functional rather than perceptual qualities of models compared with nonmodeling peers. They also demonstrated an understanding of the process of modeling in general that was similar to that of children 3 to 4 years older.

Researchers have also identified important curricular features that support the development of a more sophisticated epistemology. Curricula can facilitate the epistemological development of students when they focus on deep science problems, provide students opportunities to conduct inquiry, and structure explicit discussion of epistemological issues (see, e.g., Bell and Linn, 2000; Davis, 1998; Smith and Wenk, in press). It is also important to note that students' understanding of epistemology does not grow unproblematically from inquiry experiences. In order to advance their understanding of epistemology, learners engaged in inquiry need explicit cues to reflect on their experiences and observations and consider the epistemological implications (Khishfe and Abd-El-Khalick, 2002).

CONCLUSIONS

The research base related to children's understanding of knowledge in general and of scientific knowledge specifically is limited. Much of the work on knowledge has been carried out with college-age populations, although some studies in developmental psychology have looked at children's under-

TABLE 6-1 One Progression of Increasingly Sophisticated Metaconceptual Activities in Grades 1-6

Grade	Students' Role	Teacher's Role
1	• Explicitly state their own views about the topic under consideration • Begin to consider the reasoning used to support their views • Being to differentiate what they think from why they think it	• Finds a variety of ways in which students can externally represent their thinking about the topic • Provides many experiences for students to begin to articulate the reasoning used to support ideas/beliefs
2	• Begin to address the necessity of understanding other (usually peer) positions before they can discuss or comment on those positions • Toward the end of the year, begin to recognize inconsistency in the thoughts of others, but not necessarily in their own thinking	• Continues to provide an educational environment in which students can safely express their thoughts, without reproaches from others • Introduces concept of consistency of thinking • Models consistent and inconsistent thinking (students can readily point out when teacher is being inconsistent)
3	• Explore the idea that thoughts have consequences, and that what one thinks may influence what one chooses to see • Begin to differentiate *understanding* what a peer is saying from *believing* what a peer is saying • Begin to comment on how their current ideas have changed from past ideas and to consider that current ideas may also need to be revised over time	• Fosters metacognitive discourse among learners in order to illuminate students' internal representations • Provides lots of examples from their personal work (which is saved from year to year) of student ideas

TABLE 6-1 Continued

Grade	Students' Role	Teacher's Role
4-6	• Begin to consider the implications and limitations of their personal thinking • Begin to look for ways of revising their personal thinking • Begin to evaluate their own/others' thinking in terms of intelligibility, plausibility, and fruitfulness of ideas • Continue to articulate criteria for acceptance of ideas (i.e., consistency and generalizability) • Continue to employ physical representations of their thinking • Begin to employ analogies and metaphors, discuss their explicit use, and differentiate physical models from conceptual models • Articulate and defend ideas about "what learning should be like"	• Provides historical examples of very important people changing their views and explanations over time • Begins to use students' external representations of their thinking as a way of evaluating their ideas/beliefs (in terms of intelligibility, plausibility, and fruitfulness) in order to (a) create, when necessary, dissatisfaction in the minds of the learner to facilitate conceptual exchange or (b) look for ways of promoting conceptual capture in the mind of the learner

SOURCE: Smith et al. (2000).

standing of how knowledge is constructed. Many researchers assume that epistemology is trait-like, although some argue that it is situational—an interaction of cognitive and historical resources with environmental features that cue or elicit those resources.

Looking across the various lines of research, most children in grades K-8 do not further develop the rudimentary knowledge and skills that are so evident during the preschool years. Young children tend to move from one level of understanding to the next slowly, if at all, and by middle school few students reach higher levels of understanding, at which knowledge is viewed as problematic and claims are necessarily subjected to scrutiny for their evidentiary warrants. In large measure, this pervasive pattern probably reflects more about the opportunities to learn that children encounter in their education than a measure of what they could do under different conditions. Evidence from design studies, discussed in this chapter and to which we return in Chapter 9, suggests that, under optimal curricular and instructional conditions, children can develop very sophisticated views of knowledge. Yet the contrast is remarkable between the capabilities of preschool children and modal patterns of development in older children and the lack of sophisticated reasoning about knowledge in early adolescents.

We argue that in carefully designed, supportive environments, elementary and middle school children are capable of understanding and working with knowledge in sophisticated ways. Instruction in K-8 science can significantly advance their understanding of the nature and structure of scientific knowledge and the process by which it is constructed. Design studies, in which researchers create conditions favorable to students' learning about the scientific enterprise, suggest that elementary students can develop higher levels of how scientific knowledge develops. With appropriate supports for learning strategies of investigation, children can engage in designing and conducting investigations that enable them to understand science as a way of knowing (Gobert and Pallant, 2001; Klahr and Li, 2005; Metz, 2004; Schwartz and White, 2005; Smith et al., 2000; Toth, Klahr, and Chen, 2000). The core elements of this scientific activity involve articulating hypotheses, laws, or models, designing experiments or empirical investigations that test these ideas, collecting data, and using data as evidence to evaluate and revise them. We will discuss this literature in depth in Chapter 9.

Current science education does not typically offer the kind of educational environments that have been shown to support children's understanding of scientific knowledge. Rather, there is a tendency to overemphasize methods, often experimental methods, as opposed to presenting science as a process of building theories and models, checking them for internal consistency and coherence, and testing them empirically. This lack of attention to theory, explanation, and models may exacerbate the difficulties children have with understanding how scientific knowledge is constructed. It may, in fact, strengthen their misconceptions, such as the view that scientific knowledge is unproblematic, relatively simple to obtain, and flows easily from direct observation. While curricula may be one source of this problem, teachers' lack of understanding of science as a way of knowing may also play a role. The role of teachers and teacher knowledge in science education is taken up in greater detail in Chapter 10.

REFERENCES

Akerson, V.L., Abd-El-Khalick, F., and Lederman, N.G. (2000). Influence of a reflective explicit activity-based approach on elementary teachers' conceptions of nature of science. *Journal of Research in Science Teaching, 37*(4), 295-317.

Bell, P., and Linn, M.C. (2000). Beliefs about science: How does science instruction contribute? In B.K. Hofer and P.R. Pintrich (Eds.), *Personal epistemology: The psychology of beliefs about knowledge and knowing*. Mahwah, NJ: Lawrence Erlbaum Associates.

Burbules, N.C., and Linn, M.C. (1991). Science education and the philosophy of science: Congruence or contradiction? *International Journal of Science Education, 3*(3), 227-241.

Carey, S., Evans, R., Honda, M., Jay, E., and Unger, C. (1989). "An experiment is when you try it and see if it works": A study of grade 7 students' understanding of the construction of scientific knowledge. *International Journal of Science Education, 11*(5), 514-529.

Carey, S., and Smith, C. (1993). On understanding the nature of scientific knowledge. *Educational Psychologist, 28*(3), 235-251.

Chandler, M., Boyes, M., and Ball, L. (1990). Relativism and stations of epistemic doubt. *Journal of Experimental Child Psychology, 50*, 370-395.

Chandler, M.J., Hallett, D., and Sokol, B.W. (2002). Competing claims about competing knowledge claims. In B.K. Hofer and P.R. Pintrich (Eds.), *Personal epistemology: The psychology of beliefs about knowledge and knowing* (pp. 145-168). Mahwah, NJ: Lawrence Erlbaum Associates.

Davis, E.A. (1998). *Scaffolding students' reflection for science learning*. Unpublished doctoral dissertation, University of California, Berkeley.

Driver, R., Leach, J., Millar, R., and Scott, P. (1996). *Young people's images of science*. Buckingham, England: Open University Press.

Giere, R.N. (1991) *Understanding scientific reasoning*. New York: Holt Reinhart and Winston.

Giere, R.N. (1999). *Science without laws*. Chicago, IL: University of Chicago Press.

Gobert, J., and Discenna, J. (1997). *The relationship between students' epistemologies and model-based reasoning*. (ERIC Document Reproduction Service No. ED409164). Kalamazoo: Western Michigan University, Department of Science Studies.

Gobert, J., and Pallant, A. (2001). *Making thinking visible: Promoting science learning through modeling and visualizations*. Presented at the Gordon Research Conference, Mt. Holyoke College, Hadley, MA, August 5-10.

Grosslight, L., Unger, C., Jay. E., and Smith, C. (1991). Understanding models and their use in science: Conceptions of middle and high school students and experts. *Journal of Research in Science Teaching, 28*, 799-822.

Hammer, D. (1994). Epistemological beliefs in introductory physics. *Cognition and Instruction, 12*(2), 151-183.

Hammer, D., and Elby, A. (2002). On the form of a personal epistemology. In B.K. Hofer and P.R. Pintrich (Eds.), *Personal epistemology: The psychology of beliefs about knowledge and knowing* (pp. 169-190). Mahwah, NJ: Lawrence Erlbaum Associates.

Hewson, P., and Hewson, M.,(1988). On appropiate conception of teaching science: A view from studies of science learning. *Science Education, 72*(5), 529-540.

Khishfe, R., and Abd-El-Khalick, F. (2002). Influence of explicit and reflective versus implicit inquiry-oriented instruction on sixth graders' views of nature of science. *Journal of Research in Science Teaching, 39,* 551-578.

Kitchener, K.S., and King, P.M. (1981). Reflective judgment: Concepts of justification and their relationship to age and education. *Journal of Applied and Developmental Psychology, 2,* 89-116.

Klahr, D., and Li, L. (2005). Cognitive research and elementary science instruction: From the laboratory, to the classroom, and back. *Journal of Science Education and Technology, 14*(2), 217-238.

Kuhn, D., and Leadbeater, B. (1988). The connection of theory and evidence. The interpretation of divergent evidence. In H. Beilin, D. Kuhn, E. Amsel, and M. O'Loughlin (Eds.), *The development of scientific thinking skills.* St. Louis, MO: Academic Press.

Lederman, N.G. (1999). Teachers' understanding of the nature of science and classroom practice: Factors that facilitate or impede the relationship. *Journal of Research in Science Teaching, 36,* 916-929.

Lederman, N.G, Abd-el-Khalick, F., Bell, R.L., and Schwartz, R.S. (2002). Views of nature of science questionnaire: Towards valid and meaningful assessment of learners' conceptions of the nature of science. *Journal of Research in Science Teaching, 39*(6), 497-521.

Longino, H. (1990). *Science as social knowledge.* Princeton, NJ: Princeton University Press.

McComas, W.F., and Olson, J.K. (1998). The nature of science in international science education standards documents. In W.F. McComas (Ed.), *The nature of science in science education: Rationales and strategies* (pp. 41-52). Dordrecht, The Netherlands: Kluwer Academic.

Metz, K.E. (2004). Children's understanding of scientific inquiry: Their conceptualization of uncertainty in investigations of their own design. *Cognition and Instruction, 22*(2), 219-290.

Osborne, J.F., Collins, S., Ratcliffe, M., Millar, R., and Duschl, R. (2003). What "ideas-about-science" should be taught in school science? A Delphi study of the expert community. *Journal of Research in Science Teaching, 40*(7), 692-720.

Penner, D., Giles, N.D., Lehrer, R., and Schauble, L. (1997). Building functional models: Designing an elbow. *Journal of Research in Science Teaching, 34*(2), 125-143.

Perner, J. (1991). *Understanding the representational mind.* Cambridge, MA: Bradford Books/MIT Press.

Perry, W.G. (1970/1999). *Forms of intellectual and ethical development in the college years: A scheme.* New York: Holt Rinehart and Winston.

Reif, F., and Larkin, J.H. (1991). Cognition in scientific and everyday domains: Comparison and learning implications. *Journal of Research in Science Teaching, 28*(9), 733-760.

Roseman, J., Kesidou, S., Stern, L., and Caldwell, A. (1999). Heavy books light on learning: AAAS Project 2061 evaluates middle grades science textbooks. *Science Books and Films, 35,* 243-247.

Rudolph, J.L. (2005). Epistemology for the masses: The origins of the "scientific method" in American schools. *History of Education Quarterly, 45*(2), 341-376.

Sandoval, W.A. (2005). Understanding students' practical epistemologies and their influence on learning through inquiry. *Science Education, 89*, 634-656.

Sandoval, W.A., and Reiser, B.J. (2004). Explanation-driven inquiry: Integrating conceptual and epistemic scaffolds for scientific inquiry. *Science Education, 88*, 345-372.

Schauble, L., Glaser, R., Duschl, R., Schulze, S., and John, J. (1995). Students' understanding of the objectives and procedures of experimentation in the science classroom. *Journal of the Learning Sciences, 4*(2), 131-166.

Schwarz, C., and White, B.Y. (2005). Metamodeling knowledge: Developing students' understanding of scientific modeling. *Cognition and Instruction, 23*(2), 165-205.

Smith, C.L., Maclin, D., Houghton, C., and Hennessey, M.G. (2000). Sixth-grade students' epistemologies of science: The impact of school science experiences on epistemological development. *Cognition and Instruction, 18*(3), 285-316.

Smith, C., and Wenk, L. (in press). Relations among three aspects of first-year college students' epistemologies of science. *Journal of Research in Science Teaching*.

Sodian, B., and Wimmer, H. (1987). Children's understanding of inference as a source of knowledge. *Child Development, 58*, 424-433.

Solomon, M. (2001). *Social empiricism*. Cambridge, MA: MIT Press/Bradford Books.

Songer, N.B., and Linn, M.C. (1991). How do students' views of the scientific enterprise influence knowledge integration? *Journal of Research in Science Teaching, 28*(9), 761-784.

Taylor, M., Cartwright, B., and Bowden, T. (1991). Perspective-taking and theory of mind: Do children predict interpretive diversity as a function of differences in observer's knowledge? *Child Development, 62*, 1334-1351.

Toth, E.E., Klahr, D., and Chen, Z. (2000). Bridging research and practice: A cognitively-based classroom intervention for teaching experimentation skills to elementary school children. *Cognition and Instruction, 18*(4), 423-459.

Toth, E., Suthers, D., and Lesgold, A. (2002). Mapping to know: The effects of evidence maps and reflective assessment on scientific inquiry skills. *Science Education, 86*(2), 264-286.

7

Participation in Scientific Practices and Discourse

Main Findings in the Chapter:

- *The norms of scientific argument, explanation, and the evaluation of evidence differ from those in everyday life. Students need support to learn appropriate norms and language for productive participation in the discourses of science.*
- *Children's experiences vary with their cultural, linguistic, and economic background. Such differences mean that students arrive in the classroom with varying levels of experience with science and varying degrees of comfort with the norms of scientific practice.*
- *It may be hard for teachers to recognize the strengths that diverse learners bring to the science classroom. However, all students can be successful in science and bring resources that can be built on to develop scientific proficiency.*
- *Motivation and attitudes toward science play a critical role in science learning, fostering students' use of effective learning strategies that result in deeper understanding of science. Classroom instruction and the classroom context can be designed in ways that enhance motivation and support productive participation in science.*

In this chapter, we examine research related to Strand 4: participate productively in scientific practices and discourse. We begin with a discussion of talk and argument. Argumentation is a central activity of scientists, and students need to learn both the language and norms for argumentation in science. This discussion of talk and argument leads naturally into consideration of the role of cultural habits and values in learning science. Science brings its own norms for both social and cognitive participation, which often differ quite markedly from children's experiences in everyday settings. Finally, we consider how motivation and identity play a role in science learning and successful participation in science.

TALK AND ARGUMENT

According to Bazerman (1988), the central activity of scientists is argumentation in communities of practice for the purpose of persuading colleagues of the validity of one's own ideas and the ideas of others (see Latour, 1987). The focus of these arguments is on establishing agreement about the truth of symbolic objects. For example, Bazerman (1988) analyzed Newton's journal articles over a period of years and concluded that experiments are communicated in a way meant to ensure that his interpretations would seem both logical and inevitable to readers. Newton employed a host of rhetorical devices, from the order of experiments reported (which often did not match their actual sequence) to the wording of sentences, all orchestrated to maximize the likelihood that readers would literally come to see things his way.

In spite of its centrality in science, genuine scientific argumentation is rarely observed in classrooms. Instead, most of the talk comes from teachers, and it seems oriented primarily toward persuading students of the validity of the scientific worldview (Ogborn et al., 1996). As Mehan (1979) described in his now-classic analysis of the structure of talk in school, the tacit turn-taking rules that guide the interaction of teachers and students seem guaranteed to preclude argument of any kind, and perhaps even genuine conversation. Mehan reported that the discourse structure he most frequently observed was one he called the initiate-response-evaluate triad. This familiar form of exchange begins with a teacher asking a question, usually one to which the answer is already known. A student is called on and responds, and the teacher then follows up with a comment that communicates an evaluation of the response. These sequences are intended to find out if the student can provide the answer expected by the teacher, not to communicate anything previously unknown, put forth a claim, justify or debate a point, or offer a novel interpretation.

Many teachers are uncomfortable with argument, perhaps understandably, given that many teach in contexts in which much of their time is spent mediating conflict and persuading students of the value of civil exchange. Skill and persistence are required to help students grasp the difference between scientific argument, which rests on plausibility and evidence and has the goal of shared understanding, and everyday argument, which relies on power and persuasiveness and assumes that the goal is winning. It is not straightforward to get a middle schooler to see the distinction between disagreeing with an idea and disagreeing with a person.

Moreover, orchestrating effective scientific argument requires having sufficient knowledge of both children and content to perceive on the fly what is scientifically fruitful in students' talk. Young students tend to use language that is ambiguous, fragmentary, or even contradictory, especially in heated conversation, so the content and structure of their arguments can be difficult to follow. Yet if the educational goal is to help students understand not just the conclusions of science, but also *how* one knows and *why* one believes, then talk needs to focus on how evidence is used in science for the construction of explanations. "A prominent, if not central, feature of the language of scientific enquiry is debate and argumentation around competing theories, methodologies, and aims. Such language activities are central to doing and learning science. Thus, developing an understanding of science and appropriating the syntactic, semantic, and pragmatic components of its language require students to engage in practicing and using its discourse" (Duschl and Osborne, 2002, p. 40).

As described in Chapter 6, Gertrude Hennessey, who taught science to students in all grades at her small, rural elementary school, made the development of argument an explicit goal of instruction, starting with first graders. Her goals for these young children were modest, focused primarily on helping students become adept at stating their own beliefs and providing reasons for them. By the fourth grade, however, students were expected to understand and appeal to the scientific criteria of intelligibility, plausibility, fruitfulness, and conceptual coherence for evaluating their evolving beliefs. By sixth grade, students were expected to be actively monitoring the beliefs of their peers, considering the fit of competing explanations to the patterns of evidence that they were observing in their investigations (Hennessey, 2002).

Even understanding that more than one explanation is possible and that alternative explanations should be examined and entertained may take some getting used to (Kuhn, 1991). To keep this awareness at the center of students' attention, it may be helpful to feature alternative beliefs and explanations, socioscientific issues, and problem-based learning situations as occasional topics of classroom discussion. Eichinger et al. (1991) found that productive argumentation in classrooms is more likely to occur when students are permitted and encouraged to talk and work directly with each other, rather than always having their talk mediated through the teacher. These researchers favored collaborative problem-solving groups as a structure for encouraging peer-to-peer discourse, but they also noted that these groups are not successful unless the teacher works actively to support classroom norms that emphasize responsibility, tolerance, and the construction of arguments based on theory and evidence. Without teacher intervention, students do not spontaneously adopt either the general social norms or the specific scientific epistemic grounds for conducting productive dialogic discourse (Osborne et al., 2001). Herrenkhol and Guerra (1998) examined the effectiveness of directly teaching specific audience roles for encouraging productive scientific argumentation in the elementary grades. As small teams of fourth graders reported the results of their investigations to the whole class, the audience members were asked to assume responsibility for checking on the presenters by taking one of the following roles: (1) asking clarification questions about predictions and theories, (2) challenging claims about their results, or (3) raising questions about the relationships among their predictions, theories, and results. When students were assigned these roles, the discourse patterns in the classroom showed increased negotiation of shared understanding, monitoring of comprehension, challenges to others' perspectives, and coordination of theories and evidence.

In addition to its emphasis on discourse patterns, such as forms of scientific argument, science is also associated with a style of language use that does not match everyday kinds of talk. Specialized kinds of activities, like science, are often associated with specialized forms of language. Science, mathematics—and, for that matter, ham radio and drug selling—are activities conducted by organized groups of people who tend to communicate in particular linguistic styles, sometimes called "registers" (Halliday, 1988). Scientific language tends to emphasize the passive voice, especially in its textual forms, and as a result, people are rarely present in science talk or text, as either agents or participants (Lemke, 1990). Scientific language often features abstract nouns that are derived from verbs (e.g., "the revolution of the earth around the sun") and technical terms that have different meanings than in everyday use (e.g., "force," "energy"). Narrative and dramatic accounts are avoided, as are colloquial expressions and ambiguous words, such as pronouns with unclear referents. The impression lent by these features of scientific style is that the text is communicating a simple and veridical description of the way the world actually is—a straightforward reading of the book of nature (Olson, 1994), rather than a complex social activity conducted by humans. For these reasons, Lemke (1990) suggests that teachers work deliberately to provide opportunities for students to practice at "talking science." This goal may be accomplished through a variety of means, such as teaching students how to combine scientific terms in complex sentences, discussing their commonsense theories on science topics, teaching students the genres of science writing, and bridging colloquial and scientific language, for example, by asking students to translate back and forth between scientific and colloquial statements or questions.

CULTURAL VALUES AND NORMS[1]

Scientific thinking is both like and unlike the forms of thinking that individuals employ in their everyday lives. For example, in both science and everyday problem solving, people make inferences about the relationships between causes and effects by detecting and evaluating patterns of covariation between potential causes and outcomes (Kelley, 1973; Shultz, 1982). However, it is much less common for people to deliberately apply strategies and heuristics (such as the control-of-variables strategy) to definitively and systematically rule out factors that are *not* causal, although one does observe this form of thinking in certain specialized contexts, for example, those that call for accurate diagnosis (e.g., car repair, medicine). Moreover, causal relationships that go beyond simple, one cause/one effect can be very difficult for people to detect (Perkins and Grotzer, 2000). Similarly, people do not simply hold a catalog of unrelated beliefs; instead, they use their knowledge to make inferences that are internally consistent and that support explanations and predictions about novel cases (Gopnik and Meltzoff, 1997). Even third graders prefer explanations that are logically consistent (Samarapungavan, 1992). However, this does not necessarily mean that novices are explicitly aware of their beliefs and maintain or discard them by systematically appraising their adherence to the criteria that scientists deliberately apply when they evaluate alternative theories.

Because scientific and everyday thinking do not overlap perfectly, students sometimes find it confusing to grasp the rules of the game as they move between contexts. For example, it has been observed that when they are presumed to be designing and conducting experiments to learn about the causal structure of a complex system, children frequently are doing something else altogether—in some cases, trying to replicate outcomes that they consider interesting or favorable (Kuhn and Phelps, 1982; Tschirgi, 1980; Schauble, Klopfer, and Raghavan, 1991). Negotiating the sometimes subtle transitions between everyday thinking and the thinking valued in domains like science is a challenge for all students. Moreover, it may be particularly difficult for students who have had less experience with the forms of reasoning and talk that are privileged in American middle-class schools. Mainstream students (those who are white, middle- or upper-class, and native speakers of standard English) are more likely than culturally or linguistically diverse students to encounter ways of talking, thinking, and interacting in schools that are continuous with the practices (including knowledge, language, skills, and reasoning) and the expectations that they bring from home.

---

[1]This section draws on the commissioned paper by Ellice Forman and Wendy Sink, "Sociocultural Approaches to Learning Science in Classrooms."

Any discussion of culture needs to include a caution about the inappropriateness of portraying individuals as possessing trait-like thinking styles typical of cultural, racial, or gender categories. In place of this oversimplified and stereotypical view, Gutierrez and Rogoff (2003) propose that one conceives of individuals as developing a wide range of repertoires of practice—ways of behaving, thinking, and interpreting—for engaging with the varieties of communities and institutions that they encounter in their everyday lives. From this perspective, each person is continually developing an ever-growing multicultural repertoire, fashioned by participating in their everyday rounds of practical activity, which involve historically evolving cultural practices and tools (Cole, 1996; Erickson, 2004). Children are not passive recipients who simply receive or are molded by culture; instead, as they encounter cultural practices and routines, they are affected by them but also transform them, so that the relationships between culture and personal meaning are always fluid and complex.

That said, we note that people's histories vary, and one's fluidity in negotiating the transition across cultures and settings may be simultaneously supported and constrained by one's history. This is important, because classrooms are not neutral settings; they are "saturated with specific cultural and communicative norms" (Foster, Lewis, and Onafowora, 2003, p. 263). An implication is that the educational success of immigrant or U.S.-born racial/ethnic minority students may depend on their access to cultural and communicative norms that come for free or at much less cost to other students. The structure of classroom norms is often left tacit, making it difficult for students to figure out the rules on their own, especially if these ways of thinking, talking, and behaving are not as frequently encountered in their home communities (Ladson-Billings, 1995; Delpit, 1995).

For example, it is common for Yup'ik children in Alaska to learn by observing experienced adults and participating actively as helpers in adult work and other activities. Verbal interaction is not central to the learning process; observation and participation are considered more important (Lipka, 1998). Similarly, Rogoff and colleagues (2003) have identified a form of learning that they call "intent participation," in which children learn from keen observation, with little direct instruction. Rogoff et al. report that this pattern of learning tends to be prevalent in communities that are less stratified by age than those in the United States, communities in which children enter contexts of adult activity, including work, with relatively few barriers to their presence or full participation. The strong emphasis in school on explicit verbal instruction may be disconcerting to children from backgrounds that favor intent participation or other forms of learning. Moreover, the specific patterns and uses of discourse, such as the practice of asking questions whose answer is already known to the questioner, may also seem unfamiliar and possibly even bizarre to some.

Lee and Luyks (2006) point out that, as yet, there is little research focused directly on how cultural norms and values may either affect or be capitalized on for the learning of disciplinary knowledge, such as science. For the most part, research on student diversity and research on science learning have been separate literatures that do not frequently contact each other. Similarly, instruction for English language learners typically focuses primarily on English language and literacy development and does not give as much attention to instruction in content domains, such as science (National Research Council, 1997).

However, the research that does exist suggests that two principles can provide some guidance. First is the need to make visible and inspectable the norms and patterns of thinking that constitute the rules of the game in the science classroom, rather than leaving them implicit. If what is valued is left for students to figure out, then those who have had greater home experience with those patterns of thinking will have a clear advantage. Varying solutions to the problem of making the rules of the game understandable have been advocated, although as yet research does not support whether some may be more effective than others.

Lee and Fradd (1996, 1998) suggest that when introducing disciplinary forms of activity, such as scientific inquiry, that may be unfamiliar to students, teachers should begin with explicit, structured, direct instruction. Over time, as students' grasp of the objectives and procedures develops, teachers can cede increasing control and initiative to them. The goal is to establish and maintain *instructional congruence*, which Lee (2002) describes as mediating the nature of academic disciplines with students' language and cultural experiences to make science accessible, meaningful, and relevant. Students need opportunities to explicitly consider and master new ways of thinking, while teachers balance challenge and comfort by ensuring that students understand that their own home norms and practices are valued even as they encounter some that are less familiar.

Lucas et al. (2005) pursued a somewhat different approach to achieving the same goal. Specifically, they made the development, critique, and revision of norms for scientific thinking an ongoing instructional enterprise in a sixth grade classroom over the course of an academic year. Early in the fall, students proposed, debated, and came to agreement on classroom criteria for evaluating "what counts as a good scientific question" and "what we think is persuasive evidence." For example, everyone agreed that a good question was one to which one did not already know the answer, and that more interesting questions were ones for which one couldn't just ask someone or look up the answer. The resulting list of criteria was used as a focal class reference as students worked in small teams to design and then pursue investigations in pond ecology.

However, by midyear, students began to argue that the criteria needed to be revised, because new ideas about good questions and good evidence were coming to light as they evaluated their own work and the work of other teams. For example, students argued that they should amend the list by adding the criterion that a good question encourages "piggybacking"— their term for the idea that good questions are inspired by (or piggyback on) the findings of others and in turn, inspire related additional questions. This change reflected the students' growing understanding that a frequent source of new and interesting questions was the methods pursued by or the findings of other teams. Such shifts in their criteria for questions and evidence accompanied the shift from conceiving of investigation as an activity conducted independently to advance one's own knowledge toward understanding that a larger community can share responsibility for building and evaluating a publicly shared base of related knowledge.

If clarifying the norms and thinking patterns characteristic of science is the first important principle for supporting learning for all students, the second is the value of capitalizing on the continuities between students' everyday thinking, knowledge, and resources and those of practicing scientists. Ann Rosebery and Beth Warren have worked for a decade and a half at identifying key points of contact between students' ways of knowing and scientific ways of knowing. Their phrase "points of contact" is intended to capture the recognition that there are both continuities and discontinuities between students' thinking, tool use, and talk and that of science.

In their Cheche Konnen project, conducted with Haitian Creole students and their teachers (the name is translated as "search for knowledge"), Warren and Rosebery observed that the children regularly and spontaneously evoked analogies, arguments, and narratives as a means of making sense of the phenomena they were exploring. For example, one young student who was investigating animal behavior—in this case, the preference of ants for different kinds of habitats—imaginatively projected himself into the habitat, assuming an "ant's eye view," a perspective that resulted in his raising doubts about one of the key attributes of comparison in the design of the investigation. His original intention had been to set up an experiment to establish whether ants prefer an environment that is dark to one that is brightly lit, but as this student imagined himself as an ant crawling through the soil, he began to wonder how either side of the chamber—lit or unlit—could possibly appear "light" to an ant wandering around underneath the soil. As he pointed out, "When we put dirt in there, they—they were a little bit walking around but almost all of them were under the dirt, in the darkness" (Warren et al., 2001, p. 541).

Researchers who observe scientists and mathematicians at work have pointed out that, for professionals, too, imagination, narrative, and projection of oneself as an actor into the context of the investigation appear to serve as important resources for meaning making and discovery (Ochs, Gonzales, and Jacoby, 1996). Over the 15 years of its existence, the Cheche Konnen program has been demonstrating that urban, language-minority students can engage in high-level scientific reasoning and problem solving if they are taught in ways that respect their interests and sense-making (Hudicourt-Barnes, 2003).

PRODUCTIVE PARTICIPATION

Engagement with science begins with willingness to participate in the science classroom, but it must go beyond simply participating to participating in ways that advance science learning. Engle and Conant's (2002) definition of "productive disciplinary engagement" is a useful frame for thinking about active engagement in the classroom that is grounded in disciplinary norms for both social and cognitive activity. In their view, productive disciplinary engagement refers to classrooms in which "there is contact between what students are doing and the issues and practices of a discipline's discourse" (Engle and Conant, 2002, p. 402). Furthermore, "students' engagement is productive to the extent that they make intellectual progress. What constitutes productivity depends on the discipline, the specific task and topic, and where students are when they begin addressing a problem" (p. 403). They further distinguish how engagement and disciplinary engagement might be distinct from productive disciplinary engagement.

Engle and Conant define engagement in terms of students actively speaking, listening, responding, and working and high levels of on-task behavior. Greater engagement can be inferred when more students in the group make substantive contributions to the topic under discussion and their contributions are made in coordination with each other. Engagement also means that students attend to each other, express emotional involvement, and spontaneously reengage with the topic and continue with it over a sustained period of time. Finally, it means that few students are involved in unrelated or off-task activities.

These hallmarks of engagement do not, however, ensure that students are engaged in meaningful ways with the discipline of science. Disciplinary engagement expands to include scientific content and experimental activities (including argumentation based on logic and data patterns). For disciplinary engagement to occur, there must be "some contact between what students are doing and the issues and practices of a discipline's discourse" (Engle and Conant, 2002, p. 402). Herrenkohl and Guerra (1998) suggest that some identifying features of disciplinary engagement in science include (1) monitoring comprehension, that is, students asking questions to be sure that they fully understand perspectives posed by other students; (2) challenging others' perspectives and claims; and (3) coordinating bits of knowledge that can be construed as coordinating theories with evidence.

Finally, to be productively engaged in the discipline, students must make intellectual progress. Whether progress can be considered productive depends on the discipline, the specific task and topic, and where students begin. Productive disciplinary engagement encompasses the additional criteria of demonstrated change over time in student investigations, complexity of argumentation, and use of previous investigations to generate new questions, new concepts, and new investigations.

In this section, we discuss the characteristics of individuals and classrooms that play a role in shaping students' engagement with science. These include motivation, attitudes, identity, interactions between students' values and norms and those of the science classroom, and, finally, characteristics of instruction that foster productive participation. We note that students' motivation, attitudes, and identity toward science develop partly as a consequence of their experience of educational, social, and cultural environments. The educational environment in particular has an important influence on how students view science, their beliefs about their own ability to do science, and whether they feel supported to participate fully in the scientific community of the classroom. Consequently, we see productive participation as partly situation or context specific rather than as a stable personality trait that does not vary across settings.

Motivation, Attitudes, and Identity

Students' motivation, their beliefs about science, and their identities as learners affect their participation in the science classroom and have consequences for the quality of their learning. More specifically, results of both experimental and classroom-based studies suggest that students' own goals for science learning, their beliefs about their own ability in science, and the value they assign to science learning are likely to influence their cognitive engagement in science tasks (Lee and Anderson, 1993; Pintrich, Marx, and Boyle, 1993). Motivation, attitudes, and identity encompass cognitive components, such as beliefs about oneself and about science; emotional or affective components, such as values, interests, and attitudes; and behavioral components, such as persistence, effort, and attention.

Researchers studying motivation have developed a dizzying array of theoretical frameworks, making it challenging to develop a coherent picture of motivation, attitudes, and identity and the factors that shape them. The wide array of constructs that researchers have developed in their attempts to understand the components of motivation and attitudes have been organized by reviewers of the literature into a few broad categories (for examples, see Pintrich, Marx, and Boyle, 1993; Wigfield et al., 2006; National Research Council and Institute of Medicine, 2004). We chose to use the three dimensions developed in the recent National Research Council report *Engaging Schools* (2004): components that relate to (1) the students' feeling "I can do this"; (2) those that relate to the feeling "I want to do this"; and (3) those that relate to the feeling "I belong and this is an important part of who I am."

Beliefs About Oneself and About Science ("I Can Do Science")

In general, when children answer the question, Can I do this task? in the affirmative, they try harder, persist longer, perform better, and are motivated to select more challenging tasks (Wigfield et al., 2006). There is some evidence that a sense of being competent and efficacious as a science learner does influence learning. In a study of sixth and seventh grade science classrooms, students who reported feeling highly efficacious in science and who had a strong sense of competence in science tended to use deep learning strategies and were more focused on learning (Anderman and Young, 1994). Some researchers have suggested that students' perceptions of their ability to learn science might interact with the process of conceptual change, so that if they have confidence in their own learning and thinking strategies, they may be more likely to change their own conceptions (Pintrich, Marx, and Boyle, 1993).

Perceptions of ability usually vary from subject to subject and may vary from one context to another (National Research Council, 2004). Students will not exert effort in academic work if they are convinced they lack the capacity to succeed or have no control over outcomes (Atkinson, 1964; Eccles et al., 1983; Skinner, Wellborn, and Connell, 1990; Skinner, Zimmer-Gembeck, and Connell, 1998, cited in National Research Council, 2004). Students who have negative views of their competence and low expectations for success are more anxious in learning contexts and fearful of revealing their ignorance (Abu-Hilal, 2000; Bandalos, Yates, and Thorndike-Christ, 1995; Harter, 1992; Hembree, 1988, cited in National Research Council, 2004). Belief about the degree to which intellectual ability in a domain is fixed or malleable have also emerged as an import component of motivation. Americans tend to have a concept of intelligence or ability as inherited rather than as developed through effort (Chen and Stevenson, 1995; Dweck, 1999; Stevenson and Lee, 1990). A student who believes, for example, that ability in science is fixed and that she has low ability in it has little hope for success and therefore little reason to try.

Gender differences in competence beliefs are reported as early as kindergarten or first grade, especially in such gender role–stereotyped domains as science. For example, boys hold higher competence beliefs than girls for mathematics and sports, even after all relevant differences in skill level are controlled. In contrast, girls have higher competence beliefs than boys for reading and English, music and arts, and social studies (Jacobs et al., 2002). The extent to which children endorse the cultural stereotypes regarding which sex is more likely to be talented in a given domain predicts the extent to which girls and boys distort their ability self-concepts and expectations (Eccles and Harold, 1992). However, these gender differences are relatively small when they are found (Marsh, 1989).

Another perspective on the role of beliefs about competence is offered by research on stereotype threat. Steele (1997) proposed stereotype vulnerability and disidentification to help explain the underachievement of stereotyped groups. He and his colleagues describe a process by which some students in a group may disidentify with a particular domain, like school or science, due to widely held stereotypes about their lack of ability in it. To protect their own sense of self, some students disidentify with the domain and stop trying to achieve in it. Those students in the group who remain identified with the domain—that is, it is important to them and they want to succeed in it—may then suffer the effects of stereotype threat. This threat produces lowered performance in the domain, particularly in situations in which the stereotypes about their groups are made salient. Research based on this theory offers evidence that the process operates for black students in school in general and for women in stereotypically male domains, such as mathematics. These results have clear implications for performance in science, for which people tend to hold stereotypes about who has natural aptitude and who does not.

A key mediator of experiencing stereotype threat appears to be beliefs about the nature of intelligence. In a recent experimental intervention with college students, researchers found that by encouraging black students to adopt a mind set in which they viewed their own intelligence as malleable, they were able to increase their enjoyment and engagement in academics as well as their grades compared with controls (Aronson, Fried, and Good, 2002).

Goals, Values, and Interest ("I Want To Do Science")

Even if students believe they can succeed in science, they will not exert effort unless they see some reason to do so. They may have very different reasons for engaging in academic work, and typically there is a very complex set of reasons for engaging in any one task. Researchers have used a number of theoretical frameworks to explain the psychological processes involved in students' decisions to engage in a particular task.

Goals. Goals represent the different purposes that students may adopt in different achievement situations. Researchers working within this theoretical framework distinguished two broad orientations that students can have toward their learning. A learning orientation (also called a task-involved or mastery orientation) means that the student is focused on improving skills, mastering material, and learning new things. A performance orientation (also called an ego orientation) means that the student focuses on maximizing favorable evaluations of his competence and minimizing negative evaluations. Both goals have been observed among students in elementary and middle school science classrooms (Anderman and Young, 1994; Lee and Brophy, 1996; Meece, Blumenfeld, and Hoyle, 1988).

A number of studies have shown that these two different goal orientations can lead to different patterns of cognitive engagement (Pintrich, Marx, and Boyle, 1993). Research on adoption of mastery goals shows consistent positive consequences for learning. When children are mastery oriented they are more highly engaged in learning, use deeper cognitive strategies, and are intrinsically motivated to learn. This relation has been shown in science classrooms (Anderman and Young, 1994; Lee and Brophy, 1996; Meece, Blumenfeld, and Hoyle, 1988).

Which goals children adopt in a classroom are influenced by their own beliefs, especially beliefs about ability, as well as their experiences in classroom settings. Children holding an incremental view of intelligence tend to have mastery or learning goals, whereas children holding an entity view tend to have performance goals (Dweck and Legget, 1988). The classroom context appears to have a strong influence on which goals students adopt. When tasks are more challenging and meaningful, students tend to adopt mastery goals. In addition, classrooms that provide students with choice or control over their activities and emphasize gaining understanding rather than outperforming other students foster a mastery orientation.

Values. An individual's valuing of a task, in conjunction with her competence beliefs, influences performance as well as choices about continued investment in the activity. For example, people will be most likely to enroll in courses and choose careers in which they think they will do well and that have high task value for them. In fact, the value placed on a task predicts course plans and enrollment decisions more strongly than self-concept or expectancy of success on the task.

There are age-related declines in children's valuing of certain academic tasks that vary by domain. In one of the few longitudinal studies conducted over 12 years, children's valuing of language arts declined most during elementary years and then leveled off. Their valuing of mathematics declined the most during the high school years (Jacobs et al., 2002; Fredericks and Eccles, 2002).

There are also gender differences in the value children place on such activities as sports, social activities, and academic subjects (Eccles et al., 1989, 1993; Wigfield et al., 1991). Early work indicated that boys begin to value mathematics more than girls in early adolescence. However, more recent studies show that boys and girls value mathematics equally during adolescence (Jacobs et al., 2002). However, girls are less interested in science, with the exception of biology and engineering, than are boys (Wigfield et al., 2002).

Culture and ethnicity can influence parents' behaviors and children's motivation through values, goals, and general belief systems (for example, see Garcia Coll and Pachter, 2002; Gutman and Midgley, 2000; Luster, Rhoades, and Haas, 1989). Cultural differences can affect motivation through variations in valued activities (e.g., athletic versus musical competence), valued goals (e.g., communal goals versus individualistic goals), and approved means of achieving one's goals (e.g., competitive versus cooperative means).

Intrinsic motivation and interest. Individuals who are intrinsically motivated do activities for their own sake and out of interest in the activities. This is usually contrasted with being extrinsically motivated—that is, doing activities for instrumental or other reasons, such as receiving a reward. Some research shows that students who are intrinsically interested in an activity are more likely than students who are not intrinsically interested to see challenging tasks as worthwhile (Pittman, Emery, and Boggiano, 1982), think more creatively (Amabile and Hennessey, 1992), exert effort (Downey and Ainsworth-Darnell, 2002; Miserandino, 1996), and learn at a conceptual level (Ryan, Connell, and Plant, 1990).

Classroom practices appear to have an impact on students' intrinsic interest. Guthrie and colleagues have demonstrated positive effects on motivation of a program called concept-oriented reading instruction (CORI). CORI integrates reading with science inquiry and includes four instructional strategies to enhance motivation: support for student autonomy, support for competence, learning goals, and real-world interaction (Guthrie et al., 1996, 2000). One study of CORI involved third and fifth grade classrooms in three schools. Teachers were assigned to teach either CORI or to continue with traditional instruction. At the end of the school year, students in CORI reported greater curiosity for reading science than students in traditional instruction (Guthrie et al., 2000). They also reported using more cognitive strategies for reading comprehension. In additional research on the program, students in CORI classrooms also showed improved comprehension of science texts and higher scores on standardized tests of science content (Guthrie et al., 2004).

Interest is closely related to the notion of intrinsic motivation, although interest is generally seen as being more specific in focus. Researchers distinguish between individual and situational interest. Individual interest is a relatively stable stance toward certain domains, like science; situational interest is determined by specific features of an activity or task. In sixth grade science classrooms, Lee and Brophy (1996) found evidence that students' interest and motivation to learn were both domain general and situational. For example, students' interest varied from task to task even within a single unit on matter and molecules.

Interest is tied to the quality of learning (Alexander, Kulikowich, and Jetton, 1994; Hidi, 2001; Renninger, Ewen, and Lasher, 2002: Schiefele, 1996, 1999). For example, personal interest influences students' selective attention, effort and willingness to persist at a task, and acquisition of new knowledge (Hidi, 1990). Situational interest is more influenced than personal interest by characteristics of the classroom and the nature of the task. For example, challenge, choice, novelty, fantasy, and surprise can increase students' situational interest (Malone and Lepper, 1987). Recent studies suggest that interest is particularly predictive of achievement when there is a context that allows for choice. For example, interest in mathematics predicts achievement only at higher grade levels when students have a choice between more or less advanced courses (Koller, Baumert, and Schnabel, 2001).

Research on the development of interest indicates that children tend to have general or universal interests at first, which become more specific relatively quickly (Eccles, Wigfield, and Schiefele, 1998; Todt, 1990). Between ages 3 and 8, gender-specific interests emerge (Eccles, 1987; Ruble and Martin, 1998). For example, Johnson et al. (2004) found that among 4-year-olds, boys were more likely to have strong individual interests in conceptual domains such as dinosaurs or dogs than were girls. Girls' interests were generally more aligned with the arts (drawing, painting) or with activities related to forming and elaborating on social relationships (pretend play, dolls). Between ages 9 and 13, emerging self-concept is assumed to be linked more directly to social group affiliation and cognitive ability, leading to occupational interests consistent with one's social class and ability self-concepts (Cook et al., 1996). After age 13 or 14, students develop more differentiated and individualized vocational interests based on a notion of their internal, unique self. The development of vocational interests is thus a process of continuous elimination of interests that do not fit the individual's emerging sense of self, which includes gender, social group affiliation, ability, and then personal identity (Todt, 1990).

Identity ("I Belong")

Identity involves how people view themselves, how they present themselves, and how others see them (Holland et al., 1998; Wenger, 1998). A child's identity as a learner is contested and influenced by different practices in everyday interactions, as well as in the cultural institutions he uses (Bruner,

1996; Ogbu, 1995). Research on identity and learning in specific domains builds on the premise that how one learns and what one learns are fundamentally related to the kind of person one wants to become.

Developing an identity that includes excelling in science may be more challenging for some students than others. The culture of science is foreign to many students, both mainstream and nonmainstream, and the challenges of science learning may be greater for students whose cultural traditions are discontinuous with the ways of knowing characteristic of science and school science (Cobern, 1996; Jegede and Okebukola, 1991; Lee, 1999). It is also true, however, that nonmainstream students frequently bring values and practices to the classroom that can be seen as continuous with scientific practices. However, such experiences that could serve as intellectual resources for new learning in science classrooms may not be easily recognized.

The challenge for these students in learning science is "to study a Western scientific way of knowing and at the same time respect and access the ideas, beliefs, and values of non-Western cultures" (Snively and Corsiglia, 2001, p. 24). The ability to make cultural transitions is critically important to nonmainstream students' academic success. Giroux (1992), among others, has used the notion of *border crossing* to describe this process. To succeed academically, nonmainstream students must learn to negotiate the boundaries that separate their own cultural environments from the culture of science and school science (Aikenhead, 2001; Jegede and Aikenhead, 1999).

Even within the cultural mainstream, relatively few children's primary socialization is so science-oriented as to be perfectly continuous with the demands of school science. Thus, border crossing between the culture of science and the culture of the everyday world is demanding for all students in science classes (Driver et al., 1994). At times, students may find themselves caught in conflicts between what is expected of them in science classes and what they experience at home and in their community. If they appear too eager or willing to engage in science inquiry, they may find themselves estranged from their family or peers. If they appear reluctant to participate, they risk marginalization from school and subsequent loss of access to learning opportunities. Although some students may successfully bridge the cultural divide between home and school, others may become alienated and even actively resist learning science.

In order to manage these differences, a child from a marginalized culture may temporarily adopt an identity for science learning experiences (Heath, 1982). Better understanding how children come to integrate science into their existing culture, rather than temporarily adopting an identity, may make it possible to create formal and informal science learning environments that are more accessible and meaningful.

Classrooms That Promote Productive Participation

Findings from research on motivation, attitudes, and identity converge with findings from research on engagement with science to highlight the importance of the classroom in fostering productive participation. Engle and Conant argue that the preconditions for productive disciplinary engagement involve providing appropriately challenging activities, allowing students to take authority over their learning but making sure that their work can be scrutinized by others (teachers and students), and using criteria acceptable to scientific disciplines (e.g., logical consistency, explanatory power). In addition, students need to have access to the resources they need (texts, laboratory equipment, recording devices) to evaluate their claims and communicate them to others.

One study (Cornelius and Herrenkohl, 2004) explicitly employed the notion of productive disciplinary engagement and connected it to analyses of participant structures and discourse. In their study of a pair of sixth grade girls investigating sinking and floating, the researchers found evidence that the students took an active role in generating ideas, engaging in scientific argumentation with their peers, and learning how to use persuasive discourse to convince others of the validity of those ideas.

Other studies have demonstrated that K-8 students in both urban and suburban public schools can engage in such scientific activities as investigating floating and sinking (Herrenkohl et al., 1999; Lee and Fradd, 1996; Palincsar et al., 2001; Varelas, Luster, and Wenzel, 1999); ecology (Hogan and Corey, 2001; Rosebery, Warren, and Conant, 1992); the classification and growth of plants and animals (Brown, Reveles, and Kelly, 2005; Lehrer and Schauble, 2004; Lehrer et al., 2000; Warren and Rosebery, 1996); motion down inclined planes (Lehrer et al., 2000); and density functions of material kind (Lehrer et al., 2001).

Most of the above studies employed ethnographic case analyses of a small number of classrooms or groups of students. A few studies employed a mixture of quantitative and qualitative analyses (Herrenkohl and Guerra, 1998; Lee and Fradd, 1996; Palincsar et al., 2001). The smallest number of studies focused on students in grades K-2 (e.g., Lehrer, Schauble, and Petrosino, 2001); the largest number of studies examined students in grades 5 or 6.

These studies tend to define disciplinary engagement differently and tend to employ different tasks or focus on different participant populations, making it difficult to easily summarize results across studies (other than to show that young children, poor students, and students with mild disabilities are capable—under the right conditions—of high-level disciplinary engagement with scientific concepts and procedures in formal educational settings). Most of the studies reviewed demonstrate that disciplinary engagement can be achieved, but few appear to demonstrate productive disciplinary engagement (notable exceptions include Herrenkohl et al., 1999; Lehrer et al., 2001; Palincsar et al., 2001; Rosebery, Warren, and Conant, 1992).

CONCLUSIONS

As this chapter illustrates, science learning involves much more than individual cognitive activity. It is an inherently social and cultural process that requires mastery of specialized forms of discourse and comfort with norms of participation in the scientific community of the classroom. However, the rules for engaging in arguments and evaluating evidence that students learn in their everyday lives are sometimes dissimilar and even contradictory to those employed in science. Students often need support or explicit guidance to learn scientific norms for interacting with peers as they argue about evidence and clarify their own emerging understanding of science and scientific ideas. Genuine scientific argumentation with peer-to-peer interaction is rarely observed in science classrooms. Instead, teachers tend to dominate in a pattern of the teacher posing a question, the students responding, and the teacher following with an evaluative comment. Supporting argument in the science classroom requires a departure from this typical pattern.

Variations in students' cultural and linguistic backgrounds translate into quite different learning histories and stances toward science. Making the norms and patterns of thinking in science visible in the classroom is one approach to supporting science learning in diverse student populations. Another is to capitalize on the continuities between students' everyday thinking, knowledge, and resources and those of practicing scientists.

For all students, motivation and attitudes toward science play an important role in science learning. Becoming proficient in science requires students to actively engage in scientific tasks and participate in scientifically meaningful ways. Willingness to participate is shaped by students' own beliefs, their previous experience with science, and aspects of the science classroom. For example, students' belief in their ability in science, the value they place on science, their desire to master science, and their interest in science all have consequences for the quality of their engagement in the classroom and subsequent learning.

In turn, instruction can be designed in ways that foster a positive orientation toward science and promote productive participation in science classrooms. Such approaches include offering choice, providing meaningful tasks and an appropriate level of challenge, giving students authority over their learning while making sure their work can be examined by others, and making sure they have access to the resources they need to evaluate their claims and communicate them to others.

REFERENCES

Abu-Hilal, M.M. (2000). A structural model of attitudes towards school subjects, academic aspiration and achievement. *Educational Psychology, 20*, 75-84.

Aikenhead, G.S. (2001). *Cross-cultural science teaching: Praxis.* A paper presented at the annual meeting of the National Association for Research in Science Teaching, St. Louis, MO, March 26-28.

Alexander, P.A., Kulikowich, J.M., and Jetton, T.L. (1994). The role of subject-matter knowledge and interest in the processing of linear and nonlinear texts. *Review of Educational Research, 64*, 201-252.

Amabile, T.M., and Hennessey, B.A. (1992). The motivation for creativity in children. In A.K. Boggiano and T.S. Pittman (Eds.), *Achievement and motivation: A social-developmental perspective* (pp. 54-72). New York: Cambridge University Press.

Anderman, E.M., and Young, A. (1994). Motivation and strategy use in science: Individual differences and classroom effects. *Journal of Research in Science Teaching, 31*, 811-831.

Aronson, J., Fried, C.B., and Good, C. (2002). Reducing the effects of stereotype threat on African American college students by shaping theories of intelligence. *Journal of Experimental Social Psychology, 38*(2), 113-125.

Atkinson, J.W. (1964). *An introduction to motivation.* New York: D. Van Nostrand.

Bandalos, D.L., Yates, K., and Thorndike-Christ, T. (1995). Effects of math self-concept, perceived self-efficacy, and attributions for failure and success on test anxiety. *Journal of Educational Psychology, 87*, 611-623.

Bazerman, C. (1988). *Shaping written knowledge: The genre and activity of the experimental article in science.* Madison: University of Wisconsin Press.

Brown, B.B., Reveles, J.M., and Kelly, G.J. (2005). Scientific literacy and discursive identity: A theoretical framework for understanding science learning. *Science Education, 89*, 779-802.

Bruner, J. (1996). *The culture of education.* Cambridge, MA: Harvard University Press.

Chen, C., and Stevenson, H.W. (1995). Motivation and mathematics achievement: A comparative study of Asian-American, Caucasian-American, and East Asian high school students. *Child Development, 66*, 1215-1234.

Cobern, W.W. (1996). Constructivism and non-Western science education research. *International Journal of Science Education, 18*(3), 295-310.

Cole, M. (1996). *Cultural psychology: A once and future discipline.* Cambridge, MA: Belknap Press of Harvard University Press.

Cook, T.D., Church, M.B., Ajanaku, S., Shadish, W.R., Jr., Kim, J., and Cohen, R. (1996). The development of occupational aspirations and expectations of inner-city boys. *Child Development, 67*(6), 3368-3385.

Cornelius, L.L., and Herrenkohl, L.R. (2004). Power in the classroom: How the classroom environment shapes students' relationships with each other and with concepts. *Cognition and Instruction, 22*(4), 389-392.

Delpit L. (1995). *Other people's children: Cultural conflict in the classroom.* New York: W.W. Norton.

Downey, D.B., and Ainsworth-Darnell, J.W. (2002). The search for oppositional culture among black students. *American Sociological Review, 67*, 156-164.

Driver, R., Asoko, H., Leach, J., Mortimer, E., and Scott, P. (1994). Constructing scientific knowledge in the classroom. *Educational Researcher, 23*(7), 5-12.

Duschl, R.A., and Osborne, J. (2002). Supporting and promoting argumentation discourse in science education. *Studies in Science Education, 18,* 39-72.

Dweck, C. (1999). *Self-theories: Their role in motivation, personality, and development.* Philadelphia, PA: Taylor and Francis.

Dweck, C., and Legget, E. (1988). A social-cognitive approach to motivation and personality. *Psychological Review, 95,* 256-273.

Eccles, J.S. (1987). Adolescence: Gateway to gender-role transcendence. In D.B. Carter (Ed.), *Current conceptions of sex roles and sex typing: Theory and research.* New York: Praeger.

Eccles, J., Adler, T., Futterman, R., Goff, S., Kaczala, C., Meece, J., and Midgley, C. (1983). Expectancies, values, and academic behaviors. In J.T. Spence (Ed.), *Achievement and achievement motivation* (pp. 75-146). San Francisco, CA: W.H. Freeman.

Eccles, J., and Harold, R. (1992). Gender differences in educational and occupational patterns among the gifted. In N. Colangelo, S.G. Assouline, and D.L. Ambroson (Eds.), *Talent development: Proceedings from the 1991 Henry B. and Jocelyn Wallace national research symposium on talent development* (pp. 2-30). New York: Trillium Press.

Eccles, J.S., Wigfield, A., Flanagan, C.A., Miller, C., Reuman, D.A., and Yee, D. (1989). Self-concepts, domain values, and self-esteem: Relations and changes at early adolescence. *Journal of Personality, 57*(2), 283-310.

Eccles, J., Wigfield, A., Harold, R.D., and Blumenfeld P. (1993). Age and gender differences in children's self- and task perceptions during elementary school. *Child Development, 64*(3), 830-847.

Eccles, J.S., Wigfield, A., and Schiefele, U. (1998). Motivation to succeed. In N. Eisenberg (Ed.), *Handbook of child psychology: Social, emotional, and personality development, fifth edition* (pp. 1017-1095). New York: Wiley.

Eichinger, D., Anderson, C.W., Palinscar, A.S., and David, Y.M. (1991). *An illustration of the roles of content knowledge, scientific argument, and social norms in collaborative problem solving.* Paper presented at the annual meeting of the American Educational Research Association, April, Chicago, IL.

Engle, R.A., and Conant, F.R. (2002). Guiding principles for fostering productive disciplinary engagement: Explaining an emergent argument in a community of learners classroom. *Cognition and Instruction, 20,* 399-483.

Erickson, F. (2004). Culture in society and in educational practices. In J. Banks and C.M. Banks (Eds.), *Multicultural education: Issues and perspectives* (5th ed.). New York: Wiley.

Foster, M., Lewis, J., and Onafowora, L. (2003). Anthropology, culture, and research on teaching and learning: Applying what we have learned to improve practice. *Teachers College Record, 105*(2), 261-277.

Fredericks, J.A., and Eccles, J.S. (2002). Children's competence and value beliefs from childhood through adolescence: Growth trajectories in two male-sex-typed domains. *Developmental Psychology, 38*(4), 519-533.

Garcia Coll, C.T., and Pachter, L.M. (2002). Ethnic and minority parenting. In M.H. Bornstein (Ed.), *Handbook of parenting* (vol. 4, pp. 1-20). Mahwah, NJ: Lawrence Erlbaum Associates.

Giroux, H.A. (1992). *Border crossings: Cultural workers and the politics of education.* New York: Routledge.

Gopnik, A., and Meltzoff, A.N. (1997). *Words, thoughts, and theories.* Cambridge, MA: MIT Press.

Guthrie, J., Van Meter, P., McCann, A., Wigfield, A., Bennett, L., Poundstone, C., Rice, M., Faibisch, F., Hunt, B., and Mitchell, A. (1996). Growth of literacy engagement: Changes in motivation and strategies during concept-oriented reading instruction. *Reading Research Quarterly, 31,* 306-332.

Guthrie, J., Wigfield, A., and VonSecker, C. (2000). Effects of integrated instruction on motivation and strategy use in reading. *Journal of Educational Psychology, 92,* 331-341.

Guthrie, J., Wigfield, A., Pedro Barbosa, P., Perencevich, K.C., Taboada, A., Davis, M.H., Scafiddi, N.T., and Tonks, S. (2004). Increasing reading comprehension and engagement through concept-oriented reading instruction. *Journal of Educational Psychology, 96,* 403-423.

Gutierrez, K.D., and Rogoff, B. (2003). Cultural ways of learning: Individual traits or repertoires of practice. *Educational Researcher, 32*(5), 19-25.

Gutman, L.M., and Midgley, C. (2000). The role of protective factors in supporting the academic achievement of poor African American students during the middle school transition. *Journal of Youth and Adolescence, 29,* 223-248.

Halliday, M.A.K. (1988). On the language of physical science. In M. Ghadessy (Ed.), *Registers of written English: Situational factors and linguistic features* (pp. 162-178). London, England: Pinter.

Harter, S. (1992). The relationship between perceived competence, affect, and motivational orientation within the classroom: Processes and patterns of change. In A.K. Boggiano and T.S. Pittman (Eds.), *Achievement and motivation: A social-developmental perspective* (pp. 77-114). New York: Cambridge University Press.

Heath, S.B. (1982). What no bedtime story means: Narrative skills at home and school. *Language Socialization, 11,* 49-76.

Hembree, R. (1988). Correlates, causes, and treatment of test anxiety. *Review of Educational Research, 58,* 47-77.

Hennessey, M.G. (2002). Metacognitive aspects of students' reflective discourse: Implications for intentional conceptual change teaching and learning. In G.M. Sinatra and P.R. Pintrich (Eds.), *Intentional conceptual change.* Mahwah, NJ: Lawrence Erlbaum Associates.

Herrenkohl, L., and Guerra, M. (1998). Participant structures, scientific discourse, and student engagement in fourth grade. *Cognition and Instruction, 16*(4), 431-473.

Herrenkohl, L.R., Palincsar, A.S., DeWater, L.S., and Kawasaki, K. (1999). Developing scientific communities in classrooms: A sociocognitive approach. *Journal of the Learning Sciences, 8*(3-4), 451-493.

Hidi, S. (1990). Interest and its contribution as a mental resource for learning. *Review of Educational Research, 60*(4), 549-571.

Hidi, S. (2001). Interest, reading, and learning: Theoretical and practical considerations. *Educational Psychology Review, 13*(3), 191-209.

Hogan, K., and Corey, C. (2001). Viewing classrooms as cultural contexts for fostering scientific literacy. *Anthropology and Education Quarterly, 32*(2), 214-243.

Holland, D., Lachicotte, W., Skinner, D., and Cain, C. (1998). *Identity and agency in cultural worlds.* Cambridge, MA: Harvard University Press.

Hudicourt-Barnes, J. (2003). The use of argumentation in Haitian Creole science classrooms. *Harvard Educational Review, 73*(1), 73-93.

Jacobs, J.E., Lanza, S., Osgood, D.W., Eccles, J.S., and Wigfield, A. (2002). Changes in children's self-competence and values: Gender and domain differences across grades one through twelve. *Child Development, 73*(2), 509-527.

Jegede, O.J., and Aikenhead, G.S. (1999). Transcending cultural borders: Implications for science teaching. *Research in Science and Technology Education, 17,* 45-66.

Jegede, O.J., and Okebukola, P.A. (1991). The effect of instruction on socio-cultural belief hindering the learning of science. *Journal of Research in Science Teaching, 28,* 275-285.

Johnson, K., Alexander, J., Spencer, S., Leibham, M., and Neitzel, C. (2004). Factors associated with the early emergence of intense interests within conceptual domains. *Cognitive Development, 19,* 325-343.

Kelley, B.B. (1973). The process of causal attribution. *American Psychologist,* 107-128.

Koller, O., Baumert, J., and Schnabel, K. (2001). Does interest matter? The relationship between academic interest and achievement in mathematics. *Journal for Research in Mathematics Education, 32*(5), 448-470.

Kuhn, D. (1991). *The skills of argument.* New York: Cambridge University Press.

Kuhn, D., and Phelps, E. (1982). The development of problem-solving strategies. In H. Reese (Ed.), *Advances in child development and behavior* (vol. 17, pp. 1-44). New York: Academic Press.

Ladson-Billings, G. (1995). Toward a theory of culturally relevant pedagogy. *American Educational Research Journal, 32*(3), 465-491.

Latour, B. (1987). *Science in action: How to follow scientists and engineers through society.* Cambridge, MA: Harvard University Press.

Lee, O. (1999). Science knowledge, world views, and information sources in social and cultural contexts: Making sense after a natural disaster. *American Educational Research Journal, 36*(2), 187-219.

Lee, O. (2002). Science inquiry for elementary students from diverse backgrounds. In W. Secada (Ed.), *Review of research in education* (vol. 26, pp. 23-69). Washington, DC: American Educational Research Association.

Lee, O., and Anderson, C.W. (1993). Task engagement and conceptual change in middle school science classrooms. *American Educational Research Journal, 30,* 585-610.

Lee, O., and Brophy, J. (1996). Motivational patterns observed in sixth-grade science classrooms. *Journal of Research in Science Teaching, 33*(3), 303-318.

Lee, O., and Fradd, S.H. (1996). Interactional patterns of linguistically diverse students and teachers: Insights for promoting science learning. *Linguistics and Education: An International Research Journal, 8,* 269-297.

Lee, O., and Fradd, S.H. (1998). Science for all, including students from non-English language backgrounds. *Educational Researcher, 27*(3), 12-21.

Lee, O., and Luykx, A. (2006). *Science education and student diversity: Synthesis and research agenda.* New York: Cambridge University Press.

Lehrer, R., Carpenter, S., Schauble, L., and Putz, A. (2000). Designing classrooms that support inquiry. In J. Minstrell and E. van Zee (Eds.), *Inquiring into inquiry learning and teaching in science* (pp. 80-99). Washington, DC: American Association for the Advancement of Science.

Lehrer, R., and Schauble, L. (2004). Modeling natural variation through distribution. *American Educational Research Journal, 41*(3), 635-679.

Lehrer, R., Schauble, L., and Petrosino, A.J. (2001). Reconsidering the role of experiment in science education. In K. Crowley, C. Schunn, and T. Okada (Eds.), *Designing for science: Implications from everyday classrooms and professional settings* (pp. 251-277). Mahwah, NJ: Lawrence Erlbaum Associates.

Lehrer, R., Schauble, L., Strom, D., and Pligge, M. (2001). Similarity of form and substance: Modeling material kind. In S.M. Carver and D. Klahr (Eds.), *Cognition and instruction: Twenty-five years of progress* (pp. 39-74). Mahwah, NJ: Lawrence Erlbaum Associates.

Lemke, J.L. (1990). *Talking science: Language, learning and values.* Norwood, NJ: Ablex.

Lipka, J. (1998). *Transforming the culture of schools: Yup'ik Eskimo examples.* Mahwah, NJ: Lawrence Erlbaum Associates.

Lucas, D., Broderick, N., Lehrer, R., and Bohanan, R. (2005, Nov/Dec). Making the grounds of scientific inquiry visible in the classroom. *ScienceScope, 29*(3), 39-42.

Luster, T., Rhoades, K., and Haas, B. (1989). The relation between parental values and parenting behavior: A test of the Kohn hypothesis. *Journal of Marriage of the Family, 51*, 139-147.

Malone, T.W., and Lepper, M.R. (1987). Making learning fun: A taxonomy of intrinsic motivations for learning. In R.E. Snow and M.J. Farr (Eds.), *Aptitude, learning, and instruction: Cognitive and affective process analysis* (vol. 3, pp. 223-253). Hillsdale, NJ: Lawrence Erlbaum Associates.

Marsh, H.W. (1989). Age and sex effects in multiple dimensions of self-concept: Preadolescence to early adulthood. *Journal of Educational Psychology, 81*, 417-430.

Meece, J.L., Blumenfeld, P.C., and Hoyle, R.H. (1988). Students' goal orientations and cognitive engagement in classroom activities. *Journal of Educational Psychology, 80*, 514-523.

Mehan, H. (1979). *Learning lessons: Social organization in the classroom.* Cambridge, MA: Harvard University Press.

Miserandino, M. (1996). Children who do well in school: Individual differences in perceived competence and autonomy in above-average children. *Journal of Educational Psychology, 88*, 203-214.

National Research Council. (1997). *Improving schooling for language-minority children: A research agenda.* D. August and K. Hakuta (Eds.). Washington, DC: National Academy Press.

National Research Council and Institute of Medicine. (2004). *Engaging schools: Fostering high school students' motivation to learn.* Committee on Increasing High School Students' Engagement and Motivation to Learn. Board on Children, Youth, and Families, Division of Behaviorial and Social Sciences and Education. Washington, DC: The National Academies Press.

Ochs, E., Gonzales, P., and Jacoby, S. (1996). When I come down I'm in a domain state: Talk, gesture, and graphic representation in the interpretive activity of physicists. In E. Ochs, E. Schegloff, and S. Thompson (Eds.), *Interaction and grammar*. Cambridge, MA: Cambridge University Press.

Ogborn, J., Kress, G., Martins, I., and McGillicuddy, K. (1996). *Explaining science in the classroom*. Buckingham, England: Open University Press.

Ogbu, J.U. (1995). Cultural problems in minority education: Their interpretations and consequences-part one. *Urban Review, 27*, 189-205.

Olson, D.R. (1994). *The world on paper*. New York: Cambridge University Press.

Osborne, J.E., Erduran, S., Simon, S., and Monk, M. (2001). Enhancing the quality of argument in school science. *School Science Review, 82*(301), 63-70.

Palincsar, A.S., Magnusson, S.J., Collins, K.M., and Cutter, J. (2001). Making science accessible to all: Results of a design experiment in inclusive classrooms. *Learning Disability Quarterly, 24*, 15-32.

Perkins, D.N., and Grotzer, T.A. (2000). *Models and moves: Focusing on dimensions of causal complexity to achieve deeper scientific understanding*. Paper presented at the annual conference of the American Educational Research Association, April, New Orleans, LA.

Pintrich, P.R., Marx, R.W., and Boyle, R.A. (1993). Beyond cold conceptual change: The role of motivational beliefs and classroom contextual factors in the process of conceptual change. *Review of Educational Research, 63*(2), 167-199.

Pittman, T.S., Emery, J., and Boggiano, A.K. (1982). Intrinsic and extrinsic motivational orientations: Reward-induced changes in preference for complexity. *Journal of Personality and Social Psychology, 42*, 789-797.

Renninger, K.A., Ewen, L., and Lasher, A.K. (2002). Individual interest as context in expository text and mathematical word problems. *Learning and Instruction, 12*, 467-491.

Rogoff, B., Paradise, R., Mejia Arauz, R., Correa-Chavez, M., and Angelillo, C. (2003). Firsthand learning through intent participation. *Annual Review of Psychology, 54*, 175-203.

Rosebery, A.S., Warren, B., and Conant, F.R. (1992). Appropriating scientific discourse: Findings from language minority classrooms. *Journal of the Learning Sciences, 2*(1), 61-94.

Ruble, D.N., and Martin, C.L. (1998). Gender development. In W. Damon (Ed.), *Handbook of child psychology: Vol. 3* (pp. 933-1016). New York: Wiley.

Ryan, R.M., Connell, J.P., and Plant, R.W. (1990). Emotions in non-directed text learning. *Learning and Individual Differences, 2*, 1-17.

Samarapungavan, A. (1992). Children's judgments in theory-choice tasks: Scientific rationality in childhood. *Cognition, 45*(1), 1-32.

Schauble, L., Klopfer, L.E., and Raghavan, K. (1991). Students' transition from an engineering model to a science model of experimentation. *Journal of Research in Science Teaching, 28*(9), 859-888.

Schiefele, U. (1996). Topic interest, text representation, and quality of experience. *Contemporary Educational Psychology, 21*(1), 3-18.

Schiefele, U. (1999). Interest and learning from text. *Scientific Studies of Reading, 3*, 257-279.

Shultz, T.R. (1982). Rules of causal attribution. *Monographs of the Society for Research in Child Development, 47*(1).

Skinner, E.A., Wellborn, J.G., and Connell, J.P. (1990). What it takes to do well in school and whether I've got it: The role of perceived control in children's engagement and school achievement. *Journal of Educational Psychology, 82*, 22-32.

Skinner, E.A., Zimmer-Gembeck, M., and Connell, J. (1998). Individual differences and the development of perceived control. *Monographs of the Society in Child Development, 63*(2-3), 1-220.

Snively, G., and Corsiglia, J. (2001). Discovering indigenous science: Implications for science education. *Science Education, 85*, 6-34.

Steele, C. (1997). A threat in the air: How stereotypes shape intellectual identity and performance. *American Psychologist, 52*, 613-629.

Stevenson, H., and Lee, S.Y. (1990). Contexts of achievement. *Monographs of the Society for Research in Child Development, 55*(1-2), Serial No. 221.

Todt, E. (1990). Development of interest. In H. Hetzer (Ed.), *Applied developmental psychology of children and youth.* Wiesbaden, Germany: Quelle & Meyer.

Tschirgi, J.E. (1980). Sensible reasoning: A hypothesis about hypotheses. *Child Development, 51*, 1-10.

Varelas, M., Luster, B., and Wenzel, S. (1999). Meaning making in a community of learners: Struggles and possibilities in an urban science class. *Research in Science Education, 29*(2), 227-245.

Warren, B., Ballenger, C., Ogonowski, M., Rosebery, A.S., and Hudicourt-Barnes, J. (2001). Rethinking diversity in learning science: The logic of everyday sense-making. *Journal of Research in Science Teaching, 38*(5), 529-552.

Warren, B., and Rosebery, A.S. (1996). "This question is just too, too easy!" Students' perspectives on accountability in science. In L. Schauble and R. Glaser (Eds.), *Innovations in learning: New environments for education* (pp. 97-126). Mahwah, NJ: Lawrence Erlbaum Associates.

Wenger, E. (1998). *Communities of practice: Learning, meaning and identity.* Cambridge, MA: Cambridge University Press.

Wigfield, A., Battle, A., Keller, L., and Eccles, J. (2002) Sex differences in motivation, self concept, career aspiration and career choice: Implications for cognitive development. In A. McGillicuddy-De Lisi and R. De Lisi (Eds.), *Biology, society and behaviour: The development of sex differences in cognition* (pp. 93-124). Westport, CT: Ablex.

Wigfield, A., Eccles, J.S., MacIver, D., Reuman, D.A., and Midgley, C. (1991). Transitions during early adolescence: Changes in children's domain-specific self-perceptions and general self-esteem across the transition to junior high school. *Developmental Psychology, 27*, 552-565.

Wigfield, A., Schiefele, U., Eccles, J., Roeser, R.W., and Davis-Kean, P. (2006). Development of achievement motivation. In W. Damon and N. Eisenberg (Eds.), *Handbook of child psychology: Social, emotional, and personality development* (6th ed., vol. 3). New York: Wiley.

PART III

Supporting Science Learning

In the preceding chapters we have developed a complex picture of student learning in science. It shows that children come to school with powerful and sophisticated ways of reasoning about the material world that enable them to function effectively in many arenas. It also shows that their reasoning is limited in important ways; it is based on a limited range of experiences, and it lacks the predictive and explanatory power of expert scientific reasoning. Finally, this picture shows that with appropriate instruction children can make significant progress toward more sophisticated scientific reasoning, and we know some key principles that inform the design of that instruction. These results are products of a sustained dialogue among developmental and education researchers.

However, this research dialogue and its results have not significantly influenced science education policy and practice. This is in part because science education policy and practice are legitimately concerned with issues that are peripheral to the research dialogue; for example, by what scientific knowledge is most valued by the American public. In many cases, it is clear that policy and practice could be more effective if they were influenced by the research. Curriculum documents and textbooks fail to recognize the importance of children's prior experience, underestimating both their capacities for reasoning and the difficulties posed by scientific conceptions. In instruction, knowledge and practice are separated in ways that diminish the power of scientific reasoning. Teachers must often rely on models of instruction that are demonstrably ineffective. Clearly, children in America would benefit if policy makers, curriculum developers, and practitioners made more effective use of research results.

One key reason that policy makers and practitioners fail to do this is the complexity and fragmentation of the research literature. The studies we review in this report, drawn from a range of literatures, were mostly short in duration and limited in scope, focusing on a few students or a few classrooms, learning about some small part of the vast domain of science. These studies are also embedded in a research discourse that is complicated and often inaccessible to nonspecialists. There are reasons for the difficulty of the discourse. Science learning really *is* complex, and the research on learning cannot be reduced to a few "what works" bullet points without losing much of its value.

In Part III, we begin to take up the challenge of interpreting research on learning so as to inform policy and practice in science education. We begin in Chapter 8 with a proposal for reorganizing the K-8 science curriculum in a way that is more aligned with current understanding of children's learning in science. The hallmark of this approach is the investigation of a smaller set of core ideas and practices in science over an extended period of time. Instructional sequences that weave together the four strands and thereby coordinate conceptual learning with science practices and discourse require adoption of curriculum and assessment models that function over months, years, and grade bands.

In Chapter 9, we turn to a consideration of instruction and assessment. Our review of the research on learning combined with the four-strand framework has implications for how one thinks about the design of the classroom learning environment. Research on learning shows how important it is to include learning opportunities that develop children's abilities to obtain and reason with evidence, to develop and evaluate explanations, to develop and evaluate standards of evidence, to represent and communicate scientific data and ideas, and to engage in argumentation practices. Thus, although we argue in Part II that children are very capable learners, this does not preclude the fact that carefully thought out instructional supports and mediation are needed to help develop scientific practices and ways of knowing.

In Chapter 10 we broaden our view to consider the knowledge and tools that teachers need in order to enact high-quality instruction. We analyze the knowledge base of current in-service K-8 science teachers, and we describe what these teachers would need to know about science, teaching, and learning in order to teach science as we have discussed it in this report. We also examine the means of advancing teacher knowledge through a range of opportunities to learn. These include programs of professional development, workplace learning, and use of instructional systems that provide clear instructional guidance for teachers and provide them with timely feedback on their teaching and strategies for improvement.

8

Learning Progressions

Main Findings in the Chapter:

- *Many standards and curricula contain too many disconnected topics that are given equal priority. Too little attention is given to how students' understanding of a topic can be supported and enhanced from grade to grade. As a result, topics receive repeated, shallow coverage with little consistency, which provides a fragile foundation for further knowledge growth.*
- *Findings from research about children's learning and development can be used to map learning progressions in science. That is, one can describe the successively more sophisticated ways of thinking about a topic that can follow and build on one another as children learn about and investigate a topic over a broad span of time (e.g., 6 to 8 years).*
- *Steps in these progressions are constrained by children's knowledge and skill with respect to each of the four strands. Reaching the hypothetical steps described in the progressions is also dependent on teachers' knowledge and the effectiveness of their instructional practices.*
- *Learning progressions are a promising direction for organizing science instruction and curricula across grades K-8. However, further research and development is needed to identify and elaborate the progressions of learning and instruction that can support students' understanding of these core ideas across the disciplines of science.*

Science learning presents a special challenge to educators because of both the diversity and the complexity of mature scientific knowledge and the fact that it rests on organized conceptual frameworks and sophisticated knowledge construction and evaluation practices that are fundamentally different from the concepts and meaning-making practices that children bring to school. Although children bring a wealth of resources to the science learning task (see Part II), those resources must be built on, enriched, and transformed if they are to learn science with understanding. One challenge is to understand what is most important to teach (given limited time and resources) at the K-8 level: What might be the most important "core ideas" that both empower students to understand the distinctive value of science and prepare them for further learning in science? Another challenge is to understand the pathways—or learning progressions—by which children can bridge their starting point and the desired end point. Given the complexity and counterintuitive nature of the end point, such learning must necessarily occur over a long period of time, work on multiple fronts, and require explicit instruction. Yet at present, curriculum sequences are not typically guided by such long-term vision or understanding, nor is there clear agreement, given the wealth of scientific knowledge, about what might be truly foundational and most important to teach.

In this chapter we develop the idea of *learning progressions* as an approach to research synthesis that could serve as the basis for a dialogue that includes researchers, assessment developers, policy makers, and curriculum developers. Learning progressions are descriptions of the successively more sophisticated ways of thinking about a topic that can follow one another as children learn about and investigate a topic over a broad span of time (e.g., 6 to 8 years). They are crucially dependent on instructional practices if they are to occur. In the chapter we (a) discuss key characteristics of learning progressions, contrasting them with current approaches to defining curriculum and assessment and describing some of the challenges in developing them; (b) use current work on a learning progression as an example of both the problems and possibilities in this approach; and (c) discuss implications and further questions.

CURRENT APPROACHES IN POLICY AND PRACTICE

At present, most decisions about instruction and curriculum sequences in science have not been guided by a long-term understanding of learning progressions that are grounded in the findings of contemporary cognitive, developmental, education, and science studies research (much of this research is reviewed in Part II). Two approaches that have influenced policy and practice are (1) approaches characterizing learning in terms of science process skills and (2) approaches to listing important conceptual knowledge in standards documents.

Science Process Skills

Some scope and sequence suggestions that have been influential in the design of elementary science curricula and texts (e.g., the task analyses of the processes of science and of learning done by psychologist Gagne, which led to the sequence of process skills proposed by the curriculum *Science: A Process Approach* in the 1960s) are based more on rational task analyses than on findings about how children learn meaningful scientific concepts. These proposed "learning hierarchies" focused on building competence with domain-general processes rather than helping children build frameworks of interrelated science concepts. They had an appeal to teachers and curriculum developers because they broke complex tasks down into simpler elements, identified 14 basic process skills that were proposed to develop in a certain sequence and to underlie scientific thinking, and provided many specific exercises for children to practice these skills. But because they ignored the crucial role of meaning, content, and context and treated science instead as a series of disembodied "skills," they were often carried out as meaningless procedures (Baroody et al., 2004; Mintzes, Wandersee, and Novak, 1997). For example, children practiced making observations of a variety of types or making measurements without a concern for understanding what they were observing or measuring. As we have shown in Chapter 5, knowledge is intimately intertwined with scientific reasoning.

Ultimately, however, children failed to develop meaningful understanding under science-as-process instructional programs, and researchers recognized how little these domain-general "skills" actually generalized. Another criticism of these scope and sequence proposals was that they were based on faulty developmental assumptions about children's reasoning and learning capacities (e.g., that young children are concrete rather than abstract thinkers and capable only of observation rather than explanation; Metz, 1995; see our discussion in Chapter 3). Consequently, only a small subset of science process skills (e.g., observing, measuring, predicting) were practiced in the early elementary grades, with more advanced skills (e.g., formulating hypotheses, controlling variables, interpreting data) introduced only in the upper elementary and middle school grades, and many other important sense-making practices of science (practices involving modeling, representation, discourse, and argumentation) were omitted entirely. Given that current research has highlighted the interaction between domain-specific knowledge and reasoning, the importance of modeling, representational practices, and discourse in promoting conceptual understanding, and the capacity of young children to engage in a wide range of these meaning-making practices, a very different approach to describing learning sequences is needed, one that that is more centrally grounded in building an understanding of conceptual frameworks (see discussion of this issue in Part II).

Although Gagne's original formulation of science as a collection of content-free process has largely been rejected by science educators, its legacy persists in both policy and practice. Many textbooks and curriculum documents still have separate sections on scientific inquiry, science processes, or "the scientific method." Many classroom teachers follow the lead of these resources, teaching skills and inquiry techniques separately from the conceptual content of their courses.

Curriculum Standards

Other approaches to guiding curriculum include writing national, state, and district science standards. These standards are an important start (at codifying values), but they generally were based on values and the personal experiences of their writers rather than research on children's learning or detailed conceptual analyses of scientific knowledge and practice. Current national, state, and district standards do not provide an adequate basis for designing effective curriculum sequences for several reasons. First, they contain too many topics without providing guidance about which topics may be most central or important. National standards such as the *National Science Education Standards* (*NSES*) (National Research Council, 1996) or *Benchmarks for Science Literacy* (American Association for the Advancement of Science, 1993) do help to pare down the number of science topics to be covered. However, they still retain many more topics than can be covered and do not identify the most central or important topics. For example, a comparison of the *NSES* with curriculum in high achieving countries that participated in the Third International Mathematics and Science Study (TIMSS) reveals that the *NSES* call for much broader coverage of topics with little sequencing across grades (Schmidt, Wang, and McKnight, 2005). Second, they typically present the key ideas as simple declarative statements without explaining how those understandings need to be grounded in experience with the material world or in reasoning practices. Third, they are not sequenced in ways that recognize research on the development of children's understanding. Project 2061's *Atlas of Science Literacy* (American Association for the Advancement of Science, 2001) does provide a guide for interconnection between important concepts in science with some sequencing. The analysis is based primarily on the structure of knowledge in the disciplines of science with some attention to what scientific ideas children can understand at a given grade level. We propose a sequencing that is more deeply informed by research on children's learning such that the sequences are grounded also in what we know about the ideas children bring to the classroom that can form the foundation for developing understanding of scientific ideas. As we explain later in the chapter, these foundational ideas sometimes do not closely resemble the scientific ideas they can support.

Fourth, while they recognize the central role of involving students in the culture of scientific practice to build scientific knowledge, they do not fully articulate how students' participation in science practices can be integrated with learning about science concepts. Finally, although many standards documents include at least the first three of the four strands of scientific proficiency that we use to organize this report, these strands are generally described separately, so the crucial issue of how advances in one strand are linked to and support children's learning in the other strands is not addressed.

Curriculum and Instruction in K-8 Science Classrooms

As currently described and enacted in U.S. K-8 science classrooms, curriculum—the sequence and series of tasks and assignments posed to students—rarely builds cumulatively and in developmentally informed ways, from students' early knowledge and resources toward scientifically accepted theories and concepts. Although there are some curricular materials that pursue this approach, they tend to cover a limited slice of content and are often restricted in duration to periods spanning a few to several weeks of instruction. It is highly unlikely that brief periods of uncoordinated instruction are going to achieve the goal of helping students generate a scientifically informed epistemology, a deep and well-structured knowledge base, and a firm understanding of the purposes and methods of science.

Analyses of science curricula in the United States indicate that they are generally poorly designed for the purpose of effective knowledge building. Evaluations recently conducted under the leadership of the American Association for the Advancement of Science (AAAS) Project 2061 staff suggest that the major commercial textbook series, which do at least take a multiyear perspective to sequencing instruction, have major flaws of various kinds, including content, motivation, and attention to student prior conceptions (Kesidou and Roseman, 2002). The AAAS analysis indicates that curriculum is rarely framed around the big ideas. Indeed, the big ideas are largely lost in the curriculum. Roseman, Kesidou, Stern, and Caldwell (1999), authors of the AAAS report, concluded (p. 2):

> [T]he textbooks covered too many topics and didn't develop any of them well. In addition, the texts included many classroom activities that either were irrelevant to learning key science ideas or didn't help students relate what they were doing to the underlying ideas.

Valverde and Schmidt's (1997) comparison of U.S. science curriculum with the 10 countries performing best on the tests of science achievement in the Trends in International Mathematics and Science Study provide further support for the AAAS conclusions, as well as the results of these curricular patterns on student learning. They found that U.S. science curricula constitute a relatively extreme case of broad and superficial coverage, with little attention to building links across concepts. The U.S. science texts covered many more topics than the texts of the high-achieving countries. In their words, "breadth of topics is presented in these textbooks at the expense of depth of coverage. Consequently, U.S. textbooks are limited to perfunctory treatment of subject matter" (p. 62). More specifically, Valverde and Schmidt point to the failure of U.S. science curriculum to build connections between the abundant knowledge pieces presented in the curriculum and the resultant epistemic messages this conveys about the structure of the discipline (pp. 62):

> The unfocused curriculum of the United States is also a curriculum of very little coherence. . . . U.S. textbooks and teachers present items one after the other from a laundry list of topics from state and local district guides . . . . This is done with little or no regard for establishing the relation between various topics or themes on the list. The loss of these relationships between ideas encourages children to regard these disciplines as no more than disjointed notions that they are unable to conceive of as belonging to a disciplinary whole.

An increasingly popular approach to science curriculum in U.S. school districts is the use of science kits. Individual kits may provide students with a 6- or 8-week experience that, in some cases, provides a coherent set of experiences that build logically. While kits can bring some coherence to science curriculum (at least at the level of the unit), the cumulative effect of a kit-based approach to science can be very problematic. In many cases, students receive a series of brief exposures to a collection of unrelated topics (the rainforest, rocks and minerals, weather) presented in modular units or kits. The sequence of presentation hardly matters, as the ideas do not build in any meaningful way. Although we know of no research that has explicitly probed the learning research base of kits, their presentation of science topics as essentially interchangeable and noncumulative raises serious concerns. Kit-based curricula appear to be sensitive to a number of practical concerns, including variability in standards from locale to locale, so that a teacher can never count on a student's having knowledge prerequisite to a new set of concepts. It also maximizes flexibility, so that teachers with low content knowledge can easily skip over topics that are too unfamiliar. However, it also sacrifices the potential long-term benefits of carefully crafted curricula that strategically build on student skills and their knowledge base.

Curriculum needs restructuring to much more adequately support building robust science knowledge. It is not sufficient to teach lots of pieces of science knowledge. The curricular scaffolding of robust knowledge in the form of cohort knowledge structures, organized around core ideas, is critical for supporting science proficiency (see Chapter 4 for discussions of conceptual change and building knowledge structures). K-8 science curriculum needs to much more adequately build robust science knowledge of this form.

Deciding how research can guide standards and curriculum has also proved to be a difficult process. Which studies are trustworthy? Should one take evidence that few students *have* learned a concept at a given age as evidence that few students *can* learn? Conversely, should one take evidence of successful teaching in a few classrooms as justification for including content in standards?

DEFINING LEARNING PROGRESSIONS

Learning progressions are descriptions of the successively more sophisticated ways of thinking about a topic that can follow one another as children learn about and investigate a topic over a broad span of time (e.g., 6 to 8 years). They are crucially dependent on instructional practices if they are to occur. That is, traditional instruction does not enable most children to attain a good understanding of scientific frameworks or practices, but there is evidence that the proposed learning sequences could occur with appropriate instructional practices.

The more effective instructional practices aim to build understanding through involving students in a variety of practices, including gathering data through observation or experiment, representing data, reasoning—with oneself and others—about what data mean, and applying key ideas to new situations. At the same time, bringing about understanding of scientific frameworks is difficult, so innovative instructional practice is most effective when sustained over a period of time. The timescale of most innovative teaching interventions has typically been relatively short (on the order of 2 or 3 months for a specific topic). Thus, our ideas about longer term learning progressions are conjectural—ideas about how understanding could be developed given sustained and appropriate instructional practices—while at the same time based on research syntheses and open to empirical investigation in future research. That is, they are plausible hypotheses, greatly constrained by the findings of research. More specifically:

• Learning progressions are anchored on one end by what is known about the concepts and reasoning of students entering school. There is now a very extensive research base at this end (see Chapter 3), although much of it is not widely known or used by the science education community, which often relies on older (outdated) characterizations of preschool and elementary schoolchildren's competence from the (earlier) developmental literature.

• At the other end, learning progressions are anchored by societal expectations (values) about what society wants middle school students to understand about science. They are also constrained by research-based conceptual and social analyses of the structure of the disciplinary knowledge and practice that is to be learned. Analysis of disciplinary knowledge is important in helping to identify the core ideas in science—those of greatest explanatory power and scope—that it may be most important to teach, because they provide central frameworks for further learning. Examples of such core ideas are the atomic-molecular theory of matter and evolutionary theories of life's diversity. In addition, analysis of disciplinary knowledge helps identify the network of ideas and practices on which those core ideas rest, and hence what will be important component ideas to develop as part of their construction.

• Learning progressions propose the *intermediate* understandings between these anchor points that are reasonably coherent networks of ideas and practices and that contribute to building a more mature understanding. It is important to note that some of the important precursor ideas may not look like the later ideas, yet they crucially contribute to their construction. For example, realizing that objects are composed of materials and have some properties because they are made of that material is a critical first step toward understanding atomic-molecular theory. By thinking hard about what initial understandings need to be drawn on in developing new understandings, learning progressions highlight important precursor understandings that might otherwise be overlooked by teachers and educators.

The intellectual exercise of constructing learning progressions requires one to synthesize results from disparate (often short-term) studies in ways that begin to address questions of how longer term learning may occur; learning progressions suggest priorities for future research, including the need for engaging in longer term studies based on best bets suggested by these research syntheses; and they present research results in ways that make their implications for policy and practice apparent. Ultimately, well-tested ideas about learning progressions could provide much needed guidance for both the design of instructional sequences and large-scale and classroom-based assessments.

Key Characteristics

The learning progression approach has four characteristics that are mostly absent from accounts of domain-general developmental sequences and current standards documents.

• *Use of the current research base:* We suggest that learning progressions should make systematic use of current research on children's learning (reviewed in Part II) to suggest how well-grounded conceptual understanding can develop. For more on how the research can be used, see the example developed below.

• *Interconnected strands of scientific proficiency:* Learning progressions consider the interaction among the strands of scientific proficiency in building understanding (know, use, and interpret scientific explanations of the natural world; generate and evaluate scientific evidence and explanations; understand the nature and development of scientific knowledge; participate productively in scientific practices and discourse) and always involve students with meaningful questions and investigations of the natural world.

• *Organization of conceptual knowledge around core ideas:* Learning progressions recognize that the first strand of scientific proficiency (understanding and using scientific explanations) involves far more than learning lists of facts. Scientific understanding is organized around conceptual frameworks and models that have broad explanatory power. The purpose of concepts is to extend understanding—to allow one to predict, understand, and explain phenomena one experiences in the world—as well as to solve important problems. It is therefore important to explicitly recognize these frameworks and to help children develop them through instruction that involves model building and conceptual change.

• *Recognizing multiple sequences and web-like growth:* Learning progressions recognize that all students will follow not one general sequence, but multiple (often interacting) sequences around important disciplinary-specific core ideas (e.g., atomic-molecular theory, evolutionary theory, cell theory, force and motion). The challenge is to document and describe paths that work as well as to investigate possible trade-offs in choosing different paths.

Design Challenges

In the development of learning progressions that are research-based and reflect the variety of ways that children can learn meaningfully about a topic, there are three challenges, none of which can be completely overcome with the existing research base: (1) describing a student's knowledge and practice at a given point in the learning progression, (2) describing a succession of ways students can understand a topic that show connections between ways and respect constraints on their learning abilities, and (3) describing the variety of possibilities for meaningful learning for students with different personal and cultural resources or different instructional histories. We discuss each of these challenges below.

We wish to develop descriptions of students' knowledge and practice that will ultimately include all four strands of scientific proficiency (see Box 2-1) and that recognize the complex organization of meaningful scientific knowledge and practice. Furthermore, we would like to describe children's knowledge and practice in ways that help us to see the continuities—and the discontinuities—between the reasoning of children of different ages. Inevitably, these descriptions must fail in some way; no organizational scheme can fully capture the organization of a child's knowledge or its connections with her practices, with systems and phenomena in the material world, and with developmental changes over time. The various approaches to describing core ideas and strands in children's reasoning discussed in this book represent various compromises that emphasize some aspects of the organization of their reasoning while obscuring others.

In addition to describing children's knowledge and practice at a given age, learning progressions aspire to describe how that knowledge and practice could change over time, with successive understandings representing an achievable advance from earlier ones. This presents multiple challenges. We wish to describe both continuities and discontinuities in children's thinking, as well as successional trends over time. The choices we make will inevitably emphasize some of those continuities and discontinuities while obscuring others. In addition, each phase must represent an achievable advance from the one before. The strongest evidence for a suggested advance comes in the form of teaching experiments that demonstrate how students can move from one set of understandings to the next or longitudinal studies showing systematic progressions in students' understanding. When this kind of empirical evidence is not available, we can suggest stages that represent reasonable advances across all four strands of scientific proficiency.

Finally, no single learning progression will be ideal for all children, since they have different instructional histories, bring different personal and cultural resources to the process of learning science, and learn in different social and material environments. The best learning progressions are those that make effective use of the resources available to different children and in different environments. This is the challenge that we are farthest from responding to effectively with the current research base.

INITIAL WORK ON LEARNING PROGRESSIONS

What might such long-term learning progressions look like? Recently, two design teams that were composed of scientists, science educators, and experts on children's learning were asked to use existing research to construct possible learning progressions for two important theories in natural science: the atomic-molecular theory (Smith et al., 2004) and evolution (Lehrer, Catley, and Reiser, 2004). These two theories are unquestionably core ideas in modern science for many reasons. Each is well tested, validated, and absolutely central to its discipline. Each integrates many different findings and has exceptionally broad explanatory scope. Each is the source of coherence for many key concepts, principles, and even other theories in the discipline. Each provides insight into the development of the field, guides new research, and can be understood in progressively more complicated ways. Each enables creative links to be made between disciplines. For example, atomic-molecular analyses are important in physics, chemistry, biology, and geology. In that way, understanding and describing matter at an atomic-molecular level is truly foundational for later learning in any science. Evolutionary theory is also integrative of many disciplines, ranging from genetics to ecology and geology, and foundational to all aspects of modern biology, geology, and psychology.

Significantly, there were important similarities in the approaches taken by the two design teams that resonate with findings from current research and that might prove valuable to other (future) design efforts. First, the learning progressions were organized around big ideas of disciplinary importance—major theoretical frameworks in modern science—rather than very abstract or domain-general core ideas, such as systems, interactions, model, and measurement, that are considered important cross-cutting themes in the science standards documents. This disciplinary approach fits with the increasing recognition of the importance of specific content and context in thinking and learning and the power of theories to define and organize understandings of particular domains, something that domain-general ideas by their nature don't have the power to do (see Chapters 3, 4, and 5 for discussions of conceptual knowledge and its role in scientific thinking).

Second, both design teams identified a number of high-level (abstract) ideas that go into building these disciplinary core ideas, but which, unlike the scientific theories themselves, were more accessible at the start of schooling. These foundational ideas, although not elaborated or well-tested theories themselves, can nonetheless be a source of coherence, providing a framework for organizing children's learning of new facts, inquiry, and explanation. Thus, both the atomic-molecular theory and the theory of evolution were seen as *emergent* core ideas, creative syntheses that required the progressive elaboration and transformation of these foundational ideas as they were increasingly grounded in empirical data, integrated, and intercoordinated with each other. In these ways, both design teams acknowledged that even young children have important domain-specific ideas that serve as a foundation for their learning and that the development of complex scientific ideas involved both continuities and discontinuities in children's thinking (two themes discussed in Chapters 3 and 4).

For example, although the idea of evolution via natural selection is a complex emergent idea, it builds on and integrates a wide variety of ideas that are accessible to investigation even by young children, including ideas about:

(a) *Biodiversity:* The existence of different kinds of living things (i.e., the diversity of species);

(b) *Structure/function (adaptation):* Living things have structures that serve important biological functions (and hence can promote adaptation);

(c) *Ecology/interrelationships:* Living things populate a habitat and interact with other things in that habitat (e.g., predator/prey relationships);

(d) *Variation:* Individuals (within a species) vary in their properties;

(e) *Change* in living things can occur at different scales of time and organization (e.g., growth is change in individuals over the life cycle; populations may also change in characters across multiple generations); and

(f) *Geologic processes:* The earth has changed in regular ways over time (e.g., mountain formation, erosion, layering of sediments, volcanic eruptions; fossils found trapped in different layers of the earth provide clues about the earth's past).

In the case of the atomic-molecular theory, although the very notions of atoms, molecules, chemical substance, and chemical and physical change are complex emergent ideas, even children entering school make a distinction between objects and the materials they are made of, are elaborating on their knowledge of the properties of objects and materials, and thus have resources for beginning to explain why objects have the characteristics they do and for beginning to track some underlying constancies and changes in objects and materials across various transformations (e.g., dividing into pieces, reshaping).

Third, in keeping with the science-as-practice models discussed earlier, both design teams recognized that understanding an idea involves engaging in a wide range of practices that support using and developing that idea. Hence it was important to specify the nature of those practices, both in order to support the design of effective learning environments and appropriate assessments of student learning. These practices are of a wide variety of sorts, including being able to use ideas to question, describe, classify, identify, predict, measure/compare, explain, represent (or symbolize) ideas and data using a variety of cultural tools, design studies, evaluate ideas/make arguments, etc. Furthermore, although it was recognized that practices would become more complex and intercoordinated in the course of learning, even young children were seen as able to engage with a rich set of practices right from the start (see Chapter 3). Thus, in contrast to the skill progressions outlined in *Science: A Process Approach*, the focus was on meaning-making (knowledge construction) practices enacted and supported in a cultural context (not isolated, disembodied skills), with explanation, evaluation, and symbolization recognized as central practices right from the start.

Finally, both design teams assumed that understanding of the core ideas of science also involves understanding their epistemology (i.e., the data patterns and knowledge construction and evaluation practices that serve to give rise to those core ideas) and that even young children would have some initial epistemological ideas that could be built on, enriched, and transformed in the course of science learning (see Chapters 3 and 6). Hence the foundational ideas used to structure the learning progressions included foundational epistemological ideas as well as the foundational domain-specific ideas previously discussed. In the case of the learning progression for evolution, those epistemological ideas were characterized as of two broad sorts: (1) ideas about forms of argument (which would be elaborated over the learning progression to include understanding of both model-based and historical arguments) and (2) knowledge of specific mathematical and representational tools that can be used to enrich one's descriptions of nature (which would be elaborated to include the tools of measurement, data creation, representations of distributions, Venn diagrams, cladograms, etc.). In the case of the learning progression for the atomic-molecular theory, the designers focused on the elaboration of the core epistemological ideas of measurement, models, and evaluation of ideas using data and argument.

Including important foundational ideas about epistemology (to be built on and elaborated in the course of the learning progressions) is in keeping with current research findings that children have a capacity for metacognitive reflection: that is, they can ask themselves not only "What do I know?" or "What should I do?" but "How do I know?" "Why should I do it?" Furthermore, there is increasing evidence that flexible and adaptive use of practices is greatly aided by explicit understanding of the reasons for those practices. Current research also makes clear that these deeper epistemological understandings do not come for free with the mere use of practices (Roth, 2002). Rather, they require explicit reflection and discussion of these issues. Significantly, recognizing the importance of engaging students with these issues has led to changes in how the practices themselves are taught.

This work on constructing learning progressions is new, still partial and incomplete, and has not had a chance to be discussed and critiqued by the larger community. We present one example in greater detail here—work on a learning progression for matter and atomic-molecular theory—because of the somewhat larger research base in this area for K-8 students and to illustrate what such an approach might look like and how it is different from current practice. Also, this example shows how core ideas permit cross-domain integration (in this case, spanning domains as different as the physical and life sciences) and has implications for developing an informed citizenry able to understand current practical issues and policy debates (environmental issues and problems). Currently, other design teams are working on learning progressions for other core ideas (genetics, matter cycling). We think more work on describing such large-scale learning progressions is going to be crucially important to the improvement of science education in the United States.

A LEARNING PROGRESSION FOR THE ATOMIC-MOLECULAR THEORY OF MATTER

As mentioned above, research on children's learning is currently fragmentary, falling well short of suggesting a complete sequence of steps in learning about matter or any other topic. We therefore need to make principled use of the research to suggest the general nature of a learning progression that would lead to understanding and to fill in the gaps when research is not available. In developing a learning progression for the atomic-molecular theory of matter, we suggest reasonable steps that are constrained by three of the four strands of scientific proficiency: (a) students' existing concepts, (b) their knowledge construction and evaluation abilities, and (c) their understandings of science as a way of knowing. (Research focusing on the fourth strand, productive participation in science, currently is not easily integrated with research focusing on the first three within a learning progression focused on matter.)

Thus, in describing the learning progression, we discuss how it reflects the interactions among these three kinds of constraints and how competence in the first three strands of scientific proficiency can develop interactively. We also discuss some of the research base for the steps in the progression, the way it challenges some aspects of existing practice and provides guidance for ways of elaborating the science standards, as well as important limitations in the existing progression and questions raised for future work.

Grades K-2

Developing an Understanding of Materials and Measurement

The learning progression developed by Smith et al. (2004) identifies several ideas (concepts, resources, abilities) that children have at the start of elementary school that enable them to begin their initial exploration of three basic questions. The learning progression is described in part as the progressively more sophisticated answers that children can give to these questions (the overview table in Appendix A describes the learning progression in these terms):

1. What are things made of and how can one explain their properties?
2. What changes and what stays the same when things are transformed?
3. How do we know?

For starters, even preschool children make some distinction between material and object levels of description and have learned words to label things at both levels: kinds of objects (e.g., boats, cars, beds, balls, kites) and kinds of materials (e.g., water, milk, play dough, wood, plastic). Children also have rich vocabulary for describing the properties of things based on commonsense impressions—for example, size (big/small), weight (heavy/light),[1] texture (soft/hard, rough/smooth), color (red/blue), shape (round/square), taste (sweet/salty), smell—and have some initial ideas about which properties may pattern at object or material kind levels. They not only are fluent language speakers (which allows them to use language to form and express ideas in symbolic form) but they also have some facility at counting, drawing, and building or making things (which extends the resources they have for symbolizing things). Thus, they can use their existing ideas to engage in a variety of practices, including asking questions, describing and representing their observations, identifying and classifying things, making arguments, and proposing explanations (see the chapters in Part II for a review of research that supports these claims).

At the same time, the proposed learning progression acknowledges the extensive research that shows young children's initial conceptual knowledge of materials, of physical quantities such as weight and volume, and of the knowledge construction practices of science are still quite limited. For example, although young children are learning names for some kinds of materials, descriptions at the level of objects is much more salient and important in their everyday life, and their knowledge of and experience with different materials is still quite limited (Krnel, Watson, and Glazar, 1998; Krnel, Glazar, and Watson, 2003).

Furthermore, although young children may implicitly treat materials as homogeneous constituents of objects in some circumstances, this understanding is still fragile and unarticulated. Indeed, there are many situations in which they deny that an entity broken into tiny pieces is still the same kind of stuff in part because it no longer looks like the same stuff (Dickinson, 1987; Krnel, Glazar, and Watson, 2003). Their knowledge of object properties is limited to those accessible to commonsense impressions, so many of

---

[1]We have used "weight" rather than "mass" to describe the measured property of matter because it is the property that students measure and conceptualize at a younger age. We recognize that at some point students should learn to distinguish between weight as gravitational force and mass as a measure of the amount of matter. Even at the middle school level, though, this distinction probably is not critical for an understanding of atomic-molecular theory.

the most enduring and essential characteristics of materials (density, boiling and melting points, thermal and electrical conductivity, solubility, etc.) are not yet known to them (Johnson, 1996; Smith, Carey, and Wiser, 1985; Wilkening and Huber, 2002). Related to this, their knowledge construction and evaluation practices are based on casual everyday observations using their commonsense impressions, not on careful measurement, modeling, and extended argument. At the outset of school, they have had limited experiences using instruments to measure things, and they have even less understanding of the deeper reasons for using instruments or of explicit criteria for judging what makes a good measurement (Lehrer, Jenkins, and Osana, 1998).

Hence, the overall goal at the K-2 level is to have children clarify, extend, systematize, and even begin to problematize their understandings of common materials and important physical quantities (especially weight and measures of spatial extent). Curriculum developers need to be mindful that children are ready to tackle these issues, while at the same time realizing that they are still conceptually difficult for them. They need to realize that central to helping students make progress with these issues is not just providing them with new facts or experiences, but also introducing them to cultural tools and practices that enable them to extend and restructure their understandings.

One specific goal is to extend children's knowledge of materials and help create a richer notion of material kind as a dense causal nexus: that is, to realize that objects are constituted of materials and have some properties because they are made of that material. For example, children can be presented with objects made of a range of different materials (or containers with a range of different liquids). They can be asked to organize, describe, and classify the things by the kind of material they think they are made of and to defend their classifications. They can be asked to describe the properties of the objects and compare them in their properties, using new tools for organizing their descriptions, such as Venn diagrams and attribute/value charts.

In addition, they can consider why objects behave as they do in situations that implicate the materials they are made from. For example, they can compare the properties of two cups (one made of plastic and the other glass) and consider how each will respond when dropped and why. Or they might compare the properties of two balls (one made of metal and another of rubber) and consider how they respond when dropped and why. They can be introduced to common names for certain materials and asked how they could tell if something else was made of that material. They can predict how the observable properties of things might change or stay the same if an object is reshaped, divided into little pieces, or heated until melted, and whether they think it will still be the same kind of material. They then carry out those transformations and record and interpret what happens. For example, they might melt a chocolate bunny and be asked to describe how it has changed. They can also be asked whether they think it is still chocolate, whether it still has the same amount of stuff, whether it has the same weight, and to make arguments about how they can tell.

In the course of these activities, not only will they be learning about how to form meaningful classifications, to carry out simple investigations, and to represent and record data in useful ways, but also they will deepen their understanding of materials. They will learn that not all properties of chunks stay the same when cut into pieces and that there are at least two ways of trying to trace (or track) the identity of different materials over time—by historical continuity (i.e., by following where it came from, or what was done to it, such as grinding) or by consideration of its observable properties.[2] Originally, children might be more inclined to use commonsense properties than historical tracing. Historical tracing is important (especially across decompositions, such as grinding into smaller pieces) because it helps build an explicit idea of a material as an underlying constituent. By engaging children with considerations of what happens to materials with decomposition, they come to identify materials not just by their common perceptual features, but as constituents that can maintain their identity (and certain properties) even when they become arbitrarily small. They also begin to realize that not all large-scale properties of materials are preserved during that decomposition (i.e., some emerge when there is enough stuff or under certain conditions).

Another (related) goal identified for this period is to extend children's descriptions beyond commonsense perceptions—especially for important physical magnitudes like weight and volume—by engaging them with the problem of constructing measures for a variety of quantities so that they can develop an explicit theory of measure that underlies the practice of measurement. Measurement is an important scientific practice that contrasts with everyday practice and grows out of concern with having data that can be described in precise objectively reproducible (or verifiable) ways and made amenable to mathematical representation and manipulation. It also greatly aids in finding lawful patterns in data—patterns that would be totally obscured if one relied on commonsense impressions. Yet many aspects of the underlying logic of measurement are not initially obvious to students and can be hidden by simply teaching them how to use preexisting or standard measuring procedures or instruments. Thus, learning to measure should in-

---

[2]Of course, as chemists can attest, the problem of tracking the identity of materials is complex, and neither of the strategies children use is infallible. In fact, in some situations (chemical reactions), one substance will cease to exist and another come into being. In addition, many of the observable properties that children use are not the most reliable or valid cues to material identity.

volve much more than developing procedural competence; it should also involve developing a conceptual understanding of measurement (Lehrer, Jenkins, and Osana, 1998).

Even infants and preschoolers make judgments about how big or heavy something is, but these judgments are grounded in their commonsense impressions, not yet informed by explicit measurement procedures. Furthermore, although these commonsense impressions are useful in everyday life, they provide a poor basis for scientific practice. For example, felt weight is influenced by a host of physical variables and hence is not a very precise, reliable, or valid measure of the objective weight of objects. For these reasons, scientists have developed a wide range of measuring instruments that enable them to measure important physical variables. These measures also enable them to potentially deal with entities that are not on a scale that is accessible to commonsense impressions—both the very large and the very small.

As mentioned above, devising measuring instruments and figuring out how to use or apply mathematical ideas to one's physical concepts is by no means a trivial undertaking for students for multiple reasons. First, one needs to identify a physical situation that responds to the physical variable in question—for example, balance scales respond to weight, and alcohol in thermometers responds to temperature. Second, one needs to create a unit for that quantity of fixed size that one can use to "cover" the measurement space, which one then can count. Third, one needs to consider how to deal with fractional units. In cases in which no direct indicator for the quantity in question exists, one may need to derive a unit by mathematical combination of other units. Thus, some measurements are simpler to devise than others and may be foundational in the sense that one uses one measurement in deriving others. They also may be useful entry points for considering the basic issues that arise in measurement (i.e., constructing a theory of measurement that can inform one's understanding of the issues faced in constructing measures).

All of these possibilities occur in the learning progression for matter and constrain its proposed sequences. Thus, the proposed learning progression builds on the research of Lehrer, Schauble, and their colleagues who have investigated instructional sequences for building an understanding of the measurement of important physical quantities. In their work, learning to measure length and area provides an important foundation that aids in children's later construction of measures of volume and weight. Their classroom studies (replicated many times in different classrooms) have shown that not only are K-2 children capable of inventing initial measures of length and area (e.g., see Lehrer, Jenkins, and Osana, 1998), but also that doing so enables them to engage with basic epistemological issues about measurement (understanding the 0 point, equal partition, fractional units, the need to cover the measurement space, etc.). These are issues that even much older children often fail to understand if they are taught merely to use measurement systems developed by others. Furthermore, children who have developed these epistemological understandings of measure are able to build on these understandings in tackling the more difficult problems of measuring weight and volume (Lehrer, Jaslow, and Curtis, 2003). For these (and other) reasons, engaging K-2 children with these epistemological issues is made central to the proposed learning progression.

Because the measurement of weight and volume is more complex, students should not work on measuring those quantities (quantitatively) until the appropriate foundation has been laid. However, one problem that K-2 children are ready for working on involves figuring out that balance scales are responsive to weight (rather than, say, the size of objects, number of objects, or kind of material an object is made of), although the task is by no means trivial for children at this age (Metz, 1993). Working on this problem enables them to have two ways of making judgments: felt weight judgments (using their hands) and weight comparisons (using pan balances). It also allows children to confront an important epistemological issue: Which is a more reliable and valid (qualitative) measure of the weight of two objects, their hands or a balance scale? They can explore this question in a variety of ways: for example, by making repeated comparisons of the same objects under different conditions to see if they get the same outcome (e.g., after they have hefted a heavy object), or considering cases in which their felt weight judgments are at odds with those of the balance scale because of size/weight illusions, etc. By debating and engaging with this issue, they may come to more deeply value and trust pan balance measurements and begin to restructure their understanding of weight as an objectively defined (rather than subjectively assessed) physical magnitude. (They can also consider these issues for length and area—for example, by exploring the Muller-Lyer optical illusions.)

How This Differs from Current Practice

Very little if anything is expected to be accomplished in science during the K-2 years in most U.S. elementary school classrooms, where the overwhelming focus is on developing early literacy and numeracy. Most science activities are short (one lesson long) rather than coherent units. There is frequent shifting from topic to topic rather than a coherent building. In fact, the shift between topics may be confusing to students. For example, students might do an activity involving identification of materials one day; on another, they might identify or describe solids, liquids, and gases—both as part of their matter unit. This is potentially confusing to students at this age because, lacking a clear concept of matter (or forms of matter), they may mistakenly think of solids, liquids, and gases as kinds of materials. Phenomena are often selected—such as sinking or floating or evaporation—more by their surprise or attention-getting value than with a thought about what students will conceptually understand by exploring them. In fact, students are often presented with phenomena that they have no real means of understanding at this grade. Finally, students are often simply introduced to standard measurement procedures, without engaging them in trying to understand the underlying logic of those procedures.

In contrast, the proposed learning progression outlines a set of conceptual goals that can be investigated in a more sustained, mutually reinforcing manner, based on a principled interpretation of research on children's interpretations of matter and materials. In particular, we note that the research enables us to identify phenomena and topics for discussion that will help students make progress with respect to each of the first three strands of scientific proficiency:

- *Understanding and using scientific explanations of the natural world.* Children can learn to make the critical distinction between objects and the materials of which the objects are made. They can begin using observable properties to describe materials and transformations in materials and consider what properties of objects may depend on (and thus be explained by) the kind of materials they are made of.

- *Generating and evaluating scientific evidence and explanations.* Children can begin the process of building the measurement skills and understandings that will be essential to developing scientific concepts of material kind and of such properties as mass, volume, and density. They can actively investigate properties of materials and transformations in materials and being to understand that some transformations (e.g., grinding into little pieces, melting) lead to changes in some perceptible properties of materials without fundamentally changing the identity of the material or the amount of material.

- *Understanding how personal and scientific knowledge are constructed.* Children can develop important epistemological understandings of measurement and of transformations of materials. They can consider how reliable measurements can be generated and the circumstances in which measurements are more useful or trustworthy than personal impressions. They can also consider ways in which both history and observation are used to understand transformations that destroy objects (e.g., breaking, dividing, melting) but may leave the materials of which the objects are made intact.

Thus the strands of scientific proficiency can be used in conjunction with the research to identify serious work that can enable K-2 students to lay a foundation, especially in their early work on measurement, and their exploration of materials that will continue to have payoff in the later grades. The design of the approach to measurement, which emphasizes modeling and epistemological understandings rather than mere computations, has implications for the design of early mathematics instruction as well. The approach emphasizes the importance of developing important domain-specific concepts and foundational epistemological ideas as a base from which to build in later grades.

Grades 3-5

Developing an Explicit Macroscopic Understanding of Matter

Work in grades K-2 to elaborate children's understanding of specific materials prepares them to move up a level of abstraction and develop an initial macroscopic understanding of matter at this next age band. Students now can consider not just the salient properties that distinguish different kinds of materials, but ask the question of whether there are some properties that all material entities have in common. In this way, they can be led (with relevant instructional practices) to articulate a general concept of matter that was initially implicit in their notion of material kind. In so doing, a new causal nexus—matter—is developed as students come to realize that objects made of different materials "have weight and occupy space because they are made of something (pieces of stuff) that continues to exist, take up space, and have weight across a broad range of transformations" (Smith et al., 2004, p. 46). Some core ideas important to develop at this age band include understanding that:

- Objects are made of matter that takes up space and has weight.
- Solids, liquids, and air are forms of matter and share these general properties.
- There can be invisible pieces of matter (i.e., too small to see with the naked eye).
- Matter continues to exist when broken into pieces too tiny to be visible.
- Amount of matter and weight are conserved across a range of transformations, including melting, freezing, and dissolving (Smith et al., 2004, p. 45).

Research has shown that elementary schoolchildren are beginning to develop an intuitive (abstract) notion that there is "an amount of stuff" in objects that can remain constant across changes in surface appearance. For example, in their classic conservation studies, which have been replicated many times by others, Piaget and Inhelder (1974) poured liquid from a short, fat container into a tall, thin one and asked children if there was the same amount of liquid in both containers or if one had more. Similarly, they took a ball of clay and rolled it out into a thin sausage shape or divided it into several smaller pieces and asked if there was still the same amount of clay in the ball, the sausage, and the set of pieces. They found that young elementary schoolchildren were developing the idea that the amount of stuff remained the same despite the striking changes in surface appearances, changes that typically led younger preschool children to deny that the amounts could be the same. In this way, they showed that elementary schoolchildren were increasingly capable not only of thinking about the particular qualities (or characteristics) of a material, but also of its underlying amount.

At the same time, research also provides extensive evidence that children's notion of "amount of stuff" is still inchoate in many ways—not yet based on a clearly articulated notion of matter that is tightly interrelated with their notions of taking up space and having weight nor clearly (explicitly) understood as an additive quantity itself (Carey, 1991; Smith, Solomon, and Carey, 2005; Smith, Carey, and Wiser, 1985). So, for example, children often judge that some material objects (such as a piece of Styrofoam, a small piece of clay) weigh nothing at all, a difficulty that for many students persists well into the middle school years (Smith et al., 1997; Smith, 2005). In addition, they also often judge that when an object is repeatedly divided into littler pieces (so tiny that they are no longer visible) that the matter itself has disappeared (Smith et al., 2004; Yair and Yair, 2004). Further evidence that having weight is not criterial in their conceptions of matter stem from analysis of the instances they judge as being made of matter as well as from their explicit definitions of matter. In fact, elementary schoolchildren often fail to include many instances as matter that clearly have weight (e.g., liquids or biological entities such as a flower, dog, or meat) as well as overextend to include entities that are associated with matter but are not matter itself (e.g., fire, electricity) (Carey, 1991; Stavy, 1991). Consistent with their noncanonical classifications, their explicit definitions of matter fail to identify taking up space or having weight (mass) as criterial for being matter. Instead, they either simply list examples, focus on commonsense perceptual properties (it is something that one can see, feel, or touch) or on its having some physical effect, or noninformatively say it is something that one can use or make things from (Carey, 1991; Stavy, 1991).

These difficulties mutually support each other. Part of the problem is with children's conception of weight. To the extent that children rely on feeling objects to determine weight differences—hence the core of their weight concept is felt weight, rather than being an objective measurable quantity—it is not obvious that all material objects do have weight or that weight itself is an additive quantity. In fact, many light objects feel like they weigh nothing at all. In addition, felt weight judgments are affected by both absolute weight differences and pressure differences in one's hand (a small object made of a dense material can feel much heavier than a large object made of a less dense material), further obscuring their understanding of weight as an extensive quantity. Part of the problem may stem from the limitations in their conception of matter itself. To the extent that it is defined only in terms of limited particular examples, or in terms of properties of large-scale chunks, rather than as a constituent that continues to exist, take up space, and have weight with decomposition, children cannot conceptualize "amount of matter" as an underlying additive quantity. Furthermore, without knowing that all matter has weight, they will have no way of precisely measuring amount of matter or telling whether the amount of matter has really changed across some transformations (e.g., when an ice cube is melted, when a sugar cube dissolves in water).

The preceding analysis, however, suggests that these difficulties are by no means insuperable for elementary schoolchildren. Instead, it highlights the very practices that they can engage in that will help them restructure their conceptions of weight and taking up space as measurable objective quantities and allow them to build a sound macroscopic conception of matter at this time. It also highlights why building such an understanding is truly foundational, in that it opens up new avenues for tracing the existence of matter over time and different transformations. Given the importance of these understandings for further scientific investigations, as well as the evidence that elementary schoolchildren are very capable of developing them with appropriate instruction, it seems critical to make it a goal for curricula at this time.

One set of practices that will support their reconceptualization of weight and taking up space is learning to measure weight and volume, especially if children engage with learning to measure as a form of modeling and explicitly confront key epistemological issues. That is, students are not taught measurement as a set of disembodied procedures (e.g., being told the volume of a rectangular cube is the length × width × height, or the weight of an object is a digital read from a scale). Instead, students are involved in the active construction of mathematical models of those quantities as additive magnitudes, and they have to think through problems of identifying a relevant unit, iterating that unit, covering the measurement space, etc. As previously discussed, children's initial work in K-2—learning about materials, learning to measure length and area, learning that balance scales can measure weight—prepares them for taking this next step. The research of Lehrer, Jaslow, and Curtis (2003) has documented that with this kind of instruction in earlier grades, even third graders can develop robust understanding of the measurement of weight and volume. Significantly, the researchers found that children use many of the explicit ideas they have developed about measure from their earlier work on length and area (e.g., ideas about the need to identify a fixed unit, equal partition, and fractional unit, as well as constructing two-dimensional arrays) in their new investigations. They note that although children must still work through these (and other) issues for the new quantities in question, they work through these issues more quickly than they did for the earlier quantities. Hence, they suggest meaningful transfer has occurred by allowing children a speed-up in working through new problems, not a side-stepping of the problems themselves. (For example, in constructing a measure of volume, students need to confront the new problem of imagining a three-dimensional array. Work with multiple forms of representation and coordinating among these different representations is crucial to this process.)

Having developed these tools, children can use them to deepen their exploration of the characteristics of matter and measurements. For example, they can use a scale to measure the weight of an object (e.g., a clay ball), and then be asked how much the object would weigh if it were half its size or one-quarter its size. Then they could carry out investigations to check their predictions. In carrying out these investigations, different groups of children need to measure the weight of the ball and its volume (to confirm they have made it half or a quarter its size) multiple times. In the process, they will have to decide how to handle variability in their data and wrestle with the idea of measurement error. They can also be asked to extrapolate to a much smaller piece—say a piece 1/100th the size. If the initial piece weighed 1 gram, what would a piece 1/100th that size weigh? If the scale didn't tip down, does that mean it weighs nothing at all? How could they investigate it further? This kind of thought experiment allows students to use mathematical reasoning and conceptual arguments to go from what they know to what they think should be. For example, they might argue that, as long as there is some amount of stuff, it must weigh something, although it may be only a tiny, tiny bit; one cannot take a string of nothings and get something. In this way, they can add features to their conceptual representation that follow inferentially rather than through direct observation. It also allows them to confront important issues about precision of measurement. After students have had a chance to discuss these issues, they might be challenged to think of ways of constructing more sensitive scales.

Children can also use explicit modeling to interrelate notions of volume and weight and construct a distinct notion of density as they pursue the question of why objects made of different materials weigh what they do. In this case, they can work with families of objects of different size made of different materials. There are a variety of ways in which instruction can successfully proceed.

Lehrer et al. (2001) had fifth grade students construct graphical representations of measured weights and volumes of objects made of different materials, interpolate a "best fit" line, and interpret the slope of the line; these investigations built on prior mathematical investigations in which students investigated similarity of form in families of rectangles of different proportions and drew graphical models of them. Smith and colleagues (1992, 1997) involved students in constructing visual dots-per-box models of materials, exploiting visual analogies with quantitative potential.

Central to each approach is engaging students with model-based reasoning. For example, students construct representations (visual or graphical) that show the relation between two quantities, derive new implications from these representations, and evaluate them against further data. Significantly, Lehrer et al. (2001) have found that the notion of density itself, notoriously a difficult notion for even much older children, becomes accessible to fifth grade elementary school students when taught this way.

Indeed, their work has documented sophisticated model-based reasoning in a variety of domains (e.g., modeling the growth of plants, the workings of an elbow) among third to fifth grade elementary school students who have had prior experience with modeling (Lehrer and Schauble, 2000). In each of these cases, students are not simply using models to depict some feature they have observed (the approach taken more often by younger children), but to investigate phenomena and derive new inferences. Note too that by differentiating weight from density, students enrich their understanding of a distinguishing property of materials, as well as enhance their ability to explain the weight of an object as a joint function of its volume and density.

Finally, students can also investigate more precisely whether the weight of objects changes or stays the same with melting, freezing, and dissolving. They can be asked to make arguments from these investigations about whether they think matter has been added or lost across these transformations. They can engage in further exploration and design investigations to determine if air is matter (e.g., weighing a basketball before and after air has been pumped into or out of it). They can use their emerging understanding of matter to identify and classify a range of entities as either matter or not matter.

How This Contrasts with Current Practice

Too often curricula rush to tell students about atoms and molecules in the elementary grades before a sound (embodied) macroscopic understanding of matter is in place. In addition, curricula often do not recognize that conceptual restructuring is needed to build this macroscopic understanding of matter—they assume it is obvious or already in place—and hence do not use teaching practices that make it more likely that restructuring will occur. For example, almost totally absent from science classrooms is any systematic use of modeling or model-building activities that call for students to use new representational tools (including relevant mathematical tools and understandings) to make predictions that are tested against observations and iteratively revised.

Instead, most elementary science classrooms simply present new ideas in science in declarative form—as definitions that should be memorized and learned—and teach students about measurement as a set of simple procedures. Thus, they teach students that solids, liquids, and gases are matter without considering whether they have a notion of matter that allows this grouping to make sense. They teach them some procedures for making weight and volume measurements, without considering whether children have a conceptual understanding of what they are doing when they make measurements or alternative ideas about weight and volume that need restructuring. They move from one set of topics to another, which are not deeply connected to each other (thinking this will maintain interest), rather than pursue topics or investigations that mutually reinforce each other.

In contrast, the proposed learning progression suggests ways that children can continue to develop the conceptual and procedural knowledge that will enable them to reason flexibly about matter. The research on children's learning is used to suggest logical progressions that connect the first three strands of scientific proficiency:

- *Understanding and using scientific explanations of the natural world.* Children can build on their understanding of materials to develop a generalized conception of matter, recognizing weight and volume as key properties that all materials have in common and density as a distinguishing characteristic of material kinds. In order to do this, they must develop more robust conceptions of weight and volume, based on measurement rather than sense impressions, and they must recognize these characteristics as essential to the definition of matter. They must also reason in principled ways about transformations in materials and amounts of materials that are too small for direct measurement of their properties. As they consider these problems, they can provide deeper explanations of why objects weigh what they do (in terms of the density of the kind of material and the volume of the material). They are also laying the groundwork for tracing matter through physical and chemical changes and for a robust understanding of atomic-molecular theory.

- *Generating and evaluating scientific evidence and explanations.* Children can engage in measurements of weight and volume not merely as procedures, but as ways of actively modeling matter and its properties. As they use their measurements of weight and volume to compare related objects and materials and to trace materials through such transformations as dividing and melting, they develop both improved measurement skills and a robust evidence-based understanding of matter and its properties.

- *Understanding how personal and scientific knowledge are constructed.* A key characteristic of the activities suggested in this learning progression is that they engage students in developing scientific arguments from evidence. Their developing understanding is based neither on the authority of teacher and text nor on unmediated personal experience. Instead, they engage in systematic data collection and principled reasoning to construct new understandings both of matter and of the foundations of scientific knowledge.

Thus the strands of scientific proficiency can be used in conjunction with the research to develop understandings in upper elementary school students that build on their learning in grades K-2 and that lay the foundations for reasoning about matter using atomic-molecular models in middle school.

Grades 6-8

Developing an Initial Understanding of the Atomic-Molecular Theory

Children's macroscopic understandings of matter (now grounded in a well-articulated set of measurable quantities) provide a framework from which they can ask still deeper explanatory questions and, in response to these questions, construct another layer of explanation (i.e., in terms of atoms and molecules). For example, what is the nature of matter and the properties of matter on a very small scale? Is there some fundamental set of materials from which other materials are composed? How can the macroscopically observable properties of objects and materials be explained in terms of these assumptions? These deeper questions arise only as puzzles requiring further explanation if students have a rich, embodied, and sound macroscopic understanding of matter on which to build (Snir, Smith, and Raz, 2003). But given such macroscopic understandings and prior experience with model-based reasoning, students are ready to take on the challenge of investigating, describing, and explaining a host of new phenomena as well as reexplaining and more deeply understanding phenomena with which they are already familiar. In addition, armed with new insights provided by knowledge of the existence of atoms and molecules, they can conceptually distinguish between elements (substances composed of just one kind of atom) and compounds (substances composed of clusters of different atoms bonded together in molecules). They can also begin to imagine more possibilities that need to be considered in tracking the identity of materials over time, including the possibility of chemical change.

One set of puzzling phenomena for students to explain is how the volume of something can change in situations in which its mass or weight has been conserved. Of course, to even describe these situations, students need to not only clearly distinguish the quantities of weight and volume, but also have ways of accurately measuring them to be sure that one has clearly changed without the other. In addition, to be puzzled by this state of affairs, students have to have developed some clear expectations about materials and how they should behave. These are exactly the kinds of expectations that they have been developing in grades 3-5, as they are learning to measure both weight and volume and coming to understand that matter has weight and takes up space.

There are a large number of situations in which this basic data pattern (of volume change but weight conservation) can be readily observed by students. Some involve solids, some involve liquids, some involve gases, and still others involve a change of state. In the course of teaching, students should be exposed to all these situations. For starters, however, consider one phenomenon that research has shown to be especially intriguing and puzzling for middle school students and how it can be used to invite initial debate and discussion about whether matter is fundamentally particulate or continuous (Snir, Smith, and Raz, 2003).

The phenomenon involves mixing two equal volumes of water and alcohol, which are both colorless liquids. If you mix a given volume of water (say 50 ml) with a given volume of alcohol (also 50 ml), the resultant mixture of water and alcohol is only about 96 ml, not 100 ml, which is what students would have expected. Students immediately suspect that some liquid has been lost in the transfer. To rule out this possibility, it can be shown that there has been no loss of material: the weight of the mixture is equal to the weight of the two component parts. In addition, to allow students to more fully study the mixing itself, the two liquids can each be colored (with different food coloring) so students can watch more clearly what happens as they mix. Just as before, they can collect data showing that the total weight, but not the total volume of the system has been conserved. They can also see that if the (blue) colored water is mixed with the (red) colored alcohol, the two liquids intermingle and intermix, turning a uniform purple throughout. A number of provocative questions can be raised about this simple demonstration, including:

- How can two (continuous) liquids intermix?
- Why is the volume of the mixture less than the sum of the volumes of its parts?
- Why is the weight of the mixture equal to the sum of the weights of its parts?

Students are very intrigued (and surprised) by this demonstration, and in searching for possible explanations, they can be asked: What might matter be like at a very tiny scale (much too small to directly observe), in order for this to be? Students can consider a number of alternative models of the situation, based on different assumptions about what matter is like at such a small scale. For example: Would it be continuous all the way down (i.e., no gaps or breaks)? Would there be discrete but tightly packed particles (i.e., no spaces between the particles)? Would there be discretely spaced particles of different sizes? For each alternative, they can then work through the consequences of those assumptions—what would be predicted to happen in this situation—on each set of assumptions. They can then consider how well each imagined alternative can actually explain the three main facts.

Note that, to even engage with this issue, students have to be able to imagine that if matter were repeatedly divided in half until it was in a piece too small to see, some matter would still be there—it wouldn't simply disappear if it were no longer visible. Research has shown that as students move from thinking about matter in terms of commonsense perceptual properties (something one can see, feel, or touch) to defining it as a constituent, that takes up space and has weight, they are increasingly comfortable with making this assumption. In this way, the framework they are developing in grades 3-5 is preparing them for theorizing at this level. In addition, they need to engage in "hypothetico-deductive" model-based reasoning: they must conjecture about (and represent) what matter is like at a level that they can't see, make inferences about what follows from different assumptions, and evaluate the conjecture based on its fit with a pattern of results. Significantly, two small-scale research studies have shown that middle school students are able to (enthusiastically) discuss these issues, especially when different models (for several puzzling phenomena) are implemented on a computer and they are put in the position of judging which models can account for the facts (Snir, Smith, and Raz, 2003). Indeed, this approach led students who had relevant macroscopic understandings of matter to see the discretely spaced particle model as a better explanation than alternatives (e.g., continuous models and tightly packed particle models). Furthermore, class discussions allowed students to make an important ground rule for evaluating models more explicitly: models were evaluated on the basis of their consistency with an entire pattern of results and their capacity to explain how the results occurred rather than on the basis of a match in surface appearance. In this way, discussions of these simulations were used to help them build important metacognitive understanding of an explanatory model.

Describing and explaining the behavior of air or other gases—for example, understanding that (macroscopically) they compress and expand and searching for underlying (more microscopic) explanations of how that happens—provides another fertile ground for appreciating the explanatory power of assuming that matter is fundamentally particulate rather than continuous (Lee et al., 1993; Nussbaum, 1998). Of course, these investigations bear on students' emerging ideas about the nature of matter only if they understand that gases are material, something the proposed learning progression recommends that students begin to investigate at the previous age band. At the same time, coming to understand the behavior of gases in particulate terms should help consolidate student understanding that gases are matter and enable them to visualize their (unseen) behavior. In other words, developing macroscopic and atomic-molecular conceptions can be mutually supportive. Direct support for this assumption was provided in a large-scale teaching study with urban sixth grade students that compared the effectiveness of two curriculum units. One unit focused more exclusively on teaching core elements of the atomic-molecular theory, without addressing student misconceptions about matter at a macroscopic level. The other included more direct teaching of relevant macroscopic and microscopic concepts and talked more thoroughly about how properties of invisible molecules are associated with properties of observable substances and physical changes. The latter unit led to much greater change in understanding phenomena at both macroscopic and molecular levels (Lee et al., 1993).

Furthermore, as the extensive research of Nussbaum and colleagues with seventh and eighth grade students attests, such instruction is especially effective if students are involved in classroom debates and discussion about essential (metaphysical) ideas, alternative theories, and larger epistemological issues (Nussbaum, 1998). For example, how could a vacuum exist? Why wouldn't matter be automatically sucked into empty space? If there are discretely spaced particles, what holds them together? How do particles move and interact (e.g., do they obey laws of mechanical causality)? Such classroom debate and discussion allow classroom experiments to become more meaningful and informative to students. In addition, thought experiments are used to help students contrast descriptions at the particulate and macro level. For example, students are asked to imagine that a small dwarf (tinier than the smallest particle of matter) stuck a needle into a particle of water or a particle of gas. Would water leak out? Would the gas burst out and make a hissing sound? In this way, they can contrast the behavior of an individual particle of water (or gas) and a macroscopic fluid. One sequence of activities (involving debates, analogies, experiments, and thought experiments) is used to lead students to explain the compressibility of air in terms of a model of vacuum and particles. Another sequence is designed to help them explain the elasticity of air in terms of the continual and random movement of particles. This model in turn helps them to understand air pressure and the diffusion of gases. Thus, central to building an understanding of the atomic-molecular theory is engaging students in cycles of model building while developing their appreciation of the deeper metaphysical and epistemological commitments of atomic-molecular theory. A 3-year longitudinal study showed the much greater effectiveness of this curricular approach in helping students internalize and use the atomic-molecular theory than more traditional didactic instruction (Margel, Eylon, and Scherzo, 2006).

Still other phenomena that have been effectively used to initiate discussions of the particulate nature of matter with middle school students concern explaining the different properties of solids, liquids, and gases (Driver et al., 1995; Lee et al., 1993); thermal expansion of solids, liquids, or gases (Snir, Smith, and Raz, 2003; Lee et al., 1993); changes of state (Lee et al., 1993); dissolving (Lee et al., 1993); the transmission of smells (Nussbaum, 1998); and why materials cannot (chemically) combine in any proportion (Snir, Smith, and Raz, 2003). Based on the findings of this research, the learning progression proposes that during this age band, students can be meaningfully introduced to the following core tenets of atomic molecular theory:

(a) Existence of discretely space particles (atoms).
(b) There are empty spaces between atoms (idea of vacuum).
(c) Each atom takes up space, has mass, and is in constant motion.
(d) The existence of over 100 different kinds of atoms; each kind has distinctive properties including its mass and the way it combines with other atoms or molecules.
(e) Atoms can be joined (in different proportions) to form molecules or networks—a process that involves forming chemical bonds between atoms.
(f) Molecules have different characteristic properties from the atoms of which they are composed.

The learning progression also proposes that students should practice using these tenets in cycles of building, testing, and revising models of a wide range of particular situations.

This same body of research indicates that it takes considerable time and effort to introduce students to these tenets in a meaningful manner. For example, Nussbaum's teaching units on the behavior of gases involved over 30 (45-minute) lessons; Lee et al.'s teaching for a broad range of phenomena spanned 10 weeks of sixth grade. However, it may be important to take that time at the middle school level for several reasons. First, understanding the atomic-molecular theory opens up many productive new avenues of investigation about matter. For example, it opens up the whole topic of chemical change, which research suggests is not really accessible to students with only macroscopic criteria for identifying substances (Johnson, 2002). It also helps students much more clearly understand what stays the same and what changes in the water cycle (Lee et al., 1993). Second, many important topics that are discussed elsewhere in the science curriculum, including biology and earth science, depend on these understandings: topics like osmosis and diffusion, photosynthesis, digestion, decay, ecological matter cycling, the water cycle, and the rock cycle, to name just a few. Finally, it provides an opportunity for students to begin to develop an understanding of and respect for the tremendous intellectual work and experimentation that underlies developing a well-tested, successful scientific theory.

How This Contrasts with Current Practice

Current texts often have separate chapters for "Properties of Matter," "Changes in Matter," and "Atomic-Molecular Theory." Atomic-molecular theory is often presented as a set of facts (declarative knowledge) about atoms and molecules, disconnected from any concrete everyday experiences that it may help explain. There is often no attempt made to acknowledge the counterintuitive nature of the claims or to show the usefulness of the theory. As a result, as research on student misconceptions makes abundantly clear, the majority of students fail to internalize the core assumptions of the theory, and they have little understanding of such important ideas as chemical change (see Driver et al., 1995, for reviews). As Schwab and others have argued, science is typically taught as "rhetoric conclusions" rather than as a complex process for making sense of the world (in the words of Niels Bohr, a way of "extending our experience and reducing it to order") that rests on certain metaphysical and epistemological assumptions. Because of this, students do not appreciate what a tremendous intellectual construction a scientific theory really is, why it deserves great respect, and why it cannot be challenged by another idea that does not attempt to meet those epistemological standards. In an important sense, without constructing an understanding of those epistemological standards, students will not know the grounds on which they should believe important scientific theories.

In contrast, the proposed learning progression outlines a set of conceptual goals that can be investigated in a more sustained, mutually reinforcing manner, based on a principled interpretation of research on children's interpretations of matter and materials. In particular, we note that the research enables one to identify phenomena and topics for discussion that will help students make progress with respect to each of the first three strands of scientific proficiency:

(a) *Understanding and using scientific explanations of the natural world.* The learning progression develops atomic-molecular theory as a useful set of conceptual tools that resolve a wide variety of puzzles concerning properties of matter and changes in matter. Description at this level can explain conservation of matter and weight, the composition of materials (elements, compounds), the appearance and disappearance of specific materials, the constancy of materials across change of state, etc. These puzzles are real puzzles for children only if they already have a robust macroscopic understanding of matter and its measured properties. Furthermore, students must master several basic tenets of atomic-molecular theory and use them successfully before the power of atomic-molecular models is apparent.

(b) *Generating and evaluating scientific evidence and explanations.* The arguments from evidence that support atomic-molecular theory depend on children's abilities to measure such properties of matter as mass and volume consistently and accurately, as well as their commitment to ideas about the nature of these properties (for example, that mass/weight is a reliable indicator of the amount of matter). Furthermore, they must use these measurements in the context of arguments that require a commitment to logical consistency in predictions and explanations and that involve the coordinated use of model-based reasoning, analogies, and thought experiments.

(c) *Understanding how personal and scientific knowledge are constructed.* In developing an understanding of the atomic-molecular theory of matter, students need to appreciate that the epistemological standards that are central to science and that are used in deciding between competing views (e.g., explanatory scope, rigor, and precision, ability to integrate large patterns of data, generativity of new testable predictions) are actually different from those typically used in everyday life (e.g., consistency with immediate perceptual experience or initial intuitive ideas—standards less dependent on long chains of reasoning and that have a closer match with surface reality or appearance). Thus, mature scientific theories will often embrace core tenets that on the surface seem implausible or even unintelligible to the novice as long as these assumptions are needed to explain a large pattern of data, are supported by a logical chain of reasoning, and can provide detailed explanations of why surface appearances are misleading. The atomic-molecular theory is a clear case in point. The reason scientists believe in the existence of discrete tiny particles in different arrangements and constant motion (i.e., atoms and molecules) is not because of simple, direct perceptual evidence for such a theoretical analysis; rather it is because of the theory's tremendous explanatory power and scope and detailed experimental support.

Thus the strands of scientific proficiency can be used in conjunction with the research to develop understandings in middle school students that build on their learning in elementary school and that lay the foundations for reasoning about matter using atomic-molecular models in many different contexts in the life, earth, and physical sciences. With appropriate preparation and teaching, students can engage in true model-based scientific reasoning. They can come to appreciate both the power of scientific models to predict and explain a diversity of phenomena, and how those models are grounded in careful collection and evaluation of scientific evidence.

Limitations

The proposed learning progression is in several ways incomplete or speculative. Limitations stem from the fact that this is a relatively new way of thinking about organizing learning experiences, from questions that have not been examined in research, and from the kind of research available to us.

In our extended example at grades 6-8, we assume some instructional history with understanding force and motion that would feed into constructing some elements of the atomic-molecular theory. Yet the nature of that earlier work is not specified. In addition, some prior introduction to ideas about energy, its role in change, and discussion of heat would be important but, again, is not explicitly treated. The case of energy is interesting, because it points to a need for key ideas to be introduced, but perhaps not explicitly defined as they serve as important placeholder ideas. Another issue that was not addressed, in part due to the limited research base, is whether it would be productive to have earlier exploration of the formation and separation of mixtures. Thus, the heavy dependence of this learning progression on ideas about material, matter, weight, volume, density, atom, and molecule should by no means imply that these are the only important notions to be addressed. They are a subset of ideas that are important, and they exist within a broader array of ideas that are not merely related linearly, but also within a web interconnecting learning among multiple learning progressions.

The research base itself also necessarily limits the quality of our conceptualization of learning progressions. We have relied on many short-term studies and assembled these in an effort to depict learning across longer periods of time. Furthermore, these studies are primarily studies of knowledge—snapshots of students' capabilities at a given time—not depictions of learning or the change in capability over time. While our learning progression highlights the ways in which one could be doing more in elementary school to provide a productive foundation for later learning, there is little research to guide in identifying key early experiences. What are the ideas and practices that, if learned early on, would provide greater cognitive payoffs down the road?

CONCLUSIONS

We can see implications of learning progressions like the one described above for several areas of policy and practice, including curriculum and standards, assessment, and classroom instruction.

• *Curriculum and standards.* This learning progression suggests several ways in which current curricula and standards are problematic and could be improved. This learning progression suggests ways in which students of different ages could learn age-appropriate versions of core ideas with understanding, rather than addressing them in current haphazard ways. This learning progression also suggests priorities in the curriculum, helping to identify the conceptual tools and practices that are the foundation for critical learning.

• *Suggesting appropriate ages for introduction of key ideas.* For example, many textbooks and state curricula introduce atomic-molecular stories (not functional as models) as early as third or fourth grade, while the national science education standards delay atomic-molecular models until high school. This research suggests why middle school students could benefit from learning to use atomic-molecular models and what the key elements of those models might be.

• *Large-scale and classroom assessment.* This learning progression suggests the most important conceptual tools and practices to be assessed, common alternatives or misconceptions, and specific questions or tasks that could be used (for an extensive discussion of assessment in the learning progressions framework, see Smith et al., 2006).

• *Classroom instruction.* What is known about mechanisms of learning can be useful for guiding classroom instructions: key questions to address with children of different ages, important experiences that may move the process of succession forward, and key conceptual tools and practices that can be introduced and mastered.

Taken together, these literatures (on preschool understanding, mature scientific understanding, the response of children to sustained good instruction) along with societal expectations and values could form a powerful set of constraints on the development of a set of plausible learning progressions. Clearly, though, there could be more than one way to make choices about what core ideas should be the focus for learning progression analysis. Undertaking the intellectual task of thinking through detailed learning progressions for different end-state core ideas, however, might be one step in thinking through possible advantages and disadvantages of different approaches. In addition, even if we agree on focal core ideas that are the target of instruction and a learning progression that connects the two end points, it would not fully prescribe the instructional sequence. In much the same way as there are constraints on how a complex structure such as a house can be built from its starting components—for example, certain things such as the foundation and then walls must come first to provide structural support for the windows and roof—yet within those constraints there is some flexibility as well and multiple ways to build a house.

REFERENCES

American Association for the Advancement of Science. (1993). *Benchmarks for science literacy.* New York: Oxford University Press.

American Association for the Advancement of Science. (2001). *Atlas of science literacy: Mapping K-12 learning goals.* Washington, DC: Author.

Baroody, A.J., Cibulskis, M., Lai, M-l, and Li, X. (2004). Comments on the use of learning trajectories in curriculum development and research. *Mathematical Thinking and Learning, 6*(2), 227-260.

Carey, S. (1991). Knowledge acquisition: Enrichment or conceptual change? In S. Carey and R. Gelman (Eds.), *The epigenesist of mind: Essays on biology and cognition* (pp. 257-291). Hillsdale, NJ: Lawrence Erlbaum Associates.

Dickinson, D.K. (1987). The development of material kind. *Science Education, 71,* 615-628.

Driver, R., Leach, J., Millar, R., and Scott, P. (1995). *Young people's images of science.* Buckingham, England: Open University Press.

Johnson, P. (1996). What is a substance? *Education in Chemistry,* March, 41-45.

Johnson, P. (2002). Children's understanding of substances, part 2: Explaining chemical change. *International Journal of Science Education, 24*(10), 1037-1054.

Kesidou, S., and Roseman, J.E. (2002). How well do middle school science programs measure up? Findings from Project 2061's curriculum review. *Journal of Research in Science Teaching, 39*(6), 522-549.

Krnel, D., Glazar, S.A., and Watson, R. (2003). The development of the concept of "matter": A cross-age study of how children classify materials. *Science Education, 87,* 621-639.

Krnel, D., Watson, R., and Glazar, S.A. (1998). Survey of research related to the development of the concept of "matter." *International Journal of Science Education, 20*(3), 257-289.

Lee, O., Eichinger, D.C., Anderson, C.W., Berkheimer, G.D., and Blakeslee, T.D. (1993). Changing middle school students' conceptions of matter and molecules. *Journal of Research in Science Teaching, 30*(3), 249-270.

Lehrer, R., Catley, K., and Reiser, B. (2004). *Tracing a prospective learning progression for developing understanding of evolution.* Commissioned paper for the National Research Council Committee on Test Design for K-12 Science Achievement Workshop, May 6-7, Washington, DC. Available: http://www7.national academies.org/bota/Evolution.pdf [accessed November 2006].

Lehrer, R., Jaslow, K., and Curtis, C. (2003). Developing understanding of measurement in the elementary grades. In D.H. Clements and G. Bright (Eds.), *Learning and teaching measurement. 2003 yearbook* (pp. 100-121). Reston, VA: National Council of Teachers of Mathematics.

Lehrer, R., Jenkins, M., and Osana, H. (1998). Longitudinal study of children's reasoning about space and geometry. In R. Lehrer and D. Chazan (Eds.), *Designing learning environments for developing understanding of geometry and space* (pp. 137-167). Mahwah, NJ: Lawrence Erlbaum Associates.

Lehrer, R., and Schauble, L. (2000). Modeling in mathematics and science. In R. Glaser (Ed.), *Advances in instructional psychology: Educational design and cognitive science* (vol. 5, pp. 101-159). Mahwah, NJ: Lawrence Erlbaum Associates.

Lehrer, R., Schauble, L., Strom, D. and Pligge, M. (2001). Similarity of form and substance: Modeling material kind. In S. Carver and D. Klahr (Eds.), *Cognition and instruction: Twenty-five years in progress*. Mahwah, NJ: Lawrence Erlbaum Associates.

Margel, H., Eylon, B.S., and Scherz, Z. (2006). We actually saw atoms with our own eyes: Conceptions and convictions is using the scanning tunneling microscope in junior high school. *Journal of Chemical Education, 81*(4), 558-566.

Metz, K.E. (1993). Preschoolers' developing knowledge of the pan balance: From new representation to transformed problem solving. *Cognition and Instruction, 11*, 31-93.

Metz, K.E. (1995). Reassessment of developmental constraints on children's science instruction. *Review of Educational Research, 65*, 93-127.

Mintzes, J.J., Wandersee, J.H., and Novak, J.D. (1997). Meaningful learning in science: The human constructivist perspective. In G.D. Phye (Ed.), *Handbook of academic learning* (pp. 405-447). San Diego, CA: Academic Press.

National Research Council. (1996). *National science education standards*. National Committee on Science Education Standards and Assessment. Washington, DC: National Academy Press.

Nussbaum, J. (1998). History and philosophy of science and the preparation for constructivist teaching: The case for particle theory. In J.J. Mintzes, J.H. Wandersee, and J.D. Novak (Eds.), *Teaching science for understanding* (pp. 165-194). New York: Academic Press.

Piaget, J., and Inhelder, B. (1974). *The child's construction of physical quantities*. London, England: Routledge and Kegan Paul.

Roseman, J.E., Kesidou, S., Stern, L., and Caldwell, A. (1999 November/December). Heavy books light on learning: AAAS Project 2061 evaluates middle grades science textbooks. *Science Books & Films, 35*(6), 243-247.

Roth, K.J. (2002). Talking to understand science. In J. Brophy (Ed.), *Social constructivist teaching: Affordances and constraints* (Advances in Research on Teaching, vol. 9, pp. 197-262). New York: JAI Press.

Schmidt, W., Wang, H.C., and McKnight, C. (2005). Curriculum coherence: An examination of U.S. mathematics and science content standards from an international perspective. *Journal of Curriculum Studies, 37*, 525-559.

Smith, C. (2005). Bootstrapping processes in the development of students' commonsense matter theories: The role of analogical mapping, though experiments, and learning to measure. Submitted to *Cognitive Psychology*.

Smith, C., Carey, S., and Wiser, M. (1985). On differentiation: A case study of the development of the concepts of size, weight, and density. *Cognition, 21*, 177-237.

Smith, C., Maclin, D., Grosslight, L., and Davis, H. (1997). Teaching for understanding: A study of students' preinstruction theories of matter and a comparison of the effectiveness of two approaches to teaching students about matter and density. *Cognition and Instruction, 15*, 317-393.

Smith, C., Snir, J., and Grosslight, L. (1992). Using conceptual models to facilitate conceptual change: The case of weight/density differentiation. *Cognition and Instruction, 9*(3), 221-283.

Smith, C.L., Solomon, G.E.A., and Carey, S. (2005). Never getting to zero: Elementary school students' understanding of the infinite divisibility of number and matter. *Cognitive Psychology, 51*(2), 101-140.

Smith, C., Wiser, M., Anderson, C.A., and Krajick, J. (2006). Implications of research on children's learning for standards and assessment: A proposed learning progression for matter and atomic molecular theory. *Measurement: Interdisciplinary Research and Perspectives, 4.*

Smith, C., Wiser, M., Anderson, C.A., Krajick, J., and Coppola, B. (2004). *Implications of research on children's learning for assessment: Matter and atomic molecular theory.* Commissioned paper for the National Research Council Committee on Test Design for K-12 Science Achievement Workshop, May 6-7, Washington, DC. Available: http://www7.nationalacademies.org/bota/Big%20Idea%20Team_%20AMT.pdf [accessed November 2006].

Snir, J., Smith, C.L., and Raz, G. (2003). Linking phenomena with competing underlying models: A software tool for introducing students to the particulate model of matter. *Science Education, 87,* 794-830.

Stavy, E. (1991). Children's ideas about matter. *School Science and Curriculum, 91,* 240-244.

Valverde, G.A., and Schmidt, W.H. (1997). Refocusing U.S. math and science education. *Issues in Science and Technology, 14*(2), 60-66.

Wilkening, F., and Huber, S. (2002). Children's intuitive physics. In U. Goswami (Ed.), *Blackwell handbook of childhood cognitive development* (pp. 349-370). Malden, MA: Blackwell.

Yair, Y., and Yair, Y. (2004). Everything comes to an end: An intuitive rule in physics and mathematics. *Science Education, 88*(4), 594-609.

9

Teaching Science as Practice

Main Findings in the Chapter:

- *Students learn science by actively engaging in the practices of science, including conducting investigations; sharing ideas with peers; specialized ways of talking and writing; mechanical, mathematical, and computer-based modeling; and development of representations of phenomena.*
- *All major aspects of inquiry, including managing the process, making sense of data, and discussion and reflection on the results, may require guidance.*
- *Instruction needs to build incrementally toward more sophisticated understanding and practices. To advance students' conceptual understanding, prior knowledge and questions should be evoked and linked to experiences with experiments, data, and phenomena. Practices can be supported with explicit structures or by providing criteria that help guide the work.*
- *Discourse and classroom discussion are key to supporting learning in science. Students need encouragement and guidance to articulate their ideas and recognize that explanation rather than facts is the goal of the scientific enterprise.*
- *Ongoing assessment is an integral part of instruction that can foster student learning when appropriately designed and used regularly.*

Children come to school with powerful resources on which science instruction can build. Even young children can learn to explain natural phenomena, design and conduct empirical investigations, and engage in meaningful evidence-based argumentation. Through instruction, teachers can take much better advantage of the resources children bring to school than is commonly the case in K-8 science classrooms in the United States. Although K-8 science instruction has long been a subject of research, breakthroughs in research on teaching and learning have dramatically altered understanding of how children learn science and what can be done to structure, support, and develop their knowledge, use, and understanding of science.

In this chapter we focus on the classroom-level implications of the learning and instruction research. The chapter is divided into four sections. First, we begin with a description of typical instruction in U.S. K-8 science classrooms. In the second section we present the contrasting view of science as practice put forth in the instructional research, pointing to promising evidence of student learning when instruction is framed around science as practice. In the third section we look more closely at the common forms of scientific practice that students engage in across different types of instructional design, pointing to the challenges students encounter as they do so. Fourth, we characterize strategies that teachers and curriculum developers can use to promote student learning of science through practice. We close with the major conclusions that can be drawn from current research on science instruction.

In order to have a productive and meaningful discussion of science instruction, we need to be clear about what questions about science instruction research can and cannot answer. First, some pedagogical debates rest on differences in values rather than questions that are answerable through empirical research and, accordingly, cannot be resolved in this chapter. For example, one may be tempted to ask "Is inquiry better than direct instruction?" However, when comparing inquiry and direct instruction, the critical question is "Better for what?" Advocates of one or the other instructional approach may have different underlying visions for what it means to learn science. Thus, we need to be clear about what our goals for science learning are and ask how inquiry and direct instruction compare in reaching specific educational goals.

Second, this chapter does not provide a blanket endorsement of particular strategies for instruction (e.g., group work, computer-mediated activities, hands-on science, explicit instruction). These general instructional approaches are underspecified and gloss over important considerations of instructional goals. Computers, for example, can be used in many ways—to facilitate drill and practice exercises or to provide access to powerful analytical tools and real scientific data sets, such as visualizations of real-time climate data. Group work can be used to simply divide up the work among students (e.g., one handling the experimental apparatus, another taking notes) or groups may work more organically—debating evidence or coming to consensus about interpretations of empirical findings. Depending on the goals of a specific lesson, one or several instructional strategies may be appropriate, and none will be an instructional panacea. Thus, we discuss a variety of instructional interventions that incorporate inquiry, group work, computers, and explicit instruction and suggest how these strategies can be useful for reaching particular goals.

Third, our argument rests heavily on a growing number of small-scale, long-term intervention studies that demonstrate the profound learning effects that well-designed, high-quality science instruction can have, as well as a few controlled quasi-experimental studies. However, we acknowledge that we do not have strong evidence of these interventions at scale, and we adapt the nature of our claims accordingly. We point to features of instruction that are common across research programs that we view as "best bets" for organizing instruction. We recognize that instructional practice is situated in a layered and interactive system in which curriculum and assessment policy, teacher knowledge, and professional development opportunities have a profound effect on instructional quality.

The research points in fruitful directions and uncovers what is possible under certain conditions. Much work remains to be done to identify how to put the necessary conditions in place and support students' learning of the type of science articulated here. Furthermore, the studies do not allow one to conclude that a particular design approach is the most effective way to achieve a particular set of goals in contrast to other approaches. However, these studies do reveal the kinds of science classroom learning environments that are possible, what students can achieve therein, and what challenges remain to be addressed in instructional design. They help us explore what K-8 science teaching and learning could become.

CURRENT INSTRUCTIONAL PRACTICE

Typical science instruction in the United States does not support learning across the four strands of proficiency of our framework (see Box 2-1). Pursuing the strands framework implies providing students with opportunities to learn topics in depth, to use science in meaningful contexts, and to engage in scientific practices. In contrast, as noted earlier, the U.S. curriculum and standards are seen as "a mile wide and an inch deep." Typical classroom activity structures convey either a passive and narrow view of science learning or an activity-oriented approach devoid of question-probing and only loosely related to conceptual learning goals (O'Sullivan and Weiss, 1999). Further, U.S. textbooks fail to guide teachers in how to build on students' understanding, to contextualize science in meaningful problems, or to treat complex ideas other than superficially (Kesidou and Roseman, 2002; Schmidt, Houang, and Cogan, 2000).

Of course, what children learn is not solely dictated by curriculum and standards "content," but also by ways in which their encounters with curriculum are structured—the things students typically do in science class-rooms. Analyses of pedagogy in classrooms corroborate the findings about curriculum and standards. As teachers aspire to cover a broad but thin curriculum, they give insufficient attention to students' understanding and focus on superficial recall-level questions (Weiss and Pasley, 2004; Weiss et al., 2003).

The recurring activities in science classrooms offer entrée to a narrow slice of scientific practice, leaving students with a limited sense of science and what it means to understand and use science. A steady stream of reading sections from textbooks, taking notes on definitions of key terms, and taking exams that test recall, for example, leaves students with a distinct, and problematic, sense of what it means to know and do science. Linn and Eylon (in press) have characterized the typical activity structure in U.S. science classrooms as "motivate, inform, and assess" in which teachers "motivate" a scientific idea (perhaps with a surprising demonstration), present the normative view, and then assess students' understanding. This is analogous to patterns observed in U.S. mathematics classrooms (Stigler and Hiebert, 1999). Immersed in these patterns, students come to view science as a compilation of "right answers" provided and confirmed by teachers or textbooks. In class, students expect to be asked to recall facts on demand, rather than thinking about science as a sense-making activity requiring analysis, discussion, and debate (Carey and Smith, 1993; Smith et al., 2000).

In contrast to U.S. science classrooms, in Japan, a nation whose students outscore U.S. students, classroom activity patterns are quite different. Japanese students contribute their ideas in solving problems collectively and critically discuss alternative solutions to problems. Students in classroom environments like these come to expect that these public, social acts of reasoning and dialogue are a regular part of classroom life and learning across the disciplines (Linn et al., 2000; Stigler and Hiebert, 1999).

In sum, the patterns in U.S. pedagogy, curriculum materials, and curriculum standards exhibit a tendency to treat science as "final form" science (Duschl, 1990), in which science consists of solved problems and theories to be transmitted. The dynamics of the discipline—asking questions, finding ways to explore them empirically, investigating and evaluating competing alternative models, arguing—are severely lacking in the enacted U.S. curriculum, classrooms, and, most importantly, in students' expectations about science and what it means to learn and do science in schools.

The learning and instruction research suggests a dramatic departure from this typical approach, revealing that science instruction can be much more powerful and can take on new forms that enable students to participate in science as practice and to master core conceptual domains more fully. In the next section we sketch in broad brushstrokes an image of science as practice that can support K-8 students in learning science across the strands and point out how this diverges from current practice.

APPROACHES TO SCIENCE AS PRACTICE IN RESEARCH-BASED INSTRUCTIONAL DESIGN

Scientific practice itself is multifaceted, and so are instructional programs that frame science as practice. Researchers have designed and studied several instructional programs in which students develop scientific explanations and models, participate in scientific argumentation, and design and conduct scientific investigations. Although different programs may emphasize one aspect or another of the strands, they all reflect an approach to science in which students own and engage in aspects of scientific practice modeled on expert practice.

Underlying science as practice are meaningful problems that students work on. This is a crucial shift away from typical K-8 science instruction. A meaningful problems approach explores how to teach the skills in the context of their application (Collins, Brown, and Newman, 1989). As we have argued throughout this report, rather than teaching individual skills separately and having students practice them, skills can be taught as needed, in the context of a larger investigation linked to questions developed with students.

To call a problem meaningful, however, implies two senses of "meaning." One sense is that a problem is meaningful from a disciplinary perspective—it frames scientific concepts, disciplinary practices, and evidence bases that can be coordinated to articulate and examine central principles and questions within a scientific discipline. Another sense of "meaning" in meaningful problems is that these problems are made intelligible and compelling to students. For example, a problem might draw on issues related to the local ecology. Educators and materials developers can enhance the meaningfulness of problems by drawing on ones that situate learning in the context of networks of ideas and practices. While the programs of research we review take different approaches to engaging students in science practice, they all work from problems that are, in this sense, meaningful to students.

It is also important to bear in mind that here and throughout this chapter, the instructional programs we present are not mutually exclusive hypotheses about instruction. On the contrary, as becomes evident shortly, these are variations on a theme of common elements. Here we discuss the interventions themselves and evidence that children can in fact engage in science as practice in meaningful and productive ways. We do so to underscore the empirical basis of this work before going more deeply into details about the practices themselves. After providing a broad overview of the interventions and summarizing the evidence that K-8 students can in fact engage in science as practice in meaningful ways, in the next major section we return to finer-grained characterizations of what science as practice looks like in the classroom, and how it can be supported.[1]

Designing and Conducting Empirical Investigations in K-8 Classrooms

One approach to science as practice is teaching students to design and conduct empirical investigations. Testing ideas by gathering empirical evidence is a mainstay of science education. Researchers have found that, with appropriate instruction, K-8 students can engage in making hypotheses, gathering evidence, designing investigations, evaluating hypotheses in light of evidence, and in the process they can build their understanding of the phenomena they are investigating (Crawford, Krajcik, and Marx, 1999; Geier et al., in press; Kuhn, Schauble, and Garcia-Mila, 1992; Lehrer and Schauble, 2002; Metz, 2000, 2004; Schneider et al., 2002).

Contrary to current practice, which provides students with narrowly conceived, even misleading opportunities to "do science" (e.g., focusing exclusively on validating theories by following lockstep laboratory experiments or doing activities with no clear intellectual goal), these instructional programs engage children in designing and conducting scientific investigations and answering complex questions. These investigations take place over several weeks or months and require careful attention to students' initial and emerging understanding of the phenomena and instruction designed to gradually build their knowledge and skills. Metz (2004), for example, reported on second, fourth, and fifth grade students' efforts to design and conduct scientific investigations in the context of a life science unit. The unit gradually built in opportunities for children to master research methods and instrumentation as they learned about animal behavior. After 6 to 7 weeks of instruction, children were invested in the problem, knowledgeable about the domain, and familiar with tools and research design. At that point they were asked to think about a new species (crickets) and to propose researchable questions that they could examine empirically. Metz found that, with strong instructional guidance, children could design and carry out their own investigations—posing questions, determining appropriate methods of inquiry, carrying out the study, and reporting and critiquing their own results.

---

[1]As our goal is to frame the commonalities of approaches, and the current research base prohibits parsing approaches further by their relative empirical warrants, the following approaches are presented in no particular order.

Of course, students do not learn how to do science only over extended periods of time through highly integrated units of study. Some topics can be treated more discretely and students can make measurable gains in a few days of instruction and practice. An example is the Klahr and Chen (2003) report on a classroom-based experiment that tested instructional approaches to teaching a control-of-variables strategy. In a short instructional sequence, students investigated balls rolling down a ramp to determine the factors that influence the distance the balls will roll. Instruction began with an "exploration and assessment" phase, in which the children were asked to make comparisons to determine how different variables affected the distance the balls rolled after leaving the ramp. Students used a wooden ramp that allowed them to manipulate two variables: the pitch of the ramp (high or low) and the texture of its surface (rough or smooth). In this phase, the children gained a base level of understanding of the phenomena and the test apparatus and were given an opportunity to think about the problem. In this study the performance of students who received instruction far surpassed that of those who did not, and their gains were sustained over time and transferred to new problems.

Whether instruction aims at narrowly defined outcomes (as the Klahr and Chen study did) or long-term investigations and a range of integrated learning goals (as did Metz's study), there is broad agreement that children need a base level of knowledge about a domain in order to work in meaningful ways on scientific problems. Although the aims of the studies described here varied they both suggest that students need familiarity and interest in the scientific problems and that their learning requires explicit guidance. These interventions also underscore that children will often need clear statements about basic conceptual knowledge in order to succeed in conducting investigations and in learning science generally. These statements may originate from teachers "telling," or from children reading texts, or hearing from other experts. While these intervention studies suggest that students can learn science across the strands through highly scaffolded and carefully structured experiences designing and conducting investigations, we also note that having students design and conduct investigations may be particularly difficult and require a very high level of teacher knowledge and skill in order for students to master content across the strands (see, e.g., Roth, 2002).

We elaborate on the features of problems that students investigate and the support they need to succeed in the next section. The emerging evidence suggests that learning how to design, set up, and carry out experiments and other kinds of scientific investigations can help students understand key scientific concepts, provide a context for understanding why science needs empirical evidence, and how tests can distinguish between explanations.

Argumentation, Explanation, and Model Building in K-8 Classrooms

Another common approach in the research literature is to create opportunities for students to engage in other aspects of scientific activity, such as argumentation, explanation, and model building. As scientists investigate empirical regularities in the world, they attempt to explain these regularities with theories and models, and to apply those models to new phenomena. Furthermore, the scientific community reaches consensus through a process of proposing and arguing about their own and others' ideas through talk and writing, using the particular discourse conventions of the discipline. Some instructional interventions have brought these activities into the K-8 classroom. As students conduct investigations to develop and apply explanations to natural phenomena, they develop claims, defend them with evidence, and explain them, using scientific principles.

With a focus on explanation, students attempt to produce evidence that supports a particular account or claim (McNeill et al., 2006; Sandoval, 2003; Sandoval and Reiser, 2004). An emphasis on scientific argument adds the element of convincing peers of the explanation, responding to critiques, and reaching consensus (Bell and Linn, 2000; Driver, Newton, and Osborne, 2000; Duschl and Osborne, 2002; Osborne, Erduran, and Simon, 2004). A focus on model building adds the element of representing patterns in data and formulating general models to explain candidate phenomena (Lehrer and Schauble, 2000b, 2004; Schwarz and White, 2005).

Several elements emerge as critical in these approaches to argumentation, explanation, and model building. In these approaches, units of study are framed to address a question or set of questions about the natural world. The question may arise from benchmark lessons that elicit curiosity, from observations of perplexing natural phenomena, from a problem situated in the real world that can be addressed with scientific evidence, or from questions that scientists themselves are currently struggling to answer (Blumenfeld et al., 2000; Edelson, 2001; Linn et al., 1999). For example, Linn and colleagues used a documented cases of frog mutation in particular ecosystems and an overall pattern of increased mutations nationwide to frame a middle school environmental science unit. In this case there was no definitive scientific explanation for the pattern of mutated frogs; instead, students were engaged in a genuine scientific quandary and explored several competing explanations, including two leading hypotheses in the scientific community. One leading explanation entailed a type of parasite that scientists believe can physically interfere with the natural development of frog limbs, and the other involved a pesticide which, with exposure to sunlight, may interfere with the hormonal signals that control limb development. Once questions are framed and students understand and buy into them, they conduct investigations whose purpose is to explore one or more possible claims about the question. Dealing with authentic scientific debates required that the educators and researchers involved in this intervention take great efforts to make the scientific problems accessible to students without sacrificing core scientific concepts required to understand ecosystem relations, and the role of hormones in development. To focus and support student learning teachers and instructional materials narrowed the focus and provided students with a handful of factors to investigate and a method or structured choice of methods to choose from in order to explore the problem.

Interacting with Texts in the K-8 Classroom

Reading and texts are important parts of scientific practice and play an important role in science classrooms. Much of the research on students' interaction with text has been conducted by reading researchers and is often not well situated in the context of science curricula and pedagogy. A few studies do, however, consider the role of text in conjunction with scientific inquiry and the consequences for students learning.

Concept-oriented reading instruction (CORI) is a program of research in which elementary students and teachers pursued the study of conceptual issues in science of the students' choosing. In CORI, students were introduced to a complex knowledge domain, such as ecology or the solar system, for several weeks. They were then allowed to select a topic in that domain (such as a particular bird or animal) to study in depth and chose which books to read related to the topic. In the course of their inquiry about the topic, students received support in finding relevant resources, learned how to use those resources, and how to communicate what they learned to others. In conjunction with this text-based research, students participated in related inquiry, such as a habitat walk, specimen collection, feeder observations, feather experiments, and owl-pellet dissection. Students in CORI showed better reading comprehension of science-related texts and were more motivated to read about science than were students in traditional instruction (Guthrie et al., 2004).

In another line of research, Palinscar and Magnusson have explored students' and teachers' use of text in the context of guided inquiry science instruction (Palincsar and Magnusson, 2005). They describe the interplay of first- and second-hand investigations and the support they provide for the development of scientific knowledge and reasoning. In the latter stages of their research, the researchers developed an innovative text-genre (a scientist's notebook) to scaffold students' and teachers' use of text in an inquiry fashion. The innovative text is a hybrid of exposition, narration, description, and argumentation in which the imagined scientist's voice personalizes the text for the reader. Use of the text supported students' learning about the topics being studied (reflection and refraction). However, engaging students to interact with text in an inquiry fashion required careful mediation by the teachers. Likewise, teachers needed to be supported in developing instructional practices that supported the use of text as inquiry.

Evidence of Student Learning

Thus far we have briefly described science as practice as an instructional approach that presents scientific skills as integrated—the skills of data collection and analysis are encountered in places where they can be useful for learning about a phenomena. We have also contrasted this approach with prevailing patterns of current instructional practice that present content and process separately. The prevalent practice of separating process and content in instruction has often been premised on notions of what students can (and cannot) do. However, the evidence from instructional research suggests that students can in fact engage in science as practice in meaningful ways.

Elementary Grades: Inquiry and Models

The study of the inquiry skills of elementary school students by Metz (2004), described above, situates children's learning of investigating skills in the context of a study of animal behavior. In these interventions, students develop questions, discuss ways to operationalize their questions in observations, and then collect data, interpret the data, and debate conclusions. In this work, students consider and critique different interpretations of data, and consider such factors as how different measurement or experimental procedures they or other students have chosen could affect what the data reveal about the underlying question. In this way, students exhibit some proficiency in coordinating theory and evidence, distinguishing between the intuitive appeal of their conjectures (their "theory"), and what the evidence actually reveals about the truth of their conjectures.

In Metz's analysis of investigations designed and conducted by a second and a fourth-fifth split grade class, all of the students succeeded in designing and carrying out investigations. Furthermore, more than 70 percent of the second graders and 87 percent of the fourth and fifth graders demonstrated knowledge that their research was in some respects "uncertain"—a precondition of posing scientific questions and an inevitable feature of scientific work. Upon reflection, 80 and 97 percent of these students, respectively, posited a strategy to address the uncertainty in their research design. Metz's findings contrast sharply with views that young children cannot conduct scientific investigations or that they are necessarily bound to concrete experiences with natural phenomena.

Similarly, Lehrer and Schauble have worked with elementary school teachers to support students in data modeling practices (Lehrer, Giles, and Schauble, 2002; Lehrer and Schauble, 2000a, 2004, in press). In this approach, students are involved in developing questions for investigation, deciding how to measure the variables of interest, and developing data displays to represent their results. A focus of the approach is involving students in grappling with the need to represent their data in ways that communicate what they believe the data show about the question of interest, rather than giving students ready-made procedures for graphically representing their data. Students create representations and debate their relative merits for helping analyze and communicate their findings. They then revise the representations and use them as a tool to analyze the scientific phenomenon. These representations become more abstract and model-like and less literal over time. In one study, fifth grade students developed graphical representations to analyze naturally occurring variation in growing plants (Lehrer and Schauble, 2004). These students were able to develop representations that captured the properties of the distributions, and they were able to use these tools in designing and conducting investigations of such variables as light and fertilizer on plant growth. The focus on the meaning of the data representation and its use to communicate among the community of students seemed to help learners develop more sophisticated understandings of distribution as a mathematical idea, and the biological variation in their samples it represents.

Middle Grades: Problem-Based and Conceptual Change Approaches

In the middle grades, one common approach to engage students in the practices of science is problem-based or project-based science (Blumenfeld et al., 1991; Edelson, Gordin, and Pea, 1999; Edelson and Reiser, 2006; Kolodner et al., 2003; Krajcik et al., 1998; Reiser et al., 2001; Singer et al., 2000). In these approaches, a research question about a problem can provide the context for extended investigations. Students learn the target science content and processes in the context of pursuing that question. For example, students learn about the particulate nature of matter and chemical reactions while investigating the quality of air in their community (Singer et al., 2000), or they learn about how species interact in ecosystems while investigating a mystery of what killed many plants and animals in a Galapagos island system (Reiser et al., 2001). Characteristics of this approach include establishing a need for the target understanding, through a problem students find compelling (Edelson, 2001), often a real-world application. Students then investigate the problem context and attempt to apply their findings to address the original problem. Often the projects include a culminating activity in which students apply what they have learned to address the problem, for example, making a presentation or developing a poster to communicate their findings. Culminating activities provide students the opportunity to reflect on their experiences and apply their scientific understanding, for example, discussing atmospheric phenomena to argue about possible causes of global warming, or analyzing forces and motion to redesign and test model vehicles and their propulsion systems (Kolodner et al., 2003).

A slight variation on problem-based approaches is to frame more purely scientific questions, focusing instruction directly on changing students' conceptual understanding of core scientific ideas like atomic structure, speciation, and the nature of matter. These approaches stem from the research (reviewed in Chapter 4) that characterizes the types of conceptual changes that learners undergo—acquiring new concepts; elaborating existing conceptual structures; restructuring a network of concepts; or adding new, deeper levels of understanding—and discuss strategies for effecting conceptual change. A common thread across these programs of instruction is a strong metacognitive component.

Typically, activities are introduced to make students aware of their initial ideas and that there may be a conceptual problem that needs to be solved. A variety of techniques may be useful in this regard. Students may be asked to make a prediction about an event and give reasons for their prediction, a technique that activates their initial ideas and makes students aware of them. Class discussion of the range of student predictions emphasizes alternative ways of thinking about the event, further highlighting the conceptual level of analysis and creating a need to resolve the discrepancy. In addition, gathering data that expose students to unexpected discrepant events or posing challenging problems to students that they cannot immediately solve are further ways of sending signals that they need to stop and think, step outside the normal "apply" conceptual framework mode, to a more metaconceptual "question, generate and examine alternatives, and evaluate" mode.

Conceptual change shares several of the features of problem-based learning described above. In conceptual change approaches, teachers make complex scientific problems meaningful to students from the outset of study and integrate multiple strands of proficiency. They then provide students with pieces of the problem that will allow them to make incremental progress in understanding a large, complex area of science over weeks or months. The problems—whether practical, applied, or conceptual—require the integration and coordination of multiple ideas and aspects of scientific practice.

Research on these varied approaches to teaching science as practice reveals promising results. First, there is much evidence that, with appropriate support, students engage in the inquiry, use the tools of science, and succeed in complex scientific practices. For example, students engaged in problem-based learning succeed in working with complex primary data sets to uncover patterns in data and develop complex scientific arguments supported with evidence (Reiser et al., 2001). They can use scientific visualization tools to analyze primary data sets of atmospheric data and explain patterns of climate change (Edelson, 2001; Edelson, Gordin, and Pea, 1999). There is also some evidence that these project-based experiences can help students learn scientific practices. Kolodner et al. (2003) found that middle school students who practiced inquiry in several project-based science units performed better on the inquiry tasks of scientific practice (as measured by performance assessments) than students from traditional classrooms (Quellmalz et al., 1999). Students in project-based science classrooms performed better than comparison students on designing fair tests, justifying claims with evidence, and generating explanations. They also exhibited more negotiation and collaboration in their group work and a greater tendency to monitor and evaluate their work (Kolodner et al., 2003).

Analyses of students' content learning also reveal the promise of these approaches for their mastery of scientific principles. Conceptual change researchers have found that across the K-12 grade span, involving children in cycles of model-based reasoning can be a highly effective means of building their deeper conceptual understandings of core scientific principles (Brown and Clement, 1989; Lehrer et al., 2001; Raghavan, Sartoris, and Glaser, 1998; Smith et al., 1997; Stewart, Cartier, and Passmore, 2005; White, 1993; Wiser and Amin, 2001). Problem-based approaches have demonstrated that students succeed in learning complex scientific content as represented in state and national standards, using assessments like the National Assessment of Educational Progress (NAEP) and standardized state tests. For example, Rivet and Krajcik (2004) found that students in a lower income urban district achieved significant gains in both science content (e.g., balanced forces, mechanical advantage) and inquiry process skills, as measured by pre- and posttest achievement items based on state assessments and items from the Trends in International Mathematics and Science Study.

There is also some evidence of the scalability of the approach. Marx and his colleagues (2004) examined the learning gains for 4 project-based units enacted in a school district across 3 years. Again, using curriculum-based test items designed to parallel those on state and NAEP assessments, they found significant learning gains (more than 1 standard deviation in effect sizes) on both content and process items for all four units. These gains persisted and even increased across years of enactment, as the intervention scaled to 98 classrooms and 35 teachers in 14 schools. In more recent work, this research group has compared performance on the high-stakes state assessments for students in project-based classrooms with those of the rest of the district, again focusing on students from the lower socioeconomic distribution in this urban district (Geier et al., in press). Project-based students from seventh and eighth grade achieved higher content and process scores than their peers and had significantly higher pass rates on the statewide assessment. The effects of participation in the project-based classrooms were cumulative, with higher scores associated with more exposure to project-based instruction.

Taken together, these results demonstrate that instruction that situates science as practice and that integrates conceptual learning can have real benefits for learners. Students at both elementary and middle school levels can succeed in engaging in science and in learning the science content that is encountered in these contexts. The challenges students have with epistemology and coordinating theory and evidence shown in some studies do not arise in the same way in these very supportive classrooms. An important aspect of these designs is that they contain very carefully crafted support for the scientific practices. In the next sections we look more closely at practices that may help science learners master target concepts and practices.

ELEMENTS OF PRACTICE

We have argued that children should engage in meaningful problems in science class and experience science as practice and that when they do, they can realize tremendous advances in their understanding and ability to use science. Here we provide a finer grained description of elements of practices students can engage in that support their learning.

Research on the professional practices of scientists reveals a number of interacting activities that characterize their engagement (e.g., Latour, 1980; Longino, 1990; Nersessian, 2005). Scientists talk through problems in real time—through publication and through less formal written venues, such as lab books, email exchanges, and colloquia. They engage in an iterative process of argumentation, model building, and refinement. In some classrooms, students are engaged in several core practices that resemble scientific practice. Just like scientists, students ask questions, talk and write about problems, argue, build models, design and conduct investigations, and come to more nuanced and empirically valid understandings of natural phenomena. As we've said, K-8 students are neither scientists nor blank slates. They have a store of life experiences and intellectual resources, but they lack content expertise, refined knowledge of investigative methods, familiarity and acceptance of scientific norms, and deep experience working with peers on scientific problems. To do meaningful scientific work in classrooms, they require strategic supports, input, and guidance from teachers and curriculum materials.

Research reveals both the promise and challenges of teaching science as practice. As instruction taps their entering knowledge and skills, students must reconcile their prior knowledge and experiences with new, scientific meanings of concepts, terms, and practices. Similarly, they may enter classrooms with very limited or inaccurate views of science—that science is unchanging, that experiments are portals to uncovering truth, and that learning science means merely accumulating facts (Carey et al., 1989). In this section, we discuss three key features of K-8 science practice that require carefully crafted support and instruction. As students wrestle with meaningful scientific problems they (1) engage in social interaction, (2) appropriate the language of science, and (3) use scientific representations and tools. These are features that are central to scientific practice and require that teachers and instructional materials provide clear guidance and support for learners as they acquire these practices.

Science in Social Interactions

Social interaction is a central feature of both scientific practice and productive learning generally, and accordingly it plays an important, specialized role in K-8 science learning. As noted in Chapter 2, social studies of science describe a highly interactive and social practice of bench scientists in which argumentation—articulating and communicating understandings, testing ideas in a community, giving and receiving feedback, and processes for evaluating and reaching consensus—is a central feature (e.g., Latour, 1980; Longino, 1990; Nersessian, 2005). Prior reviews have also identified the importance of social interactions for learning generally. The National Research Council report on advanced study of math and science in high school, for example, found that "socially supported interactions can strengthen children's ability to learn with understanding" (National Research Council, 2001). The research studies of social interaction in K-8 science classrooms reveal both the unique challenges of drawing on and teaching productive social interaction and the promise of seriously attending to social interactions.

Children enter school with a range of resources that can be tapped to support meaningful social interaction. They also bring habituated ways of interacting with their peers that often run contrary to desirable productive social interactions that sustain science learning. For example, while science practice entails argumentation as a process for refining knowledge claims, students may view argumentation in a different light. They may see arguments as unpleasant experiences. Children may also view argument as something that is won or lost on the basis of status and authority (e.g., bigger kids may be more persuasive in a playground dispute irrespective of evidence and logic), rather than on its logical or empirical merits. Furthermore, traditional school values, such as competition among students, emerge in tension with scientific values of comparing results among peers to explore a factor's effect on other variables (Hogan and Corey, 2001).

We can expect that students will need instruction in how to work on science problems collectively. National data suggest that opportunities for meaningful social interaction are limited across U.S. student groups. These may be particularly infrequent for nonmainstream students, students in urban schools, English-language learners, and students with disabilities (Gilbert and Yerrick, 2001; Palincsar and Magnusson, 2005; Rodriguez and Berryman, 2002).

When educators succeed in creating a community of learners, in which students see their goal as one of contributing to a community understanding of scientific problems, students can reap cognitive, social, and affective benefits. For example, student learning from hands-on investigation is dramatically improved when they also present their ideas and arguments about investigations to their peers (Crawford, Krajcik, and Marx, 1999; Krajcik et al., 1998). Debating with peers can help make scientific tasks more meaningful, lead to more productive and conceptually rich classroom dialogue, and improve conceptual mastery (Brown and Campione, 1990, 1996; Herrenkohl and Guerra, 1998; Herrenkohl et al., 1999; Lehrer and Schauble, in press).

The benefits of rich social interactions apply to the range of students that populate K-8 classrooms. The program of research at the Cheche Konnen Center has demonstrated that urban English-language learners can effectively engage in high-level scientific reasoning and problem solving if taught in ways that respect their interests and modes of social interaction (e.g., Ballenger, 1997; Hudicourt-Barnes, 2003; Warren et al., 2001). For example, Hudicourt-Barnes used her knowledge of the traditional Haitian form of talk called *bay odyans* (chatting) to foster arguments or *diskisyon* (discussion) in science classrooms for Haitian students. She worked with other members of the Cheche Konnen Center to help poor bilingual students build on their interest in talking and in exploring phenomena in the world by using their indigenous form of argument (and their interests, e.g., in African drums) as a link to more conventional scientific investigations of the physics of sound, the reproductive cycle of snails, and the causes of mold. The message that culturally diverse students can participate in meaningful science discussion is echoed by Lemke (1990).

The Specialized Language of Science

Communication and argumentation about scientific ideas involves characteristic uses of language defined by the discipline: "controlled experiments," "trends in data," "correlation versus causation." Scientific discourse also requires use of special patterns of language, which enable individuals to identify and ask empirical questions, describe the epistemic status of an idea (hypothesis, claim, supported theory), critique an idea apart from its author or proponent, and specify types of critiques (e.g., concerns about a claim versus claims about evidence). For K-8 students, each of these kinds of communication may require learning new uses of language. Thus, while scientific language skills can be considered important learning goals in their own right, specialized language can also help students perform the activities of scientific practice (Lemke, 1990; Moje et al., 2001; Rosebery, Warren, and Conant, 1992).

Disciplinary language can carry specialized, technical meanings. As mentioned in Chapter 2, some words may have nonscientific, lay meanings that conflict with their scientific meanings (e.g., theory). Students need opportunities to master the specialized meanings of scientific words and to sort these from their nonscientific meanings. Using technical language appropriately may be particularly trying for students who bring different ways of using language into academic settings (Rosebery, Warren, and Conant, 1992). An important strand of instructional research is the attempt to support more productive ways of using scientific language. Such efforts involve attempts to bridge learners' ways of using language and more normative scientific discourse in doing scientific activities by supporting their language interactions (Moje et al., 2001; Rosebery et al., 1992).

Another area of research probes efforts to make explicit the social roles and associated language that governs students' interactions in scientific practice (Herrenkohl and Guerra, 1998; Herrenkohl et al., 1999; Hogan and Corey, 2001; Palincsar, Anderson, and David, 1993). Given the challenges that learners face in acquiring modes of discourse associated with science, researchers have analyzed the effects of teaching distinct roles to individuals and assigning individual students to a particular role.

Work with Scientific Representations and Tools

Finally, the representation of ideas is a central part of scientific work that carries over to instruction and is evident across programs of research on instruction. Scientists use diagrams, figures, visualizations, and mathematical representations to convey complex ideas, patterns, trends, and proposed explanations of phenomena in compressed, accessible formats. These tools require expertise to be understood and to be used to reason about underlying scientific phenomena (Edelson, Gordin, and Pea, 1999; Gordin and Pea, 1995; Lehrer and Schauble, 2004). As with the social interaction and discourse aspects of practice, work with representations and tools poses challenges for learners, but also offers promise as a vehicle to more effectively support learners and bridge the resources they bring to the classroom and more sophisticated scientific practices.

Challenges arise when representations such as graphing are taught procedurally. Current instruction often underestimates the difficulty of connecting work with scientific representations to reasoning about the scientific phenomena they represent. To exploit their utility, students need support in working with interpreting and creating data representations that carry meaning. Access to scientific data in the form of data sets, data collected through observation and experimentation, interaction with simulations, and visualizations can become an important part of providing opportunities for students to experience and reason about scientific phenomena.

SUPPORTING THE LEARNING OF SCIENCE AS PRACTICE

Having laid out central features of doing science in K-8 classrooms and the challenges that learners face, we now shift our focus to examine the ways in which teachers and instructional materials can act to support student learning. Research has uncovered several types of complementary strategies that can be part of instructional support for students learning science as practice. The areas of support build on what is known about learning in general and about science in particular. In this section we discuss the means of supporting science learning as students engage in science as practice—designing and conducting investigations, developing arguments, and building and refining models and explanations.

Our discussion of support for student learning relies heavily on forms of guidance that are, in part, embedded in curriculum materials. However, this is not to suggest that teachers are somehow less important to the process. On the contrary, no system of instruction can operate without skillful teachers. Curriculum materials, specific instructional approaches (project-based science, coherent instruction focused on conceptual change), and software tools, such as scaffolded simulations and visualization tools, offer useful structure to student learning experiences, but they cannot dictate learning. In all these examples, the teacher plays a critical role in realizing these designs. Even if the intervention is represented by carefully specified curriculum materials (e.g., Blumenfeld et al., 2000; Singer et al., 2000), the teacher plays a role in how the instructional materials are enacted. In most of these designs, teachers need to carefully orchestrate classroom discussions to establish research questions; consider hypotheses; establish classroom norms for evidence; compare results; help elucidate, question, and critique conceptual models; and so on.

In all of these cases, teachers' beliefs and understandings of the discipline and of the pedagogy shape how they interpret and put the design ideas of the materials into action (Ball and Cohen, 1996; Clandinin and Connelly, 1991). For example, Schneider, Krajcik, and Blumenfeld (2005) found a range of enactments of critical aspects of the project-based science approach (such as attention to students' prior ideas), resulting from particular teachers' interpretations of the materials. Some of these adaptations diverged from some of the important instructional characteristics intended by the designers. Yet it is not possible to script these interactions or to embed all possible alternatives in "teacher-proof" curriculum materials (Doyle and Ponder, 1977). Instead, these approaches call for careful attention to teacher learning, perhaps through researcher-teacher partnerships (as in the early design studies) in an approach, or in more formalized professional development programs as interventions develop (Blumenfeld et al., 2000; Marx et al., 1997). Teacher learning is discussed further in Chapter 10.

Sequencing Units of Study

As discussed above, science as practice frames meaningful problems that depict complex phenomena and require that students master and coordinate a range of concepts and practices. As students begin to wrestle with these problems, teachers and instructional materials necessarily provide an important sequencing function. Students cannot do everything at once from the start. After framing a complex problem and assessing students' entering capabilities to work on it, the teacher must adjust instruction to focus on smaller pieces of the problem at hand. While students are always working in the context of a large, complex problem, throughout the unit instruction emphasizes smaller, manageable pieces in their daily classroom experiences.

Let us consider how sequencing works by briefly examining the BGuILE middle school Struggle for Survival unit, a 6- to 7-week classroom examination of core evolutionary concepts through an investigation (Table 9-1). In this unit, "students learn about natural selection by investigating how a drought affects the animal and plant populations on a Galapagos island. Students can examine background information about the island, read through field notes, and examine quantitative data about the characteristics of the islands' species at various times and points to look for changes in the populations" (Reiser et al., 2001, p. 275).

While from the outset this unit frames the large-scale, complex problem of explaining the impact of a drought on plant and animal populations, it unfolds over four phases, which are sequenced to gradually ratchet up the demands of the learning experiences and the sophistication of students' reasoning about core concepts. The first phase (10 classes) sets the stage for the study by discerning students' entering knowledge of natural selection and providing requisite background knowledge (about ecosystems and the theory of natural selection) and building student motivation. In the second phase (5 classes), students learn background information specific to the Galapagos investigation. They learn about the Galapagos Islands and the methods scientists use to study ecosystems. They generate initial hypotheses,

TABLE 9-1 The Struggle for Survival Middle School Curriculum

Phase A: General Staging Activities (10 Classes)	Staging activities provide background knowledge and motivation for the investigation. Brainstorming activities reveal what students believe and understand about island ecosystems. Activities include a geography game using characteristics of tropical island as clues, student research on how animals are adapted to the local ecosystem of an island, a background video, and reading on Darwin and the Galapagos.
Phase B: Background for Investigations (5 Classes)	Activities focus directly on the Galapagos ecosystem and understanding how to investigate ecosystem data. Activities include a video introduction to the Galapagos and the methods scientists use to study the ecosystem, brainstorming about hypotheses, and a mini paper-based investigation in which students work with a small data set from the software and make a graph that backs up a claim about the data.
Phase C: Software Investigations (10 Classes)	Students investigate data using the Galapagos finches software environment, documenting their developing explanations as they progress. At the midpoint, student teams pair up and critique each other's explanations.
Phase D: Presenting and Discussing Finding (6 Classes)	Student teams prepare their reports. Each team presents their findings, and the class analyzes key points of agreement and dissension.

SOURCE: Reiser et al. (2001)

work from a small data set, and learn about the computer system they will use in the major investigation.

Only after these 15 lessons lay important conceptual groundwork, provide justification for the study of ecosystems, and build the intellectual tools and motivation that the students need, do they themselves conduct investigations of the natural selection data set. In the third phase (10 classes), students explore the data set and generate explanations for observed patterns of change in the finch populations and critique the explanations of their classmates. In the fourth phase (6 classes), student teams prepare reports, present findings, and analyze key points of agreement and disagreement across reports.

Such carefully sequenced experiences can provide an intelligible roadmap for student learners. At each turn, they develop important elements of scientific practice as they wrestle with evidence, consider different ways of looking at phenomena and interpreting evidence, and work collectively to determine what they understand and which interpretations they find compelling. Students need guidance, including explicit and direct guidance, as well as support that helps them develop the tacit knowledge of scientific practice that will inform judgments and decisions they make as they do science. We now turn to discussion of the mechanisms that teachers and curriculum designers can use to provide support to students as they work on tasks.

Embedding Instructional Guidance in Students' Performance of Scientific Tasks

Learners face many obstacles in learning science as practice, and they require support in order to engage in it productively. For example, in conducting and interpreting science, students often confuse evidence with its interpretation (the "theory/evidence" confusion), are unfamiliar with the strategy of controlling variables in order to design experiments to test a hypothesis, and do not continually reevaluate hypotheses in light of new evidence. Their entering understandings of and experiences with the physical, biological, and social worlds may confound their efforts to master new knowledge. Their prior exposure to science, including science instruction, may leave them with a distorted impression of the scientific enterprise. Explicit support is required to help students learn the practices, the concepts, and the very nature of science. Students left free to explore, as in pure "discovery learning" approaches, may continue to face these obstacles, interfering with their ability to learn through inquiry. Simple experience with inquiry alone does not lead to acquisition of better experimentation skills or conceptual mastery (Roth, 1987; Klahr, 2000). Students need firsthand experiences working on meaningful scientific problems, as developing expertise in a discipline entails developing more sophisticated strategies for solving problems

(VanLehn, 1989) and much of the knowledge involved in solving problems is tacit. Thus pure explicit instruction will fail to produce awareness, understanding, or knowledge of appropriate use of important strategies (Greeno, Collins, and Resnick, 1996).

Instead of pure discovery or pure direct instruction, students need strategic "scaffolds" that embed instructional guidance in ongoing investigations to call attention to important decision points and to make data patterns more explicit (Box 9-1). Scaffolding has been defined broadly and used to mean

BOX 9-1 Scaffolding

Scaffolding is ongoing guidance provided to students as they perform a task, which facilitates performance and learning. Scaffolding can be viewed as the additional support built around a core (baseline) version of a task to make it more tractable and useful for learning. Scaffolding is always defined relative to some assumed baseline version of the task (Sherin, Reiser, and Edelson, 2004).

The original scaffolding metaphor included the eventual removal or "fading" of the scaffolding. This aspect of scaffolding has yet to be thoroughly investigated. Most studies of scaffolding are not extensive enough to include the fading of scaffoldings. A notable exception is the recent study by McNeill et al. (2006) of scaffolds for students' evidence-based explanations. They found that middle school students in a 2-month project-based unit performed better on posttests requiring explanations if the scaffolding was gradually faded during the instructional unit, rather than if the scaffolding was continued throughout the entire unit. More research is needed to explore the time frame and approaches for fading scaffolds.

- Scaffolding can be support for students provided by a teacher, tutor, or peer (Palincsar, 1998). For example, through scripts, peers may learn to ask questions that help classmates clarify their reasoning or justify claims by linking them with evidence.
- Scaffolding can be support embedded in students' performance of a task that transforms the task to make it more tractable for learners. For example, to facilitate students use of data sets in computer-based investigations, software systems can provide more meaningful ways to refer to and manipulate data.
- Scaffolding may work to guide or structure problem solving, focusing students on important aspects of the task that are productive for learning and that they might otherwise overlook or treat superficially (Reiser, 2004).

different things; however, recent analyses of scaffolding emphasize the ways that support can be embedded in students' ongoing performance of tasks to support learning (Hogan and Pressley, 1997; Linn, Bell, and Davis, 2004; Quintana et al., 2004; Reiser, 2004; Sherin, Reiser, and Edelson, 2004). We think of scaffolding as strategic support that enables students to do scientific tasks with a higher degree of sophistication than they could without it. Scaffolding may structure students' interactions with one another or their thinking about a particular model, concept or practice, or it may guide students' interpretation of scientific tools and representations. It might also entail teachers telling things to students—giving them clear canonical explanations, or facts to build upon.

Various approaches to scaffolding scientific tasks have emerged in the literature. A central theme is to make a process or concept more explicit for learners by enabling them to do something they could not do without some crucial element provided through scaffolding. The elements might come through teacher actions, instructional materials, or actions of other students. Students might be cued to reflect, reminded to incorporate a key concept in their work, or prompted to reflect on their experiences. In this section, we describe three ways in which scaffolds can support students' learning. Scaffolding can structure experiences to draw attention to the elements of scientific practice, provide guidance in students' efforts to engage in social processes around scientific problems, and help them track the important conceptual aspects of the problems they are working on. Furthermore, these different approaches to scaffolding science learning can mutually reinforce one another and together provide necessary guidance, enabling students to perform in complex ways that they could not do without the scaffolding.

Scaffolding Scientific Process

When students learn science, they do not necessarily come to understand their experiences, observations, or science itself in ways that teachers and curriculum designers intend. In conducting investigations, students may ignore or choose not to believe unexpected results, rather than wondering why it was that an unexpected result occurred and puzzling over how to interpret it (e.g., as an error in procedure, an interesting result that should be further tested). Clear cues and guidance at strategic points in an investigation can prompt students to focus on the salient features of their experiences, observations, and the concepts they are working with to support critical engagement and movement toward desired learning outcomes.

One approach is to develop an instructional framework that can be presented and then used in ongoing fashion to structure students' work, such as the evidence-based explanation framework developed by Krajcik and his colleagues (McNeill et al., 2006; Moje et al., 2004). While evidence-based explanations in science may have a very complex structure, this instructional approach identifies the most central elements and makes them explicit to students. These elements consist of the claim, the empirical evidence in support of the claim, and the reasoning that articulates why the evidence supports the claim. This instructional framework is developed with students' input, as they learn first about evidence supporting claims and then consider how to organize a written or oral presentation to defend a claim. Teachers discuss the three elements with students, who then begin to use this framework to represent their written explanations in response to research questions. As they construct and refine these explanations, students use worksheets with scaffolding prompts that remind them of the elements and the criteria for them. This framework becomes a repeated structure that they use to guide their investigation, and it guides the synthesis of results into an explanation. Empirical studies of students' explanations reveal that students using this instructional framework improve in their ability to cite relevant data and connect it with claims within their written explanations (McNeill and Krajcik, in press). A similar approach embedded in software tools rather than paper and pencil worksheets was used in the Knowledge Integration Environment (Linn, 2000). In these tools, a checklist of tasks specifying important steps in inquiry was provided to help students coordinate the different steps in the activity. Similar approaches have been explored for scaffolding prompts to help learners articulate their experimental designs (Kolodner et al., 2003).

Another approach is to structure the tools that students use to represent their ideas in order to make the important aspects of the task more explicit. This is apparent in several software tools for argumentation. For example, SenseMaker (Bell and Linn, 2000) provides a representation that helps students develop and record their arguments. Students explicitly identify relevant evidence and code it as supporting or refuting sets of competing claims. Belvedere (Toth, Suthers, and Lesgold, 2002) supports students in constructing argument graphs, in which claims and evidence are visually distinguished, and students construct a chain of reasoning that includes claims, subclaims, and their supporting evidence. These tools can help learners develop more accurate and elaborate arguments, focusing them on the distinctions relevant for the domain (such as claim or theory versus evidence).

Scaffolding Social Interaction

We have discussed the promise and the complexity of social interactions in doing science. Scaffolding science learning through students' social interactions can harness the complexity of a scientific task and students' varied experiences and observations with it to build understanding in a student group. This type of approach has its roots in the reciprocal teaching approach to reading comprehension, which makes the process of comprehension explicit for learners (Palincsar and Brown, 1984). In reciprocal teaching of reading comprehension, for example, teachers model the important elements of comprehension, such as predicting, summarizing, and questioning, and then students begin to take on individual elements of the task. The task is essentially distributed among students, who share responsibility for its completion.

In elementary science classrooms, researchers have attempted to establish classroom versions of scientific communities (e.g., "community of learners" or "learning community" approaches), beginning with the "community of learners" (Brown and Campione, 1990, 1994, 1996) and "knowledge building" (Scardamalia and Bereiter, 1991, 1994) approaches in elementary school classrooms. Core to the approach is the notion that students are working together to build their understanding of answers to questions; the models they build can be revised as new ideas are uncovered through research; proposal and critique are essential to testing ideas in the community; and the teacher's role is to facilitate this process rather than provide authoritative answers to questions. The classroom designs attempt to realize these goals through various "distributed expertise" activity structures, such as creating research teams pursuing particular topics, jigsaw activities in which representatives of different teams (who have developed different expertise) come together in new teams to pursue new questions, and culminating activities in which teams present and critique one another's findings.

In general, the empirical research uncovers both the challenges and the promise of these approaches. Students in elementary school classrooms participate successfully in these types of learning communities. They take responsibility and ownership of the questions they pursue, and they exhibit increasing focus on discipline-appropriate peer-to-peer discourse, such as justifying and critiquing ideas and their evidence (Scardamalia and Bereiter, 1991, 1994). However, the classroom interactions are not simple to facilitate, requiring professional development for participating teachers. They also take time to become established and develop into shared classroom norms. These interventions are usually year-long collaborations between schools and researchers.

Herrenkohl and her colleagues have explored using "intellectual roles" to help make tasks more explicit to elementary schoolchildren (Herrenkohl and Guerra, 1998; Herrenkohl et al., 1999). These approaches build on the idea of supporting a task by making the process explicit, through assignment of specific responsibilities or roles for particular individuals. For example, Herrenkohl and Guerra (1998), working with two fourth grade classrooms, identified intellectual roles corresponding to particular aspects of the investigation task, such as making or checking predictions, summarizing findings, and connecting findings to theories. As the investigation proceeded, the teacher established these as important aspects of the investigation, identifying them as important jobs or roles, to be divided among the group sharing their results and among the audience listening and critiquing. As in some of the scaffolding prompts described earlier, the teacher established particular questions to ask associated with each job. For example, audience members would ask a range of results questions, such as "What helped you find your results?" "Did your group agree on your results?" Students use question prompts appropriate for their role, tailoring them to the current experiment and findings. In this way, the design attended to multiple elements of the scientific practice of investigation and argumentation, by associating the cognitive task of arguing for or critiquing an experimental result with particular types of social interactions and particular uses of language.

Herrenkohl and Guerra found that students were able to take on these roles and that they tailored their questioning as they became more sophisticated with the approach. Classroom discussions became more focused on important aspects of the scientific task (e.g., critiquing fit of evidence with hypothesis) and included more peer-to-peer rather than student-to-teacher interactions. Importantly, these peer interactions happened around issues, such as coordinating theory and evidence, that appear to be very challenging for students in the context of unstructured discovery or traditional instruction (Klahr, 2000; Kuhn, 1989; Kuhn, Amsel, and O'Loughlin, 1988).

Researchers exploring these approaches caution that these types of classroom participation structures, such as distributed expertise (Brown and Campione, 1994) and intellectual roles for science (Herrenkohl and Guerra, 1998), can become proceduralized, with students taking on particular jobs or asking questions in a superficial fashion. Hogan and Corey (2001) characterize science classrooms as having a "composite culture," which emerges as the traditional norms of schools (such as doing work to get grades, expecting the teacher to know the answers, contributing to show the teacher that one knows the answer she has previously provided) interact with the new scientific norms of knowledge building (valuing evidence, seeing questions as open, etc.) that teachers and designers are attempting to create. They emphasize the need to establish a shared understanding of these norms through ongoing discussion, identifying the need, clarifying what it means in terms of responsibilities and ways of interacting, and reflecting as the practice proceeds.

Scaffolding Conceptual Models

Instructional supports can be designed with conceptual models or dynamic simulations that make science concepts more transparent for learners, helping them connect their prior understandings with more sophisticated scientific understandings. These scaffolds can remind learners of important concepts that they need to include in their work or draw their attention to important conceptual distinctions, problematizing these issues and focusing their attention in productive ways. Interactive simulations can also highlight key concepts, helping students see concepts within a network of interrelated ideas.

Scaffolding can help students examine, scrutinize, and critically appraise their understanding of key scientific concepts. Visualizations can help learners connect patterns in data to a better understanding of the scientific phenomenon. For example, White and Fredericksen (1998) developed Thinkertools, a software environment that allows users to examine Newtonian physics, facilitates experimentation, and focuses users on salient features of key concepts. Designed for middle grade users, this system allows students to create "what if" experiments that are difficult or impossible to create in the real world—contrasting the behavior of moving objects in an environment with or without friction or in which gravity can be turned on or off. Users can manipulate the mass of balls, as well as stationary objects, which can serve as barriers to balls as they move through space. Users can assign impetuses to balls. The environment can also automatically generate accurate measurements of time, distance, and velocity. Graphical representations of variables help users visualize the results of changes in the variables' values. For example, moving balls can leave dot patterns as they move across the screen. This can make the velocity of a moving object more immediately salient as slower traveling balls leave dot patterns that are closer together and faster balls leave dot patterns at larger intervals. Students also have access to analytic tools that enable them to slow or freeze time and closely examine how a given object is moving (e.g., rate, distance, direction). These features help students control their investigation and analysis and focus their observations while they explore underlying physical principles.

Similarly, computer-based visualization tools can help learners see patterns in data that support scientific views of phenomena. Often, "seeing the data," that is, finding and interpreting coherent patterns, can be particularly challenging for students who have little familiarity with the content area and with using data in inductive ways. Scaffolds built into instruction, including computer simulations, can highlight for students the relationships between data patterns and possible explanations for phenomena.

Edelson (2001) has developed and tested computer visualization tools that enable middle school students to explore the impact of light entering the atmosphere on weather. Students use two software tools to conduct observations and observe patterns in data, from which they draw conclusions about the influence of geography on climate. WorldWatcher is a visualization and data analysis tool that is based on tools scientists use, but it is designed for learners (Edelson, Gordin, and Pea, 1999). This tool helps students see the tacit meanings that scientists see in tools and the representations that they use in the course of their work. It enables students, for example, to click on a region and automatically view numerical data. Or the software may provide links between two different weather maps, for example, by providing comparative data on average temperature for a given region during June and September. Close linking of multiple elements for students, visual representations of patterns, as well as simple summary statistics (e.g., cell-by-cell temperatures, average temperature on a given date) can help students uncover important relationships that underpin a scientific understanding of phenomena. The Progress Portfolio tool structures students' reflections, allowing them to capture, annotate, and organize information and create presentations from their data (Loh et al., 2001). It also allows them to chart their progress through the investigation. As students view data in the WorldWatcher, they are cued to reflect on relevant parts of the data representation by the Progress Portfolio. For example, students examining the influence of large bodies of water on land temperature would make focused observations of coastal areas on the world map illuminated with colored heat bands. Then they would be prompted to examine specific geographic features, to record a pattern of data, and to draw conclusions from it. Used together, these tools can help students see patterns clearly and interpret them in light of the intended learning outcomes by focusing their observations and cueing them to interpret data in scientifically viable ways.

Supporting Articulation and Reflection

Articulation and reflection are mutually supportive processes that are at the core of the scientific enterprise, and they are critical to the four strands of scientific thinking. In scientific practice, constructing and testing knowledge claims require a focus on articulating those claims, that is, developing clear statements of how and why phenomena occur. Argumentation requires articulating claims and teasing apart when there is agreement or divergence among different claims.

Reflection is critical to a complex cognitive process, such as managing an investigation. Researchers have documented that children repeat experiments and forge local interpretations of current results without connecting to prior hypotheses (Schauble et al, 1991; Klahr, 2000). To harness their investment in experimentation and focus their interpretations, children need regular opportunities to reflect. Reflection helps students monitor their understanding and track progress of their investigations. It also helps them solve problems along the way—identifying problems with current plans, rethinking plans, and keeping track of pending goals.

Supports for articulation and reflection have been a focus of instructional guidance and scaffolding design efforts. For example, in the Thinkertools work, White and Frederiksen have demonstrated students' increased success when asked to analyze and explain the products and process of their investigation (White and Frederiksen, 1998). Davis and Linn (2000) examined student learning in the context of a computer-based investigation that provided prompts asking students to reflect on their ideas as they engaged in investigations. They analyzed eighth grade students' performance as they engaged in computer-based investigations in which they collected real-time data and performed simulations and experiments. As students read articles on the computer, for example, they were prompted to state the major claim of the piece. As they evaluated claims, they were prompted to provide concrete concerns and revise claims to more accurately reflect the evidence. Students who used prompts developed greater awareness of their own knowledge and were better able to take advantage of opportunities to learn and integrate their knowledge.

Taken together, these studies (and others: see, e.g., Suthers, 2003) show that interacting with software prompts can help students articulate their understanding as well as provide rationales for decisions that they would otherwise not make explicit. This articulation and reflection is also critical to the success of collaboration, helping students converge on a consensus or uncover unknown disagreements that can determine whether groups are successful or not in their collaboration (Barron, 2003). Rather than considering reflection to be something that occurs at the end of an activity, what emerges from this work is the need for ongoing articulation of understanding and reflection on both the practices and the content of the investigation.

Formative Assessment[2]

Formative assessment practices present an additional set of strategies that are at a teacher's disposal. As we have argued throughout this volume and underscored in this chapter, students' ideas and experience in science are essential to science teaching that will help them make sense of scientific phenomena. Accordingly, teachers must have access to their ideas, as well as a range of strategies they can use to learn what students understand about a given topic. Instruction should fundamentally link what students understand at the beginning of a given unit of study to what they learn by the end. *Formative assessment* places agency for the improvement of learning on both the teacher and student as they move through a unit of instruction (Shavelson and Stanford Education Assessment Laboratory, 2003). The formative assessment literature frames the importance of better understanding classroom assessment in the move to raise standards and improve learning

---

[2]This section is based on the commissioned paper by Erin Marie Furtak titled, "Formative Assessment in K-8 Science Education: A Conceptual Review."

for all students, so that high standards may be achieved (Black and Wiliam, 1998a). Formative assessment is critical to teachers' ability to plan for, support, and assess the quality of students' experiences learning science as practice.

Teachers have the most direct access to information about student learning and are thus in a position to interpret and use it to provide them with timely feedback (Shepard, 2003; Wilson, 2005). Teachers can also use the information to monitor the effectiveness of their own teaching (National Research Council, 2001); however, formative assessment also involves students, since they need to recognize, evaluate, and react to their own learning and others' assessments of their learning (Bell and Cowie, 2001; Sadler, 1989).

Assessment becomes formative in nature—informing teaching and learning—only when the teacher uses that information to adapt instruction, or the student uses the information to influence his or her learning, or both (Black, 1998). For example, a teacher asking a planned sequence of questions might find out that students had not understood the concept to be learned in a particular lesson, and as a result the teacher might use that information to modify the subsequent lesson to reinforce the prior learning goal. In another situation, a student comparing his or her own work with an exemplar shown by the teacher might make modifications on the basis of reaching the goal made explicit in the form of the exemplar. Therefore, whether assessment is formative hinges on a criterion of *use;* that is, assessment can be considered formative when information is used to take action to advance students toward learning goals (Bell and Cowie, 2001; Black and Wiliam, 1998a; Shavelson et al., 2003).

Formative assessment can be summarized in three central questions to be answered by the student or the teacher: Where are you going? Where are you now? How are you going to get there? (National Research Council, 2001). This three-step process summarizes what has been called the "feedback loop" in formative assessment: setting a learning goal, determining the gap between the learning goal and the student's present state of understanding, and formulating feedback to close the gap.

Informal
Formative
Assessment

Formal Formative
Assessment

On-the-fly   Planned-for   Curriculum-Embedded

FIGURE 9-1   *Continuum of formative assessment.*
SOURCE: *Shavelson and Stanford Education Assessment Laboratory (2003).*

Formative assessment practice commonly takes three distinct forms, which can be thought of as a continuum (Figure 9-1). It can be on the fly, in which instruction goes a step beyond traditional classroom interactions; it becomes a method of genuine probing for understanding, rather than simply checking and evaluating the state of students' understanding (White and Gunstone, 1992). This point is especially relevant in the context of science education, in which teachers of scientific inquiry need to continuously elicit student thinking and help students consider their developing conceptions on the basis of scientific evidence. In planned-for formative assessment, ongoing formative assessment occurs in a learning environment that helps teachers acquire information on a continuing and informal basis, such as in the course of daily classroom talk. This type of classroom talk has been called an assessment conversation (Duschl and Gitomer, 1997; Duschl, 2003) or an instructional dialogue that embeds assessment into an activity already occurring in the classroom. When planned deliberately, assessment conversations become an example of planned-for assessment. Assessment conversations permit teachers to recognize students' conceptions, mental models, strategies, language use, or communication skills and allow them to use this information to guide instruction. A third type of formative assessment is referred to as "curriculum-embedded." This occurs when specific assessments are used in a curricular system at the school or school system level. We acknowledge curriculum-embedded formative assessment now as one type of formative assessment, and we discuss it in Chapter 10 as a feature of coherent instructional systems.

Formative Assessment and Student Learning

Research on the effectiveness of formative assessment across many school subjects suggests compelling results. In an extensive review of the literature that included more than 250 articles, Black and Wiliam (1998a) placed the effect size for learning gains in interventions involving aspects of formative assessment between 0.4 and 0.7.[3] These gains are observed across student achievement levels, with the highest gains for lower achieving students. Despite these encouraging findings, Black and Wiliam also found that few strong, empirical studies on formative assessment existed, and they found only one such study (White and Fredericksen, 1998) in the context of K-8 science.[4]

In that study, White and Frederiksen (1998) explored how peer and self-assessment could help to build students' understanding of scientific inquiry.

---

[3]Effect size derived only from studies with pre- and postmeasures of student learning.

[4]The only other science-specific controlled studies of formative assessment were in the context of instructional systems with embedded formative measures. Those studies are discussed in Chapter 10 under instructional systems.

Students from four middle school science classes were randomly assigned to two conditions: half to complete the reflective assessment process, and the other half to serve as a control. Students in both groups were provided with criteria for scientific inquiry processes; for example, "being systematic" and "reasoning carefully." Two of the classes used regular time during class to reflect on what they were learning and how they were learning it (e.g., using evidence from their work to support their evaluations), and the other two classes spent the same amount of time talking about how the activities could be changed. In this way, students in the reflective assessment (i.e., formative assessment) group monitored their own progress and the progress of their peers through verbal and written feedback and then were provided with opportunities to improve their performance later in the unit. The two classes of students that engaged in the reflective assessment process performed better on both project work and the unit test. Perhaps most notable, however, is the fact that lower performing students in the experimental class (as designated by score on the Comprehensive Test of Basic Skills) showed the greatest improvement in performance when compared with the control class.

Although we found no additional controlled studies of formative assessment, there is a handful of studies that provide case-based evidence of the process and value of formative assessment in science teaching. Ruiz-Primo and Furtak (2004) explored the on-the-fly formative assessment practices of three middle school science teachers and compared them with student performance. These practices were labeled as ESRU cycles, based on Bell and Cowie's (2001) model: the teacher Elicits a question, the Student responds, the teacher Recognizes the student's response, and then Uses the information collected to support student learning. *Eliciting* information focuses on the teacher's strategies such as asking questions that allow students to share and make explicit their thinking (e.g., ask the students to relate evidence to explanations). *Recognizing* students' thinking requires the teacher to listen and acknowledge their responses, explanations, or mental models (e.g., teacher repeats the student's comment to make sure it has been understood appropriately). *Using* information involves taking action on the basis of student responses to help them move toward learning goals (e.g., by responding with another question, eliciting alternate points of view, conducting a demonstration, or repeating an activity). For example, a teacher might ask a student to provide an example (*Eliciting*), the student provides an example (*Student Responds*), the teacher repeats the statement to confirm that she has understood it correctly (*Recognizing*), and then the teacher encourages the student to share his idea with another student who has a different example for the same idea (*Using*) (Furtak and Ruiz-Primo, 2005).

Most of the cycles observed in the study were classified as focusing on making predictions, interpreting graphs, and other epistemic factors, with only a few cycles observed across the three teachers that focused on conceptual development. The study found that while students' performance varied across questions and teachers, the highest level of student performance was observed in the class of the teacher with the most complete questioning cycles. However, the study also raises the question of whether the performance differences observed between classes were attributable to on-the-fly formative assessment practices alone or were a reflection of overall differences in teachers' everyday science teaching skills.

Duschl and Gitomer (1997) conducted research on planned assessment conversations in the Science Education through Portfolio Instruction and Assessment (SEPIA) project. These conversations are used to help teachers provide scaffolding and support for students' construction of meaning by carefully selecting learning experiences, activities, questions, and other elements of instruction (Duschl and Gitomer, 1997). Project SEPIA uses modeling and explicit teaching to help students "learn how to learn in science" (p. 41). Duschl and Gitomer explored how two middle school teachers worked with Project SEPIA's model of instruction. Developing a portfolio as they complete the unit, students are presented with authentic problems and proceed through an established sequence of investigations to develop their conceptual understanding, reasoning strategies related to ways of knowing in science, and communication skills.

A central element of the assessment conversation is a three-part process that involves the teacher receiving student ideas through writing, drawing, and sharing orally, so that students can show the teacher and other students what they know. The second step involves the teacher recognizing students' ideas through public discussion, and the third has the teacher using ideas to reach a consensus in the classroom by asking students to reason on the basis of evidence.[5] Project SEPIA also provides teachers with criteria for guiding students during these conversations, including a focus on relationships, clarity, and consistency with evidence, use of examples, making sense, acknowledging alternative explanations, and accuracy. Engaging students in assessment-related conversations about their work provides a context in which standards and criteria of quality are negotiated and discussed publicly (Duschl and Gitomer, 1997). The authors concluded that teachers should focus less on tasks and activities and more on the reasoning processes and underlying conceptual structures of science.

---

[5]Duschl and Gitomer's (1997) description of a three-step questioning process is very similar to that previously described in Bell and Cowie (2001) and Ruiz-Primo and Furtak (2004) as examples of on-the-fly, informal formative assessment. However, Duschl and Gitomer's study is considered an example of planned-for formative assessment because the questioning process is intended to take place in the context of planned assessment conversations. In contrast, Bell and Cowie and Ruiz-Primo and Furtak observed the questioning process in the course of everyday, on-the-fly classroom interactions.

Minstrell and vanZee (2003) describe questioning as a form of planned-for formative assessment by using questions both to diagnose the state of students' thinking and to prescribe an appropriate next step for them to take in their learning. VanZee and Minstrell's (1997) study explored how the "reflective toss" strategy Minstrell used in his high school physics classroom gave students responsibility for monitoring their own thinking and making their meanings clear. A reflective toss is defined as a question that "catches" the meaning of a student's statement and then "throws" responsibility for thinking back to the student. For example, if a student made a particular assertion, the teacher would respond with another question, such as "Now what do you mean by . . ." or "If you were to do [that] . . . , what would you do?" (p. 245). In this way, the teacher (in this case, Minstrell) used questions to find out what students were thinking, to consider with his students how their thinking fits with what physicists think, and to place responsibility for thinking back on the students. While the study took place in the high school classroom of only one teacher, it raises the important point for all levels of science instruction that a simple, planned-for questioning strategy can be an effective tool for formative assessment. The reflective toss forced students to take ownership of their ideas and to think about them further, and it also allowed the teacher to react and take action on students' ideas as they were offered to the class.

Despite substantial evidence of its positive impact on student achievement (Black and Wiliam, 1998a), research indicates that meaningful formative assessment is, in general, not a key priority for teachers (Crooks 1988; Black and Wiliam, 1998b). Most teachers limit their assessment practices to assigning grades or norm referenced marks that are unrelated to criteria and with few accompanying details or comments (Butler, 1988; Daws and Singh, 1996; Ruiz-Primo et al., 2004).

White and Frederiksen (1998) cite two important caveats to their findings related to reflective assessment: first, both students and teacher need to know that performance is being rated, not individuals, and, second, students must be given the means to understand what it is they need to do well in their performance; otherwise, ratings may be damaging. These caveats, according to White and Frederiksen, relate to the important point that if students are not given explicit feedback on how to improve their performance, they are likely to fall back on ability-related attributions for their performance—similar to Butler's (1988) findings. In addition, less advantaged students may be further discouraged if performance criteria and steps to improvement are not made clear. The authors caution that reflective assessment is an integral part of a curriculum and should scaffold the development of the skills being developed and should not simply be "added on."

Classroom-Based Assessment Practices and
Student Learning Outcomes

In the form that supports learning, assessment is a ubiquitous aspect of classroom activity and is rarely a discrete event. It involves observing students at work and listening to what they say (Hogan, Nastasi, and Pressley, 2000), being clear with criteria, and making sure the criteria capture and reflect what counts in the subject area (Resnick and Resnick, 1991). It also involves analyzing student work in light of that criteria and paying attention to what they are thinking, attending as much to their reasoning as to what they don't understand. It involves engaging students as active participants in an assessment activity or conversation, so that it becomes something they do, not merely something done to them (Duschl and Gitomer, 1997; White and Frederiksen, 1998). Finally, and most importantly, all kinds of formative assessment demand using assessment information in a way to inform teaching and learning (Black and Wiliam, 1998a).

The majority of studies cited in this review were performed in middle school classrooms. Thus it is difficult to make any kind of claim about the differences in abilities of students of varying ages to participate in formative assessment. We can confidently say that the formative assessment strategies summarized here suggest middle school students are capable of participating in and benefiting from formative assessment to various degrees. More research needs to be performed in K-5 classrooms to determine if the result is similar for students of that age.

CONCLUSIONS

This chapter has presented a range of instructional approaches that can support the four strands of our framework for science proficiency. The programs of instruction we have discussed differ in the aspect of scientific practice they choose to make central—creating well-designed experiments, making sense of scientific phenomena through experiments, applying theories to make sense of data, constructing scientific explanations and models, and convincing a scientific community through scientific argumentation. Although the aspect of scientific practice that is emphasized varies, several common themes are in evidence across these interventions.

The four strands of scientific proficiency come together in instructional approaches that involve learners in scientific practice. Rather than treating scientific content, scientific processes, epistemology, and participation independently in instruction, these proficiencies can be brought together as complementary aspects of science by engaging learners in such practices as investigation, argumentation, explanation, and model building. Teaching science as a practice brings these proficiencies together as they support one another—students develop powerful scientific ideas through developing and testing knowledge claims and applying their understandings of the nature of science to guide and evaluate those processes. The practice of developing and defending knowledge claims involves students in participating in a scientific community as they learn from and attempt to convince their peers of scientific claims.

Thus the practice of science is multidimensional, involving of course scientific reasoning, but also the social interaction that can realize these scientific processes (e.g., scientific arguments are to persuade peers of the claims and their interpretation) and the specialized discourse that provides the precision to communicate about these scientific tasks (e.g., language for evaluating explanations on plausibility, simplicity, and fit with evidence). Instructional interventions can profitably go beyond a focus on scientific content and reasoning processes and can help learners understand the epistemological underpinnings of scientific knowledge building by involving learners in the types of social interactions and discourse through which they can create and evaluate knowledge in their own scientific community.

Providing carefully structured opportunities for students to engage in investigations and other key elements of scientific practice can advance their learning in science. Approaches vary in whether students are being asked to develop principles or to enrich their understanding of presented principles by applying them to make sense of data (theory building versus theory application). However, students encounter problems along the way, as they plan and carry out investigations or apply principles across a range of examples of targeted scientific phenomena. All major aspects of inquiry—managing the process, making sense of data, and articulation and reflection—may require guidance. The design efforts we have discussed in this chapter explore what resources students bring to instruction that can be built on, what kinds of guidance are needed, and how best to embed that guidance in the doing of the scientific investigation.

Across these approaches there is a consistent emphasis on eliciting and building on students' prior understandings. Earlier, we reviewed the types of understandings that students bring into science learning situations—prior conceptions about scientific phenomena, such as density, gravity, and diversity in living things, as well as epistemological understandings about the nature of science, such as what makes a convincing argument or what counts as scientific data. Instruction needs to build incrementally toward more sophisticated understandings and practices, eliciting these prior understandings, uncovering questions to be explained, and linking these to experiences with experiments, data, and phenomena to expand students' conceptions. Support for practices may take the form of explicit structure that can make the practice more explicable or providing criteria that can help motivate and guide scientific work.

We have also shown that scaffolding is needed to support students' engagement in scientific practice. Young students can engage in aspects of scientific practice, but they need explicit support to do so effectively. In the design of instructional materials and their use by teachers, scaffolding pursues a balance between giving learners real responsibility for performing aspects of the scientific work, perhaps in a simplified version of the practice, while providing the structure that learners need to be able to succeed. Scaffolding can provide a structure that makes the process more explicit (e.g., by helping students understand and monitor whether their claims are supported with evidence) and more manageable (e.g., by providing a representation of inquiry steps for them to track their progress in an investigation), and it can prompt students to evaluate their thinking at critical points in a problem (e.g., by providing prompts for important reflective questions).

Finally, discourse and classroom discussion in which students engage in articulation and reflection are key to many of these approaches. Students are encouraged to articulate their understandings and are helped to realize that explanation rather than facts are the goal of the scientific enterprise. Ongoing nudging is important in encouraging students to articulate their ideas and test their consistency, coherence, and accuracy. Managing investigations is complex and requires monitoring, and reflection is key to staying on track and changing direction when needed.

REFERENCES

Ball, D.L., and Cohen, D.K. (1996). Reform by the book: What is—or might be—the role of curriculum materials in teacher learning and instructional reform? *Educational Researcher, 25*(9), 6-8.

Ballenger, C. (1997). Social identities, moral narratives, scientific argumentation: Science talk in a bilingual classroom. *Language and Education, 11*(1), 1-14.

Barron, B. (2003). When smart groups fail. *Journal of the Learning Sciences, 12*(3), 307-359.

Bell, B., and Cowie, B. (2001). *Formative assessment and science education.* Dordrecht, The Netherlands: Kluwer Academic.

Bell, P., and Linn, M.C. (2000). Scientific arguments as learning artifacts: Designing for learning from the web with KIE. *International Journal of Science Education, 22*, 797-817.

Black, P. (1998). Formative assessment: Raising standards inside the classroom. *School Science Review, 90*(291), 39-46.

Black, P., and Wiliam, D. (1998a). Assessment and classroom learning. *Assessment in Education, 5*(1), 7-74.

Black, P., and Wiliam, D. (1998b). Inside the black box: Raising standards through classroom assessment. *Phi Delta Kappan, 80*(2), 139-148.

Blumenfeld, P., Fishman, B.J., Krajcik, J., Marx, R.W., and Soloway, E. (2000). Creating usable innovations in systemic reform: Scaling-up technology-embedded project-based science in urban schools. *Educational Psychologist, 35*, 149-164.

Blumenfeld, P., Soloway, E., Marx, R., Krajcik, J., Guzdial, M., and Palincsar, A.S. (1991). Motivating project-based learning: Sustaining the doing, supporting the learning. *Educational Psychologist, 26,* 369-398.

Brown, A.L., and Campione, J.C. (1990). Interactive learning environments and the teaching of science and mathematics. In M. Gardner, J.G. Greeno, F. Reif, A.H. Schoenfeld, A. diSessa, and E. Stage (Eds.), *Toward a scientific practice of science education* (pp. 111-139). Hillsdale, NJ: Lawrence Erlbaum Associates.

Brown, A.L., and Campione, J.C. (1994). Guided discovery in a community of learners. In K. McGilly (Ed.), *Classroom lessons: Integrating cognitive theory and classroom practice* (pp. 229-270). Cambridge, MA: MIT Press.

Brown, A.L., and Campione, J.C. (1996). Psychological theory and the design of innovative learning environments: On procedures, principles, and systems. In L. Schauble and R. Glaser (Eds.), *Innovations in learning: New environments for education* (pp. 289-325). Mahwah, NJ: Lawrence Erlbaum Associates.

Brown, D.E., and Clement, J. (1989). Overcoming misconceptions by analogical reasoning: Abstract transfer versus explanatory model construction. *Instructional Science, 18,* 237-261.

Butler, R. (1988) Enhancing and undermining intrinsic motivation: The effects of task-involving and ego-involving evaluation on interest and performance. *British Journal of Educational Psychology, 58,* 1-14.

Carey, S., Evans, R., Honda, M., Jay, E., and Unger, C. (1989). "An experiment is when you try it and see if it works": A study of grade 7 students' understanding of scientific knowledge. *International Journal of Science Education, 11,* 514-529.

Carey, S., and Smith, C. (1993). On understanding the nature of scientific knowledge. *Educational Psychologist, 28*(3), 235-251.

Clandinin, D.J., and Connelly, F.M. (1991). Teacher as curriculum maker. In P.W. Jackson (Ed.), *Handbook of research on curriculum* (pp. 363-401). New York: Macmillan.

Collins, A., Brown, J.S., and Newman, S.E. (1989). Cognitive apprenticeship: Teaching the crafts of reading, writing, and mathematics. In L.B. Resnick (Ed.), *Knowing, learning, and instruction: Essays in honor of Robert Glaser* (pp. 453-494). Hillsdale, NJ: Lawrence Erlbaum Associates.

Crawford, B.A., Krajcik, J.S., and Marx, R. (1999). Elements of a community of learners in a middle school science classroom. *Science Education, 83,* 701-723.

Crooks, T.J. (1988). The impact of classroom evaluation on students. *Review of Educational Research, 58*(4), 438-481.

Davis, E.A., and Linn, M.C. (2000). Scaffolding students' knowledge integration: Prompts for reflection in KIE. *International Journal of Science Education, 22*(8), 819-837.

Daws, N., and Singh, B. (1996). Formative assessment: To what extent is its potential to enhance pupils' science being realized? *School Science Review,* 77(281), 93-100.

Doyle, W., and Ponder, G. (1977). The practical ethic and teacher decision-making. *Interchange, 8*(3), 1-12.

Driver, R., Newton, P., and Osborne, J. (2000). Establishing the norms of scientific argumentation in classrooms. *Science Education, 84,* 287-312.

Duschl, R.A. (1990). *Restructuring science education: The importance of theories and their development.* New York: Teachers College Press.

Duschl, R.A. (2003). Assessment of scientific inquiry. In J.M. Atkin and J. Coffey (Eds.), *Everyday assessment in the science classroom* (pp. 41-59). Arlington, VA: National Science Teachers Association.

Duschl, R.A., and Gitomer, D.H. (1997). Strategies and challenges to changing the focus of assessment and instruction in science classrooms. *Educational Assessment, 4*(1), 37-73.

Duschl, R.A., and Osborne, J. (2002). Supporting and promoting argumentation discourse in science education. *Studies in Science Education, 38,* 39-72.

Edelson, D.C. (2001). Learning-for-use: A framework for integrating content and process learning in the design of inquiry activities. *Journal of Research in Science Teaching, 38,* 355-385.

Edelson, D.C., Gordin, D.N., and Pea, R.D. (1999). Addressing the challenges of inquiry-based learning through technology and curriculum design. *Journal of the Learning Sciences, 8,* 391-450.

Edelson, D.C., and Reiser, B.J. (2006). Making authentic practices accessible to learners: Design challenges and strategies. In R.K. Sawyer (Ed.), *The Cambridge handbook of the learning sciences* (pp. 335-354). New York: Cambridge University Press.

Furtak, E.M., and Ruiz-Primo, M.A. (2005, January). Questioning cycle: Making students' thinking explicit during scientific inquiry. *Science Scope,* 22-25.

Geier, R., Blumenfeld, P.C., Marx, R.W., Krajcik, J., Fishman, B., and Soloway, E. (in press). Standardized test outcomes for students engaged in inquiry-based science curricula in the context of urban reform. *Journal of Research in Science Teaching.*

Gilbert, A., and Yerrick, R. (2001). Same school, separate worlds: A sociocultural study of identity, resistance, and negotiation in a rural, lower track science classroom. *Journal of Research in Science Teaching, 38*(5), 574-598.

Gordin, D.N., and Pea, R.D. (1995). Prospects for scientific visualization as an educational technology. *Journal of the Learning Sciences, 4,* 249-279.

Greeno, J.G., Collins, A.M., and Resnick, L.B. (1996). Cognition and learning. In D.C. Berliner and R.C. Calfee (Eds.), *Handbook of educational psychology* (pp. 15-46). New York: Macmillian Library Reference Prentice Hall International.

Guthrie, J., Wigfield, A., Pedro Barbosa, P., Perencevich, K.C., Taboada, A., Davis, M.H., Scafiddi, N.T., and Tonks, S. (2004). Increasing reading comprehension and engagement through concept-oriented reading instruction. *Journal of Educational Psychology, 96,* 403-423.

Herrenkohl, L.R., and Guerra, M.R. (1998). Participant structures, scientific discourse, and student engagement in fourth grade. *Cognition and Instruction, 16*(4), 431-473.

Herrenkohl, L.R., Palincsar, A.S., DeWater, L.S., and Kawasaki, K. (1999). Developing scientific communities in classrooms: A sociocognitive approach. *Journal of the Learning Sciences, 8*(3-4), 451-493.

Hogan, K., and Corey, C. (2001). Viewing classrooms as cultural contexts for fostering scientific literacy. *Anthropology and Education Quarterly, 32*(2), 214-243.

Hogan, K., Natasi, B.K., and Pressley, M. (2000). Discourse patterns and collaborative scientific reasoning in peer and teacher-guided discussions. *Cognition and Instruction, 17*(4), 379-432.

Hogan, K., and Pressley, M. (1997). Scaffolding scientific competencies within classroom communities of inquiry. In K. Hogan and M. Pressley (Eds.), *Scaffolding student learning: Instructional approaches and issues* (pp. 74-107). Cambridge, MA: Brookline Books.

Hudicourt-Barnes, J. (2003). The use of argumentation in Haitian Creole science classrooms. *Harvard Educational Review, 73*(1), 73-93.

Kesidou, S., and Roseman, J.E. (2002). How well do middle school science programs measure up? Findings from Project 2061's curriculum review. *Journal of Research in Science Teaching, 39*(6), 522-549.

Klahr, D. (2000). *Exploring science: The cognition and development of discovery processes.* Cambridge, MA: MIT Press.

Klahr, D., and Chen, Z. (2003). Overcoming the "positive capture" strategy in young children: Learning about indeterminacy. *Child Development, 74*, 1256-1277.

Kolodner, J.L., Camp, P.J., Crismond, D., Fasse, B., Gray, J., and Holbrook, J. (2003). Problem-based learning meets case-based reasoning in the middle-school science classroom: Putting learning by design into practice. *Journal of the Learning Sciences, 12*(4), 495-547.

Krajcik, J., Blumenfeld, P.C., Marx, R.W., Bass, K.M., Fredricks, J., and Soloway, E. (1998). Inquiry in project-based science classrooms: Initial attempts by middle school students. *Journal of the Learning Sciences, 7*, 313-350.

Kuhn, D. (1989). Children and adults as intuitive scientists. *Psychological Review, 96*(4), 674-689.

Kuhn, D., Amsel, E., and O'Loughlin, M. (1988). *The development of scientific thinking skills.* San Diego, CA: Academic Press.

Kuhn, D., Schauble, L., and Garcia-Mila, M. (1992). Cross-domain development of scientific reasoning. *Cognition and Instruction, 9*, 285-327.

Latour, B. (1980). Is it possible to reconstruct the research process?: Sociology of a brain peptide. In K.D. Knorr, R. Krohn, and R. Whitley (Eds.), *The social process of scientific investigation* (vol. IV). Dordrecht, The Netherlands: D. Reidel.

Lehrer, R., Giles, N.D., and Schauble, L. (2002). Children's work with data. In R. Lehrer and L. Schauble (Eds.), *Investigating real data in the classroom: Expanding children's understanding of math and science* (pp. 1-26). New York: Teachers College Press.

Lehrer, R., and Schauble, L. (2000a). Inventing data structures for representational purposes: Elementary grade students' classification models. *Mathematical Thinking and Learning, 2*, 51-74.

Lehrer, R., and Schauble, L. (2000b). Modeling in mathematics and science. In R. Glaser (Ed.), *Advances in instructional psychology: Educational design and cognitive science* (vol. 5, pp. 101-159). Mahwah, NJ: Lawrence Erlbaum Associates.

Lehrer, R., and Schauble, L. (Eds.). (2002). *Investigating real data in the classroom: Expanding children's understanding of math and science.* New York: Teachers College Press.

Lehrer, R., and Schauble, L. (2004). Modeling natural variation through distribution. *American Educational Research Journal, 41*(3), 635-679.

Lehrer, R., and Schauble, L. (in press). Scientific thinking and science literacy: Supporting development in learning in contexts. Submitted to *Handbook of Child Psychology.*

Lehrer, R., Schauble, L., Strom, D., and Pligge, M. (2001). Similarity of form and substance: Modeling material kind. In S.M. Carver and D. Klahr (Eds.), *Cognition and instruction: Twenty-five years of progress* (pp. 39-74). Mahwah, NJ: Lawrence Erlbaum Associates.

Lemke, J.L. (1990). *Talking science: Language, learning, and values.* Norwood, NJ: Ablex.

Linn, M.C. (2000). Designing the knowledge integration environment. *International Journal of Science Education, 22*(8), 781-796.

Linn, M.C., Bell, P., and Davis, E.A. (2004). Specific design principles: Elaborating the scaffolded knowledge integration framework. In M.C. Linn, E.A. Davis and P. Bell (Eds.), *Internet environments for science education.* Mahwah, NJ: Lawrence Erlbaum Associates.

Linn, M.C., and Eylon, B.-S. (in press). Science education: Integrating views of learning and instruction. In P.A. Alexander and P.H. Winne (Eds.), *Handbook of educational psychology* (2nd ed.). Mahwah, NJ: Lawrence Erlbaum Associates.

Linn, M.C., Lewis, C., Tsuchida, I., and Songer, N.B. (2000). Beyond fourth-grade science: Why do U.S. and Japanese students diverge? *Educational Researcher, 29*(3), 4-14.

Linn, M.C., Shear, L., Bell, P., and Slotta, J.D. (1999). Organizing principles for science education partnerships: Case studies of students' learning about "rats in space" and "deformed frogs." *Educational Technology Research and Development, 47*(2), 61-84.

Loh, B., Reiser, B.J., Radinsky, J., Edelson, D.C., Gomez, L.M., and Marshall, S. (2001). Developing reflective inquiry practices: A case study of software, the teacher, and students. In K. Crowley, C.D. Schunn, and T. Okada (Eds.), *Designing for science: Implications from everyday, classroom, and professional settings* (pp. 279-323). Mahwah, NJ: Lawrence Erlbaum Associates.

Longino, H.E. (1990). *Science as social knowledge: Values and objectivity in scientific inquiry.* Princeton, NJ: Princeton University Press.

Marx, R.W., Blumenfeld, P.C., Krajcik, J.S., Fishman, B., Soloway, E., Geier, R., and Tali Tal, R. (2004). Inquiry-based science in the middle grades: Assessment of learning in urban systemic reform. *Journal of Research in Science Teaching, 41*(10), 1063-1080.

Marx, R.W., Freeman, J., Krajcik, J.S., and Blumenfeld, P. (1997). Professional development of science teachers. In B. Fraser and K. Tobin (Eds.), *International handbook of science education.* Dordrecht, The Netherlands: Kluwer Academic.

McNeill, K.L., and Krajcik, J. (in press). Middle school students' use of appropriate and inappropriate evidence in writing scientific explanations. In M. Lovett and P. Shah (Eds.), Thinking with data: *The proceedings of the 33rd Carnegie symposium on cognition.* Mahwah, NJ: Lawrence Erlbaum Associates.

McNeill, K.L., Lizotte, D.J., Krajcik, J., and Marx, R.W. (2006). Supporting students' construction of scientific explanations by fading scaffolds in instructional materials. *Journal of the Learning Sciences, 15*(2), 153-191.

Metz, K.E. (2000). Young children's inquiry in biology: Building the knowledge bases to empower independent inquiry. In J. Minstrell and E.H. vanZee (Eds.), *Inquiry into inquiry learning and teaching in science* (pp. 371-404). Washington, DC: American Association for the Advancement of Science.

Metz, K.E. (2004). Children's understanding of scientific inquiry: Their conceptualization of uncertainty in investigations of their own design. *Cognition and Instruction, 22*(2), 219-290.

Minstrell, J., and vanZee, E. (2003). Using questioning to assess and foster student thinking. In J.M. Atkin and J.E. Coffey (Eds.), *Everyday assessment in the science classroom* (pp. 61-73). Arlington, VA: National Science Teachers Association.

Moje, E.B., Collazo, T., Carrillo, R., and Marx, R.W. (2001). "Maestro, what is 'quality'?": Language, literacy, and discourse in project-based science. *Journal of Research in Science Teaching, 38*, 469-498.

Moje, E.B., Peek-Brown, D., Sutherland, L.M., Marx, R., Blumenfeld, P., and Krajcik, J. (2004). Explaining explanations: Developing scientific literacy in middle-school project-based science reforms. In D. Strickland and D.E. Alvermann (Eds.), *Bridging the gap: Improving literacy learning for preadolescent and adolescent learners in grades 4-12.* New York: Teachers College Press.

National Center for Education Statistics. (2006). *Highlights from the TIMSS 1999 video study of eighth grade science teaching.* Washington, DC: Author. Also available: http://nces.ed.gov/pubs2003/2003011.pdf [accessed July 2006].

National Research Council. (2001). *Classroom assessment and the national science education standards.* J.M. Atkin, P. Black, and J. Coffey (Eds.), Committee on Classroom Assessment and the *National Science Education Standards.* Center for Education. Washington, DC: National Academy Press.

Nersessian, N. (2005). Interpreting scientific and engineering practices: Integrating the cognitive, social, and cultural dimensions. In M. Gorman, R. Tweeny, D. Gooding, and A. Kincannon (Eds.), *Scientific and technological thinking* (pp. 17-56). Mahwah, NJ: Lawrence Erlbaum Associates.

Osborne, J., Erduran, S., and Simon, S. (2004). Enhancing the quality of argumentation in school science. *Journal of Research in Science Teaching, 41*(10), 994-1020.

O'Sullivan, C.Y., and Weiss, A.R. (1999). S*tudent work and teacher practices in science.* Washington, DC: National Center for Education Statistics. Also available: http://eric.ed.gov/ERICWebPortal/Home.portal?_nfpb=true&_pageLabel=Record Details&ERICExtSearch_SearchValue_0=ED432472&ERICExtSearch_SearchType_0=eric_accno&objectId=0900000b8009872b [accessed January 2007].

Palincsar, A.S. (1998). Keeping the metaphor of scaffolding fresh—a response to C. Addison Stone's "The metaphor of scaffolding: Its utility for the field of learning disabilities." *Journal of Learning Disabilities, 31*(4), 370-373.

Palincsar, A.S., Anderson, C., and David, Y.M. (1993). Pursuing scientific literacy in the middle grades through collaborative problem solving. *Elementary School Journal*, 93, 643-657.

Palincsar, A.S., and Brown, A.L. (1984). Reciprocal teaching of comprehension-fostering and comprehension-monitoring activities. *Cognition and Instruction, 1*, 117-175.

Palincsar, A., and Magnusson, S. (2005). The interplay of first-hand and second-hand investigations to model and support the development of scientific knowledge and reasoning. In S. Carver and D. Klahr (Eds.), *Cognition and instruction: Twenty-five years of progress* (pp. 151-193). Mahwah, NJ: Lawrence Erlbaum Associates.

Quellmalz, E., Schank, P., Hinojosa, T., and Padilla, C. (1999). *Performance assessment links in science (PALS)* (ERIC Digest Series E-DO-TM-99-04). College Park, MD: ERIC Clearinghouse on Assessment and Evaluation.

Quintana, C., Reiser, B.J., Davis, E.A., Krajcik, J., Fretz, E., Duncan, R.G., Kyza, E., Edelson, D., and Soloway, E. (2004). A scaffolding design framework for software to support science inquiry. *Journal of the Learning Sciences, 13*(3), 337-386.

Raghavan, K., Sartoris, M., and Glaser, R. (1998). Why does it go up? The impact of the MARS curriculum as revealed through changes in student explanations of a helium balloon. *Journal of Research in Science Teaching, 35*(5), 547-567.

Reiser, B.J. (2004). Scaffolding complex learning: The mechanisms of structuring and problematizing student work. *Journal of the Learning Sciences, 13*(3), 273-304.

Reiser, B.J., Tabak, I., Sandoval, W.A., Smith, B.K., Steinmuller, F., and Leone, A.J. (2001). BGuILE: Strategic and conceptual scaffolds for scientific inquiry in biology classrooms. In S.M. Carver and D. Klahr (Eds.), *Cognition and instruction: Twenty-five years of progress* (pp. 263-305). Mahwah, NJ: Lawrence Erlbaum Associates.

Resnick, L.B., and Resnick, D.P. (1991). Assessing the thinking curriculum: New tools for educational reform. In B. Gifford (Ed.) *Changing assessments: Alternative views of aptitude, achievement and instruction.* Boston, MA: Kluwer Academic.

Rivet, A., and Krajcik, J.S. (2004). Achieving standards in urban systemic reform: An example of a sixth grade project-based science curriculum. *Journal of Research in Science Teaching, 41*(7), 669-692.

Rodriguez, A.J., and Berryman, C. (2002). Using sociotransformative constructism to teach for understanding in diverse classrooms: A beginning teacher's journey. *American Educational Research Journal, 39*(4), 1017-1045.

Rosebery, A.S., Warren, B., and Conant, F.R. (1992). Appropriating scientific discourse: Findings from language minority classrooms. *Journal of the Learning Sciences, 2*, 61-94.

Roth, K.J. (2002). Talking to understand science. In J. Brophy (Ed.), *Advances in research on teaching: Social constructivist teaching: Affordances and constraints* (vol. 9, pp. 197-262). Boston, MA: JAI Press.

Roth, P. (1987). *Meaning and method in the social sciences.* Ithaca, NY: Cornell University Press.

Ruiz-Primo, M.A., and Furtak, E.M. (2004). *Informal assessment of students' understanding of scientific inquiry.* Paper presented at the American Educational Research Association Annual Conference, San Diego, CA.

Ruiz-Primo, M.A., Li, M., Ayala, C., and Shavelson, R.J. (2004). Evaluating students' science notebooks as an assessment tool. *International Journal of Science Education, 26*(12), 1477-1506.

Sadler, D.R. (1989). Formative assessment and the design of instructional systems. *Instructional Science, 18*, 119-144.

Sandoval, W.A. (2003). Conceptual and epistemic aspects of students' scientific explanations. *Journal of the Learning Sciences, 12*(1), 5-51.

Sandoval, W.A., and Reiser, B.J. (2004). Explanation-driven inquiry: Integrating conceptual and epistemic scaffolds for scientific inquiry. *Science Education, 88*(3), 345-372.

Scardamalia, M., and Bereiter, C. (1991). Higher levels of agency for children in knowledge building: A challenge for the design of new knowledge media. *Journal of the Learning Sciences, 1*, 37-68.

Scardamalia, M., and Bereiter, C. (1994). Computer support for knowledge-building communities. *Journal of the Learning Sciences, 3*(3), 265-283.

Schauble, L, Glaser, R., Raghavan, K., and Reiner, M. (1991). Causal models and experimentation strategies in scientific reasoning. *Journal of the Learning Sciences, 1*, 201-238.

Schmidt, W.H., Houang, R., and Cogan, L. (2002). A coherent curriculum: The case of mathematics. *American Educator, 26*(2), 10-26, 47-48.

Schneider, R.M., Krajcik, J., and Blumenfeld, P. (2005). Enacting reform-based science materials: The range of teacher enactments in reform classrooms. *Journal of Research in Science Teaching, 42*(3), 283-312.

Schneider, R.M., Krajcik, J., Marx, R.W., and Soloway, E. (2002). Performance of students in project-based science classrooms on a national measure of science achievement. *Journal of Research in Science Teaching, 39*(5), 410-422.

Schwarz, C.V., and White, B.Y. (2005). Metamodeling knowledge: Developing students' understanding of scientific modeling. *Cognition and Instruction, 23*(2), 165-205.

Shavelson, R.J., Black, P.J., Wiliam, D., and Coffey, J.E. (2003). *On aligning formative and summative assessment.* Paper presented at the National Research Council's Assessment in Support of Instruction and Learning: Bridging the Gap Between Large-Scale and Classroom Assessment Workshop, Washington, DC, January.

Shavelson, R.J., and the Stanford Education Assessment Laboratory. (2003). *On the integration of formative assessment in teaching and learning with implications of teacher education.* Paper presented at the Biannual Meeting of the European Association for Research on Learning and Instruction, Padova, Italy.

Shepard, L.A. (2003). Reconsidering large-scale assessment to heighten its relevance to learning. In J.M. Atkin and J. Coffey (Eds.), *Everyday assessment in the science classroom* (pp. 41-59). Arlington, VA: National Science Teachers Association.

Sherin, B.L., Reiser, B.J., and Edelson, D.C. (2004). Scaffolding analysis: Extending the scaffolding metaphor to learning artifacts. *Journal of the Learning Sciences, 13*(3), 387-421.

Singer, J., Marx, R.W., Krajcik, J., and Chambers, J.C. (2000). Constructing extended inquiry projects: Curriculum materials for science education reform. *Educational Psychologist, 35*, 165-178.

Smith, C., Maclin, D., Grosslight, L., and Davis, H. (1997) Teaching for understanding: A study of students' preinstruction theories of matter and a comparison of two approaches to teaching about matter and density. *Cognition and Instruction, 15*(3), 317-393.

Smith, C.L., Maclin, D., Houghton, C., and Hennessey, M.G. (2000). Sixth-grade students' epistemologies of science: The impact of school science experiences on epistemological development. *Cognition and Instruction, 18*, 349-422.

Stewart, J., Cartier, J.L., and Passmore, C.M. (2005). Developing understanding through model-based inquiry. In National Research Council, M.S. Donovan, and J.D. Bransford (Eds.), *How students learn* (pp. 515-565). Washington, DC: The National Academies Press.

Stigler, J.W., and Hiebert, J. (1999). *The teaching gap: Best ideas from the world's teachers for improving education in the classroom.* New York: The Free Press.

Suthers, D.D. (2003). Representational guidance for collaborative learning. In H.U. Hoppe, F. Verdejo, and J. Kay (Eds.), *Artificial intelligence in education* (pp. 3-10). Amsterdam, The Netherlands: IOS Press.

Toth, E.E., Suthers, D.D., and Lesgold, A.M. (2002). "Mapping to know": The effects of representational guidance and reflective assessment on scientific inquiry. *Science Education, 86*(2), 264-286.

VanLehn, K. (1989). Problem solving and cognitive skill acquisition. In M. Posner (Ed.), *Foundations of cognitive science* (pp. 527-580). Cambridge, MA: MIT Press.

vanZee, E., and Minstrell, J. (1997). Using questioning to guide student thinking. *Journal of the Learning Sciences, 6*, 227-269.

Warren, B., Ballenger, C., Ogonowski, M., Rosebery, A., and Hudicourt-Barnes, J. (2001). Rethinking diversity in learning science: The logic of everyday language. *Journal of Research in Science Teaching, 38*(5), 529-552.

Weiss, I.R., and Pasley, J.D. (2004). What is high-quality instruction? *Educational Leadership, 61*(5), 24.

Weiss, I.R., Pasley, J.D., Smith, P.S., Banilower, E.R., and Heck, D.J. (2003). *Looking inside the classroom: A study of K-12 mathematics and science education in the United States.* Chapel Hill, NC: Horizon Research.

White, B. (1993). ThinkerTools: Causal models, conceptual change, and science instruction. *Cognition and Instruction, 10*, 1-100.

White, B., and Fredericksen, J. (1998). Inquiry, modeling, and metacognition: Making science accessible to all students. *Cognition and Instruction, 16*, 3-118.

White, R., and Gunstone, R. (1992). *Probing understanding.* London, England: Falmer Press.

Wilson, M. (2005). *Constructing measures: An item response modeling approach.* Mahwah, NJ: Lawrence Erlbaum Associates.

Wiser, M., and Amin, T. (2001). Is heat hot? Including conceptual change by integrating everyday and scientific perspectives on thermal physics. In L. Mason (Ed.), *Instructional practices for conceptual change in science domains. Learning and Instruction, 11*(special issue), 331-355.

10

Supporting Science Instruction

Main Findings in the Chapter:

- *Student learning of science depends on teachers having adequate knowledge of science. Currently, K-8 teachers have limited knowledge of science and limited opportunities to learn science. Furthermore, undergraduate course work in science typically does not reflect the strands of scientific proficiency, focusing instead primarily on Strand 1 and, in a limited sense, on Strand 2.*

- *In order for K-8 teachers to teach science as practice, they will need sustained science-specific professional development in preparation and while in service. Professional development that supports student learning is rooted in the science that teachers teach and includes opportunities to learn about science, about current research on how children learn science, and about how to teach science.*

- *Achieving science proficiency for all students will require a coherent system that aligns standards, curriculum, instruction, assessment, teacher preparation, and professional development for teachers across the K-8 years.*

We have described four intertwining strands of scientific practice that almost all K-8 students should be able to master given well-structured opportunities to learn. Robust opportunities to learn science exist when students are presented with challenging academic tasks that draw on these four strands. What would it take to ensure that all students have regular access to such opportunities to learn science? The factors impinging on the quality of classroom instruction in science include powerful influences outside school (e.g., Lareau, 2000), within school systems at the state or district level (Spillane, 1996, 2000), and at the school and classroom level (Cohen, Raudenbush, and Ball, 2001). We acknowledge this broad range of factors and choose to focus here primarily on the conditions that support student learning at, and immediately surrounding, the classroom level.

In this chapter we review what researchers have found about the influence of three critical components—teacher knowledge, teachers' opportunities to learn, and instructional systems—on students' science learning. Two questions guide our discussion of the literature in this chapter. First, what are the implications of research on student learning for school and classroom-level supports for instruction? Second, where do empirical links between classroom and school-level supports for instruction and student learning exist?

KNOWLEDGABLE SCIENCE TEACHERS

It is a truism that teachers must know the content that they are to teach. While no teacher could adequately support student learning without first mastering the content of the curriculum herself, effective teaching requires more than simple mastery. Quality instruction entails strategically designing student encounters with science that take place in real time and over a period of months and years (e.g., learning progressions). Teachers draw on their knowledge of science, of their students, and of pedagogy to plan and enact instruction. Thus, in addition to understanding the science content itself, effective teachers need to understand learners and pedagogy design and need to monitor students' science learning experiences.

Knowledge of Science

Research findings generally support the notion that higher levels of teacher subject matter knowledge contribute to higher student achievement (Chaney, 1995; Goldhaber and Brewer, 1997, 2000). This finding holds across a range of measures of teacher knowledge. Having a major or a graduate degree in a subject contributes to a teacher's effectiveness and higher student achievement (Goldhaber and Brewer, 1997, 2000; Chaney, 1995). Monk (1994) found that the number of postsecondary courses that mathematics and science teachers have taken is associated with incremental gains in student scores. Although there has been less research on the knowledge of science teachers (and of elementary science teachers in particular), the existing evidence supports this pattern. In a meta-analysis of 65 studies, Druva and Anderson (1983) found that student science achievement was positively related to both the number of biology courses and the overall number of science courses their biology teacher had taken. Monk (1994) found similar effects in mathematics and physical sciences but not in the life sciences. Goldhaber and Brewer (2000) used data from the National Education Longitudinal Study of 1988 to conduct a multiple regression analysis of 6,000 high school seniors and 2,400 mathematics and science courses. They found a relationship between teachers holding a mathematics degree and student performance, but no relationship between teachers holding a science degree and student performance. These results may have been affected by the high percentages of high school science teachers who teach out of their field, that is, a teacher with a biology degree teaching chemistry or physics.

The optimal level of subject matter training for a teacher is unclear, and there is some evidence suggesting a threshold effect—a point after which further course work provides no additional measurable impact on student learning. For example, Monk (1994) found that after a teacher had taken five college mathematics courses or four physical science courses, additional courses were not associated with additional gains in student achievement. Findings from several studies suggest that the impact on students of having a teacher with a subject matter major might vary with the level of the grade taught; the achievement of middle and high school students appears to be affected more by the amount of subject matter preparation of their teachers than that of elementary students (Rowan, Correnti, and Miller, 2002; Hawkins, Stancavage, and Dossey, 1998). Interpretation of these results, however, must consider the generally poor alignment of the content of college courses taken by teachers with the curriculum that they are expected to teach as well as by the ceiling effects in the achievement measures used in the studies. If college courses were aligned with school curriculum and if higher quality measures of student achievement were available, one might find that there are no threshold effects or that they must be higher than suggested by these studies.

There is also evidence from case studies of science teachers that teacher knowledge influences instructional practice and, in particular, that classroom discourse—an integral component of science learning environments—is sensitive to teachers' knowledge of science (Carlsen 1988, 1992; Hashweh, 1987; Sanders, Borko, and Lockard, 1993). For example, Sanders and colleagues (1993) conducted an in-depth analysis of three secondary science teachers teaching inside and outside their areas of certification. They reported that when teachers had limited knowledge of the content, they often struggled to sustain discussions with students and found themselves trying to field student questions that they could not address.

Even more than quantity of knowledge, the qualities of teachers' understanding of science are also important. If teachers are to help students achieve science proficiency, they too need to achieve proficiency across the four strands. Yet undergraduate science curricula, like those in K-12 science, tend to be biased toward conceptual and factual knowledge and reflect impoverished views of scientific practice (Trumbull and Kerr, 1993; Seymour and Hewitt, 1994). Not surprisingly, undergraduates' and prospective science teachers' views of science reflect this emphasis on science as a body of facts and scientific practice as mechanistic applications of a sequential scientific method. Hammer and Elby (2003) in their analysis of undergraduates' perspectives on learning physics found that, in contrast to the "modeling game" of practicing physicists, many undergraduate students "view physics knowledge as a collection of facts, formulas, and problem solving methods, mostly disconnected from everyday thinking, and they view learning as primarily a matter of memorization" (p. 54; see also Elby, 1999).

Prospective teachers typically view scientific practice in a similarly narrow light (e.g., Abd-El-Khalick and BouJaoude, 1997; Aguirere, Haggerty, and Linder, 1990; Bloom, 1989; Pomeroy, 1993; Windschidtl, 2004). For instance, Windshitl (2004) studied the views of pre-service science teachers as they designed and conducted studies in the context of a secondary science methods course. Study participants included 14 pre-service teachers with earned bachelors' degrees in a science. Windschitl tracked their thinking about science through regular journal entries for one semester and conducted interviews with them on their experiences in science from middle school forward. He analyzed their efforts to develop inquiry projects (beginning with formulating questions through presentations to peers) and found that they had a common folk view of science. Among other features, folk science entails construing hypotheses as guesses that have little bearing on how problems are framed and examined. Furthermore, scientific theory assumes a peripheral role in this view of science, relegated to the end of a study as an optional tool one might use to help explain results.

Observed limitations in K-8 teachers' knowledge of science are not surprising given the mixed and generally low expectations laid out in teacher certification policy at the state level. Although 80 percent of states require demonstration of subject matter competence for obtaining an elementary school certificate, most states do not stipulate what that means in terms of the content that teacher candidates should study, nor the clusters of courses they should take. Delaware, Maryland, and Maine register on the high end of requirements. Delaware and Maine both require 12 semester hours in science. In Maine, which offers a K-8 certificate, teachers must have at least 6 semester hours in science. In contrast, Hawaii and Kansas are states that do not require credit hours in science or other subject areas. Other states use tests to assess subject matter knowledge. In Arizona, for example, elementary school certified teachers must take and pass a subject knowledge assessment—although it is not possible to ascertain what proportion of any state assessment test covers science.

There is scant evidence on how elementary and middle grade teachers are typically prepared in science, as well as few controlled analyses of how teacher knowledge and skill influence student learning. Without such knowledge, we must rely on credentialing standards to characterize what base-level proficiency means in current practice.

Elementary teacher preparation accreditation standards provide a sense of the base-level expectations that certified programs hold for prospective elementary teachers' knowledge of science. The National Council for Accreditation of Teacher Education standards call for elementary preparation programs to attend to candidates' knowledge of science and technology (and how they differ), inquiry, science in personal and social perspectives, and the history and nature of science, and they stipulate that candidates should be able to use and apply concepts and inquiry. These categories are defined quite vaguely and suggest very modest expectations for prospective elementary teachers' knowledge of science. For example, the "inquiry" standard indicates that an "acceptable" elementary candidate would "demonstrate an understanding of the abilities needed to do scientific inquiry" but provides no further definition of what inquiry is, the attendant abilities, nor descriptions of performances that would be indicative of satisfactory understanding.

Science specific standards for middle school level credentialing are not typical. However, we can consider the state standards of those that do have such standards to discern what states expect middle grade teachers to know about science. Most of these states require a certain number of credit hours in the subject area of assignment (National Association of State Directors of Teacher Education and Certification, 2004). Illinois, for example, requires 18 credit hours in the subject area of assignment. Other states are less specific about teaching assignments and instead require prospective teachers to choose from a range of subjects when satisfying subject matter requirements. For instance, Georgia requires 30 semester hours in at least 2 of the teaching areas applicable to middle school, but it does not require teachers to take science courses in order to be assigned to a science teaching assignment. Similarly, in Mississippi, teachers who hold a Middle School Interdisciplinary Endorsement must complete 2 areas of content concentration consisting of a minimum of 18 credit hours in each area. Only about 15 percent of states require a major in the subject area taught as part of requirement to obtain a middle school certificate.

Clearly the scientific knowledge of K-8 teachers is often quite thin. Factors likely to contribute to this pattern are narrowly focused undergraduate course work, insufficient teacher professional development, and a credentialing process that requires little of prospective K-8 science teachers. If they are to help students reach national and state standards in science, teachers will need substantial supports in the form of better pre-service training, as well as professional development that will bolster their knowledge of the science they teach.

Understanding Learners and Learning

Beyond knowledge of science, effective science teachers need to understand the process of learning itself. This report provides substantial evidence that student learning can be harnessed when classrooms are cognizant of students' ways of thinking, their experience base, and provide challenging problems for them to engage in. Teachers' understanding of how students learn has important implications for how they structure learning experiences and make instructional decisions over time. We have described learning science as a process that entails developing self-awareness of, and building on, one's own knowledge of the natural world; participating in scientific practices; and building new understanding in a community through argumentation. Teachers, as instructional designers, need to understand student learners to make good decisions about how to teach them. They need to understand what students do when they learn, as well as the types of experiences that produce engagement and conceptual understanding. They also need to understand the unique qualities of their particular students and the unique demands of particular groups of students in their classrooms.

Teachers' Beliefs About Student Learning

Are teachers' perceptions of student learning commensurate with the learning processes we've described? The research on this matter is scarce and of uneven quality, and careful analyses of teachers' understanding of student learning are rare in the science education research literature. Limited evidence suggests that teachers' conceptions of student learning are highly dissimilar to contemporary research perspectives.

One source of evidence on this question is a large body of research on "teachers' dispositions," which examine teachers' espoused beliefs about science teaching and their instructional practices to make inferences about their views on learning. This research base offers very limited guidance, however. Despite decades of research, studies tend, almost exclusively, to use very small sample sizes (e.g., 1 to 3 teachers) and propose no clear research design (see, e.g., the review by Jones and Carter, in press). What is worse, the research is hobbled by a conflation of learning and teaching, falsely suggesting that good teaching requires highly interactive and "student centered" instruction. While we think that good science teaching necessarily includes student investigations, we reject the idea that teachers who understand learners will necessarily consistently create interactive, student-driven teaching experiences, as this research implies.

There is emerging work on "folk pedagogy" or popular belief systems about how others learn and what teachers can do to cause learning in others (Strauss, 2001), which provides some insight into how people generally, and some teachers, think about learning. This work rests on the proposition that teaching is an inherently human practice, that people all continuously are teaching one another, and in so doing they develop working (although often tacit) notions of pedagogy. Much like the folk science of children and adults, folk pedagogy is evident across age spans and diverse populations and represents a shared, working notion of learning. Individuals may not be aware of their own folk pedagogy, and it may even be incommensurate with their own espoused views of teaching and learning, constraining the range of pedagogical moves they will make.

An important component of folk pedagogy is a mental model of the learner (Strauss, 1997). In a series of studies, Strauss and colleagues have examined teachers' "explicit espoused" and "enacted" mental models of learning to try to describe what they believe students do when they learn. For example, in one study of espoused mental models, Strauss administered semi-structured interviews to science and humanities teachers, who explained their strategies for teaching material that is difficult for students. They found a common mental model of learners across teachers. Irrespective of subject matter area (e.g., science, language arts) and level of subject matter knowledge, teachers conceived of learners as consuming small portions of information in relative isolation and trying to link this to their extant prior knowledge. Strauss encapsulates the mental model metaphorically: "the entrance to the children's minds has 'flaps' that are open when children are attentive. If children are uninterested or unmotivated, the flaps go down and the material cannot enter the mind" (Strauss, 1997, p. 380). Given this view of learners, teachers saw instruction as an "engineering problem" in which their task was twofold. First, the teacher needs to get information into the mind of the child. Second, once the information is there, the challenge is how to move it to a place where it will be "stored."

Teachers' beliefs about student mental models, as described in this research, contrast with research on student learning that we have described in this report. The mental model Straus and colleagues describe calls for teachers to break the subject matter into "chunks" that can be mastered sequentially and made more enticing by manipulating an affective response. In contrast, we have argued that learning science includes participating in scientific practice in which learners engage in meaningful problems over time. In the practice view of student learning, these chunks are framed, from the outset, as important pieces of a whole that, when understood and organized, provide learners with leverage to explain, manipulate, or further explore the natural world. It is this leverage—the promise of new, meaningful ways to act—that entices students to work hard at complex scientific problems. Although there is no empirical research that examines how the teachers' mental model of students influences student learning, we draw attention to this finding because it points both to a potential stumbling point for instructional reform and a topic worthy of further research.

Teachers' Perceptions of Diverse Student Learners

Another aspect of teachers' knowledge of learners that can have real consequences for teaching is their appreciation and understanding of student diversity. Teaching that will help all students make sense of science also requires that teachers understand the particular students and the student groups they teach, including those who come from cultural backgrounds different from their own. Both societal and classroom-level factors inform students' beliefs about science and the degree to which they identify with science. Although it is not always clear how teachers would optimally manage these factors, it is clear that they can play an important role in either limiting or expanding students' understanding and appreciation of science.

In a literature review, Eisenhart, Finkel, and Marion (1996) addressed several societal factors that impinge on students' views of science. Some of the factors that they identify as contributing to the underrepresentation of women, working-class men, and people of color in science include media stereotypes of scientists, the lack of connection with female and non-Western interests and backgrounds, and the climate of degree programs and high-status scientific professions that systematically exclude women from some fields (Eisenhart et al., 1998). It is important to note that while patterns of underrepresentation and stereotypes may have a negative impact on many students, students' responses to them are not predetermined. In light of these broad societal factors, some students may position themselves to resist stereotypes by showing their capabilities in science, whereas others may appropriate the messages they receive and conclude that science is just not for them (Brown, Reveles, and Kelly, 2005; Ritchie, 2002; Smardon, 2004).

At the classroom level, the teacher may fail to recognize cultural differences or understand how they can impact students' interactions with science. In their review of the literature on prospective teachers' beliefs about multicultural issues, Bryan and Atwater (2002) conclude that most prospective science teachers enter their teacher preparation programs with little or no intercultural experience and with beliefs and assumptions that undermine the goal of providing an equitable education for all students. Furthermore, many graduate without fundamentally changing their beliefs and assumptions, despite their experiences in teacher preparation programs.

Furthermore, most teachers feel unprepared to meet the learning needs of English-language learners (National Center for Education Statistics, 1999). The research findings that draw attention to the importance of vocabulary and discourse in science practice and science learning heighten the challenge of teaching these students. Most teachers assume that English-language learners must acquire English before learning subject matter, although this approach almost inevitably leads such students to fall behind theirEnglish-speaking peers (National Research Council and Institute of Medicine, 1997).

The research on how to effectively teach science to diverse student populations is inconclusive (see Chapter 7), yet there is little disagreement that teaching science to diverse student populations presents immense challenges, and that teachers need to be knowledgeable about both classroom-level and broader societal factors that influence students' science learning.

Subject Matter Knowledge for Teaching

More than the sum of knowledge about science, learners, and learning, teacher knowledge is qualitatively distinct from that of mature nonteachers and disciplinary experts. Expert teachers have knowledge of subject matter that is peculiarly suited for instruction (Shulman, 1986, 1987; Wilson, Shulman, and Richert, 1987).[1] While scientists will understand the canon of accepted scientific theory deeply, the range of questions that are "in play," and the modes of inquiry in the field, they will not necessarily know how to make this knowledge accessible to children and other nonexperts. That is, "knowing subject matter" is a different form of knowledge than "knowing how to teach subject matter." The expert teacher must therefore master the fundamental forms of the discipline and combine these with knowledge of students and learning.

Although broad in scope, research on subject matter knowledge for teaching is primarily focused on two areas—teachers' knowledge of students' preconceptions and misconceptions of science and instructional strategies or representations for teaching science—and these categories are frequently used to describe the literature base (see, e.g., Grossman, Schoenfeld, and Lee, 2005; Hill, Rowan, and Ball, 2005; Smith, 1998; van Driel, Verloop, and de Vos, 1998).

Consider how this dual focus on content and how it is learned inform the identification of meaningful questions. In Chapter 9 we argued that quality science instruction includes exploration of meaningful scientific problems, and that teachers actively structure and guide students' learning experiences through these (even when excellent curriculum materials are available). In order for students to be engaged with meaningful scientific problems,

---

[1]For consistency we use the term "subject matter knowledge for teaching" throughout this section, although others may also use the terms "pedagogical content knowledge" (PCK), "professional knowledge," and "event-structured knowledge for teaching."

teachers must understand science from the standpoint of the learner, selecting and structuring problems that are meaningful in two senses of the word. The problem must be meaningful from the standpoint of science and be clearly connected to a body of knowledge. It also must be meaningful from the standpoint of the learners; that is, it must require something they can do (or are learning to) and they must be able to work on the problem in a purposeful manner.

Of course, subject matter knowledge for teaching is not absolute but can be understood as situated. That is, students' sense of what constitutes a meaningful problem and their approaches to making sense of scientific phenomena are not universal but reflect the varied social contexts and communities (home, school, classroom, etc.) they inhabit (Lave and Wenger, 1991). What is meaningful and stimulating to one group of students may not be for another. Furthermore in any given classroom, students will have a range of ideas and understanding of science and scientific concepts. Accordingly, skillful teachers need to apply their knowledge flexibly in practice in response to this variability (Putnam and Borko, 2000). A skillful teacher is able to draw on a range of representations of scientific ideas, select those that suit the specific instructional setting, and use her knowledge as an interpretive framework to make sense of the diverse ideas and perspectives that students express about science and scientific phenomena.

While the logic of subject matter knowledge for teaching is persuasive, there is almost no research on the empirical link between specialized teacher subject matter knowledge and student learning.[2] More than three decades of research have resulted in distinct portraits of expert/novice teachers' knowledge (Munby, Russell, and Martin, 2001) and case studies of teachers' acquisition of PCK (e.g., Zembal-Saul, Blumenfeld, and Krajcik, 2000; Smith and Neale, 1989). We can point to only one study that examines the influence of subject matter knowledge for teaching on student learning, and it is in mathematics (Hill, Rowan, and Ball, 2005).

Hill and colleagues developed measures of teachers' mathematical knowledge for teaching, which they defined as "the mathematical knowledge used to carry out the work of mathematics" (p. 373), such as explaining terms and concepts, interpreting students' statements and solutions, judging and correcting textbook treatments of topics, using mathematical representations correctly in class, and providing students with examples of mathematical con-

---

[2]Lee Shulman, one of the originators of this line of work, made this point in his introduction to Gess-Newsome and Lederman's (1999) science-specific edited volume on teacher subject matter knowledge. Shulman pleaded: "I hope that those who use these ideas now and in the future give more attention that I did to the connections between teachers' knowledge and the ultimate consequences for students' learning and development" (p. xi).

cepts, algorithms, or proofs (Rowan et al., 2001). They found that mathematical knowledge for teaching was a significant predictor of student gains and a stronger predictor than all other teacher background variables (mathematics and mathematics education course work, certification) as well as time spent on instruction (Hill, Rowan, and Ball, 2005).

This important area of emerging research is in its infancy, but it may ultimately provide important guidance for policy and practice. Research in science is even less developed than research in mathematics. However, science educators could follow the same path: operationalizing scientific knowledge for teaching, developing and validating measures, and carefully designing studies to examine its influence (although science presents an additional complexity in that multiple scientific fields and disciplines make up the science curriculum). In fact, Olson (2005) is working on a small part of this lofty challenge and has begun developing measures of subject matter knowledge for selected topics in physical science.

TEACHERS' OPPORTUNITIES TO LEARN

Current research on K-8 science learning suggests a model of instruction that contrasts starkly with current instructional practice. To move toward instruction that is consistent with the research base we review in this volume, teachers will need substantial, ongoing, and systemic supports for their own learning. In the previous section we described the forms of knowledge that excellent science teachers draw on to inform instruction. In this section we describe how teachers' experiences can be structured to support their learning, which in turn enables them to provide quality science instruction.

Teachers learn continuously from their experiences in the classroom, their interactions with colleagues, and their professional development activities. Our discussion of teacher learning opportunities reflects this reality. We describe opportunities to learn that take place in the naturally occurring functions of the school, as well as through programs specifically designed to support teacher learning and improved instruction. We first review the evidence for supporting teacher learning and the general qualities of teachers' opportunities to learn. We then discuss research on organizing teacher learning in the organizational context of schooling and in professional development programs. Next we review the literature on teachers' opportunities to learn with regard to student diversity. Finally, we discuss the use of science specialists as an alternate means of bolstering science instructional capacity.

Effective Teacher Learning Opportunities

Well-designed opportunities for teacher learning can produce desired changes in their classroom practices, can enhance their capacity for continued learning and professional growth, and can in turn contribute to improvements in student learning. In a general sense, a great deal is known about the characteristics of such opportunities for teacher learning. There is a general consensus about these characteristics among researchers and among professional and reform organizations (National Staff Development Council, 2001; American Federation of Teachers, 2002; Elmore, 2002; Knapp, McCaffrey, and Swanson, 2003). Among the more rigorous studies of professional development for teachers are those of mathematics reforms in California (Cohen and Hill, 1998, 2001; Wilson, 2003); studies of District #2 in New York City (Elmore and Burney, 1997; Stein and D'Amico, 1998); a longitudinal study of sustained professional development by the Merck Institute for Science Education (Corcoran, McVay, and Riordan, 2003); the National Science Foundation (NSF)-funded studies of systemic reform in mathematics and science (Supovitz and Turner, 2000; Weiss et al., 2003); and evaluations of the federal Eisenhower mathematics and science professional development program (Garet et al., 1999).

Drawing heavily on three previous attempts to synthesize this literature (American Educational Research Association, 2005; Elmore, 2002; Odden et al., 2002), we point to seven critical features of teachers' opportunities to learn. Research suggests that well-structured opportunities for teacher learning:

1. Reflect a clear focus on the improvement of student learning in a specific content area that is grounded in the curriculum they teach.

2. Focus on the strengths and needs of learners in the setting and evidence about what works drawn from research and clinical experience.

3. Include school-based and job-embedded support in which teachers may engage in assessing student work, designing or refining units of study, or observing and reflecting on colleagues' lessons.

4. Provide adequate time during the school day and throughout the year, including considerations of the time required for both intensive work and regular reflection on practice. Furthermore, the overall span of time for teacher professional development is several years.

5. Emphasize the collective participation of groups of teachers, including opportunities for teachers from the same school, department, or grade level.

6. Provide teachers with a coherent view of the instructional system (e.g., helping teachers see connections among content and performance standards, instructional materials, local and state assessments, school and district goals, and the development of a professional community).

7. Require the active support of school and district leaders. School leaders who participate in creating and sustaining teacher learning opportunities are better positioned to support teachers' use of new knowledge and skills.

These features provide a frame for describing, comparing, and analyzing the infrastructure of teacher learning across schools, districts, and programs of support. They imply a purpose and rigor, suggesting that teacher learning is serious business, a product of thoughtful design and collective system-wide participation, and that the rationale for participation and learning should be clear and compelling.

In the next two sections, we extend our discussion of teachers' opportunities to learn in the organizational context of schools and departments and in professional development programs. We use examples to illustrate how the features listed above are enacted in professional development and to provide further evidence of the teacher and student learning effects of well-designed teacher learning opportunities. It is important to note that the above features are derived from a diverse body of research, much of which is not specific to science. Wherever possible we draw on science-specific examples.

Teacher Learning in the Organizational Context of Schooling

For several decades, researchers have reported significant benefits of organizational changes that facilitate teacher collaboration, including increased student achievement in schools characterized by strong patterns of collaboration among teachers (Corcoran, Walker, and White, 1988; Ingersoll, 2004). When teachers work collectively in teams, work groups, or as a department, their efforts can yield important instructional results and measurable effects on student learning. Collective work and learning in groups is what Wenger (1998) and other researchers refer to as "communities of practice." A community of practice involves much more than the technical knowledge or skills associated with the work. Members of a community of practice work collectively on core tasks that members learn to execute at increasing levels of proficiency over time, drawing on support and feedback from the group. Common tasks (and the underlying knowledge that supports them) serve as the focal point of the community. In a community of teaching practice, individuals engage in the shared work of teaching. For example, they collaborate in preparing units of study, analyzing student work or videotaped lessons, developing assessments, and coaching and mentoring one another.

When teacher teams, work groups, and departments function as communities of practice, numerous studies have shown strong, desirable effects on faculty willingness to implement instructional reforms, teacher relationships with students, and student achievement outcomes. For example, the Bay Area School Reform Collaborative works at the district, school, and classroom levels to promote systematic and continuous education improvement through building and sharing professional knowledge and fostering mutual accountability and collaboration. BASRC evaluators (McLaughlin and Talbert, 2000) reported statistically significant relationships between measures of teacher community and gains in students' SAT-9 scores between 1998 and 2001, as well as strong correlations between teacher community and student survey measures of teacher-student respect, student initiative in class, and students' academic self-efficacy.

Newmann and associates (1996) reported that strong norms of teacher collaboration in schools were associated with more effective implementation of reforms and continuous improvement of practice. They found five elements to be critical to the effectiveness of professional learning groups: (1) shared norms and values, (2) focus on student learning, (3) reflective dialogue among teachers, (4) deprivatization of practice through public discussions of instructional cases and problems among colleagues, and (5) collaboration on curriculum and instruction (Louis and Marks, 1998). Anthony Bryk and Barbara Schneider (2002) studied relational trust in schools and found that building social trust among faculty and between faculty and students pays dividends in the levels of engagement around reform initiatives and improved student achievement. They argue that this is especially critical in urban settings, where the work is especially hard. While organizing groups of teachers to work together can result in functional communities that focus their efforts and resources on instructional improvement and teacher learning, merely creating group structures by no means guarantees such positive outcomes. Supovitz (2002) found that simply making structural changes that support school-level teacher groups (e.g., providing release time) may not result in collaboration around instruction or improved pedagogical decisions. Groups may develop that are not engaged in instructional improvement. McLaughlin and Talbert (2000) reported similar findings in their study of high school departments.

Developing teacher groups focused on improvement of instructional practice requires intentionality and support. For groups to work toward instructional improvement, they require time for individuals to work together, for example, shared planning periods. However, the expectations about the use of this time must also be clear. DuFour (2000) also noted the importance of active leaders who help the group identify critical questions to guide their work, set obtainable goals, monitor progress, and ensure that teachers have relevant information and data (e.g., measures of student learning).

Connecting teachers to work groups, teams, and departments that are focused on instructional reform can be an effective means of improving learning environments for students, but it will require leadership, time, and resources to develop. Collaboration, critique, and analytic discussion of practice are essential aspects of a functional teacher group, but these features are often antithetical to existing school and teacher cultures.

There is some evidence that the resources needed to develop such groups in schools may be subject matter specific. A recent study by Spillane (2005) suggests that the resources drawn on by these groups may vary across subjects, be affected by the level of teacher expertise in the subject, and be influenced by teacher perceptions about where expertise lies. Spillane found that elementary school teachers tended to have stronger group affiliations and collaborative activities around literacy. These were somewhat less well developed in mathematics and were least developed in science. He found that teachers believed that the expertise in literacy was available among their colleagues but that to access expertise in mathematics or science they had to go outside the school. As scientific capacity in the K-8 teacher workforce is often quite thin, professional communities that will support science instructional improvement may require recruiting local science teaching experts to work with teachers, or building relationships between schools and other organizations (informal science learning institutions, universities, industry) that have expertise in science and science teaching.

The evidence of science-specific subject matter specialists is less clear. In part, this reflects the lower status of science in the lower grades, where mathematics and language arts are emphasized. Here, as in previous sections, by and large, the research base is not specific to science but was drawn from studies in the context of literacy and mathematics. There may be additional features and challenges of building science teacher teams or work groups, but to date, these are not well documented in the science education literature.

Professional Development Programs

Besides the school structures and norms that support quality science instruction, professional development programs also support teacher learning and instructional improvement. We know that supports for science teacher learning should be grounded in the work teachers do *in* schools and informed by local policies, constraints, and resources. However, the faculties of many K-8 schools lack the science-specific expertise necessary for instructional improvement—deep knowledge of science, learning, subject-specific knowledge for teaching. Accordingly, in order for groups of teachers to engage in instructionally meaningful science-specific learning activities, they will require substantial guidance and input from external support providers.

Building on our characterization of student learning and the instruction that promotes it, we describe specific programmatic efforts to ignite improvements in K-8 teachers' knowledge of scientific practice and understanding of students' subject matter ideas, as well as efforts to provide them with focused lessons honed to address students' learning challenges.

Research on teacher learning in professional development is at an early phase and is arguably lagging in science compared with mathematics and literacy (Borko, 2005). However, there is a handful of case studies (e.g., Crawford, 2000; Rosebery and Puttick, 1998; Smith and Anderson, 1999) that describe the features of high-quality science teacher professional development that engages teachers in doing science, as well as some analyses of its impact on instructional practice and student learning. These serve as examples for researchers to build on and as food for thought for policy makers and professional development providers.

Doing Science

Many, perhaps most, K-8 science teachers have limited science backgrounds and have had little or no direct experience "doing science." An important trend in teacher professional development is to provide teachers with intensive firsthand experiences in the disciplines. Researchers have documented such programs across the core school subjects, including science (Wilson and Berne, 1999). Providing K-8 science teachers with unique learning opportunities that involve the "doing" of scientific activities is particularly interesting, as many report very limited exposure to science course work and inquiry experiences in particular. In science these experiences provide teachers with opportunities to think scientifically, to analyze phenomena, and to engage in meaningful discourse with peers. Moreover, in these settings, science teachers gain experiences with a broad range of scientific issues, including the generation of researchable questions and working as a community to interpret evidence and determine what counts. All the while, these experiences are connected to instructional practice as they are situated in K-8 curricula.

Rosebery and Puttick (1998) describe an example of long-term teacher professional development that is rooted in teacher inquiry experiences. They present an in-depth longitudinal case study of how one novice elementary school teacher, Elizabeth, developed her understanding of physical science topics and science itself through her participation in workshops that engaged groups of K-8 science teachers in doing science. Elizabeth, like many elementary school teachers, had no postsecondary science experience to speak of. She joined a group of teachers in a professional development program that took place during the summer and was run by educators and researchers from the Cheche Konnen Center. She and her peers, over a period of 3 years, worked on explaining qualitative phenomena such as "Why do helium balloons float?" This was a question taken up early in Elizabeth's first summer workshop. For Elizabeth and her peers, it served as the basis of ongoing discussion, generation of a range of experimental trials, and practice at organizing and interpreting evidence to characterize physical phenomena. Over a period of 3 years, Elizabeth returned to the summer institutes, and researchers tracked her teaching. Her experiences in the summer institute were systematically linked to the kinds of experiences and discussions she developed with her students. In the institute she learned central concepts of physical science, how to engage in scientific inquiries herself, and, through structured discussions with peers, how to enact such instruction in her own elementary school classroom.

Understanding Student Ideas

In order to make sense of the natural world, children need to become aware of, build on, and refine their own ideas. Accordingly, their ideas about science become a central component of science instruction that teachers need to understand and act on. To support student sense-making in instruction, teachers need to know how students think, have strategies for eliciting their thinking as it develops, and use their own knowledge flexibly in order to interpret and respond strategically to student thinking. Teacher professional development can serve as a context for helping them understand students' ideas about the subject matter to inform their teaching.

Although there is little research on science teachers' opportunities to learn student ideas, there is strong evidence from mathematics suggesting that teachers can learn how to work productively with student ideas about the subject matter. A program of research on "cognitively guided instruction" at the University of Wisconsin has shown that teacher professional development designed to support understanding of student ideas can have profound effects on teachers' knowledge and instructional practice and, importantly, that this knowledge translates to measurable learning gains for students (Carpenter et al., 1989; Fennema et al., 1996). The researchers supported these findings experimentally, tracked them longitudinally, and used case studies to learn how individual teachers acquire and utilize knowledge of student ideas to inform instruction.

Engineering Instructional Improvement

Fishman et al. (2003) describe yet another way of thinking about supporting instruction through professional development. Rather than bolstering teachers' experiences in science or explicitly building their understanding of student reasoning, they offer a pragmatic approach focused on instruction. In the context of a multiple-year study of local systemic reform in the Detroit Public Schools, Fishman and colleagues studied the implementation of new middle school curriculum over several years. Teachers received initial training in the new problem-based learning curriculum. The new curriculum depicted science in real-world contexts that were readily accessible and of interest to students, drew on computational technologies, and provided "benchmark lessons" for especially difficult content. Researchers then monitored whether teachers taught the new units and collected student performance on relevant exam items to determine how successful the instruction in those units had been.

Their research entailed analyzing pre- and post-instruction student assessments over multiple years of instruction. In year 1, researchers analyzed student data to identify key concepts in which students made modest or no gains (postinstruction). Once these were identified, researchers developed and presented teacher workshops that showcased benchmark lessons designed to ensure student learning of those identified areas. In year 2, researchers again analyzed student learning of those key concepts, as well as instructional practice and teachers' perception of their own understanding of the content. They compared year 1 gains with year 2 gains.

In analyses of the first year of student learning data in a unit on water quality, researchers noted that students struggled with problems asking them to refer to two-dimensional maps, a fundamental skill for many of the concepts they wanted students to master, including representing water sheds, envisioning and describing points of contamination, and characterizing directional patterns of effluence. In the summer that followed, the research staff provided explicit training on teaching mapping skills, and had teachers do benchmark lessons in professional development workshops. In the following year, researchers found that these focused interventions on key topics resulted in positive changes in teachers' self-report of understanding and comfort with the topic, observed changes in instructional practice (the teachers enacted the benchmarking lessons), and statistically significant improvements in student learning in the second student cohort on key topics.

These studies provide a glimpse of some emergent and promising approaches to science-specific K-8 teacher professional development. Although the evidence base for professional development that is specific to science is less developed, we have inferred from the broader body of professional development research to point to practices that show promise and are worthy of further analysis. The studies we have described highlight important features of teacher professional development: these approaches are rooted in subject matter that teachers teach, focused on student learning, rooted in activities of teachers' work, take place over extended periods of time, and are actively supported by school system administrators.

Despite emerging evidence that the continuous improvement of practice and student performance requires sustained high-quality opportunities for teacher learning, few school districts provide teachers with curricular-based institutes, mentoring and coaching, and opportunities for examination of and reflection on classroom practice required to deepen their subject-matter expertise and pedagogical content knowledge. Far too many providers of professional development—from school districts to textbook publishers to professional organizations to reform groups—continue to rely on stand-and-deliver, one-shot workshops, and menu-driven conferences and conventions. While most of them acknowledge that the transfer of new skills and knowledge into practice requires more than what they are providing, too few teachers have access to the kinds of learning opportunities they need (Porter et al., 2000).

Teacher Learning Opportunities That Focus on Diverse Student Groups

A small number of studies examine the professional development of science teachers of racial/ethnic minority or low-income students in inner-city schools and urban school districts. As noted previously, while there is broad agreement that diverse student populations bring distinct experiences and identities vis-à-vis science to the classroom, there is little agreement in the field as to the most effective means of teaching diverse student populations. Accordingly, the content of teacher learning described in this section is varied. Some of these interventions focus on the unique qualities and challenges of working with diverse student groups (e.g., Lee et al., 2005), while others reflect approaches that are not specialized to diverse student groups per se (e.g., Boone and Kahle, 1998). Across approaches, professional development for teachers of diverse student populations shows promising results, including positive impact on students' science and literacy achievement, and on narrowing of achievement gaps among demographic subgroups (Amaral, Garrison, and Klentschy, 2002; Cuevas et al., 2005; Lee et al., 2005).

Teachers of English-language learners need to promote students' English-language and literacy development as well as academic achievement in subject areas. A limited body of research indicates that professional development efforts have a positive impact on helping practicing teachers expand their beliefs and practices in integrating science with literacy development for these students. As part of an NSF-supported local systemic initiative, Stoddart et al. (2002) involved elementary school teachers of predominantly Latino English language learners. After their participation in the 5-week summer professional development program, the majority of teachers showed a change from a restricted view of the connections between inquiry science instruction and second language development to a more elaborated reasoning about the different ways that the two could be integrated. Hart and Lee (2003) provided professional development opportunities to elementary school teachers serving students from diverse backgrounds. The results indicate positive change in teachers' beliefs and practices in teaching science to language-minority students. At the end of the school year, these students showed statistically significant gains in science and literacy (writing) achievement, enhanced abilities to conduct science inquiry, and narrowing of achievement gaps (Cuevas et al., 2005; Lee et al., 2005).

Amaral, Garrison, and Klentschy (2002) examined professional development in promoting science and literacy with predominantly Spanish-speaking elementary school students as part of a district-wide local systemic reform initiative. Over 4 years, the inquiry-based science program gradually became available to all teachers at all elementary schools in the school district. They were provided with professional development, in-classroom professional support from resource teachers, and complete materials and supplies for all the science units. Results indicated that the science and literacy (writing) achievement of language-minority students increased in direct relation to the number of years they participated in the program.

Kahle and colleagues conducted a series of studies to examine the impact of standards-based teaching practices (i.e., extended inquiry, problem solving, open-ended questioning, and cooperative learning) on the science achievement and attitudes of urban black middle school students (Boone and Kahle, 1998; Kahle, Meece, and Scantlebury, 2000). As an NSF-supported statewide systemic initiative, the Ohio professional development programs consisted of 6-week summer institutes and six seminars during the academic year. The results indicate that professional development designed to enhance teachers' content knowledge and use of standards-based teaching practices not only improved science achievement but also reduced inequities in achievement patterns for urban black students.

These studies suggest that, despite disagreement among researchers on the specific qualities of science instruction that advance student learning with diverse student populations, given opportunities to learn a range of new strategies for teaching these students, teachers can improve their practice and improve student learning. However, the relative benefits of one approach over another are not clear and will need to be examined.

Science Specialists

School leaders may opt to invest in a cadre of specialized science educators—science specialists, teacher leaders, coaches, mentors, demonstration teachers, lead teachers—rather than, or in conjunction with, organized forms of teacher opportunities to learn described above. We use the term "science specialist" to capture varied arrangements of organizing and distributing teacher expertise (Loucks-Horsley et al., 1998; Lieberman, 1992). District staff or principals may make decisions about how they spend their time and what responsibilities they assume, or science specialists themselves may use their own professional judgment in determining to do so. Subject matter specialist teachers may serve as leaders of groups of teachers—working with individual teachers in classroom settings, working with groups of teachers in professional development settings, or working with teachers, administrators, community members, or students on issues or programs that indirectly support classroom teaching/learning experiences (Lord and Miller, 2000). Alternately, they may assume instructional duties for a subject, in this case science, for an entire K-5 school or certain grade level. This practice is not common in U.S. elementary schools, although some countries typically rely on science specialists from as early as second grade.

Evidence of the effects of subject matter specialists is limited and the results are mixed. Teacher leaders, for example, were a central component in 14 of 19 districts included in Kim and colleagues' (2001) evaluation of the urban systemic initiatives. In this context, teacher leaders did a range of things, including planning, instruction, and working in the classroom with teachers, as well as organizing and running professional development activities. Kim found that the urban systemic initiatives had demonstrable effects on teacher practice and student learning outcomes in both mathematics and science. The role of teacher leaders in this sense was correlated with student learning effects. However, it was part of a systemic approach to reform, and specific contributions of the teacher leaders were not identified. Although evidence suggests an important role for teacher leaders in influencing peers' practice and there is correlational evidence of an effect on student learning, there has been little careful analysis of the effects of teacher leaders on student learning. The research does suggest that positive outcomes of teacher leaders are contingent on a carefully crafted role in the education system, as Lord and Miller (2000, p. 8) observed:

> Teacher leadership is part of an entire district infrastructure for mathematics and/or science reform. Districts with coherent curriculum programs, professional development that supports teachers' thoughtful and skillful use of curriculum, accountability systems that hold all teachers and administrators responsible for teaching the curriculum, and assessments that provide appropriate measures of what students are expected to learn are most likely to have effective teacher leadership.

We identified no studies that examined the use of science specialists who assume instructional duties in grades K-5. We also call attention to the fact that science specialists are commonly used internationally from early elementary grades onward. This is a common practice in high-performing nations in international comparisons such as the Trends in International Mathematics and Science Study and the Programme for International Student Assessment. Using science specialists may be a particularly useful strategy in schools and systems in which current K-5 teachers lack knowledge and comfort with science.

COHERENT INSTRUCTIONAL SYSTEMS

Marc Tucker (2004) has observed that one of the key differences between the U.S. education system and systems in countries whose students regularly outperform U.S. students is that they are instructionally coherent. He describes these educational systems as follows (p. 203):

> They had instructional systems that could properly be called systems. The list is now familiar: clear standards; high-quality examinations designed to assess whether the standards had been met; curriculum frameworks specifying what topics and concepts were to be taught at each grade level; a standard required curriculum (with very few electives), typically through the ninth or tenth year of school; instructional materials that fit the curriculum frameworks; and training designed to prepare teachers to impart the official curriculum successfully.

Tucker labels these conditions coherent instructional systems, and he goes on to say that true coherence requires more than formal alignment of standards, curriculum, and assessments. He says that coherence occurs when the culture of schools and all the elements of practice, large and small, are "in harmony with one another" (p. 208). He continues (pp. 208-209):

> [Coherence] is what happens when the school makes sure that the parents know what standards the students are expected to meet, how their children are doing, and what they can do to help where the help is most needed. It is what happens when the master schedule is set up so that student time is allocated to the tasks on which they are furthest behind and so that teacher time is allocated to the students who need the most help. Finally, it is what happens when tests or examinations are designed to assess whether the students learned what they were supposed to learn from the courses they took, which were in turn derived from a curriculum that is referenced to the standards they are supposed to meet. It is a matter of making sure that every aspect of the school's functioning is organized to advance its stated purposes.

This argument has a persuasive logic, and there is some empirical support for it. Beginning with the effective schools studies, researchers have found that focus, unity of purpose, and a shared vision of outcomes are related to gains in student learning (Smith and O'Day, 1991; Bryk, Lee, and Holland, 1993; Hill and Celio, 1998). However, no one had examined the importance of instructional coherence at the school level as defined by Tucker until Newman et al. (2001) investigated whether elementary schools in Chicago that had improving instructional coherence showed improvements in student achievement. They found that such schools made higher gains over multiple years than schools that were lower on measures of instructional coherence.

Do public schools have coherent instructional systems in science? The available evidence suggests that overall they do not, but that they are making some progress toward creating them. Banilower et al. (2006) reported that the schools and districts participating in NSF-funded local systemic change initiatives made some progress toward providing teachers with more support for reformed classroom practice in science and also made limited progress with aligning policies with science standards. Progress was limited because so many external factors—state and federal policies, private funding, etc.—influenced local policies. This section elaborates two core components of an instructional system: curriculum materials and benchmarking assessment systems.

Curriculum Materials

As we have discussed, the current store of curriculum materials for K-8 science teachers is quite uneven. Analysis of science textbooks suggest that, by and large, those used in American classrooms are of a low quality. These texts typically lack coherent attention to concepts in favor of including many topics, and they rarely provide teachers with guidance about how students think about science (Kesidou and Roseman, 2002). Full-scale K-8 or K-12 systems of science curricula do not typically provide the coherence or teacher guidance that is necessary to support high-quality instruction. Short of comprehensive curriculum packages, many primary and middle schools use commercially available science modules or kits for select units or in particular grades. These kits can facilitate teaching science as practice, although they are limited in some important respects.

Designed to teach major concepts and the scientific process by engaging students in guided inquiry, curriculum kits or modules are aligned with the national standards. Ideally, local decision makers would have at their disposal a plethora of reliable data and guidance to make decisions about selecting and using modules. Useful information would include evidence of their effectiveness with similar student populations, careful analysis of apparent alignment with state standards, and clear indications of the skills and training their teachers would need in order to use these materials effectively. Such information is not widely available.

Although rich empirical data on the effectiveness of curriculum modules is not available, both the American Association for the Advancement of Science's Project 2061 and the National Research Council have produced useful guides to facilitate curriculum materials selection. *Selecting Instructional Materials* (National Research Council, 1999), for example, describes how school districts, schools, or groups of science teachers can systematically develop internal capacity to make informed decisions in selecting instructional materials. It also provides processes and tools that can guide their collective work: description of the facilitator role, methods for training reviewers, how to carry out reviews, as well as forms that can be used in these processes. Involving teachers in systematic analysis of curriculum materials can have real benefits, including identifying high-quality materials, providing teachers who participate in the review process with knowledge of the curriculum and bolstering their capacity to critically analyze curriculum materials.

Managing curriculum modules may also present challenges. Modules typically include consumable materials that must be replaced after they are used. Since the modules are expensive, schools often ask teachers to share them, and replenishing the supplies becomes a problem. Teachers often have trouble finding the necessary supplies and either do not use the modules or use them inappropriately. A solution to this problem is for districts or schools to set up systems for replenishing the modules and distributing them across classrooms or "materials resources centers." These centers shift the burden of preparing materials from the individual teacher to a specialized unit in the system. They provide space, deliver materials to schools, and ensure that both reusable and consumable materials are included and adequately stocked before they are delivered to teachers.

One potential limitation to shared kits is that reliance on them can limit the degree of school and district-level coordination of instruction as kits are frequently shared within or across schools. For example, if four schools share two sets of kits, it would be difficult to teach the units in a clearly defined, developmental learning progression across classrooms. What is more, when teachers at a given grade level are working on topics asynchronously, it can complicate efforts to pool the intellectual resources of the group. Science teacher learning communities that collaborate on planning, teaching, and assessing science instruction will typically work on a common set of tasks that are relevant to their current unit of instruction. Working on different modules at different times of the year could complicate and weaken collaborations.

Benchmarking Assessment Systems

There is growing interest in improving the means by which teachers monitor the progress of their students. Policy makers, school leaders, and teachers are becoming interested in the use of benchmarking assessments that provide practitioners with regular feedback on student learning, so that their progress can be judged either continually or periodically, and information about student learning can inform instructional decisions in a timely fashion. By providing teachers with feedback in the short term about student learning, these systems are designed to influence teaching in ways that other testing systems (e.g., high-stakes testing) do not.

Benchmarking assessments or curriculum-embedded formative assessments created in the context of a curriculum are designed to elicit student thinking and are referenced specifically to an interpretive framework. While few science-specific studies of benchmarking assessments have been completed, there is a large research base on benchmarking assessment systems in other subject matter areas. Some well-developed programs that are based heavily on benchmarking assessments have shown positive student learning effects. Success for All, for example, uses reading tests at 6-week intervals to determine the effectiveness of reading instruction and to regroup students for subsequent instruction. Instruction based on the principles of mastery learning, a system developed by Benjamin Bloom in which students are allowed to progress on the basis of demonstrating proficiency on a set of formative assessments, has been shown to have a significant positive effects for lower achieving students and for inexperienced teachers (Block and Burns, 1976; Guskey and Gates, 1986; Whiting, Van Burgh, and Renger, 1995).

There are a few published studies of science-specific benchmarking programs and others are in progress. Currently the Berkeley Evaluation and Assessment Research Center (BEAR) (2005) is creating embedded assessments for the Full Option Science System. The assessments are being developed to help teachers of students in grades 3-6 assess, guide, and confirm student learning in science. These assessments make use of construct maps, which model levels of student understanding of a particular construct (e.g., students' ability to reason with evidence) on the way to developing proficiency (Wilson, 2005). BEAR has helped to develop and refine the associated assessment frameworks, items, scoring guides, and other elements of the system and will later provide support in the process of psychometric data analyses.

In a recently completed study, the Stanford Education Assessment Laboratory explored Black and Wiliam's (1998) contention that formative assessment would increase student learning by developing curriculum-embedded assessments for the Foundational Approaches to Science Teaching (FAST) curriculum (Yin, 2005). The first unit of FAST guides students through a series of investigations to culminate in an explanation of floating and sinking on the basis of relative density. Assessments were embedded at key conceptual "joints" in the curriculum, following a developmental trajectory of understanding density that students were expected to experience. Twelve sixth and seventh grade teachers were selected from a pool of FAST-trained volunteers. Teachers were matched in pairs according to school characteristics, and one member of each pair was then randomly assigned to a control group, which would teach FAST as they normally did, while the other was assigned to an experimental group, which would implement the curriculum-embedded assessments. The experimental group teachers attended a 5-day workshop, where they were trained to implement the curriculum-embedded assessments following the interpretive framework for formative assessment. Multiple measures of student learning were administered to all students of teachers in both the control and experimental groups. Pretests consisted of a multiple-choice achievement test and a science motivation questionnaire. Posttests included the achievement test and the motivation questionnaire, as well as a performance assessment, a predict-observe-explain assessment, and an open-ended question assessment.

Results of the study indicated that the teachers and their contexts were extremely influential on students' motivation, achievement, and conceptual change; teacher effects overshadowed the treatment effect. Possible interpretations suggest that some experienced teachers implemented their own informal formative assessment strategies regardless of the treatment group they belonged to; some experimental teachers, despite the 5-day workshop, could not implement the curriculum-embedded assessments as intended.

Although benchmarking assessment systems show promising student learning results, the quality of assessment systems is uneven. Stern and Ahlgren (2002) analyzed assessments provided in middle school curriculum materials. The study included only comprehensive middle school science programs—that is those that covered 3 years of instruction and were in wide use by school districts and states. Two two-member teams independently analyzed the curriculum materials and accompanying assessments. With respect to curriculum-embedded assessments, the analysis revealed that all materials received poor scores in terms of providing guidance for teachers to use students' responses to modify instruction. Those curriculum-embedded assessments that were aligned with the curriculum materials usually focused on terms and definitions that could be easily copied from the text. Few questions were included that were able to sufficiently elicit students' understanding, and even when those questions were included, the materials failed to provide interpretive frameworks for the teachers to interpret students' responses.

The use of benchmarking assessment is clearly not a silver bullet. Effects are highly dependent on a number of factors. Bangert-Drowns et al. (1991) found in a meta-analysis of 58 experiments that while periodic feedback generally improved student performance, the type of feedback students received had the largest effect. Feedback that helped students to correct errors and reflect on the original learning goals had the greatest positive impact. Comments unique to a particular student's performance relative to an absolute standard appear to motivate students to achieve at higher levels, while responses that include solely grades or praise (or no feedback at all) seem to have little effect on student achievement, and some evidence would indicate a small negative effect from these types of feedback (Butler, 1987, 1988).

In a meta-analysis of 21 studies, teachers who had specific instructional processes to follow based on test outcomes and who had received explicit directions about how to share information with students based on the data from the assessments demonstrated significantly higher growth in student achievement than those teachers who used their own judgment about how to respond to the data (Fuchs and Fuchs, 1986).

Teachers may need clear guidance about how to use evidence from benchmarking systems, but there is no "teacher proof" curriculum. Well-designed benchmarking systems are closely integrated with instruction and may lighten its immense cognitive load. But they require informed, professional teachers who make key decisions to structure and support student learning. For benchmarking assessment systems to support quality instruction and improvements in student learning, teachers must understand the desired stages of progression for students of varying ages and skill levels in the particular discipline being taught.

CONCLUSIONS

Advancing high-quality science instruction that supports student understanding across the strands of science proficiency will require teachers and schools to take action to improve teacher knowledge and practice, support and focus instruction in productive directions, and build systems that measure and sustain ongoing improvement in teaching and learning. Research can guide practice to some extent, although important questions require additional research.

Researchers have identified, in general terms, what expert teachers know about their discipline, how to teach it, and, to a lesser extent, what they understand about student learning. Empirical links between what teachers know and student learning, however, are emergent and can be complicated to establish. As research advances in this area, more precise definitions are needed of the knowledge that is necessary for teaching and the aspects of knowledge that provide the greatest student learning return. With this understanding in hand, educators will be better positioned to craft teacher credentialing policy and design teacher learning experiences.

There is broad agreement that well-designed opportunities for teacher learning can produce desirable changes in instructional practice and improved science learning for students. Furthermore, research has identified features of quality teacher learning opportunities that can be realized through a diverse array of organizational structures (mentoring and coaching, teacher work groups, expert- and teacher-led programs of professional development) combined with distinct learning outcomes (topic-specific learning strategies, conducting and teaching inquiry science, conducting science discussions, analyzing student work, planning instruction). Well-designed opportunities for teacher learning can benefit diverse student groups, including those that have traditionally been underserved.

Although there is abundant evidence to support subject-specific teacher learning opportunities, the comparative advantages of one approach or another are not clear. There may be unique learning potential or capacity to influence practice that arises in teacher work groups, or programs that focus on analyzing student work, for example. Future research will need to examine the potential and comparative advantage of distinct approaches. Given the consensus view that teacher learning should be framed in the context of the science that teachers actually teach, approaches should probably be considered in light of local resources and constraints. For example, given the dearth of K-5 teachers who specialize in science, most elementary schools will benefit from the participation of qualified expert teachers and other science teacher educators.

In addition to significantly bolstering K-8 science teachers' opportunities to learn, schools and school systems can benefit from developing and refining instructional systems that focus and support science instruction. It may be some time before schools have and can use a comprehensive K-8 (or K-12) learning progression like that described in Chapter 7 as the basis of curriculum. However, they can begin to make important steps in that direction by carefully selecting and modifying curricular materials so that they present central scientific ideas across grades. In addition, schools can use existing benchmarking assessment systems that provide teachers with timely feedback on students' ideas and guidance on structuring instruction in order to build on and advance students' thinking toward intended learning outcomes.

REFERENCES

Abd-El-Khalick, F., and BouJaoude, S. (1997). An exploratory study of the knowledge base for science teaching. *Journal of Research in Science Teaching, 34,* 673-699.

Aguirere, J.M., Haggerty, S.M., and Linder, C.J. (1990). Student teachers' conceptions of science, teaching, and learning: A case study in preservice science education. *International Journal of Science Education, 12,* 381-390.

Amaral, O., Garrison, L., and Klentschy, M. (2002). Helping English learners increase achievement through inquiry-based science instruction. *Bilingual Research Journal, 26*(2), 213-239.

American Educational Research Association. (2005). Studying teacher education: *The report of the AERA panel on research and teacher education.* M. Cochran-Smith and K.M. Zeichner (Eds.). Mahwah, NJ: Lawrence Erlbaum Associates.

American Federation of Teachers. (2002). *Principles for professional development.* (Report 39-0176). Washington, DC: Author.

Bangert-Drowns, R.L., Kulik, C., Kulik, J.A., and Morgan, M.T. (1991). The instructional effect of feedback in test-like events. *Review of Educational Research, 61*, 213-238.

Banilower, E.R., Boyd, S.E., Pasley, J.D. and Weiss, I.R. (2006) *Lessons from a decade of mathematics and science reform: A capstone report for the local systemic change through teacher enhancement initiative.* Chapel Hill, NC: Horizon Research.

Berkeley Evaluation and Assessment Research Center. (2005). *Assessing science knowledge (ASK).* Available: http://bearcenter.berkeley.edu/research.php [accessed January 2005].

Black, P., and Wiliam, D. (1998). Assessment and classroom learning. *Assessment in Education, 5*(1), 7-74.

Block, J., and Burns, R. (1976). Mastering learning. *Review of Research in Education, 4*, 3-49.

Bloom, J.W. (1989). Preservice elementary teachers' conceptions of science: Science, theories and evolution. *International Journal of Science Education, 11*, 401-415.

Boone, W.J., and Kahle, J.B. (1998). Student perceptions of instruction, peer interest, and adult support for middle school science: Differences by race and gender. *Journal of Women and Minorities in Science and Engineering, 4*, 333-340.

Borko, H. (2005). *Professional development for all teachers: Achieving educational excellence and equity in the era of accountability.* Presidential Invited Session at the annual meeting of the American Educational Research Association, Montreal.

Brown, B.B., Reveles, J.M., and Kelly, G.J. (2005). Scientific literacy and discursive identity: A theoretical framework for understanding science learning. *Science Education, 89*, 779-802.

Bryan, L., and Atwater, M. (2002). Teacher beliefs and cultural models: A challenge for science teacher preparation programs. *Science Education, 86*, 821-839.

Bryk, A.S., Lee, V.E., and Holland, P.E. (1993). *Catholic schools and the common good.* Cambridge, MA: Harvard University Press.

Bryk, A.S., and Schneider, B.L. (2002). *Trust in schools: A core resource for improvement.* New York: Russell Sage Foundation.

Butler, R. (1987). Task-involving and ego-involving properties of evaluation: Effects of different feedback conditions on motivational perceptions, interest, and performance. *Journal of Educational Psychology, 79*(4), 474-482.

Butler, R. (1988). Enhancing and undermining intrinsic motivation: The effects of task-involving and ego-involving evaluation on interest and involvement. *British Journal of Educational Pyschology, 58*, 1-14.

Carlsen, W.S. (1988). *The effects of science teacher subject-matter knowledge on teacher questioning and classroom discourse.* Unpublished doctoral dissertation, Stanford University.

Carlsen, W.S. (1992). Closing down the conversation: Discouraging student talk on unfamiliar science content. *Journal of Classroom Interaction, 27*, 15-21.

Carpenter, T.P., Fennema, E., Peterson, P.L., Chiang, C., and Loef, M. (1989). Using knowledge of children's mathematical thinking in classroom teaching: An experimental study. *American Educational Research Journal, 26*, 499-532.

Chaney, B. (1995). *Student outcomes and the professional preparation of eighth grade teachers in science and mathematics.* Rockville, MD: Westat.

Cohen, D., and Hill, H.C. (1998). State policy and classroom performance: Mathematics reform in California. *CPRE Policy Briefs, 23.*

Cohen, D.K., and Hill, H.C. (2001). *Learning policy.* New Haven, CT: Yale University Press.

Cohen, D.K., Raudenbush, S., and Ball, D.L. (2001). Resources, instruction, and research. *Educational Evaluation and Policy Analysis, 25*(2), 119-142.

Corcoran, T.B., McVay, S., and Riordan, K. (2003). *Getting it right: The MISE approach to professional development.* (Research Report No. RR-055). Philadelphia: Consortium for Policy Research in Education, University of Pennsylvania.

Corcoran, T.B., Walker, L.J., and White, J.L. (1988). *Working in urban schools.* Washington, DC: Institute for Educational Leadership.

Crawford, B. (2000). Embracing the essence of inquiry: New roles for science teachers. *Journal of Research in Science Teaching, 37,* 916-937.

Cuevas, P., Lee, O., Hart, J., and Deaktor, R. (2005). Improving science inquiry with elementary students of diverse backgrounds. *Journal of Research in Science Teaching, 42*(3), 337-357.

Druva, C.A., and Anderson, R.D. (1983). Science teacher characteristics by teaching behavior and by student outcome: A meta-analysis of research. *Journal of Research in Science Teaching, 20*(5), 467-479.

DuFour, R. (2000). The leader's role in building a professional learning community. *Catalyst for Change, 29*(3), 13-15.

Eisenhart, M.A., Finkel, E., Behm, L., Lawrence, N., and Tonso, K. (1998). *Women's science learning from the margins.* Chicago, IL: University of Chicago Press.

Eisenhart, M., Finkel, E., and Marion, S.F. (1996). Creating the conditions for scientific literacy: A re-examination. *American Educational Research Journal, 33,* 261-295.

Elby, A. (1999). Another reason that students learn by rote. *Physics Education Research: A Supplement to the American Journal of Physics, 67*(7), S53-S60.

Elmore, R.F. (2002). *Bridging the gap between standards and achievement: Report on the imperative for professional development in education.* Washington, DC: Albert Shanker Institute.

Elmore, R.F., and Burney, D. (1997). *Investing in teacher learning: Staff development and instructional improvement in community school district #2, New York City.* (CPRE/NCTAF Joint Report). New York: National Commission on Teaching and America's Future and Consortium for Policy Research in Education.

Fennema, E., Carpenter, T., Franke, M., Levi, L., Jacobs, V., and Empson, S. (1996). A longitudinal study of learning to use children's thinking in mathematics instruction. *Journal of Research in Mathematics Education, 26*(4), 403-434.

Fishman, B.J., Marz, R.W., Best, S., and Tal, R.T. (2003). Linking teacher and student learning to improve professional development in systemic reform. *Teaching and Teacher Education, 19,* 643-658.

Fuchs, L.S., and Fuchs, D. (1986). Effects of systematic formative evaluation on student achievement: A meta-analysis. *Exceptional Children, 53,* 199-208.

Garet, M., Birman, B.F., Porter, A.C., Desimone, L., Herman, R., and Yoon, K.S. (1999). *Designing effective professional development: Lessons from the Eisenhower program.* Prepared under Contract (EA97001001) by American Institutes for Research for the U.S. Department of Education Office of the Under Secretary.

Gess-Newsome, J., and Lederman, N.G. (1999). *Examining pedagogical content knowledge.* Dordrecht, The Netherlands: Kluwer Academic.

Goldhaber, D.D., and Brewer, D.J. (1997). Why don't schools and teachers seem to matter? Assessing the impact of unobservables on education. *Journal of Human Resources, 32*(3), 505-523.

Goldhaber, D.D., and Brewer, D.J. (2000). Does teacher certification matter? High school teacher certification status and student achievement. *Education Evaluation and Policy Analysis, 22*(2), 129-145.

Grossman, P.L., Schoenfeld, A., and Lee, C.D. (2005). Teaching subject matter: In L. Darling-Hammond, J. Bransford, P. LePage, K. Hammerness, and H. Duffy (Eds.), *Preparing teachers for a changing world: What teachers should learn and be able to do.* San Francisco: Jossey Bass.

Guskey, T., and Gates, S. (1986). Synthesis of research on the effects of mastery learning in elementary and secondary classrooms. *Educational Leadership, 43*(8), 73-80.

Hammer, D., and Elby, A. (2003). Tapping epistemological resources for learning physics. *Journal of the Learning Sciences, 12*(1), 53-90.

Hart, J.E., and Lee, O. (2003). Teacher professional development to improve the science and literacy achievement of English language learners. *Bilingual Research Journal, 27*(3), 357-383.

Hashweh, M.Z. (1987). Effects of subject-matter knowledge in the teaching of biology and physics. *Teaching and Teacher Education, 3*(2), 109-120.

Hawkins, E.F., Stancavage, F.B., and Dossey, J.A. (1998). *School policies and practices affecting instruction in mathematics.* (NCES #98-495). Washington, DC: U.S. Government Printing Office.

Hill, H.C., Rowan, B., and Ball, D.L. (2005). Effects of teachers' mathematical knowledge for teaching on student achievement. *American Educational Research Journal, 42*(2), 371-406.

Hill, P.T., Celio, M.B. (1998). *Fixing urban schools.* Washington, DC: Brookings Institution.

Ingersoll, R.E. (2004). *Who controls teachers' work? Power and accountability in America's schools.* Cambridge, MA: Harvard University Press.

Jones, M.G., and Carter, G. (in press). Science teacher attitudes and beliefs. Submitted to *Handbook of Research on Science Teaching.*

Kahle, J., Meece, J., and Scantlebury, K. (2000). Urban African-American middle school science students: Does standards-based teaching make a difference? *Journal of Research in Science Teaching, 37*(9), 1019-1041.

Kesidou, S., and Roseman, J.E. (2002). How well do middle school science programs measure up? Findings from Project 2061's curriculum review. *Journal of Research in Science Teaching, 39*, 522-549.

Kim, J.J., Crasco, L.M., Smithson, J., and Blank, R.K. (2001). *Survey results of urban school classroom practices in mathematics and science: 2000 report.* Norwood, MA: Systemic Research.

Knapp, M.S., McCaffrey, T., and Swanson, J. (2003). *District support for professional learning: What research says and has yet to establish.* Paper presented at the annual meeting of the American Educational Research Association, April, Chicago.

Lareau, A. (2000). *Home advantage: Social class and parental intervention in elementary education* (updated ed.). Lanham, MD: Rowan and Littlefield.

Lave, J., and Wenger, E. (1991). *Situated learning: Legitimate peripheral participation.* Cambridge, MA: Cambridge University Press.

Lee, O., Deaktor, R.A., Hart, J.E., Cuevas, P., and Enders, C. (2005). An instructional intervention's impact on the science and literacy achievement of culturally and linguistically diverse elementary students. *Journal of Research in Science Teaching, 42*(8), 857-887.

Lieberman, A. (1992). Teacher leadership: What are we learning? In C. Livingston (Ed.), *Teachers as leaders: Evolving roles* (pp. 159-165). Washington, DC: National Education Association.

Lord, B., and Miller, B. (2000). *Teacher leadership: An appealing and inescapable force in school reform?* Boston, MA: Education Development Center.

Loucks-Horsley, S., Hewson, P.W., Love, N., and Stiles, K.E. (1998). *Designing professional development for teachers of science and mathematics.* Thousand Oaks, CA: Corwin Press.

Louis, K.S., and Marks, H.M. (1998). Does professional community affect the classroom? Teachers' work and student experiences in restructuring schools. *American Journal of Education, 106*, 532-575.

McLaughlin, M., and Talbert J. (2000). *Assessing results: The Bay Area school reform collaborative, year four.* Stanford, CA: Center for Research on the Context of Teaching, Stanford University.

Monk, D.H. (1994). Subject matter preparation of secondary mathematics and science teachers and student achievement. *Economics of Education Review, 13*(2), 125-145.

Munby, H., Russell, T., and Martin, A.K. (2001). Teachers' knowledge and how it develops. In V. Richardson (Ed.), *Handbook of research on teaching* (4th ed., pp. 877-904). Washington, DC: American Educational Research Association.

National Association of State Directors of Teacher Education and Certification. (2004). *The NASDTEC manual on the preparation and certification of educational personnel 2004 Ninth edition.* Whitinsville, MA: Author.

National Center for Education Statistics. (1999). *Student work and teacher practices in science.* (NCES #1999-455). Washington, DC: Author.

National Research Council. (1999). *Selecting instructional materials: A guide for K-12 science.* M. Singer and J. Tuomi (Eds.), Committee on Developing the Capacity to Select Effective Instructional Materials. Center for Science, Mathematics, and Engineering Education. Washington, DC: National Academy Press.

National Research Council and Institute of Medicine. (1997). *Improving schooling for language-minority children: A research agenda.* D. August and K. Hakuta (Eds.), Committee on Developing a Research Agenda on the Education of Limited-English-Proficient and Bilingual Students. Board on Children, Youth, and Families, Commission on Behavioral and Social Sciences and Education. Washington, DC: National Academy Press.

National Staff Development Council. (2001). *NSDC standards for staff development.* Oxford, OH: Author.

Newmann, F. (1996). *Authentic achievement: Restructuring schools for intellectual quality.* San Francisco, CA: Jossey Bass.

Newman, F.M., Smith, B., Allensworth, E., and Bryk, A. (2001). Instructional program coherence: What it is and why it should guide school improvement policy. *Education Evaluation and Policy Analysis, 23*(4), 297-321.

Odden, A.R., Archibald, S., Fermanich, M.L., and Gallagher, H.A. (2002). A cost framework for professional development. *Journal of Education Finance, 28*(1), 51-74.

Olson, M. (2005). *The relationship between teachers' knowledge and students' opportunities to learn.* Paper presented at the National Association of Research in Science Teaching Annual Conference, Dallas, TX.

Pomeroy, D. (1993). Implications of teachers' beliefs about the nature of science: Comparison of the beliefs of scientists, secondary science teachers and elementary teachers. *Science Education, 77,* 261-278.

Porter, A.C., Garet, M.S., Desimone, L., Yoon, K.S., and Birman, B.F. (2000, October). *Does professional development change teaching practice? Results from a three-year study.* (Report to the U.S. Department of Education, Office of the Under Secretary on Contract No. EA97001001 to the American Institutes for Research). Washington, DC: Pelavin Research Center.

Putnam, R.T., and Borko, H. (2000). What do new views of knowledge and thinking have to say about research on teacher learning? *Educational Researcher, 29*(1), 4-15.

Ritchie, S.M. (2002). Student positioning within groups during science activities. *Research in Science Education, 32*(1), 35-54.

Rosebery, A.S., and Puttick, G. (1998). Teacher professional development as situated sense-making: A case study in science education. *Science Education, 82*(6), 649-677.

Rowan, B., Correnti, R., and Miller, R. (2002). What large-scale survey research tells us about teacher effects on student achievement: Insights from the prospects study of elementary schools. *Teachers College Record, 104*(8), 1525-1567.

Rowan, B., Schilling, S., Ball, D., and Miller, R. (2001). *Measuring teachers' pedagogical content knowledge in surveys: An exploratory study.* Ann Arbor: University of Michigan, Consortium for Policy Research in Education.

Sanders, L.R., Borko, H., and Lockard, J.D. (1993). Secondary science teachers' knowledge base when teaching science courses in and out of their area of certification. *Journal of Research in Science Teaching, 30,* 723-736.

Seymour, E., and Hewitt, N. (1994). *Talking about leaving: Factors contributing to high attrition rates among science, mathematics, and engineering undergraduate majors.* Boulder: Bureau of Sociological Research, University of Colorado.

Shulman, L.S. (1986). Those who understand knowledge growth in teaching. *Educational Researcher*, February, 4-14.

Shulman, L. (1987). Knowledge and teaching: Foundations of the new reform. *Harvard Educational Review, 57*, 1-22.

Smardon, R. (2004). Streetwise science: Toward a theory of the code of the classroom. *Mind, Culture, and Activity, 11*(3), 201-223.

Smith, B. (1998). *It's about time: Opportunities to learn in Chicago's elementary schools.* Chicago, IL: Consortium on Chicago School Research.

Smith, D.C., and Anderson, C. (1999). Appropriating scientific practices and discourses with future elementary teachers. *Journal of Research in Science Teaching, 36*(7), 755-776.

Smith, D.C., and Neale, D.C. (1989). The construction of subject matter knowledge in primary science teaching. *Teaching and Teacher Education, 5*(1), 1-20.

Smith, M., and O'Day, J. (1991). *Putting the pieces together: Systemic school reform.* (CPRE Policy Brief). New Brunswick, NJ: Eagleton Institute of Politics.

Spillane, J. (1996). School districts matter: Local educational authorities and state instructional policy. *Education Policy, 10*(1), 63-87.

Spillane, J. (2000). Cognition and policy implementation: District policy makers and the reform of mathematics education. *Cognition and Instruction, 18*(2), 141-179.

Spillane, J. (2005). Primary school leadership practice: How the subject matters. *School Leadership and Management, 25*(4), 383-397.

Stein, M.K., and D'Amico, L. (1998). *Content-driven instructional reform in community school district #2.* Pittsburgh: University of Pittsburgh, Learning Research Development Center.

Stern, L., and Ahlgren, A. (2002). An analysis of student assessments in middle school curriculum materials: Aiming precisely at benchmarks and standards. *Journal of Research in Science Teaching, 39*, 889-910.

Stoddart, T., Pinal, A., Latzke, M., and Canaday, D. (2002). Integrating inquiry science and language development for English language learners. *Journal of Research in Science Teaching, 39*(8), 664-687.

Strauss, S. (1997). Cognitive development and science education: Toward a middle level model. In W. Damon (Series Ed.) and I. E. Sigel and K. A. Renninger (Vol. Eds.), *Handbook of child psychology, volume 4: Child psychology in practice* (5th ed., pp. 357-399). New York: Wiley.

Strauss, S. (2001). Folk psychology, folk pedagogy and their relations to subject matter knowledge. In B. Torff and R.J. Sternberg (Eds.), *Understanding and teaching the intuitive mind* (pp. 217-242). Mahwah, NJ: Lawrence Erlbaum Associates.

Supovitz, J. (2002). Developing communities of instructional practice. *Teachers College Record, 104*(8), 1591-1626.

Supovitz, J.A., and Turner, H. (2000). The effects of professional development on science teaching practices and classroom culture. *Journal of Research in Science Teaching, 37*(9), 963-980.

Trumbull, D., and Kerr, P. (1993). University researchers' inchoate critiques of science teaching: Implications for the content of preservice science teacher education. *Science Education, 77,* 301-317.

Tucker, M. (2004). Reaching for coherence in school reform: The case of America's choice. In T.K. Glennan, S.J. Bodilly, J.R. Galegher, and K.A. Kerr (Eds.), *Expanding the reach of education reforms.* Santa Monica, CA: RAND.

van Driel, J.H., Verloop, N., and de Vos, W. (1998). Developing science teachers' pedagogical content knowledge. *Journal of Research in Science Teaching, 35,* 673-695.

Weiss, I.R., Pasley, J.D., Smith, P.S., Banilower, E.R., and Heck, D.J. (2003). *Looking inside the classroom: A study of K-12 mathematics and science education in the United States.* Chapel Hill, NC: Horizon Research.

Wenger, E. (1998). *Communities of practice: Learning, meaning, and identity.* New York: Cambridge University Press.

Whiting, B., Van Burgh, J.W., and Render, G.F. (1995). *Mastery learning in the classroom.* Paper presented at Annual Meeting of the American Educational Research Association, San Francisco, CA.

Wilson, M. (2005). *Constructing measures: An item response modeling approach.* Mahwah, NJ: Lawrence Erlbaum Associates.

Wilson, S.M. (2003). *California dreaming: Reforming mathematics education.* New Haven, CT: Yale University Press.

Wilson, S.M., and Berne, J. (1999). Teacher learning and the acquisition of professional knowledge: An examination of research on contemporary professional development. *Review of Research in Education, 24,* 173-209.

Wilson, S.M., Shulman, L.S., and Richert, A.E. (1987). 150 different ways of knowing: Representations of knowledge in teaching. In J. Calderhead (Ed.), *Exploring teachers' thinking* (pp. 104-123). London, England: Cassell.

Windschitl, M. (2004). Folk theories of "inquiry": How preservice teachers reproduce the discourse and practices of the scientific method. *Journal of Research in Science Teaching, 41,* 481-512.

Yin, Y. (2005). *The influence of formative assessments on student motivation, achievement, and conceptual change.* Unpublished doctoral dissertation, Stanford University.

Zembal-Saul, C., Blumenfeld, P.C., and Krajcik, J.S. (2000). The influence of early cycles of planning, teaching, and reflection on prospective elementary teachers' developing understanding of supporting students' science learning. *Journal of Research in Science Teaching, 37*(4), 318-339.

PART IV

Future Directions for Policy, Practice, and Research

11

Conclusions and Recommendations

The emerging understanding of how children learn science in kindergarten through eighth grade paints a very different picture of a science learner than existed 20 or 30 years ago. As this report has documented, children come to school with rich knowledge of the natural world and an ability to engage in complex reasoning that provides a solid foundation for learning science. At the same time, many key ideas and ways of thinking in science are difficult if not impossible to achieve without instructional support. Successful strategies for science learning engage students in scientific tasks that explore ideas and problems that are meaningful to them with carefully structured support from teachers. Too often, however, the instructional and curricular approaches currently used in classrooms do not reflect this emerging understanding of children as competent learners who can engage in scientific tasks throughout their schooling. Instead, current approaches are often based on now outdated knowledge about cognitive development and misunderstanding of its implications concerning how to design instruction for young and novice learners.

In this chapter, the committee summarizes the major conclusions of the report. We then follow with a discussion of the key recommendations for policy and practice that flow from these conclusions. Finally, we outline a research agenda that if pursued would fill critical gaps in the knowledge base and recommends a multidisciplinary approach to the issues that have emerged in the report.

MAJOR FINDINGS AND CONCLUSIONS

We begin with a discussion of current understanding of science learners and science learning, highlighting the ideas that differ from some popularly held conceptions. These conclusions are based on evidence discussed mainly in Part II. Working from this picture of learning, we discuss what is known about effective curriculum and instruction. These conclusions flow from the new vision of learning described in Part II as well as from studies reviewed in Part III that have explicitly explored the design of effective science instruction. Finally, we move from the classroom into the larger context of the school and district to consider key factors the committee thinks influence whether and how classroom practice is informed by knowledge about how children learn science. Evidence for these conclusions is discussed mainly in Chapter 10.

Learning and Learners

The committee developed a framework for proficiency that identifies four fundamental strands of learning. In our view students who understand science:

1. Know, use, and interpret scientific explanations of the natural world.
2. Generate and evaluate scientific evidence and explanations.
3. Understand the nature and development of scientific knowledge.
4. Participate productively in scientific practices and discourse.

These strands of scientific proficiency represent learning goals for students as well as provide a broad framework for curriculum design. They address the knowledge and reasoning skills that students must eventually acquire to be considered fully proficient in science. They also incorporate the scientific practices that students need to participate in and become fluent with in order to demonstrate their proficiency. Students can understand science with increasing sophistication starting in the earliest grades. The committee thinks the development of proficiency is best supported when classrooms provide learning opportunities that interweave all four strands together in instruction.

Evidence to date indicates that in the process of achieving proficiency in science, the four strands are intertwined so that advances in one strand support and advance another. For example, learning how to design controlled experiments enables students to discover and verify knowledge about causal factors in the natural world. Conversely, an inadequate understanding of how scientific knowledge is constructed can constrain students' scientific reasoning and limit the kinds of inferences they may be drawn from evidence.

This four-strand framework represents an important departure from the dichotomy of content and process that informs much of current practice in science education. That is, teaching content alone is not likely to lead to proficiency in science, nor is engaging in inquiry experiences devoid of meaningful science content. In current practice, content and an oversimplified view of scientific processes are often the primary or even sole foci of instruction; however, the evidence indicates that this leads to a very impoverished understanding of science and masks the complex process involved in developing scientific evidence and explanations. In addition, without an understanding of how scientific evidence is obtained, evaluated, and accumulated—more sophisticated than the seven-step version of the scientific method that is often taught in U.S. schools—students are unlikely to become science-literate citizens who can critically evaluate scientific information in order to participate in public debates or make informed decisions. Students are most likely to be successful in science when the four strands are brought together in instruction.

> *Conclusion 1: The norms of scientific argument, explanation, and the evaluation of evidence differ from those in everyday life. Students need support to learn appropriate norms and language for productive participation in the discourses of science.*

Many advances in children's knowledge and understanding of science are made through a social process of constructing arguments and evaluating evidence. However, the rules for engaging in arguments and evaluating evidence that students learn in their everyday lives are sometimes dissimilar and even contradictory to those employed in science. For example, children may settle arguments outside the science classroom on the basis of appeals to authority, personal experience, social status, or physical size. In contrast, children engaged in a productive scientific argument base their claims on empirical evidence and engage in arguments in order to refine their thinking and clarify their collective understanding of phenomena. Students often need support or explicit guidance to learn scientific norms for interacting with peers as they argue about evidence and clarify their own emerging understanding of science and scientific ideas.

> *Conclusion 2: Children entering school already have substantial knowledge of the natural world, much of it implicit. In contrast to the commonly held and outmoded view that young children are concrete and simplistic thinkers, the research evidence now shows that their thinking is surprisingly sophisticated. They can use a wide range of reasoning processes that form the underpinnings of scientific thinking, even though their experience is variable and they have much more to learn.*

Recent research indicates that children of all ages can and do engage in complex reasoning about the world. This echoes a major conclusion of *How People Learn: Brain, Mind, Experience and School, Expanded Edition* (National Research Council, 2000, National Academy Press, Washington, DC) that "children lack knowledge and experience, but not reasoning ability," that is, "they are ignorant, but not stupid" (p. 112). Children reason quite well with the knowledge they do understand. Furthermore, it is now known that even preschool and kindergarten-age children have a more sophisticated knowledge of the natural world than was once assumed.

Much of the current science education curriculum is based on dated assumptions about the nature of cognitive development and learning, assumptions that lead to the suboptimal teaching of science. It has been common to view younger children as deficient in some manner, resulting in a focus on what they cannot do rather than what they can do. Cognitive development has often been characterized as a series of artificial dichotomies, in which children do or do not have a particular capacity and the transition from not having the capacity to having the capacity is understood as going through a stage. These deficit assumptions ignore the tremendous subtlety, variability, and context dependence in children's thinking and reasoning, and the important domain-specific knowledge they bring to school, especially knowledge of the natural world. In many cases, these assumptions about children's abilities lead to curriculum materials that are designed to fit with a stage-like conception of a child's abilities and inabilities, rather than to take advantage of and build on existing knowledge and reasoning skills.

Conclusion 3: What children are capable of at a particular age is the result of a complex interplay among maturation, experience, and instruction. Thus, what is developmentally appropriate is not a simple function of age or grade. What children can do is in large part contingent on their prior opportunities to learn and not on some fixed sequence of developmental stages.

Contrary to conceptions of development held 30 or 40 years ago, current research does not show a broad age trend in children's thought suggesting that young children are only able to think concretely, with abstract thought emerging only in later childhood. Instead, there is variation across children at a given age and even variation within an individual child. That is, a single child's thinking does not develop in a unitary way across all domains; at a given point in time, a child may be more sophisticated in one area and less sophisticated in another.

In addition, current research contradicts the assumption that development is a kind of inevitable unfolding and that one must simply wait until a child is cognitively "ready" for more abstract or theory-based forms of content. Instead, children need assistance to learn; building on their early capacities requires catalysts and mediation (National Research Council, 2000). Adults play a central role in "promoting children's curiosity and persistence by directing their attention, structuring their experiences, supporting their learning attempts, and regulating the complexity and difficulty of levels of information for them" (National Research Council, 2000, p. 235). In the case of the science classroom, both teachers and peers can and must fill these critical roles.

A major problem with assuming children's capacity for sophisticated reasoning will unfold with minimal support is that what they are capable of doing without instruction may lag considerably behind what they are capable of doing with effective instruction. In fact, there is more information from research about starting points than about children's potential for developing scientific proficiency under effective instructional conditions. There are very few examples of what students may be capable of by the end of eighth grade if they experience effective science instruction from the time they enter school.

> *Conclusion 4: Students' knowledge and experience play a critical role in their science learning, influencing all four strands of science understanding. Children's concepts can be both resources and barriers to emerging understanding. These concepts can be enriched and transformed by appropriate classroom experiences. Science learners require instructional support to engage in scientific practices and to interpret experience and experiments in terms of scientific ideas.*

Children's rich but naïve understandings of the natural world can be built on to develop their understandings of scientific concepts. Some areas of knowledge may provide more robust foundations to build on than others, because they appear very early and appear to have some universal characteristics across cultures throughout the world. Young children, even infants, track a wide range of relational and causal properties of the world around them. They tend to identify regularities in the world around them that can be linked to broad domains, such as physical mechanics and the living world. Various aspects of scientific thinking and investigation are also closely tied to students' understanding of the natural phenomena being considered. For example, students' beliefs about the natural world shape the hypotheses they choose to pursue and the investigations they design to test them.

Children's understandings of the world sometimes contradict scientific explanations. These conceptions about the natural world can pose obstacles to learning science. However, their prior knowledge also offers leverage points that can be built on to develop their understanding of scientific concepts and their ability to engage in scientific investigations. Thus, children's prior knowledge must be taken into account in order to design instruction in strategic ways that capitalize on the leverage points and adequately address potential areas of misunderstanding.

Some aspects of modern scientific understanding are so counterintuitive and "unnatural" that a child is highly unlikely to arrive at that understanding without explicit instruction, for example, understanding atomic-molecular theory, plate tectonics, or genetics. There are also aspects of scientific thinking in which adults still demonstrate difficulty and require support to learn. These include differentiating theory and evidence, evaluating evidence that contradicts prior beliefs, and understanding how scientific knowledge is constructed.

To move to greater proficiency, students need help with learning how to engage in science and with connecting their own ideas to scientific explanations of the natural world. Thus, topics and specific investigations within those topics must be selected with great thoughtfulness and care, and the structure and sequence of those activities must be carefully planned. Young and novice students are likely to profit from study in areas in which their personal, prior experience with the natural world can be leveraged to connect with scientific ideas. They will also need teacher assistance to engage in and pursue fruitful scientific investigations.

Studies of instructional interventions carried out over weeks or months indicate that, with opportunities to practice or explicit instruction, even elementary and middle school children can master difficult concepts in science. However, to be successful, students need carefully structured experiences, scaffolded support from teachers, and opportunities for sustained engagement with the same set of ideas over extended periods of time (weeks, months, even years).

Current approaches to adjusting science instruction for young and novice learners may actually be counterproductive. For example, limiting them to learning about discrete science facts without opportunities for discussion, reflection, or direct investigation of the phenomena can lead to a very impoverished understanding of the ideas. Developing expertise in science means developing a rich interconnected set of concepts (a knowledge structure) that moves closer and closer to resembling the structure of knowledge in the science discipline. Memorizing lists of established scientific facts does not provide the kind of engagement with ideas that will produce rich, interconnected knowledge and reasoning.

Conclusion 5: Proficiency in science involves having knowledge of facts and concepts as well as how these ideas and concepts are related to each other. Thus, to become more expert in science, students need to learn key ideas and concepts, how they are related to each other, and their implications and applications within the discipline. This entails a process of

*conceptual development that in some cases involves large-scale reorga-
nization of knowledge and is not a simple accumulation of information.
Such deep conceptual change is achieved more successfully when students receive instruction that integrates the four strands.*

The difference between students who are less or more proficient in
science is not only that the latter know more discrete facts. Instead, gains in
proficiency often consist of changes in the organization of knowledge, not
just the accretion of more pieces of knowledge. Learning an unfamiliar concept requires students to come to understand the concept's appropriate implications and applications. Moreover, enough of the surrounding conceptual or theoretical framework must be in place and understood so that students'
interpretation of the new concept will be appropriately constrained. When
students develop a coherent understanding of the organizing principles of
science, they are more likely to be able to apply their knowledge appropriately and will learn new, related material more effectively. Knowledge of the
salient factual details is necessary but not sufficient for developing an understanding of the discipline and its core ideas and principles.

Conceptual development can occur in many different ways, and some
conceptual changes are more challenging than others. For example, when
children develop commonsense frameworks that deviate substantially from
those proposed by scientists, a considerable amount of conceptual work is
required to achieve knowledge restructuring. Part of the difficulty of learning a new concept is letting go of a familiar but incorrect set of ideas. Major
changes in conceptual frameworks are often difficult to grasp because they
require learners to break out of their familiar frame and reorganize a body of
knowledge, often in ways that draw on unfamiliar ideas. Making these changes
is facilitated when students engage in metacognitively guided learning, when
teachers use a variety of techniques (such as bridging analogies, thought
experiments, and imagistic reasoning) to help students construct an understanding of new concepts, and when students have opportunities to strengthen
their understanding of the new ideas through extended application and
argumentation.

Learning science is often characterized as increasing what one knows
about concepts, ideas, and issues associated with science-related topics. Science in school is often presented as a rather flat, nonhierarchical list of
unrelated concepts. This approach is driven by an assumption that the simple
accumulation of ideas or facts increases knowledge or understanding. This
narrow construal of knowing science as simply knowing facts or understanding a specific causal mechanism can lead to underestimating the rich
knowledge of the natural world children bring to school. It also may cause
teachers to ignore the sophisticated cognitive capacities that children have
available to them that can allow them to build new knowledge. Moreover, it

underestimates what it takes for students to be able to go beyond simply repeating the memorized facts to understanding their implications in contexts beyond those in which the ideas were originally encountered.

Conclusion 6: Race/ethnicity, language, culture, gender, and socioeconomic status are among the factors that influence the knowledge and experience children bring to the classroom. This diversity offers richness and opportunities in the classroom, and it also affects the kinds of support children need to learn science.

The challenge of helping all students achieve proficiency in science is daunting in the context of an increasingly diverse student population and persistent gaps in science achievement. Children's experience varies with their cultural, linguistic, and economic background. For example, cultural differences in discourse patterns are well documented, and some students' norms for discussion and social interaction may actually be at odds with the norms in scientific practice. Such differences mean that students arrive in the classroom with varying levels of experience with science and varying degrees of comfort with the norms of scientific practice.

It may be hard for teachers to recognize the strengths that diverse learners bring to the science classroom. For example, differences among students in norms for discourse, lack of familiarity with scientific terms, or limited proficiency in English may produce the impression that some students are unable to be successful in science. However, all students bring basic reasoning skills, personal knowledge of the natural world, and curiosity, which can be built on to achieve proficiency in science. Capitalizing on these resources requires teacher sensitivity to cultural and other background differences and willingness and skill to adjust instruction in light of these differences. Adjusting for variation in students' background and experience does not mean dumbing down the science curriculum or instruction provided to certain groups of students, for example, by reducing science to sheer memorization of facts and terms.

Curriculum and Instruction

Conclusion 7: Many existing national, state, and local standards and assessments, as well as the typical curricula in use in the United States, contain too many disconnected topics given equal priority. Too little attention is given to how students' understanding of a topic can be supported and enhanced from grade to grade. As a result, topics receive repeated, shallow coverage with little consistency, which provides a fragile foundation for further knowledge growth.

Comparisons of science standards and curricula in the United States with that of countries that perform well on international science tests reveal overly broad and superficial coverage of science topics in U.S. classrooms, with little attention to building links across concepts or developing a specific concept over successive grades. Furthermore, national standards documents in the United States have a circular pattern, in which almost all concepts are covered at every grade level. This is in contrast to high-achieving countries that follow a more "spiral" curriculum, in which more challenging concepts are introduced gradually over successive grades.

Science textbooks suffer from similar problems. They tend to cover many more topics than those used in high-achieving countries. Close analysis of middle school textbooks indicates that science topics are presented as a list of unrelated items with little or no regard to the relations among them. Textbooks and the accompanying classroom activities are not consistently framed around the central ideas in the disciplines. Such organization of both standards and curricula does not match what is known about how best to facilitate student learning.

> *Conclusion 8: Sustained exploration of a focused set of core ideas in a discipline is a promising direction for organizing science instruction and curricula across grades K-8. A research and development program is needed to identify and elaborate the progressions of learning and instruction that can support students' understanding of these core ideas. The difficult issue is deciding what to emphasize and what to eliminate.*

Findings from research about children's learning and development can be used to map learning progressions in science. That is, one can describe the successively more sophisticated ways of thinking about a topic that can follow and build on one another as children learn about and investigate a topic over a broad span of time (e.g., 6 to 8 years). Steps in these progressions are constrained by children's knowledge and skill with respect to each of the four strands. Reaching the hypothetical steps described in the progressions is also dependent on teachers' knowledge and the effectiveness of their instructional practices.

The emerging research on learning progressions offers insight into how curricula, and accompanying systems for assessment, might be reorganized to better support science learning. For example, such sequences could be organized around a few central ideas in science that would be studied and developed in depth and at increasing levels of complexity across succeeding grade levels. They would be anchored at one end by what is known about the reasoning of students entering school and at the other end by expectations about what society wants middle school students to understand about science. The best candidates for the scientific ideas on which to build learning progressions are those that are central to a discipline of science, are accessible to students in some form starting in kindergarten, and have potential for sustained exploration across grades K-8.

> *Conclusion 9: Students learn science by actively engaging in the practices of science. A classroom environment that provides opportunities for students to participate in scientific practices includes scientific tasks embedded in social interaction using the discourse of science and work with scientific representations and tools. Each of these aspects requires support for student learning of scientific practices.*

The view of science as practice is emerging from research on the work of scientists as well as from research on student learning in the classroom. In this view, theory development and reasoning are components of a large ensemble of activities that includes conducting investigations; networks of participants and institutions; specialized ways of talking and writing; modeling using mechanical, mathematical, or computer-based models; and development of representations of phenomena. To develop proficiency in science, students must participate in the full range of practices.

> *Conclusion 10: Frequently, K-8 classroom investigations treat data collection and analysis as the end game of science. Instead, science is, and should be presented as, a process of building theories and models, checking them for internal consistency and coherence, and testing them empirically. Method should follow from theory, therefore presentation of scientific methodology should consider a broad range of methods, including acquiring and interpreting observational data and modeling (an important research method in astronomy, the earth sciences, and evolutionary biology), which should be reflected in the experiences provided in K-8 classrooms.*

Current science education tends to overemphasize experiment relative to the wide array of forms of scientific investigation that are in use in the sciences. Although experimentation is one fundamental form of investigation in science, it is by no means the sole or definitive means. An overemphasis on recipes for data collection procedures—whether experimental, observational, or archival—may strengthen the misconceptions that some students hold about the so-called scientific method—the image that scientific discoveries emerge unproblematically if one just faithfully follows the steps outlined in the science text. The tendency for science in school to use highly structured investigations often aimed at verifying established scientific principles exacerbates this problem.

Forms of descriptive science that rely on planned and structured observation and modeling are important ways to conduct science that are also accessible to elementary and middle school students. Moreover, some sciences, such as evolutionary biology and geology, rely heavily on historical reconstruction, a form of scientific inquiry that is underrepresented in school science.

Conclusion 11: The artificial dichotomy that pits teacher-directed instruction against discovery learning is not productive. A range of instructional approaches is necessary as part of a full development of the four strands. All students need to experience these different approaches.

Instruction occurs in sequences of designed, strategic encounters between students and science. Any given unit of study may include episodes that are highly teacher-directed as well as structured student-led activities. Across time, quality instruction should promote a sense of science as a meaningful process of building and improving knowledge and understanding. Students may generate researchable questions, design methods of interrogating these, conduct data analysis, and debate interpretations of data. Individual lessons may also focus on discrete questions, concepts, facts, or methods of investigation.

Instruction can make science processes more explicit for learners. Instruction may illustrate for students how to engage in science processes, learn to do them more effectively, and develop better understanding of the content they are investigating. Instructional supports can be designed with conceptual models or dynamic simulations that make science concepts more transparent for learners, helping them bridge from their prior understandings to more sophisticated scientific understandings.

Sustained investigations serve as a way of sidestepping the common tendency to treat content and process as separable goals. In these investigations, students both develop knowledge and explanations of the natural world and generate and interpret evidence. These investigations must be carefully selected to link to important scientific ideas. If not, hands-on investigations can turn into mindless, fun activity with little connection to important ideas in science.

Designing these contexts requires careful attention to learning goals and instructional support for engaging in the practices of science. Forms of support that have been effective include highlighting the structure of scientific tasks, modeling and shaping scientific discourse, and encouraging students to articulate and reflect on both the process and products of investigation. Without support, students may have difficulty in finding meaning in their investigations, or they may fail to see why and how they are relevant to their other ongoing work in the science classroom.

Conclusion 12: Ongoing assessment is an integral part of instruction that can foster student learning when appropriately designed and used regularly. Assessments, whether formative or summative, need to be responsive to the full range of proficiencies that are implied by the strands. Assessment needs to be aligned with the research on students' thinking as well as informed by the structure of the subject matter.

Planning, evaluating, and improving the quality of science instruction is contingent on accurately assessing students' knowledge and skills and how these develop over time. Individual teachers can conduct assessment to gauge student learning through the activities they use regularly in the course of instruction (e.g., questioning strategies, discussion, analysis of student work). Schools and school systems can administer periodic benchmarking assessments to track student learning over time and provide teachers with feedback, including suggested modifications to instruction. Well-designed assessment can have tremendous impact on students' learning of science if conducted regularly and used by teachers to alter and improve instruction.

Teachers and Schools

Conclusion 13: To create a successful science classroom, teachers need to modify and adapt curriculum materials so as to design instruction that is appropriate for a particular group of students at a particular time. Making these kinds of modifications to achieve effective instruction requires knowledge of science, knowledge of how students learn science, and knowledge of how to plan effective instruction. Many K-8 teachers have insufficient knowledge in one or all of these areas and need ongoing support to develop it.

The demands on teachers of providing effective science instruction are immense. As no curriculum can remove teacher decision making from instruction, enacting high-quality science instruction broadly will require dramatic improvements in all three areas of teacher knowledge.

First, teachers must understand the science they teach broadly and deeply, including mastery of the four strands of proficiency we have described for student learners. This broad understanding of science is not readily supported by the typical undergraduate science courses provided for aspiring teachers. Accordingly, although increasing the undergraduate science course requirements for prospective teachers may bolster teacher knowledge in some important ways, it is unlikely to provide them with sufficient understanding of science unless the courses are redesigned.

Second, teachers need to understand the current intellectual capabilities and developmental trajectories of their students. As instruction should tap students' existing and emergent skills and build on their conceptual knowledge base, teachers need to understand how students think, what they are capable of doing, and what they could reasonably be expected to do under supportive instructional conditions, and how to make science more accessible and relevant to them.

Third, teachers need specialized science knowledge about teaching science in order to bring their understanding of science and students' capabilities together in well-crafted learning experiences. To plan instruction and monitor student progress, teachers need to understand how to elicit and interpret students' understanding. They must be able to harness their understanding to inform instruction both in real time and throughout the academic year. They need to understand what students find confusing or difficult as well as what they find interesting. Furthermore, teachers need a repertoire of instructional strategies, curricular examples, and knowledge of curricular and reference materials to draw on in planning and providing instruction.

Developing these three areas of knowledge requires professional development that is both rich in science content and closely linked to teachers' classroom practice.

> *Conclusion 14: Achieving science proficiency for all students will require a coherent system that aligns standards, curriculum, instruction, assessment, teacher preparation, and professional development for teachers across the K-8 years.*

In effective science classrooms, curriculum, instruction, and assessment form an instructional system that is integrated. In these classrooms, students encounter a curriculum that engages them with scientific knowledge and practice in challenging and stimulating ways and flows logically and coherently across grades K-8. Current science curriculum standards have provided some focus and long-term vision for curriculum sequencing. However, they are still too numerous, loosely integrated across topics and aspects of science (e.g., inquiry practices and science concepts), and insufficiently specified to drive a cohesive instructional system. Moreover, new research on student learning suggests that there are areas in which the standards underestimate students' capabilities to learn and do science.

A well-designed instructional system provides students with opportunities to learn science that are aligned with summative assessments. In these systems, day-to-day instructional decisions are informed by classroom-based formative and benchmarking assessment practices that provide snapshots of students' emerging understanding.

Professional development that supports quality science instruction is ongoing, rooted in the science that teachers teach, and relevant to their classroom contexts. It provides teachers with opportunities to think and work collectively on instructional problems, supporting their efforts to tailor curriculum and instruction to classroom contexts. Professional development that supports instructional improvement rests on school- and system-level commitments that are manifest in actively involved leadership and the establishment of regular times throughout the school day for teachers' collaboration.

Diversity and Equity in Science Education

The committee is unanimous in emphasizing the pressing need to understand the sources of inequity in science education and to identify strategies for eradicating these inequities. However, we concluded that, given the complexity of the issue and the state of the evidence base, it would be premature to formulate a set of specific findings and recommendations in this area.

The committee began its deliberations with a focus on learning and instruction at the classroom level. The evidence makes clear that all students, regardless of background, have the capabilities needed to engage with and be successful in science. Evidence from research also indicates that students from varied cultural, linguistic, and socioeconomic backgrounds bring different resources to the classroom, which must be attended to in instruction (see Conclusion 6). In fact, many studies demonstrate that it is possible for traditionally underserved children to learn science with understanding with improved instruction. Yet there is little or no agreement in the literature about the degree to which instruction should be modified for children from different backgrounds, nor what such modifications should look like. For this reason, the committee was unable to arrive at conclusions or recommendations related to instruction for diverse student populations. We did agree, however, that further research is needed to examine the effectiveness of different instructional approaches, whether these approaches are complementary or competing, and whether each approach is more effective in different instructional contexts (see the section below called "Agenda for Research and Development" for further discussion).

As the committee began to look beyond instruction to consider additional sources of achievement gaps and inequities in science education, the importance of systemic issues—such as inequities across schools in qualifications of teachers, facilities, and resources—became apparent. As we began to explore the relevant research literature, it became clear that it is difficult to tease out which systemic issues are unique to science education and which are pervasive issues that cut across all subject areas. What is more, the complex interplay among cultural, linguistic, and socioeconomic issues is difficult to document and understand. Given the scope of this study and limited time, the committee was unable to undertake a thorough review of this body of evidence. For these reasons, we did not develop conclusions or recommendations related to the systemic issues that contribute to inequities in science education. We stress that inequities in the quality of instruction, the qualifications of teachers, resources, facilities, and time devoted to science are unacceptable and must be addressed. We identify this as a critical area for further research (see research agenda section below for further discussion). While current research does not provide sufficient guidance we urge policy makers, education leaders, and school administrators to join researchers in examining and revising policies and practices in schools and districts so that existing inequities are better understood and can be eliminated.

RECOMMENDATIONS FOR POLICY AND PRACTICE

Based on our findings and conclusions, a new view of science education is needed for K-8 schools. It should build on the new insights and reconceptualizations about how children learn science provided by the past 30 years of research in cognitive and developmental psychology and science education. These insights about learning require changes in standards, curricula, instruction, and assessment so that they are organized around the four-strand model of science learning and build the core ideas of science in a cumulative fashion across the K-8 grades. In this section, the committee lays out key steps toward realizing this new vision of science education.

Our recommendations for action are grounded in the evidence base reviewed in this report. However, in some areas the research base is not robust enough to offer a detailed, step-by-step roadmap for improving all aspects of science education. Given the urgent need for improvement and the potential power of approaches identified in emergent research, the committee focused on "best bets" for the next steps of policy, research, and practice. These best bets represent the most promising directions forward, based on the best research evidence available. They require additional documentation through continued research and careful evaluation of implementation. Through a substantial research and development effort that includes evaluation of school, district, and state initiatives, these best bets can be transformed into well-researched alternatives for policy and practice.

In framing our recommendations for policy and practice, the committee takes the perspective that science standards, curriculum, assessment, instruction, and teacher professional development should be conceived of, designed, and implemented as a coordinated system. In this view, standards and curriculum should lay out specific, coherent goals for important scientific ideas and practices that can be realized through sustained instruction over several years of K-8 schooling. Assessment should provide teachers and students with timely feedback about students' emergent thinking that, in turn, supports teachers' efforts to improve instruction. Teacher preparation and professional development should be focused on developing teachers' knowledge of the science they teach, how students learn science, and specific methods and technologies that support science learning for all students.

Standards, Curricula, and Assessment: What to Teach and When

Recommendation 1: Developers of standards, curriculum, and assessment need to revise their frameworks to reflect new models of children's thinking and take better advantage of children's capabilities. Standards and many widely used curriculum materials fail to reflect new evidence about children's thinking, particularly the cognitive capabilities of younger children, which are greater than previously assumed.

Recommendation 2: The committee thinks that the next generation of standards and curricula at both the national and state levels should be structured to identify a few core ideas in a discipline and elaborate how these ideas can be grown in a cumulative manner over grades K-8. Focusing on core ideas requires eliminating ideas that are less central to the development of science understanding. Selection of the core ideas should be guided by their status as foundational ideas in the disciplines of science that connect to many related scientific ideas, as well as the potential for sustained exploration at increasingly sophisticated levels across grades K-8. While existing national and state standards have been a critical first step in narrowing the focus of science in grades K-8, they do not go far enough. Future revisions to the national standards—and the subsequent interpretation of these standards at the state and local levels and by curriculum developers—need to clearly identify the knowledge and practices that are most central to the disciplines and describe how these can be developed over successive grades based on current models of children's learning.

Recommendation 3: Developers of curricula and standards need to present science as a process of building theories and models using evidence, checking them for internal consistency and co-

herence, and testing them empirically. To this end, discussions of scientific methodology need be introduced in the context of pursuing specific questions and issues rather than as templates or invariant recipes. Similarly, the methodology students encounter in the classroom needs to reflect the range of investigatory forms in science. This requires expanding beyond a focus on experiments to incorporate examples from disciplines of science that employ observational methods or historical reconstruction.

Instruction: How to Teach

Recommendation 4: Science instruction should provide opportunities for students to engage in all four strands. This requires policy makers, education leaders, and school administrators to ensure that adequate time and resources are provided for science instruction at all grade levels for all students. They must also ensure that teachers have adequate knowledge of science content and are provided with adequate professional development.

Recommendation 5: State and local leaders in science education should provide teachers with models of classroom instruction that incorporate the four strands. These models should incorporate examples of instruction that provide opportunities for interaction in the classroom, where students carry out investigations and talk and write about their observations of phenomena, their emerging understanding of scientific ideas, and ways to test them.

Professional Development: Supporting Effective Science Instruction

We call for a dramatic departure from typical professional development practice both in scope and kind. Teachers need opportunities to deepen their knowledge of the science content of the K-8 curriculum. They also need opportunities to learn how students learn science and how to teach it. Teachers need to know how children's understanding of core ideas in science builds across K-8, not just at a given grade or grade band. They need to learn about students' entering conceptual ideas and ideas about science itself. They need to learn how to assess children's developing ideas over time and how to interpret and respond (instructionally) to the results of assessment. Teachers need opportunities to teach science as an integrated body of knowledge and practice (the strands of scientific proficiency).

Teacher preparation and professional development that sensitize teachers to the capabilities of all learners and which develop teachers' capacity to effectively teach science to diverse student populations are urgently needed. In order to provide adequate opportunities for all students to learn science, teachers need preparation and professional development in how to respond to variation among students. They also need to know how to recognize and build on the strengths and needs that students of diverse cultural and linguistic backgrounds bring to the classroom. This should be a central feature of science teacher preparation courses and ongoing teacher professional development.

Providers of professional development should align their programs with the key conclusions and recommendations in this report. They should pay particular attention to the four strands of scientific proficiency, building on core ideas in science over long periods of time, and current research on how students learn science.

> **Recommendation 6: State and local school systems should ensure that all K-8 teachers experience sustained science-specific professional development in preparation and while in service. Professional development should be rooted in the science that teachers teach and should include opportunities to learn about science, about current research on how children learn science, and about how to teach science.**

> **Recommendation 7: University-based science courses for teacher candidates and teachers' ongoing opportunities to learn science in service should mirror the opportunities they will need to provide for their students, that is, incorporating practices in all four strands and giving sustained attention to the core ideas in the discipline. The topics of study should be aligned with central topics in the K-8 curriculum so that teachers come to appreciate the development of concepts and practices that appear across all grades.**

> **Recommendation 8: Federal agencies that fund providers of professional development should design funding programs that require applicants to incorporate models of instruction that combine the four strands, focus on core ideas in science, and enhance teachers' science content knowledge, knowledge of how students learn science, and knowledge of how to teach science.**

AGENDA FOR RESEARCH AND DEVELOPMENT

In our synthesis of the research evidence, we have drawn on varied programs of research across multiple fields, all of which can be brought to bear on the question of how children learn science. Integrating across bodies of evidence is necessary because the problem of how best to design science instruction to support a deep understanding of science is inherently interdisciplinary. In some cases the committee considered programs of research that were explicitly concerned with science learning and instruction in school settings. In other cases the research was designed to investigate fundamental questions about how children come to understand and respond to the world around them. Making sense of such a broad body of research that is often informed by different theories and different methodologies is challenging.

A critical question for continuing to advance understanding of how to support science learning and instruction in schools is how to organize programs of research so that they explicitly address problems of educational practice in schools while advancing fundamental understanding of children's learning in science. Two key elements of such a program that need to be thought through are (1) What is the nature of the teams of individuals who should be brought together to conduct this work? and (2) How can some common intellectual ground be developed so that a dialogue can begin across the varied research traditions?

The committee agrees that there is a glaring lack of an infrastructure for research, development, and implementation in science education that is informed by research on fundamental aspects of learning and teaching but takes up problems and questions that are grounded in the realities of practice. This research and development effort must be closely tied to schools and classrooms. Research and development partnerships must include teachers, administrators, curriculum developers, providers of professional development, and district- and state-level supervisors. Funding streams must support studies at various levels, including design and development work to identify promising approaches, small-scale testing of initial concepts under controlled conditions to establish viability, classroom-based research in a few classrooms or schools, replication to explore the implications of varying conditions, longitudinal studies, and finally implementation and evaluation on a large scale.

Critical Areas for Research and Development

Learning Across the Four Strands

The four-strand framework represents a departure from the way research on science learning has been organized in the past. Researchers have tended to focus on either domain-specific learning or domain-general reasoning related to Strands 1 and 2 in our model. More recent work has begun to look at Strands 3 and 4, and further research is needed in these areas. For example, an area that needs increasing attention is related to students' understanding of how scientific knowledge is constructed and how they come to understand and negotiate different knowledge communities. That is, how do children start to navigate the terrain of knowledge around them? How do they know who is credible and who is not? How do they determine who is a trustworthy source? Also of interest is a related set of questions about students' understanding of the status of their own knowledge, such as, How do you know when you don't know?

Much more research is also needed to further elaborate the interconnections between the four strands—for example, studies of the interplay between domain-specific and domain-general knowledge over the course of development. Understanding interconnections between the strands and how instruction might better leverage these interconnections is of particular interest for informing instructional models based on the four strands.

Identifying Core Ideas and Developing Learning Progressions

Developing learning progressions to structure science standards, curricula, instruction, and assessment is a promising direction for science education, but an extensive research and development effort is needed before learning progressions are well established and tested. A major first step is to identify the most generative and powerful core ideas for students' science learning (i.e., those that have broad reach across science disciplines and provide the best leverage for students' future study of science) through a cross-disciplinary research program. From these core ideas a series of learning progressions can be developed and tested. Research and development necessary to establish the empirical basis for learning progressions across the domains of science will need to include multiple phases, including focused studies of children's learning under controlled conditions, small-scale instructional interventions, classroom-based studies in a variety of contexts, and longitudinal studies.

Longitudinal studies over multiple ages are particularly important. In a given domain and across domains, a better understanding is needed of continuities and discontinuities in students' understanding across grades K-8. That is, what are the legacies of early development, and what is new and different as children develop and encounter different experiences both inside and outside the classroom? What are the mechanisms behind the changes? Finally, for a given set of related concepts, the research should examine the trade-offs of different learning sequences or instructional approaches as well as the instructional support needed to help students move through the progression.

Curriculum and Instruction

Studies of instruction and the links to student learning are needed to develop instructional models that integrate the four strands. Research is also needed to develop a better understanding of whether and how instruction should change with children's development. Clear depictions of scientific practice across K-8 and variations among particular practices across consecutive years of instruction (e.g., younger versus older children's argumentation) should be developed. One mechanism for deepening the understanding of effective instruction is through replication of classroom-based research on instruction (e.g., design studies). Two additional areas of particular need are (1) the development of tools to help teachers diagnose students' understanding and cue-productive instructional options for teachers to advance it and (2) the characteristics of instruction that best serve diverse student populations.

Research on curriculum materials is also a critical area. Such studies should systematically analyze the effects on learning of variation in conditions, such as student populations, school settings, teacher knowledge, and forms of professional development, as well as the dimensions on which curricula vary (i.e., comparing curriculum focused on content knowledge, on contextualized science problems, on modeling). Longitudinal studies of different curriculum approaches under varied conditions would be particularly useful.

Professional Development and Teacher Learning

A substantial commitment is needed to empirical research on the practices of building expertise in science teaching. These include using science specialist teachers (in K-5), mentoring, teacher work groups, instructional materials designed to support teacher learning, and long-term professional development. It is important to understand how local circumstances enable or limit the effect of these models. This research needs to establish an empirical relationship between professional development and student learning.

Evaluation and Scale-Up

Evaluation of current and emerging instructional practices and curriculum materials is a critical part of the research and development cycle. We stress that it is preferable to develop a substantial research base documenting the effectiveness of a particular approach before it is taken to scale. Often, however, this is either not done in practice, or it is not feasible given the pressing needs of schools and districts for immediate solutions. In such cases, systematic evaluation efforts should be tied to large-scale implementation of instructional practices and curriculum materials that are widely implemented before adequate small-scale testing is complete. Such evaluations must be carried out in partnerships with school systems and states. Capitalizing on the increased availability of student data due to the reporting demands of the No Child Left Behind Act of 2001 (H.R. 1) might be a useful way to investigate the impact of particular approaches at scale.

Diversity and Equity

Research on supporting science learning for culturally, linguistically, and socioeconomically diverse students is an area of critical need. This includes research on instruction, curriculum assessment, and professional development. For example, alternative instructional approaches have been proposed to promote science learning with nonmainstream students with promising results. Further research is needed to examine the effectiveness of each approach, whether these approaches are complementary or competing, and whether each approach is more effective in different instructional contexts. In addition, research on curriculum models that incorporate effective approaches to instruction for diverse students is necessary.

More work is also needed on understanding systemic factors involved in creating inequitable learning opportunities in science. For example, differences across schools in teacher qualifications, resources devoted to science, and time for science instruction should be explored. The interactions of culture, ethnicity, language, and socioeconomic status in shaping students' opportunities to learn science are also important areas for further research.

We live in a time when science is a ubiquitous part of civic and political life. The pressing issues of today—global warming, pandemics, alternative fuels, use of biometric information to fight terrorism—require a scientifically informed citizenry as never before in the nation's history. Calls for a better prepared scientific and technical workforce have become more urgent in the context of increasing globalization and fears that a diminished capacity for innovation will make the United States less competitive in a global market. With the convergence of these issues, the quality of science education in this country takes on tremendous importance. Yet students' performance in science is disappointing, and recent improvement efforts have proven insufficient. What is more, non-Asian minority and disadvantaged students are consistently among the bottom-performing groups, trailing economically advantaged and white students. Such achievement gaps are unacceptable in view of the increasing diversity of the American population, the reality that science permeates society at all levels, and overwhelming evidence that children from all backgrounds have the capacity to become proficient in science.

To improve science education in the United States, changes are urgently needed throughout the system. The evidence reviewed in this report provides a compelling framework for how science education can be reshaped to take account of research on how best to support children's science learning. Admittedly, further research is needed, especially to advance the strands framework, elaborate the learning progressions, increase understanding of effective approaches to instructional design, and determine how best to support teachers. Nevertheless, the research base reveals that current approaches are inadequate, and it provides a roadmap for moving forward. Beginning with what is now known about how children learn science, the direction for teaching and for the education of teachers is clear.

Appendixes

Appendix A

Overview of Learning Progressions for Matter and the Atomic-Molecular Theory

Questions & Big Ideas[a]	Components of Big Ideas	K-2 Elaboration of Big Ideas
1. What are things made of and how can we explain their properties? **1. Objects[b] are constituted of matter, which exists as many different material kinds. Objects have properties that can be measured and depend on the amount of matter and on the material kinds they are made of.**	**Existence of matter and diversity of material kinds.**	Objects are made of specific materials. There are different kinds of materials. The same kind of object can be made of different materials.
	Objects have properties that can be measured and explained. Three important properties are mass, weight, and volume.	Objects have certain properties—weight, length, area, and volume—that can be described, compared and measured. (Only preliminary exploration and construction of volume measurement at this time.)
	Material kinds have characteristic properties that can be measured and explained.	The properties of materials can be described and classified. (Only readily observable properties, such as color, hardness, flexibility, are investigated at this time.)

3-5 Elaboration of Big Ideas	6-8 Elaboration of Big Ideas
Objects are made of matter that takes up space and has weight.	Matter has mass, volume, and weight (in a gravitational field), and exists in three general phases, solids, liquids, and gas.
Solids, liquids, and air are forms of matter and share these general properties.	
There can be invisible pieces of matter (too small to see).	Materials can be elements, compounds, or mixtures.
There are many different kinds of materials.	**1AM. All matter is made of a limited number of different kinds of atoms, which are commonly bonded together in molecules and networks. Each atom takes up space, has mass, and is in constant motion.**
Weight is an additive property of objects that can be measured (e.g., the weight of an object is the sum of the weight of its parts).	Mass is a measure of amount of matter and is constant across location; weight is a force, proportional to mass and varies with gravitational field.
Volume is an additive property of an object that can be measured.	Solids, liquids, and gases have different properties.
The weight of an object is a function of its volume and the material it is made of.	**1AM. The mass and weight of an object is explained by the masses and weights of its atoms. The different motions and interactions of atoms in solids, liquids, and gases help explain their different properties.**
Materials have characteristic properties that are independent of the size of the sample.	Materials have characteristic properties independent of size of sample (extends knowledge to include boiling/freezing points and to elaborate on density).
(Extends knowledge to less obvious properties such as density, flammability, or conductivity at this time.)	**1AM. The properties of materials are determined by the nature, arrangement, and motion of the molecules that they are made of.**

Questions & Big Ideas	Components of Big Ideas	K-2 Elaboration of Big Ideas
2. What changes and what stays the same when things are transformed? **2. Matter can be transformed, but not created or destroyed, through physical and chemical processes.**	**Mass and weight are conserved across a broad range of transformations.**	There are some transformations (e.g., reshaping, breaking into pieces) where the amount of stuff and weight is conserved despite changes in perceptual appearance.
	Material kinds stay the same across some transformations and change across others.	Material kind stays the same when objects are reshaped or broken into small pieces. Freezing and melting changes some properties of materials but not others.

3-5 Elaboration of Big Ideas	6-8 Elaboration of Big Ideas
Matter continues to exist when broken into pieces too tiny to be visible. Amount of matter and weight are conserved across a broader range of transformations (e.g., melting, freezing, and dissolving).	Mass and weight (but not volume) are conserved across chemical changes, dissolving, phase change, and thermal expansion. **2AM: Mass and weight are conserved in physical and chemical changes because atoms are neither created nor destroyed.**
Materials can be changed from solid to liquid (and vice versa) by heating (or cooling) but are still the same kind of material. Combining two or more materials can produce a product with properties different from those of the initial materials.	Some transformations involve chemical change (e.g., burning, rusting) in which new substances, as indicated by their different properties, are created. In other changes (e.g., phase change, thermal expansion) materials may change appearance but the substances in them stay the same. **2AM: In chemical changes new substances are formed as atoms are rearranged into new molecules. The atoms themselves remain intact.** **2AM: In physical changes, molecules change arrangement and/or motion but remain intact, so the chemical substance remains the same.**

Questions & Big Ideas	Components of Big Ideas	K-2 Elaboration of Big Ideas
3. How do we know? **3. We can learn about the world through measurement, modeling, and argument.**	**Good measurements provide more reliable and useful information about object properties than common-sense impressions.**	Measurement involves comparison. Good measurements use iterations of a fixed unit (including fractional parts of that unit) to cover the measured space completely (no gaps). Measurements are more reliable than common-sense impressions.
	Modeling is concerned with capturing key relations among ideas rather than surface appearance.	Some properties of objects can be analyzed as the sum of component units. (Students are involved with the implicit modeling of extensive quantities through the creation of measures.)
	Arguments use reasoning to connect ideas and data.	Ideas can be evaluated through observation and measurement.

[a]In this table, the term "big idea" corresponds to "core idea" used throughout the report. The committee adopted the term core idea to differentiate the learning progressions idea from other initiatives that use the term big idea.
[b]As mentioned in the text, we use the term "object" in the broad sense to refer to any bounded material entity, not just solids.
SOURCE: Smith et al. (2006).

3-5 Elaboration of Big Ideas	6-8 Elaboration of Big Ideas
Although measurements are more reliable than commonsense impressions, measurements can be more or less precise and there is always some measurement error. Instruments, such as microscopes, can extend our ability to observe and measure.	Our senses respond to combinations of physical properties, rather than isolated ones. For this reason, they are not good measures of those physical properties. Sources of measurement error can be examined and quantified. We can learn about the properties of things through indirect measurement (e.g., water displacement) as well as using powerful tools (microscopes). **3AM. Atoms are too small to see directly with commonly available tools.**
Graphs, visual models, simple algebraic formulas, or quantitative verbal statements can be used to represent inter-relations among variables and to make predictions about one variable from knowledge of others.	Models can propose unseen entities to explain a pattern of data. **3AM: The properties of and changes in atoms and molecules have to be distinguished from the macroscopic properties and phenomena for which they account.**
Hypotheses and data are distinct. We make stronger arguments for our ideas when they fit a pattern of data rather than simply one observation. We can clarify our ideas by more precisely stating the conditions under which they are true.	Good arguments involve getting data that help distinguish between competing explanations. **3AM. We learn about properties of atoms and molecules indirectly, using hypothetico-deductive reasoning.**

Appendix B

Biographical Sketches of Committee Members and Staff

Richard A. Duschl (*Chair*) is professor of science education at Rutgers University. Prior to joining the Rutgers faculty, he held the chair of science education at King's College London, and prior to that was professor of science education at Vanderbilt University. One focus of his research examines how the history and philosophy of science can be applied to science education. A second focus of his research is the design of instructional sequences that promote assessment for learning. This research has led to many new ideas about how formative assessment strategies can help learners and teachers make scientific thinking visible. He also has expertise in informal science education and in earth science education. Duschl publishes widely in U.S. and international journals on inquiry, science teaching, learning, cognition, and assessment. He has served as editor of *Science Education* and was a member of the National Research Council (NRC) committee that wrote the *Inquiry Addendum for the National Science Education Standards.* He has a Ph.D. from the University of Maryland at College Park.

Charles W. Anderson is a professor in the Department of Teacher Education at Michigan State University. Anderson's primary research interests are in using conceptual change and sociocultural research on student learning to improve classroom science teaching. He has published numerous articles and book chapters on this and related issues, as well as developing science teaching materials that are based on research on student learning. Anderson was coauthor of *Matter and Molecules,* Project 2061's top-rated middle school science teaching materials. He served as lead consultant to the state of Michigan for the development of its state science objectives. He also led the development of the life science component of the Michigan Educational Assessment Program. He is past president of the National Association for Research in Science Teaching. He has been coeditor of the *Journal of Research in Science Teaching* and associate editor of *Cognition and Instruction* and currently serves on the editorial board of the *American Educational Research Journal*. He recently served as design team member for the NRC's Committee on Test Design for K-12 Science Achievement. He has a Ph.D. in science education from the University of Texas at Austin.

Thomas B. Corcoran codirects the Consortium for Policy Research in Education at the University of Pennsylvania, where he has led evaluations of the Merck Institute for Science Education, the Annenberg Challenge in Philadelphia, team-based schooling in Cincinnati, and the America's Choice Comprehensive School Design. Previously, he served as the policy advisor for education for New Jersey Governor Jim Florio, director of school improvement for research for better schools, and director of evaluation and chief-of-staff of the New Jersey Department of Education. He is a member of the MacArthur Foundation's Network on Teaching and Learning and a member of the Research Committee of the International Baccalaureate Organization. His major research interests are the use of evidence to inform policy and practice in public education, policies for expanding access to challenging curriculum, the development and use of clinical expertise about teaching, the efficacy of different approaches to professional development, and the impact of changes in work environments on the productivity of teachers and students. He has an M.Ed. from the University of London (1963).

Kevin J. Crowley is associate professor of education and cognitive psychology at the University of Pittsburgh's Learning Research and Development Center, where he also directs the Center for Learning in Out-of-School Settings. His research interests focus on the development of children's scientific thinking in informal, formal, and everyday settings, focusing on how they develop knowledge and skill in such contexts as museums and on the web and how to best coordinate their experiences in science. He has been a visiting fellow at the Department of Psychology and Education at Nagoya University in Japan. He has a Ph.D. in psychology from Carnegie Mellon University (1994).

Frank C. Keil is professor of psychology and linguistics at Yale University and master of Morse College. Previously, he held the William R. Kenan, Jr., endowed chair in psychology at Cornell University. His research focuses on how people come to make sense of the world around them. Much of this research involves asking how intuitive explanations and understandings emerge in development and how they are related to notions of cause, mechanism, and agency. His work also explores how children and adults learn to navigate the division of cognitive labor that integrates both formal and informal scientific understanding. He received the National Institutes of Health multiyear MERIT award in 2003, which provides long-term support for outstanding investigators. He has been a Guggenheim fellow and a fellow at the Center for Advanced Study in the Behavioral Sciences. He has a Ph.D. in psychology, with an emphasis in developmental psychology, from the University of Pennsylvania (1977).

David Klahr is professor in the Department of Psychology at Carnegie Mellon University, where he served as department head from 1983 to 1993 and is currently director of the interdisciplinary Training Grant in Educational Research. His early work addressed cognitive processes in such diverse areas as multidimensional scaling, voting behavior, college admissions, consumer choice, peer review, and problem solving. He pioneered the application of information-processing analysis to questions of cognitive development, formulating the first computational models to account for children's thinking processes. His current research focuses on cognitive development, scientific reasoning, and cognitively based instructional interventions in early science education. He served on the NRC Committee on Research in Education and the committee responsible for the report *Knowing What Students Know.* He is currently on the governing board of the Cognitive Development Society and an associate editor for *Developmental Psychology.* He has a Ph.D. in organizations and social behavior from Carnegie Mellon University (1968).

Okhee Lee is a professor in the School of Education at the University of Miami, Florida. Her research areas of interest include science education, language and culture, and teacher education. One of her current research projects implements instructional interventions to promote science learning and English language and literacy development for elementary school students from diverse languages and cultures. She received a 1993-1995 National Academy of Education Spencer Post-doctoral Fellowship and was a 1996-1997 fellow at the National Institute for Science Education, Wisconsin Center for Education Research, University of Wisconsin-Madison. She serves on editorial boards for major education research journals as well as advisory boards for science education reform projects. Lee currently serves as a member of the NRC's Board on Science Education. Lee has a Ph.D. in educational psychology from Michigan State University (1989).

Daniel M. Levin is a science teacher at Montgomery Blair High School, an ethnically diverse school in the Washington, DC, area. He taught middle school science for a number of years and is now a high school biology and chemistry teacher. He is currently on leave from the school and is acting as a professional development school coordinator for the University of Maryland while he pursues an advanced degree there. He has also held positions as a research biologist at the National Institutes of Health and at Harvard University. He has undertaken a number of professional activities in science education, including serving as research assistant in the Cognition and Technology Laboratory at the University of Maryland, writing curricula in biology, and participating in a summer institute for teachers at the National Institutes of Diabetes, Digestive, and Kidney Research. He has a B.A. in biology and anthropology from Brandeis University and an M.A. in teaching from Towson State University, and he is currently pursuing a Ph.D. in science education at the University of Maryland.

Kathleen E. Metz is associate professor of cognition and development at the Graduate School of Education, University of California, Berkeley. Her research interests center on children's scientific cognition, where developmental and instructional perspectives intersect. She is also interested in children's intuitions about rudimentary statistical constructs that are involved in data-based inquiry. At the postdoctoral level, she studied cognitive development with Jean Piaget's successor, Bärbel Inhelder, at the University of Geneva, Switzerland, and she was an Alfred P. Sloan fellow in cognitive science, working with Herbert Simon at Carnegie Mellon University. Her career spans work as a classroom teacher, a curriculum developer, a teacher educator, and a cognitive science researcher. She serves on the advisory board of the National Sciences Resources Center. She served on the planning committee for the NRC workshop on Mathematical and Scientific Development in Early Childhood. She has an Ed.D. from the University of Massachusetts in human development and teacher education.

Helen R. Quinn is professor of physics at Stanford University, where she also serves as education outreach manager at the Stanford Linear Accelerator Center. Quinn is a theoretical physicist who was elected to the National Academy of Sciences in 2003. She was president of the American Physical Society in 2004. In addition to her scholarship in physics, Quinn is interested in science education and the continuing education of science teachers. She was an active contributor to the California State Science Standards development process. She is past president of the nonprofit Contemporary Physics Education Project. Previously she served as a member of the NRC's Committee on Physics of the Universe and on the Federal Coordinating Committee on Science, Mathematics and Technology Education. She has a Ph.D. in physics from Stanford University (1967).

Brian J. Reiser is professor of learning sciences at the School of Education and Social Policy at Northwestern University. His research concerns the design and study of investigation environments and inquiry support tools for science. These projects explore the design of computer-based learning environments that scaffold investigation and scientific argumentation about biological phenomena and the design of inquiry support tools that help students organize, reflect on, and communicate about the progress of their investigations. This work is being conducted as part of the initiatives of the Center for Learning Technologies in Urban Schools, which is working to understand how to make learning technologies a pervasive part of science classrooms in urban schools. Reiser is also a member of the core faculty of the Center for Curriculum Materials in Science, a collaboration of Project 2061, Michigan state, Northwestern University, and the University of Michigan. He serves on the editorial boards of *Interactive Learning Environments* and the *Journal of the Learning Sciences*. He recently served as a design team member for the NRC's Committee on Test Design for K-12 Science Achievement. He has a Ph.D. in psychology from Yale University (1983).

Deborah L. Roberts is an experienced teacher of elementary and middle school science who currently serves as science instructional specialist with the Montgomery County, Maryland, public schools. Until 2004, for many years, she taught science and mathematics in grades 1 through 8. In 2001 she was named Carnegie Academy for the Scholarship of Teaching and Learning K-12 scholar. Throughout her career as a classroom teacher, she has also been active in education research. She has presented research on teaching at the American Educational Research Association, the National Association for Research in Science Teaching, the National Science Teachers Association, and other national and regional science teaching and research venues. Her current position entails writing and developing curriculum with classroom teachers, training teachers in inquiry science teaching methods, and supervising elementary science instruction across the district. She also teaches pre-service courses in science curriculum and is currently pursuing a Ph.D. in science education at the University of Maryland, College Park.

Leona Schauble is professor of education at Vanderbilt University. Her research interests include the relations between everyday reasoning and more formal, culturally supported, and schooled forms of thinking, such as scientific and mathematical reasoning. Her research focuses on such topics as belief change in the contexts of scientific experimentation, everyday reasoning, causal inference, and the origins and development of model-based reasoning. Prior to her work at Vanderbilt, she worked at the University of Wisconsin, the Learning Research and Development Center at the University of Pittsburgh, and the Children's Television Workshop in New York. Schauble recently served as a member of the Strategic Educational Research Partnership, an NRC-affiliated venture designed to construct a powerful knowledge base, derived from both research and practice that will support the efforts of school people at all levels with the ultimate goal of significantly improving student learning. Schauble has a Ph.D. in developmental and educational psychology from Columbia University (1983).

Heidi A. Schweingruber *(Co-Study Director)* is a senior program officer for the Board on Science Education (BOSE). She was a program officer on the NRC study that produced *America's Lab Report: Investigations in High School Science* and is currently directing a congressionally mandated review of NASA's precollege education programs. Prior to joining the NRC, she was a senior research associate at the Institute of Education Sciences in the U.S. Department of Education where she served as a program officer for the preschool curriculum evaluation program and for a grant program in mathematics education. She was also a liaison to the Department of Education's Mathematics and Science Initiative and an adviser to the Early Reading First program. Before moving into policy work, she was the director of research for the Rice University School Mathematics Project, an outreach program in K-12 mathematics education, and taught in the psychology and education departments. She has a Ph.D. in psychology (developmental) and anthropology, and a certificate in culture and cognition from the University of Michigan (1997).

Andrew W. Shouse *(Co-Study Director)* is an educational researcher and policy analyst whose interests include teacher development, science education in formal and informal settings, and communication of educational research to policy and practice audiences. In his current position as senior program officer with the NRC's BOSE, he is director of Learning Science in Informal Environments, a synthesis study of the literatures on learning science in nonschool settings (sponsored by NSF). He is co-study director (with Heidi Schweingruber) of Science Learning in Kindergarten Through Eighth Grade, a synthesis of the multidisciplinary literature on science learning, which will provide strategic guidance for future research and development in science education (sponsored by NSF, NIH, and the Merck Institute for Science Education) and director of the Science Learning in Kindergarten Through Eighth Grade practitioner project (a "translation" of the Science Learning in Kindergarten Through Eighth Grade report findings for a diverse practice audience). Prior to joining the NRC, Dr. Shouse worked as an educational research and evaluation consultant, science center administrator, and elementary and middle grades teacher. Dr. Shouse received his Ph.D. in curriculum, teaching, and educational policy from Michigan State University.

Carol L. Smith is associate professor of psychology at the University of Massachusetts, Boston. She is interested in understanding how concepts develop and change, in both children and scientists, and why some science concepts are very hard for students to understand. Her research focuses on characterizing students' initial commonsense theories in some domains (which often contain concepts that are incommensurable with the scientists' concepts) and understanding the processes by which students can restructure and change these concepts. She has examined the role of several practices in facilitating conceptual change in schooling contexts, and how different schooling contexts affect students' general conceptions of the nature of science, learning, and knowledge. She recently served as a design team member for the NRC's Committee on Test Design for K-12 Science Achievement. She has a Ph.D. in personality and developmental studies from Harvard University (1976).

Index

H

Haiti, 266
Harvard University, 173
Hawaii, 299
Helicobacter pylori, 29
High-stakes testing, 319
Historical context of U.S. science education,
    12–18
    emergence of standards-based reform,
        15–18
    legacy of the 1960s science curriculum
        reforms, 12–15
Historical tracing, 229
*How People Learn: Brain, Mind, Experience
    and School,* 22, 42, 336
Human body, children's understanding of,
    68, 99, 111
Hypotheses. *See also* Theory and hypothesis
    causal, 140
    considering, 268
    evaluating alternative, 76
    formulating, 131–132
    revising, 132
"Hypothesis-oriented" approaches, 135
"Hypothetico-deductive" model-based
    reasoning, 241

I

Ideas, young children's understanding of,
    78–79
Identity, 195–201
    ability to "do science," 196–197
    beliefs about oneself and about science,
        196–197
    desire to "do science," 197–200
    feeling of "belonging," 200–201
    goals, values, and interest, 197–200
Illinois, 300, 317
Implicit reasoning, 77
Indeterminacy, 141
Individual cognitive activity, 3, 203
Individual interest, 199
Induction, 74
Infants' understanding of the physical world,
    57–59
Inference strategies
    cognitive, 75, 103
    multiple, 142

Infrastructure, needed for researching
    science education, 351
Inquiry
    as evidence of student learning in the
        elementary grades, 260–261
    experiences with, 179
Institute of Medicine, 196, 304
Instruction in K-8 science classrooms, 217–
    219, 247
    aims of, 257
    approaches and strategies, 252–253
    designing, 3
    explicit, 94
    factors affecting quality of, 296–297
    how to teach, recommendations for
        policy and practice, 349
    importance of, 130, 149–152
    improving, 17
    major findings and conclusions
        concerning, 340–344
    professional development programs in,
        312–314
    research and development needed in,
        352–353
    suboptimal, 55
Instructional congruence, 192
Instructional support, importance of, 133
Intellectual roles, 275
"Intent participation," 191
Interactions. *See also* Social interactions
    and force, 97
    multidimensional, 6, 178, 349
    with simulations, 268
    with texts in K-8 classrooms, 259–260
Interest
    development of, 200
    individual, 199
    situational, 199–200
Interpretation, ambiguity involved in, 39,
    174–175
Intervention studies, 148–150, 253, 255, 257,
    268
Intraindividual variability, 4, 134, 142
Intrinsic motivation and interest, in the
    desire to "do science," 199–200
Investigations
    evaluating evidence in the context of,
        140–142
    sustained, 343
Israel, 99
Iterative processes, 27